# TERROR

## THE NEW ANTI-SEMITISM
## AND THE WAR AGAINST THE WEST

# FIAMMA NIRENSTEIN

*English translation by Anne Milano Appel*

SMITH AND KRAUS GLOBAL

A Smith and Kraus Book
Published by Smith and Kraus, Inc.
177 Lyme Road, Hanover NH 03755
www.smithandkraus.com

First Edition: March 2005
Manufactured in the United States of America
10 9 8 7 6 5 4 3 2 1

*Text design by Kate Mueller, Electric Dragon Productions*
*Cover design by Julia Gignoux, Freedom Hill Design*
*Author photo by Ofer Eshed*

ISBN 1-57525-377-1 paper
ISBN 1-57525-347-X cloth

*To my dear friends and family*

*who gave me courage*

8-10-05 Jerusalem

To Charles,
with a lot of
thanks, happy
to see you in
Jerusalem again!!
Come back soon

Fiamma

# CONTENTS

# PART II  Intifada Two: An Anatomy

# PREFACE

art II is based on articles published in the newspaper *La Stampa*, later revised, along with articles I wrote as a contributor to the magazine *Panorama*, also later revised. Pieces published in *Commentary, Liberal, Shalom,* and *World Net Daily* also appear.

The first article in Part I (It Is Not Easy to Talk About the New Anti-Semitism) and Conclusion are excerpts from my book *Gli anti-semiti progressisti: La forma nuova di un odio antico (Anti-Semites, Progressives: The New Form of an Ancient Hate).* Thanks to Maggie Brewer for her translation of that material.

A warm note of thanks to the editor of *La Stampa*, Marcello Sorgi, and to the editors of *Commentary* magazine. My thanks also to the editor of *Panorama*, Carlo Rossella, and to Neal Kozodoy, Ferdinando Adornato, Massimo Caviglia, and Joseph Farah.

—*Fiamma Nirenstein*

# INTRODUCTION

In 1967 I was a young Communist like most Italian youngsters. Bored by my rebellious behavior, my family sent me to a kibbutz in the upper Galilee, Neot Mordechai. I was quite satisfied there. The kibbutz used to give some money every month to the Vietcong. When the Six Day War began, Moshe Dayan spoke on the radio to announce it. I asked: "What is he saying?," and the comrades of Neot answered: "Shtuyot"—silly things. During the war, I took children to shelters; I dug trenches and learned simple shooting and acts of self-defense. We continued working in the orchards but were quick to identify the incoming MiGs and the outgoing Mirages, chasing one another in the sky of the Golan Heights.

When I went back to Italy, some of my fellow students stared at me as somebody new, an enemy, a wicked person who would soon become an imperialist. My life was about to change. I didn't know that yet because I simply thought that Israel rightly won a war after having been assaulted with an incredible number of harassments. But I soon noticed that I had lost the innocence of the good Jew, of the very special Jewish friend, their Jew: I was now connected with the Jews of the state of Israel, and slowly I was moved away from the dodecaphonic, psychoanalytic, Bob Dylan, Woody Allen, Isaac Bashevis Singer, Philip Roth, Freud shtetl, the coterie that sanctified my Judaism in left-wing eyes.

I have tried for a long time to bring back that sanctification, and they tried to give it back to me because we desperately needed each other, the left and the Jews. But today's anti-Semitism has overwhelmed any good intention.

Throughout the years, even people who, like me, had signed petitions asking the Israeli Defense Forces (IDF) to withdraw from Lebanon have become "unconscious fascists," as a reader of mine wrote me in a letter filled with insults. In one book it was simply written that I was "a passionate woman who fell in love with Israel, confusing Jerusalem with Florence." One Palestinian told me that if

I see things so differently from the majority, this plainly means that my brain doesn't work too well. Also, I've been called a cruel and insensitive human rights denier who doesn't care about Palestinian children's lives. A very famous Israeli writer told me on the phone a couple of months ago: "You really have become a right-winger." What? Right-winger? Me? An old feminist, human rights activist, even a Communist when I was young? Only because I described the Arab-Israeli conflict as accurately as I could and because sometimes I identified with a country continuously attacked by terror, I became a right-winger? In the contemporary world, the world of human rights, when you call a person a right-winger, this is the first step toward his or her delegitimization.

Jews born after the Holocaust learn a very clear message: Evil has come to Jews mostly from the right, from the Catholic Church during a large part of its history, and certainly from Nazism and Fascism. The history of the Holocaust placed evil on the right. And because the Jews are the living torches of how bad the right can be, they legitimize the left by their mere existence.

The left blessed the Jews as the victims par excellence, always a great partner in the struggle for the rights of the weak against the wicked. In return for being coddled, published, filmed, and considered artists, intellectuals, and moral judges, Jews, even during the Soviet anti-Semitic persecutions, gave the left moral support and invited it to cry with them at Holocaust memorials. Today, the game is clearly over. The left has proved itself the real cradle of contemporary anti-Semitism.

When I speak about anti-Semitism, I'm not speaking of legitimate criticism of the state of Israel. I am speaking of pure anti-Semitism: criminalization, stereotyping, and specific and generic lies that have fluctuated between lies about the Jews (conspiratorial, bloodthirsty, dominating the world) to lies about Israel (conspiratorial, ruthlessly violent), starting most widely since the beginning of the second intifada in September 2000 and becoming more and more ferocious since Operation Chomat Magen (Defensive Shield), when the IDF reentered Palestinian cities in response to terrorism.

The basic idea of anti-Semitism today, as always, is that Jews have a perverted soul that makes them unfit, as a morally inferior people, to be regular members of the human family. Today, this *Untermensch* ideology has shifted to the Jewish state: a separate, unequal, basically evil stranger whose national existence is slowly but surely emptied and deprived of justification. Israel, as the classic evil Jew, according to contemporary anti-Semitism, doesn't have a birthright but exists with its "original sin" perpetrated against the Palestinians. Israel's heroic history has become a history of arrogance.

Nowadays anti-Semitism's narrative focuses much more on the Deir Yassin massacre than on the creation and defense of Kibbutz Degania; more and more on the suffering of the Palestinian refugees than on the surprise of seeing five armies in 1948 denying Israel's right to exist just after being established by the United Nations; much more on the Jewish underground resistance organizations, the Lechi and the Irgun, than on the heroic battle along the way to Jerusalem. The caricature of the evil Jew is transformed to the caricature of the evil state. And now the traditional hook-nosed Jew carries a gun and kills Arab children with pleasure.

On the front pages of European newspapers, Sharon munches Palestinian children, and little Jesuses in cradles are threatened by Israeli soldiers. This new anti-Semitism has materialized in unprecedented physical violence toward Jewish persons and symbols, coming from organizations officially devoted to human rights. Its peak occurred at the U.N. summit in Durban when anti-Semitism officially became the banner of the new secular religion of human rights, and Israel and Jews became its official enemy.

Jews, and the international community in general, have been caught unawares and have failed to denounce this new trend of anti-Semitism. Nobody is scandalized when Israel is accused daily, without explanation, of excessive violence, of atrocities, of cruelty. Everybody is tormented about the necessity of painful attacks against terrorist nests, often located among families and children. Still, every country has the right to defend itself. Only the Jews in history have been denied the right of self-defense, and so it is today. Why is the war on terrorism often looked upon as a strategic problem, which the world still must solve (look at the U.S. war against Afghanistan and Iraq) and Israel is treated like a guilty defendant for fighting it? Is it not anti-Semitism when you act as if Jews must die quietly? Why is Israel officially accused by the human rights commission in Geneva of violating human rights, while, China, Libya, and Sudan have never ever been accused? Why has Israel been denied a fixed place in regional groups in the United Nations, while Syria sits on the Security Council? Why can everybody join a war against Iraq except Israel, despite the fact that Saddam has always threatened Israel with complete destruction? When sovereign states and organizations threaten death to Israel, why does nobody raise the question at the United Nations? Has Italy been threatened by France or Spain like those Iranian leaders who openly say that they will destroy Israel with an atomic bomb? And what is said when many world newspapers and television and radio stations and Palestinian school textbooks recommend kicking the Jews out of Israel and killing them all over the world using terrorist bombers? The international community doesn't consider this a problem. Israel is an "unterstate," denied the basic rights of every other state to exist in honor and peace. The Jewish state is not equal.

Like the mythical Medusa, this new anti-Semitism has a face that petrifies anyone who looks at it. People don't want to admit it, don't even want to name it, because doing so reveals both the identity of its perpetrators and its object. Even Jews don't want to call an anti-Semite by his name, fearing disruption of old alliances. Because the left has a precise idea of what a Jew must be, when Jews don't match its prescription, it asks: How do you dare be different from the Jew I ordered you to be? Fighting against terrorism? Electing Sharon? Are you crazy? And here the answer of Jews and Israelis is the same: We are still very shy, very concerned about your affection. So, instead of requesting that Israel become an equal nation and that Jews become equal citizens in the world, we prefer standing with you shoulder to shoulder, even when you have come out with hundreds, thousands of anti-Semitic statements. We prefer to stand with you at Holocaust memorials cursing old anti-Semitism, while you accuse Israel, and therefore the Jews, of being racist killers.

Let's take a well-known example: A famous Italian journalist, the former director of Corriere Della Sera, was named president of RAI, which is a very important job. RAI, the state-owned television network in Italy, is an empire that shapes Italian public opinion and manages billions of dollars. The nominee's last name, Mieli, is Jewish. Mieli is a widely appreciated journalist and historian who enjoys enormous and well-deserved prestige. But when he was appointed, the same night, the walls of RAI headquarters were filled with graffiti.

RAI means Radio Televisione Italiana—Italian Radio and Television. The graffiti authors wrote the word *raus* over it. They drew a Star of David over the A of the acronym RAI, and transformed RAI to Radio Televisione Israeliana—Israeli Radio and Television. The phrase is a perfect cross-section of what we are talking about: *raus* and the use of the Star of David are the classic signs of traditional anti-Semitic contempt and hate, and the words Radio Televisione Israeliana, putting Israel in the center of the picture, is a clear indication of how Israel is the focus of the left-wing anti-Semitic hate today.

Surprisingly, or perhaps predictably, such a blatant expression of anti-Semitism caused very little reaction from both the Italian authorities and the Italian Jewish community. The aggression and threat to such a famous intellectual gave rise to weak exclamations in a subdued tone and was treated like a minor issue in a debate centered on more relevant ones, such as the management of RAI and its political meaning.

Another notable example: A group of professors at Ca Foscari University, the prestigious Venetian institution, signed a petition calling for a boycott of Israeli professors and researchers. The content of the document is irrelevant, but the reaction it provoked among the Jewish community is very interesting. One prominent Venetian Jew, when asked for his opinion, said: "They're making a serious mistake. Those professors don't realize that they are reinforcing Sharon's policy with their boycott." Such an absurd reaction is clear proof of the failure within the Jewish world to understand this totally new type of anti-Semitism that focuses on the state of Israel.

Another document, this time a letter by a group of professors at the University of Bologna "to their Jewish friends," was published with a large number of signatures. Here is an excerpt: "We have always considered the Jewish people an intelligent and sensitive one because they have been selected [that's right, selected!] by the suffering of persecution and humiliation. We have school friends and some Jewish students whom we have helped and educated, taking them to high academic levels, and today many of them teach in Israeli universities. We are writing because we feel that our love and appreciation for you is being transformed into a burning rage. We think that many people, also outside the university feel the same. You have to realize that what was done to you in the past, you are now doing to the Palestinians. If you continue on this path, hatred for you will grow throughout the world."

The letter is an excellent summary of all the characteristics of the new anti-Semitism. There is the pre-Zionist definition of the Jewish people as ones who suffer and have to suffer by nature, a people who are bound to bear the worst persecutions, without anyone lifting a finger to help, and who are therefore worthy of compassion and solidarity. And there is the well-established, democratic, militarily powerful, and economically prospering state of Israel, which is the antithesis of this stereotype. The "new Jew," who tries not to suffer and who, above all, can and wants to defend himself, immediately loses all his charm in the eyes of the left.

But it was different before the map of Middle East was painted in red by the Cold War and Israel was declared the long arm of U.S. imperialism. The rising new-born Israel, until the 1967 war, was built on an ideology that allowed and even obliged the left to be proud of the Jews and the Jews to be proud of the left, even when Israelis were fighting and winning hard wars. The Jews who survived Nazi-Fascist persecution, the persecution of the right, created a socialist state inspired by the values of the left—work and collectivism—and by doing so again sanctified the left as a shelter for victims.

In exchange for this, the Jews were granted legitimization. But in fact, the Jews were enormously important for the left. The people of Israel were a living accusation of the anti-Semitism that marked the *Shoah*, the Nazi-Fascist anti-Semitism; and now they were building collective farms and an omnipotent trade union! To some degree, this absolved Stalinist anti-Semitism or gave it a much smaller importance than it really had. The Jews became indispensable for the left: look at the passionate and paternalistic tone of the Bologna professors as they seem to plead: "Come back, our dear Jews. Be ours again. Let us curse Israel together and then take a trip together to the Shoah memorials."

But the contradiction has become even ontologically unbearable: How can you cry with the survivors of Jews killed by Nazis when the living Jews are accused of being Nazis themselves? Somebody on a European radio program said that after the diffusion of the images of Muhammed al Dura, Europe could finally forget the famous picture of the boy in the Warsaw ghetto with his hands raised. This statement, often repeated in other forms, means obliterating the

Holocaust by conflating Israel and Nazism—accusing Jews of racism, genocide, and the ruthless elimination of civilians, women, and children and an utterly unwarranted eruption of cruelty and the most brutal instincts. It means pretending to believe blindly, without investigation, the Palestinian version of a highly disputed episode and of many many others; it means taking for granted the "atrocities" that the Palestinian spokespersons always talk about and ignoring every proof or fact that doesn't serve this position.

Well, people can, and always have, take for granted the prejudices about Jews; everyone is free to think whatever he wants. But we the Jews must reserve our moral right to hold such people accountable: In our eyes, they will plainly be anti-Semites. We will have to say to them: When you lie or use prejudices and stereotypes about Israel and the Jews, you are an anti-Semite, and I'll fight you. We must not be intimidated by the professors who tell us in their letter: "We have helped you poor Jews who lacked everything, a nonexistent nation, in the Diaspora and in Israel, to stay alive. Without us you are nothing. And therefore be careful: if you continue with your treachery we'll annihilate you. You don't exist if you don't know your place, and your place is nowhere." They'll say that it is a legitimate criticism about the state of Israel. The truth is that a big part of these criticisms are simply lies, just as when Suha Arafat, wife of Yasir Arafat, claimed that Israel poisoned Palestinian waters, or when Arafat claimed that Israel use depleted uranium against the Palestinian people and that Israeli women soldiers show up naked in front of the Palestinian warriors to confuse them. It's just the same as when you say that the Israeli army purposely shoots children or journalists.

As a journalist, I must mention the significant contribution of the mass media to this new anti-Semitism. Since the beginning of the intifada, freedom-fighter journalists, grown in the Guevara and Fedayeen campus, have given the Israeli-Palestinian conflict one of the most biased coverage in the history of journalism. Here are the main problems that lead to distorted reporting of the intifada:

1. Lack of historic depth in attributing responsibility for its outbreak. In other words, failure to repeat the story of the Israeli offer of a Palestinian state and of Arafat's refusal, which, in essence, is a refusal to accept Israel as a Jewish state and which continues the almost seventy-year-old Arab rejection of partition of the land of Israel

between Arabs and Jews as recommended by the British in 1936, decided by the United Nations in 1947, and always accepted by the Jewish representatives.

2. Failure, right from the very first clashes at the checkpoints, to assign responsibility for the first deaths to the fact that, unlike in the first intifada, in the second the IDF faced armed fighters hiding in the midst of the unarmed crowd.

3. Failure to recognize the enormous influence of the culture on the Palestinians—from the systematic education in Palestinian schools to the mass media, which vilifies Jews and Israelis and idealizes terrorist acts of murder and mayhem.

4. Describing the deaths of Palestinian children without identifying the circumstances in which those deaths occurred. Equating Israeli civilian losses to those of Palestinians, as if terrorism and the war against it are the same thing and as if intentional killing is the same as the deplorable consequences of a difficult and new type of fighting.

5. Using Palestinian sources to certify events, as if Palestinian sources were the most reliable. I am thinking of Jenin, of the unconfirmed reports that passed to printed pages and television screens as truth. In contrast, Israeli sources, which are very often reliable, are seen as subservient, prejudiced, and unworthy of attention, despite the country's aggressive free and open journalism and the equally determined criticism of government policies by opposition parties, conscientious objectors, commentators, and journalists.

6. Manipulation of the order in which the news is given and of the news itself. The headlines give the number of Palestinians killed or wounded in most articles, at least in Europe, before describing the gunfights and their causes, and linger on the ages and family stories of the terrorists. The purposes of the IDF actions, such as capturing terrorists, destroying arms factories, the hiding places of terrorists, and the bases for attacks against Israel, are rarely mentioned. On the contrary, Israel's operations are often described as completely uncalled for, bizarre, wicked, and useless.

7. Manipulation of language, taking advantage of the great confusion about the definition of terrorism and terrorist. This, too, is an old issue, connected to the concept of the freedom fighter, so dear to my generation. A few days ago, at a checkpoint, I was doing some interviews. It soon became clear to me that using the word *terrorist*

was to each one of my Palestinian interlocutors a capital political and semantic sin. The press has learned this very well: The occupation is the cause of everything; terrorism is called resistance and does not exist per se. Terrorists who kill women and children are called militants or fighters. An act of terrorism is often "a fire fight," even when only babies and old men are shot inside their cars on a highway. It is also interesting to note that a young *shahid* is a source of deep pride for the Palestinian struggle, but if you ask how a child of twelve can be sent to die and why young children are indoctrinated to do such acts, the answer is: "Come on, a child can't be a terrorist. How can you call a twelve-year-old boy a terrorist?"

This is perhaps the most crucial point: Given the fact that there is a ferocious debate on the definition of terrorism, it is widely accepted that terrorism is a way of fighting. This is a semantic and even substantial gift of the new anti-Semitism, where it is natural for a Jew to be dead. Namely, intentionally targeting civilians to cause fear and disrupt the morale of Israel is not a moral sin. It doesn't raise world indignation, and if it does, it hides in its folds some or much sympathy for the terrorist aggressor. What the European press fails to or doesn't want to understand is that terror is a condemned and forbidden way of fighting, regardless of the specific, political goal it tries to achieve.

8. The media have promoted the extravagant concept that the settlers, including women and children, are not real human beings. They present settlers as pawns in a dangerous game they choose to play. Their deaths are almost natural and logical events. In a way, they asked for it. On the other hand, when a Hamas commander is killed, even though he obviously "asked for it," an ethical, philosophical debate arises on the perfidy of extrajudicial death sentences. This would certainly be a licit debate, were it not for the grotesque double standard on which worldwide press bases it.

9. Not to go overlooked is that censorship and corruption within the Palestinian Authority and the physical elimination of its political enemies is hardly ever covered.

The points listed above all point in one direction: Durban. Here, the human rights movements, which later demonstrated on the streets against the war in Iraq, chose Israel as their primary target and enemy. This choice constitutes a great success for Palestinian propaganda, but also a very serious signal of weakness from the movements themselves. The ideologically and politically cornered left chose to adopt as universal a controversial and sectorial struggle, marked heavily by terrorism. A left incapable of confronting the capitalist globalization system decided to appoint the state of Israel as its main target. In a word, the left decided to make Israel pay for what they think America should pay. Isn't this real cowardice?

In addition , there is the issue of how the United Nations and its outrageous policy has helped this process, and how Europe has coddled it because of its ancient sense of guilt toward Israel and its hate for the United States, Israel's friend and ally. This matter alone deserves an entire book. Denouncing this new human rights anti-Semitism is psychologically a terribly arduous task for Israel and for Diaspora Jews. It is even more difficult because between the Jews and the left there is a divorce that the latter does not want. The left wants to continue being considered the paladin of good Jews. It pretends to continue mourning the Jews killed in the *Shoah*, crying together with the Jews shoulder to shoulder. And it does so because this gives it the moral authorization to go a second later and speak of the "atrocities" of Israel. After writing about the atrocities of Israel, the good European leftist will talk to you with vivacity about the fascinating *shtetl* culture and the sweetness of Moroccan Jewish dishes.

Until we break the silence, we the Jews give leftists the authorization to deny us the right to a nation of our own and to defense of our people from unprecedented anti-Semitism. Just as the left curses Israel—this left of human rights, pacifism, and protest against the death penalty, war, and racial and gender discrimination—it praises suicide terrorists and the caricatures of Sharon worthy of the Sturmer. And no leftists will ever sit as a human shield in an Israeli coffeehouse or in a Jerusalem bus.

Still, this new anti-Semitism has a peculiar characteristic: It allows conversion. This kind of anti-Semitism, unlike Nazi anti-Semitism, is more like the older theological anti-Semitism, for it gives the Jews the option to renounce the devil (Israel, or sometimes Sharon). Whoever declares a sense of revulsion toward Israel's conduct is allowed to set foot again in the civil society, the one of common sense, civilized conversation, groups of good people full of goodwill who fight for human rights.

If we want to obtain something, if we decide that it is about time to fight, we must renounce liberal impostors. We have to know how to say that the free press is a failure when it lies, and that it does lie.

We have to say that all human rights are violated when a people is denied the right of self-defense, and that right is denied of Israel. Human rights are also violated when a nation is subjected to systematic defamation and made a legitimate target for terrorists. We have to stop what we have accepted since the day the state was born, namely, that Israel be viewed as a different state in the international community.

Another very important point is that of all the parameters of anti-Semitism now used, one is the confusion between Israeli and Jew. Supposedly, it is wrong to insinuate that the Jews act in the interests of the state of Israel and not their own state. The more a country confuses the two terms, the more anti-Semitic it is considered, and therefore one would imagine that Jews combat this prejudice. This is a serious conceptual error. Since both the state of Israel and Jews have been made the object of the worst kind of prejudice, Jews everywhere should consider their being identified with Israel a virtue and honor. They should assert that identification with pride. If Israel is, and it is indeed, the focal point of anti-Semitic attacks, our attention must be concentrated there. We must measure the moral character of the person we are speaking to on that basis: If you lie about Israel, if you cover it with bias, you are an anti-Semite. If you're prejudiced against Israel, then you're against the Jews.

This doesn't mean criticizing Israel and its policies is forbidden. However, very little of what we hear about Israel is lucid criticism. Prejudice and bias, not Sharon's personality, is the major reason for criticism. The self-defined critics are not the pious interlocutors for the Jews that they pretend to be. So we must tell them: From now on you cannot use the human rights passport for free; you cannot use false stereotypes. You must demonstrate what you assert—that the army ruthlessly storms poor Arab villages that have nothing to do with terrorism; that it shoots children on purpose; that it kills journalists with pleasure. You cannot? You called Jenin a slaughter? Then you are an anti-Semite, just like the old anti-Semites you pretend to hate. You have to convince me that you are not an anti-Semite, now that we know that you do not condemn terrorism, that you have never said a word against the contemporary caricatures of hooked-nosed Jews with a bag of dollars in one hand and a machine gun in the other.

Israel is in shock over the new anti-Semitism. All the theories that claimed classic anti-Semitism would abate with the creation of the state of Israel and that, in the long run, it would be extinguished have been destroyed. Furthermore, Israel has actually become the sum of all the evil, the proof that the protocols and the blood libels were right. The Palestinians are turned into Jesus, crucified; the war in Iraq or in Afghanistan waged by the United States is part of the Jewish plan of domination. Jews all over the world are threatened, beaten, even killed to pay the price of Israel's existence.

Israel and the Jews have today only one certainty: Now that Jews have their own means of defense, a new *Shoah* is no longer possible. Still, we have to pass from the idea of our possible physical elimination to that of possible moral elimination. The only way to face this threat is to fight fearlessly, on our own terrain, using all the historic and ethical weapons that Israel possesses. No shame, no fear, and no sense of guilt. Israel has the chance to prove itself for what it really is: the outpost of the fight against terrorism and the defense of democracy. That is no small thing. But we the Jews pose as victims and hide from this chance because using it puts us in conflict with our ancient sponsors and their legitimization. We have to realize that legitimization is really in our own hands and we never used it.

The watchwords of the Jews should be *Jewish pride,* in the sense of pride in our history and national identity, wherever we are. Jewish pride means that we have to claim the unique identity of the Jewish people and its right to exist. We must act as though it has never been acknowledged, because today, once again, it no longer is. In defending this identity we have to be, as Hillel Halkin says, as tough as can be and as liberal as no one else is. No left and no right. We won't give the left the power to decide where we stand. We will decide our alliances by ourselves according to the actual position of our potential partners.

*This speech was delivered by Fiamma Nirenstein on April 14, 2003, at the Yivo Institute in New York*

# Part I

## THE NEW ANTI-SEMITISM

## It Is Not Easy to Talk About the New Anti-Semitism

It is not easy to talk about the new anti-Semitism, which has Israel at its core, because the topic is anathema. It sometimes embarrasses even my oldest friends. It seems over the top, bad mannered—it seems like an excuse to defend Israel at all costs. And it becomes even grittier when one links it to terrorism, trying to explain that anti-Semitism is a substantial ideological part of terrorism. The subject is not even acceptable when one speaks of it from Jerusalem, where my work as a journalist brought me several years ago and from where I look at my homeland, Italy, with great nostalgia, but where the fact of being Jewish has been able to become fully meaningful. During these tough years of the intifada, I have been very lucky. I have been the lookout on a terrace from which history is set starkly against the dunes, against the profile of the mosques of Jerusalem, and against the skyscrapers of Tel Aviv—without shadows, tragically gleaming like a sword—in its truth.

And I have liked that, even though it has cost me a great deal living in the shadow of death and suffering, and even though I have seen what I hope the world will never have to see again. I have liked living here because this country, contrary to what many people imagine, is a hope for a daughter of the human rights culture, as I am. That is to say that its resistance in the face of terrorism and a war without quarter and without light is a promise for the whole of humanity. If it manages to resist, of course. No country has, in fact, had to support so much in advance of the rest of the world, the blows inflicted by terror with imaginative precision. This plague devastates the entire world, and no country is a better example of how to tackle it fearlessly with determination and perseverance—and, perhaps in the future, beat it—without losing its humaneness, democracy, unity, and joie de vivre and also without losing—in the midst of criticisms from the entire international community, which demands a surrender—the courage to continue fighting, even though voluntarily tying a hand behind its back.

Israel in fact has an army that could have long ago taught a hard, irreparable lesson to those who have persecuted it with terror. Instead, it tries to face, with a sense of moderation, an enemy that is ready for any unthinkable gesture to annihilate it. The Israeli soldier is the only one who has the order to shoot only and exclusively if his life or that of his companion-in-arms beside him is in jeopardy. Even if mistakes have been made—and a not indifferent number of Palestinian civilians have lost their lives—the reason should not be sought in any confusion or lack of moral sense of the army. And even less so in crazy orders from above to shoot at civilians and to target them in a premeditated manner. Except for the undisciplined impulses of some individuals, I believe that no shot has ever been deliberately fired against an innocent passer-by. When civilians obviously not involved in a conflict fall, criminal inquiries are immediately started. The army has remained on guard against itself even in situations when probably no other army would have done so.

If anything, the lack of moral sense that some wish to attribute to Israel should be sought in Palestinian society. It is a bridgehead of that part of the Arab world that refuses to accept any type of dialogue, practices a death culture (and never mind whether it is a question of Sunni, as in the Palestinians' case, or of Shiites) linked to the jihadist interpretation of religion as a weapon. It consequently makes it an indispensable part of the Arab and Palestinian fight for liberation and celebrates terrorists as martyrs for the faith and as models for education of the young. It is a society that sends civilians and children ahead and proclaims "Our fortune is that we love death more than we do life," reducing mothers to machines who can no longer grieve for their children. Certainly, Sheikh Yassin did not send Mohammed Atta out against the Twin Towers—but the mentality with which he has sent hundreds of young men to blow themselves up and dozens of women to kill Israelis is that of the martyrdom cult, with no pity either for the enemy or for his own people.

The substantial integrity of the Israeli soul is reflected in the immensity of the moral problems that Israel has had to face at every dawn for nearly sixty years, since it is the only country that has suffered the scourge of terrorism since its origin and, as Yossi Klein Ha Levy wrote in the *Jerusalem Post* in January 2004, whose "existence is considered to be offensive by its enemies." How to stop the continuous entry of people determined to kill into kibbutzs' dining rooms, school buses, cinemas, and pizzerias? How to avoid massacres when, to arrest the perpetrators and instigators, it is necessary to search in populous towns and villages? What stand to take in the face of an enemy who hides assassins in hospitals and uses ambulances to transport suicide terrorists and explosives, who knows no moral limits, who sends women who, according to their culture, have "lost their honor" to blow themselves up, and who plans massacres via dissemination of the AIDS virus? How to address so much horror? The territorial dispute with the Palestinians, the idea of partition (unless one considers Arafat's secret but evident determination to expel all Jews, either with brute force or applying the right to return, to be legitimate), is certainly a secondary element compared with the overall Arab rejection of Israel and of the colonialist and sinful West, which, in its eyes, Israel embodies. In reality, Israel is the only country that would have voluntarily handed over a large portion of the lands forming part of its historical heritage and part of its capital in exchange for peace. What counts more than Jerusalem for Jewish history and religion? And yet Barak had already handed over more than half of it when the Palestinian jihad's attack took place. It is the only country that—even though it has obtained only war from an attitude that, to say the least, is flexible—has reached the conclusion, on both the right and left wing, that when the counterpart is absent, instead of taking advantage of this, instead of warring, it is better to withdraw its forces and its citizens and leave room for a new attempt at pacification via territorial cession. Sharon and Peres are very much of the same opinion, while I write, and I do not know whether this is promising for peace, but it is certainly irrefutable proof of the fact that this country has continued to seek a pacific solution, even in the face of unspeakably bloody attacks, and to remain united.

And yet Israel is the butt of daily denigration, the butt of the most strongly shared vituperation. And when I ask myself why, I try to find strength in the face of the terrible answer, balm for my soul, and I find it: Israel is in fact an encouraging example for all democracies. When I see the people who, in the morning, walk the streets of Jerusalem and pass those stations of the Via Dolorosa that Jews have had to endure—from the blackened stop of an exploded bus to a café newly rebuilt (and already full) after twenty deaths there, from the devastated supermarket to the pizzeria (that, too, once again in full operation) where entire families have been pulverized—there is no more convincing spectacle to demonstrate the marvelous strength of liberty and democracy. Going out into the wind, alone and free, is so wonderful that you have to do it, and while you do so, you fight and win for your life just as if you were at war. Nothing can keep you at home; you just have to run (or go to the café, or to the meeting of your seminar at the bar of Mount Scopus Hebrew University, or to your political or dance group) to celebrate your life in democracy. Civilian society beckons to you, and it is too interesting to renounce: You cannot not go to the cinema or a concert, or to the Knesset, even when the human bombs explode. The appointment with your friends at the restaurant, when there is a get-together on the eve of the Jewish Sabbath, is mad in terms of the danger—but it is something that cannot be renounced because this is freedom. On television, programs expressing a fanatical passion follow one after the other: a karaoke program where everyone sings at the tops of their voices, another program in which a famous disc jockey, joking about himself, talks of his success at a transvestite festival in Brazil with thousands of people ("They raised four Israeli flags, and I thought, my word! Forget about the territories, we've occupied Brazil!"), or the speed with which antigovernment jokes are made in one comic talk show after the other—all these things can only be explained by a courageous hunger for life. And if, to stop a terrorist who wants to kill customers, people must be ready to throw themselves at the terrorist to save the others, that's all right; it's part of the game.

Civilian society at war with terrorism needs heroes. Unfortunately, episodes of personal courage are indispensable when the last bulwark is the body of a waiter or a bus driver. It is wonderful to see that even a society so profoundly at war produces—and certainly not only the left wing—so much sense of humor between the tears that, still today, the popular Israeli hero is not a champion either of bellicose values or of expansionist ideals, and not even of a rigid mentality. He is normally a simple and ironic boy, nearly never as rich as boys in Europe, never spoilt by material things, but indulgently cared for by his parents; a young man who loves to enjoy himself, teasingly scorning the constituted order of things and roaming around until five in the morning. But he has clear ideas on one fact: The enemy is he who wants to kill you, who wants to destroy your home. His country has to be defended and not abandoned in the jaws of terror. And he is ready to give his life for others. He is never a racist, saving in cases immediately punished severely, even if the enemy has always been Arabian. Just think what we would say about—taking any example—the Chinese, if they had always been our enemies. Here, no: If at a school or in the army, a master were to dare to speak of the Arabs disparagingly, in generalized terms, he would end up on trial, or fired, or outcast. And yet the young Israeli—perhaps because his educational framework plays an important role in the army's team discipline and solidarity, perhaps because the country is so small—cannot allow himself to be lulled by would-be good-naturedness, which makes it impossible to detect danger. And when he sees it, he generally knows how to face up to it. He warns his companions and even reports when he sees someone else do stupid things—exaggerating or overacting. This does not mean that it does not happen, but he who surrenders to stupid machismo is generally considered to be a real idiot and is even sent away from his *plugah* or company in the army, and in society he becomes part of socially noncore groups.

Israelis went on an excursion to the flowered plains even during this Passover of 2004. Some two million people defied sixty warnings from the security forces of street attacks to touch the water of the springs that soon, with the heat, would dry up. People still crowd the entrances to the nature reserves and buy their tickets because, after nearly sixty years of wars, they are still crazy with joy at having a piece of land to cultivate. They have not lost the sense of the incredible adventure of founding, after so many centuries and millennia of persecution, a democratic Jewish state, and they continue to think, between one war and another, between one terrorist attack and another, that their real nature as a people lies in those five minutes when they manage to be a nation like all the others—maybe winning or losing a sports competition. The people who celebrate Passover Day, with all their qualities and defects, go on excursions also out of patriotism, as well as to enjoy the sun: for an Israeli, enjoying the sun is a sign of patriotism. What has been seen here on the buses—the slaying of children, the elderly blown to pieces—would make even the most thick-skinned European lose the desire to stay in the sun with the crowds. But Israel has resisted.

After three and a half years of intifada, Israel has thus in no way lost its soul, as suggested by those who are its enemies or who have lost their way on their own road because it has simply been worn away by terrorism. On the contrary, one is struck by the Israeli government's equilibrium when it ponders whether or not to pull out of

Gaza and leave the Judea and Samaria settlements, with the prospect of handing over its land to someone who can, and certainly wants to, use it as a base for terrorism. And yet Israel continues to ponder evacuation; decides to leave; continues to care for Palestinian patients in hospitals; builds a defensive fence (indispensable to halt terrorists) or shifts it by several kilometers as requested; continues to confront itself with the United Nations and the European Union without becoming impatient, not even in the face of definitely biased stances. In various cases, it replants the olive trees of someone who has to remain on the other side of this momentary barrier, repeating that a tree regrows but a person remains killed forever; it reopens as soon as it can the check points closed when a few hours or few days before a terrorist had entered by those very routes. But Israel institutes stringent rules, videos, and courses to explain to the frightened and stressed soldiers how to behave when a boy draws near with a cart that could be loaded with explosives; and it reports soldiers who have fired for no apparent reason.

After all, Sharon is a leader who has stated that it is "morally impossible" to continue dominating another people and who is certainly aware of the vertical growth of the people dominated, who have one of the world's highest population growth rates. All this is systematically denied—and yet it is there, laid out for everyone to see. But the problem is that in Israel there are the Jews, and this is only the first of the problems. The second one is that, because of a cursed circumstance, Israel is in the front ranks of the war that frightens everyone most: Terrorism's global war against the West and our war against terrorism, a war to which Europe has no desire to commit itself, even though it is in it up to its neck.

Each day, from my computer, besides the day's news, two piles of printed sheets accumulate on my table. Half of them concern, or comment on, events of terrorism, blood, madness—young people killed, dismembered, blinded, lamed; trains, buses, and pizzerias blown up; praises and condemnations of terrorism. At every latitude, men, women, and children; Christian and Jewish families; Americans and Israelis, but also Filipinos, Balinese, and Spaniards disappear—in pieces—from this earth. The other half concerns anti-Semitism, often mixed with anti-Americanism: demented, astounding statements by poets and politicians; illogical reactions to events that instead require concentration and thought; unthinking heat-of-the-moment remarks; institutions of no mean size (the United Nations, the European Union, the French government, the Historical Museum of Stockholm, many universities of ancient fame) that have made a truly monumental hash of it, institutions withdrawing hands, rushing to limit the damage, or insisting and maintaining that boycotting Israeli scholars is a right and a duty. And again, denials from ordinary people, from intellectuals, journalists, and politicians, who say that anti-Semitism does not exist, that the cartoon showing Sharon nude with his mouth dripping with the blood of Palestinian children is just "a legitimate criticism of the state of Israel."

In these three years, the piles of paper and the horror have grown in parallel, vertically. They accumulate and stratify the European soul and culture—and soon they might crash down on top of us. Every country where a synagogue is burned has to face up to a barbarism that will cause its own parliament to be pelted with stones. Those who foolishly maintain that if we were to let Middle Eastern dictatorships and their championing of terrorism calmly proliferate, that if Israel were to obey, bow its head, maybe even to the point of disappearing, this would contribute to peace; those who maintain that Yassin was nothing more than a poor, old paraplegic even though he killed hundreds of Jews and preached their extermination; and those who insist on only seeing the Palestinians as a people fighting against occupation, even when they take stands identical to those that once led to the extermination of the Jews— they all risk finding themselves, one day, forced to bow their heads to the point of letting their democracies be destroyed.

It has already happened. World War II set the globe on fire, and its ideological core was anti-Semitism. And that is the core of the terrorist war too. The blood libel that is broadcast by Palestinian, Egyptian, and Syrian television at a local level and Al-Manar and Al-Jazeera at a global level and *The Protocols of the Elders of Zion* have become the greatest titillation of the global Wahhabite jihad. It is not the Koran, which has a thousand interpretations and a thousand faces; it is the death-driven dementia of terror that needs the nourishment of Jewish blood. Even though terrorism targets are many and various and spread throughout the world; even though terrorists strike or try to strike Christians, Jews, Muslims, Americans, Arabs, Filipinos, Europeans, Asians, and Africans; and even though not all the attacks are openly anti-Semitic (though good number of them are, as in Argentina, Djerba, Mombasa, Istanbul, and Montreal, and as in all attacks on synagogues, Jewish cemeteries, and Jews wearing kippah), we can say, with a good degree of assurity, that all terrorists are anti-Semitic.

The anti-Western terrorist uses the Israeli Jew, and Jews in general, as his good reason for attacking the society that is his host. It is his visiting card to capture sympathies of various types—the sympathy of those who think that, by handing over Israel (that is, the Jews), peace will be achieved, of those who hate Jews, and of those who think that the Israeli-Palestinian conflict is global terrorism's true cause, including the terrorism of bin Laden, Shiite and Sunni terrorism, and the terrorism in Iraq, Iran, and Syria. The Jew, as the terrorist sees and shows him, is the latter's psychotic and homicidal invention, just as Süss (of the film *The Jew Süss*) was Hitler's invention, his good reason for identifying Jews as blood- and power-thirsty and therefore to be eliminated in a total war against a world dominated by the Jews' secret conspiracy. In reality, the Jew is certainly not the reason for the terrorist's madness, but the latter's homicidal fury has a prime target in the Jews—and it is pathetic and horrifying to see how convincing he is for the weak and for the liberal-minded—a distinction that at times is meaningless.

"When I was a boy I worked for a catering company to earn a bit of money," writes a certain Alessandro to a mailing list of breastfeeding Italian mothers. "I asked why the sets of plates were divided and was told that one set was for the Jews who refused to eat impure food. . . . As long as there are people in the world who think like that, we will never be at peace." He writes this to the mothers, uncensored and without a line of explanation, this man who sees in Jewish dietary rules a sign of aggression, racism, and a desire for war. He has heard it said that the Jews in Israel kill Palestinians for entertainment, that they slaughter children out of pure racism or a desire for power, indeed for world power, which they are seeking to achieve via the United States—or the United States via Israel. It does not matter; the flags, in any case, are burnt together. It is sufficient to make a brief visit to the Internet sites of terrorist organizations, mainly Islamist, to see how terrible explosions, projects for Islamic domination, Twin Towers collapsing, Judaic noses, satanic representations of Jews, negations of the Holocaust together with the definition of Nazi applied to the Jews, are bundled together with Bush presented as an evil idiot. This Islamist promise to burn and then dominate the world and the terrorists' anti-Semitism and anti-Americanism are one and the same thing. Those who fight one, also fight the other.

This intertwinement is long standing: Terrorism's fundamentalist and totalitarian nature considers the liberalism and democratic inspiration at the heart of Jewish history to be its enemies. Terrorism has always made elimination of the Jews a preferential aim in its strategy and also an occasion of special joy. When Arafat mentioned the Hudaibija truce and then the breaking of that truce while speaking of the Oslo agreements, he touched the hearts of Muslims because the Koran describes the episode of the breaking of the truce and consequent massacre when talking of betrayal. The reference was not only clear but was also faithfully imitated. When reference is made to the Jews as "sons of dogs and monkeys," it is the Koran that is being quoted. When it is said "Follow the Jew and kill him, the rock and bush hiding him will denounce him," it is the Koran that is being quoted. Sheikh Haj Amin al-Husseini, when he sympathized with Hitler's Nazi massacre, also had as his terms of reference not only the hate created by the Jewish presence in the Holy Land and its growth, but also quoted the sacred writings. Those writings gave him the theoretical basis for his anti-Semitism.

And yet in the 1960s the Koran as such did not cause terrorism. Today Al Qaeda, the Islamic revolution, and the Wahhabite movement have reshuffled the cards on the table. It is their interpretation of the Koran, their use of its quotations, that has to be thanked for the current situation in which the whole world is fighting in a clash of decisive historical importance. And the quotations so fashionable today and the episodes of persecution of Jews believed to be absolute truths in Islamic history are sufficient for these movements to maintain that, for the Islamic world's emancipation, subjugation, or elimination of the Jews as a nation—and now one by one as repulsive and aggressive human beings—is indispensable.

In March 2004 a young student at Jerusalem's Hebrew University was shot dead in the street by terrorists lying in wait. The Martyrs' Brigades of Al Aqsa joyfully claimed responsibility for the murder of another Jew. When it emerged that the boy killed was an Israeli Arab, they apologized for the incident, which consisted not of shooting at a boy who was running, not of firing against another human being who also happened to be Israeli, but only the victim's religion: the boy killed—what a mistake!—was not a Jew. This is called anti-Semitism of course, and nothing else. It justified terrorism, in exactly the same way that it justifies it for religious organizations. The pus has spread from Islamic fundamentalism to the new pan-Arabism: Kill the Jews wherever they are; they are the epitome of what is worst. Sheikh Yassin was already saying it in the 1980s: They can live in our land, which is naturally Palestine inclusive of Israel, since what right does the Jewish state, the collective Jew, have to exist? The Jew has the right to live as a *dhimmi* (non-Muslim in a Muslim country) only, otherwise we can only offer him flight or death, Yassin used to say. When the suicide terrorist explodes, no target hit is so merrily celebrated as a Jewish one, never are so many candies handed out. Striking the Jews and, immediately after them in the jihad order of priorities, the Americans is not just a sign of power, it is a sign of the triumph of divine justice. And while the armed confrontation takes place on these two fronts, on the European front there is a conquest—demographic, economic, ideological, and also, in the end, with bombs—that is not less important.

The spinning top today has gained unprecedented momentum starting from bin Laden's theorization of the war against the Jews and the crusaders. Later on, after the Twin Towers attack, bin Laden launched a further complementary and indispensable message when—sitting on a carpet together with his second Zawahiri, against the background of bare rocks and wild bushes, as ascetic as a seventeenth-century picture of Mohammed—he talked of pagans, hypocrites, and of the perfidious Jews. He announced the historical task of destroying America and, as noted by Bernard Lewis, spoke of the "humiliations," of the "bloodshed," and of the "desecration of holiness" suffered by Islam for eighty years. The Muslim world, which knows its history better than we know ours, instantly understood that bin Laden was talking of Kemal Atatürk's laical and modernization revolution in Turkey and of the fall of the caliphate, of the Islamic disaster under the hand of apostates and enemies. Bin Laden was also referring to the revolutions following World War I, which marked an uprising against the ruinous culture, the liberal Western world: the age of the new antiliberal prophets, who incited the masses, disappointed by what they considered to be the failure of the European Judeo-Christian dream, to rebel. And together with this—and bin Laden certainly did not forget it—came anti-Semitism, not new, as ferocious as ever, and, ultimately, even more fierce in Christian Europe. Bin Laden's reference to the 1920s thus had two sides: the desire for revolutionary times under the aegis of Islam and, together with this, repudiation of and the promise of destruction for any Islamic regime drawing close to the West and moving toward democracy.

Anti-Semitism has been the natural ingredient of all terrorist incitement. The Islamism originating it has chosen a Koranic interpretation that relentlessly insists on Jews' inferiority and cruelty and on the need to fight and eliminate them as part of the international conspiracy. "The Jews today avenge their forefathers, sons of monkeys and pigs. . . . Some demand their property back in the Medina. . . . They are extremists, they are the ones that are terrorists, they deserve death and we deserve life. . . . They take our holy places and our lands by force. . . . In the light of their massacres . . . we will fight them with the help of Allah. The Jews are those about whom Allah—who knows them best of all—says 'Terrorize them more than Allah himself does.' Oh Muslims, it is Allah who says it: You see it by yourself, but the Arabs and Muslims must know that it is a Koranic truth. The Creator of the sky and the earth so establishes. Allah knows that they love life: no one is more closely attached to life than they are. Never mind what type of life it is: even if it is a life of humiliation, disgrace, and subjection, they preserve it. This makes them poor in spirit and cowardly. The Jews disseminate their poison in Arab countries; they live in the Middle East, like a cancer, and they cannot give up spreading their fire of war among Arabs and Muslims, and that is what they do." So says one of the many speeches made in the world's mosques: This one was made on March 12, 2004, by Sheikh Ibrahim Muderis, an employee of the Palestinian Authority's Awkaf (Islamic affairs and religious endowments) Ministry, and in it he also explained that Jews should be destroyed in three phases, as done by Mohammed in the Medina. The Jews' unworthiness was genetic and theological—and this is the general set of anti-Semitism—they had to be eliminated. Moreover, "They thrust the global superpowers against Arab countries. Israel incites the United States against Syria. Syria thus finds itself facing heavy pressure [to dismantle terrorist bases on its soil] and we say to them: 'Be patient and Allah will be with you.' People of Syria, brothers of the Lebanon, of Jordan, of Egypt, of countries throughout the world—we will never abandon them for as long as they combat this cancer."

Associating Israel, the state of the Jews, with the idea of Jews as criminals, along with the long arm of imperialism, is a potent trigger, intrinsic to terror. Europe today has the misfortune that this ideology—which has spread along the immigration routes of Islam—has been embraced, albeit certainly not in the same terms and with different nuances, by the liberal movements of our times, by the NGOs, left-wing parties, and pacifists. At the time when Hitler was preparing extermination camps as well as war, French socialists were asking themselves, as Paul Berman notes, whether, after all, their traditional anticapitalism criticisms against the Jews, against the rich financiers and warmongers, could not and should not be considered legitimate: Weren't the Jews in favor of war for their own benefit? Should Leon Blum himself be exempt from criticism of his support for the war just because he was Jewish? Today, anti-Semitism is transformed by those French socialists' descendants into liberal criticism of Israeli society and of its friends, of its oppression of the Palestinian world, and of the United States' possible oppression of Afghanistan and Iraq—and so we are made to forget the true history of the conflict.

But is it not indeed this ad-libbing interpretation of history, of the guilty and the innocent, of the personages' characters, of the characteristics and intentions of its leading players that creates anti-Semitism and a totalitarian society? The complete distortion and misrepresentation of intentions and meanings lies at the base of anti-Semitism and anti-Americanism—that terrorists are a reaction to injustice; the United States and Israel are keen to dominate and crush and massacre civilians; the United States is only after oil and wealth and behaves unilaterally. In Europeans' frenzied desire to mock George W. Bush, they fail to understand his historical intuition. What a pity: We Europeans found ourselves faced with the American intuition that the only way of beating terrorism was to democratize the Arab world—undoubtedly an extremely difficult route to take but obligatory, unless we want to arrive at a total and certainly undesirable confrontation—and we have mostly been capable of doing nothing more than feebly cheeping about our fear of becoming involved in a war that in any case concerns us, whether we like it or not. In Iraq we were immediately scared of the shock waves that, after thirty-six years of dictatorship, were logical to expect. When people ask me what I think of the population's misery and poverty, I cannot stop being astounded by the ingenuousness or artfulness of that question. With the policy of robbery and total negligence implemented by Saddam to the people's detriment, how could anyone expect the situation to be righted in a year? It is already miraculous that, in that period of time, work has started on infrastructures for electricity, water, telephones, hospitals, and schools. Similarly, I am amazed by the presumption that it is possible for public order to be maintained and the accusation that the United States and the emergency government have not been doing so. Iraq is broken up into ethnic and religious groups, has always been dominated by a murderous minority, and today is the meeting point of the whole of world terrorism, particularly that of the Hezbollahs financed by Iran and of Al Qaeda. They, together with Saddam's Sunnis, fear, more than anyone else, the advent of democracy.

The reaction to the possibility of a democracy in the Middle East is as terrible as the terrorist war—and both of them are inevitable. In Palestine, Arafat caused Abu Mazen to flee from his post when the latter stated that he wanted to combat terrorism and to use banks and not cash payments to pay the police forces, which, instead of acting as private militias, as they do today (almost 12 percent of the Palestinians who died during the intifada have died at the hands of their fellow countrymen in the confusion and reciprocal feuds), would have at long last had to assure security. It is hard to accept order and reformist change, and strong powers do not intend to allow it. And yet something has happened, something important. Following the victory in Afghanistan, after the war in Iraq and the capture of Saddam, the Gulf states started their timid democratization. Libya has renounced (so it says) weapons of mass destruction; Saudi Arabia has called its first general local elections; and the underground democratic movement in Iran has become braver and has also spread among the clerics. In the meantime, Afghanistan's reconstruction has continued. Even an Iraqi constitution has been created that awards no special advantage to any one group but gives everyone access to rights never possessed before under the horror of Saddam's regime.

Certainly there is furious resistance from terrorism, from Saddam's ex-followers, and from that part of the Shiite world on which

Iran is placing all its bets. And how could it be any different since the match is of such vital importance? And yet, as soon as things turned out to be complicated (as anyone with experience of terrorism would expect—terrorism is the nest of vipers where all secret international relations entwine and slink and all the strangest economic connections occur, where the corruption and dirt of tyrannies accumulate and interests unite in the most abysmal of all desires—the desire for death and power), we have often preferred—in an effort to underline the ingenuousness, mistakes, and imperialism of Bush—to act as an amplifier for the heirs of Saddam, who fear the war crimes trial, or for the delegates of international terrorism, who have all gathered in Iraq, the place where a new victory of Kemal Atatürk—democracy in the Arab world, the great danger for global terrorism—must be prevented at all costs. The United States in great difficulty, Bush in crisis, sixty Americans dead in a month, the coalition off the rails—so wrote newspapers in Europe with a certain gusto, while other articles hoped for the saving grace of the United Nations—as if this were none of our business. Europeans won't acknowledge that any failure in Iraq is a failure that can destroy us all and reassure terrorists and fundamentalists, whereas democracy is the victory of our civilization and of peace itself.

And instead we are so stupid and blind as to have whole movements and miles of printed paper that preach withdrawal of the United States from Iraq, that basically sentence U.S. defeat. And yet democracy would prevent reproduction of the flight to the dream palace of Gouad Ajami, that illusory construction produced in the Middle Eastern world's psychic and physical captivity, which refuses all responsibility and blames the entire international community for the Arab world's failure, which envelopes everything in a postcolonial haze to criminalize, curse, and sentence the others to death.

The diamond spearhead of this pitiful fantasy, the preferred weapon that bewitches everyone, is twofold: suicide terrorism and the anti-Semitism of blood libel and the accusation of global domination accompanied by anti-Americanism, where an America befuddled by its own power lets itself be tricked by a conspiracy of diabolical Jews, the same ones as in *The Protocols of the Elders of Zion*.

Suicide terrorism is not a recent invention in the Islamic world, but it has never reached its current peak. There are amazed debates on why it exists and from where its great ease of action comes, its adaptability in the big new battle to dominate the world. From where does this incredible desire to kill themselves erupt, to see or encourage their children to die, and where is the birthplace of the erotic pleasure of pulling the explosive's cord or of being hooked up to a mobile telephone that, with its ring, will cause not only a mass murder but also the death of a young boy or of a mother?

The founder of the Israel Anti-Terrorist Center of Herzliya, Professor Ehud Sprinzak, who died recently, maintained that it was above all a choice dictated by megalomania of the political and religious type, a form of glorification, of the illusion of exercising huge power over the lives of many people and over politics, of being the creator of one's own destiny, choosing the heroic road that leads to paradise, imposing one's lesson on the world. Another interpretation—that of Professor Ariel Merari, a psychoanalyst who has personally analyzed thousands of individual cases—finds no particularities in the terrorist personality but instead a "banality of evil," sometimes with fideistic features (the seventy-two *urì* or virgins awaiting the martyr in heaven, the martyr's right to choose the relations to take with him to heaven), and suggests, as the all-important factor, the social dimension that channels you toward the decisive act with no way out, through a corridor of emotional blackmail, illusions, and social honors that are impossible to renege, on pain of disgrace worse than death. The latter interpretation has many historical confirmations, whereas the first one does not consider the humility typical, for example, of the mujaheddins of bin Laden and of bin Laden himself, with his stick, his tunic, and his eyes constantly lowered, or of Arafat, who—despite rolling in public income, besides the billions of dollars accumulated with the power of weapons—on a personal basis wears only military uniforms and does not like entertainment.

Another fundamental interpretation is the religious one of Yigal Karmon. Karmon, president of the Middle East Media Research Institute (MEMRI), thinks that Islam, right from ancient times and in its fundamental texts, has extolled the sacrifice of one's self in battle while killing the largest possible number of enemies and that this was a consequence of Mohammed's need to strongly motivate his followers in a world already divided into great powers (the Persians, Constantinople) and by religion, which threatened to crush him instantly. In modern times the difficulty for Islam to recapture the world after centuries of failures is equally huge and is directly proportional to the immense theoretical and theological effort that justifies and encourages suicide: whence a series of fatwas that assure increasingly wonderful prizes and even the absence of pain in accomplishing the extreme deed, right "from the first drop of blood." The political effort of representing heavenly bliss via video clips and in textbooks (even in Europe, for example in the Islamic schools in France) goes hand in hand with glorification of the poor and exploited Islam (the one that people know in reality) in the face of the arrogant Zionist and American enemy. These are three ways of seeing the problem. Others have been considered, and there are elements of truth in all of them. Daniel Pipes, an eminent historian, is convinced, for example, that the root of suicide terrorism lies in Wahhabism, the dominant current of Islamic thought and that of bin Laden. He holds that moderate Islam—now directly hit by extremist Islam—is the most effective antidote to Islamist terrorism.

When the so-called engineer, Yahya Ajash, was responsible for hundreds of victims on Jerusalem's buses in two months (the peace process was in full swing) and was then killed by the Israelis, I went to interview his family in a village set among the olive trees—very poetic—on the West Bank: his home totally renovated at the community's expense and full of devoted friends; a nice wife and a little boy reared to hero-worship his father and photographed with a little machine gun; the patriarchal atmosphere; the overflattering portraits of the terrorist, by then almost certainly in paradise; the nostalgic memories of Yahya's excellence at the mosque as an extremely young scholar of the Koran; even the large matrimonial bed to prove the virility very evidently missed by the beatified widow. Megalomania, social order and honor, religion—they were all there.

What certainly was not there was social desperation, which I have seen in only a very few cases of suicide terrorism, never, for example, in my visits to prisons where I met terrorists who had repented. Maybe just once in a meeting outside a shop in Bethlehem with a would-be terrorist whom I do not think ever achieved his desire. Desperation is instead the core explanation for terrorism given in Europe, indeed the only explanation. When televisions throughout the world showed a young boy with his TNT belt, everyone hastened to explain that the boy and his family were people who had nothing to lose, that life for them was "not life." This is a totally mistaken thought about a society that does not fear—but indeed desires—death interpreted as martyrdom. No one wondered why the mother, talking about her fourteen-year-old son who was found with his TNT belt, his life saved by Israeli soldiers, said: "I condemn those who have encouraged a boy to commit suicide. But if he wants to do so when he is eighteen years old, I will instead be proud. I would not mind it." Why? Perhaps because, when the boy reaches eighteen years of age, the family's social conditions will be desperate and today they are not? Maybe because the mother will be less of a mother in a few years' time? The truth is that the mother was alluding to terrorism's internal rules, the ones that none of us understand, according to which a Palestinian mother is certainly not happy for her son to die because of juvenile unhappiness or lack of integration (the little terrorist said that at school "no one liked him"), but rather because she considers it an honor, a form of social advancement, and a religious duty.

Desperation is not at the heart of terrorism: It is a concept that serves only to justify it and instead is at the heart of the philosophy of the world, which, at all costs, wants to avoid the war forced on us. We liberals feel compassion and solidarity for the desperate ones of the earth; their sufferings are synonymous with their reasons. Justification of terrorism, relating it to the Israeli occupation, to the West's imperialist policy, to U.S. unilateralism, and so on, is a nonanalytical but very cogent attitude, and above all it is cowardly because it rejects all responsibility for terrorism's victims, in effect putting the blame on them for having triggered desperation in the enemy.

Western self-condemnation, which prefers the Americans and Jews as the detonating causes of terrorism, is the demented dominant thinking of today's huge human rights party. This group, consisting, as stated earlier, of international organizations, street movements, NGOs, and some left-wing parties, is totally distorting itself in its spasmodic effort to defend every illiberal and fascist motivation. It dresses up as desperate the billionaire Middle Eastern dictatorships and terrorists, making terrorism, which denies all and any human and civil rights, into a fountain of human rights. It is not the first time that this has happened in the history of humanity: the illusion of defending the people, extolling horrible dictators is, on the contrary, typical of large mass movements. Stalin was for a long time the sun of the future; Mussolini and Hitler attracted the underprivileged masses, or those who considered themselves to be such;

Fidel Castro is still today the object of legendary veneration. Bin Laden is a figure whose motivations people try to understand and who is sometimes even admired and adored by the young Arabs who, having emigrated to Europe, see him as a symbol of the future power of Islam. Saddam Hussein who has killed, it is thought, four hundred thousand of his fellow countrymen, has often been depicted as a victim of American arrogance.

So it is that human rights defenders, who ought to be left wing, have become ominously similar to those who destroy and denigrate those rights. Freedom movements—and let us not deceive ourselves—have become movements for the defense of authoritarian and murderous regimes, for lack of freedom of the press, for women's oppression, and for the elimination of minorities. Anti-Semitism—and I myself am particularly sorry about this—has become left wing, or at least liberal (in the American sense), in the same way that liberals believe terrorists must be understood based on their history as an exploited and suffering people. Sheikh Yassin was a poor old tetraplegic and also a spiritual leader (I have seen it written in many newspapers and I have heard it shamelessly repeated on television). The children that Palestinian terrorism sends into the streets with their TNT belts, victims of ruthless propaganda and social forces that have also destroyed all possibility of development, are the result of Jewish cruelty. In the background is the American empire, which in the left wing's eyes is largely responsible for the terrorism in Iraq and the nonconclusion of the Israeli-Palestinian conflict, in the same way that U.S. imperialist policy is responsible for Israel's actions against the poor innocent Palestinians.

Among the many differences in the way in which September 11 has been considered and the way in which suicide terrorism—which to date has caused 1,000 dead in Israel (equivalent to 10,000 in Italy)—is viewed, there is a common denominator: Since the time when their slaughter became the high road of terrorist policy, both the peoples hit by terrorism and their respective ruling classes have been deplored without respite, as if the fact of being so hated were the sign of undeniable and gigantic guilt. In the liberal mind, the one sick with power, ferocity, and bellicose dementia is not the suicide terrorist; he is not aggressive and dangerous. The ones who are aggressive are those who, with their evil conduct, have caused terror and who subsequently react. Paradoxically, the terrorist becomes democratic, as does the anti-Semite who accuses Israel of being the cause of all ills. The liberal—if I am allowed this intentional exaggeration—turns into a terrorist.

If one considers that Syria, a country that openly supports terrorism, is part of the U.N. Security Council, this gives a terrifying political measure of what has happened. King Abdullah of Jordan accused Syria of having let Al Qaeda's trucks, packed with TNT, through its frontiers for a major attack on his people. According to the United States, Syria has introduced men and weapons into Iraq for the war against the Americans. When faced with the request to increase the Anti-Terrorism Commission's actions, Syria quoted the 1998 Arab Convention for the repression of terrorism as a cogent document for distinguishing between terrorism and the right of peoples to fight against foreign occupation. In the 2002 report, Syria quotes the definition to explain to the U.N. Anti-Terrorism Commission that, given this unquestionable point, the fight against terrorism cannot be undertaken by the United Nations due to lack of a definition. And Syria is in fact right: The definition of terrorism is immensely confused and it is logical that the United Nations has never given it a precise definition; it is a substantive part of its present nature. Because it would indicate that the automatic majorities that, de facto, protect the countries financing terrorism no longer existed. And unfortunately that is not the case. At the very time of possible condemnation of terrorism by virtue of an unequivocal definition, this would show that the United States and Israel were not isolated, but that the countries backing terrorism were. And instead no condemnation of a terrorist attack in Israel has ever been passed in the United Nations, with the excuse that it would have to be accompanied by similar condemnation of the occupation, absurdly considered equivalent—so much for international legality—to an act of terrorism.

How to react is an even more confused issue. Block the funds of the Hezbollahs and of Hamas? But how? They have been collected to help poor and needy populations, widows, the wounded, and children. Control the mosques' messages? Even consider mosques to be sanctuaries for terrorists? But that is a patent violation of religious freedom. Control broadcasters such Al-Manar or Al-Jazeera, the handbills, the libels, and the press in general so that they do not spread messages of incitement to terrorize? Impossible, it is a violation of the freedom of information. Control the funds donated (above all by Europe) for textbooks and educational development, so that they do not serve just to create new terrorists? Already done, certainly, but the books still invite children to become suicide terrorists and the TVs and newspapers financed by us are still bilges of violent and murderous messages. Rome, however, was not built in one day, and already some books are no longer in the old Jordanian version. Are they worse than before? They will change; in the meantime, we see that there is a will to change, that something has happened. Then consider how difficult it is to defend yourself physically from those attacking you, since treatises on antiterror strategy do not yet exist and there is no Geneva Convention that is suited to the new war. It is preferable to condemn Israel when it seeks to stop the terrorists using the old strategic rules, those according to which, rightly, civilians are untouchable. Every step seems to be a violation of common sense and of the compassion that one should have for the weak and oppressed, whereas today's weak and oppressed are those who are attacked by terrorism, not vice versa.

To the liberal mind, combating terrorism is a controversial point—for heaven's sake do not touch peoples' right to self-determination. Their logic has nothing to do with good sense; they ceaselessly express hope of intervention by the United Nations—which to date is only a discouraging arena for the incessant political war between some democratic governments and authoritarian governments, mostly Muslim, and part of Europe, which fears them or takes economic advantage of them. It is incredible that the United Nations is considered the source of an international wisdom able to solve problems, especially in Iraq and the Middle East, after it showed itself incapable of saving just one of the eight hundred thousand Tutsi butchered in Rwanda or after the sorry figure it cut in Kosovo. It is incredible to consider it an equitable judge after the General Assembly's solemn and crazy declaration that "Zionism is racism." The United Nations cannot—because it does not want to—stop terrorism in Iraq. It sees the conflict in Iraq as an anti-American and, above all, anti-Israeli bullfight, and therefore in no way can it have anything to do with terrorism, which is the greatest cause of the Middle Eastern conflict. The United Nations is an organism that manages conflicts to favor just one side; it can neither fight terrorism nor comprehend the phenomenon. On the contrary, anyone who dares to defend him- or herself triggers the assembly's immediate condemnation. Today the United Nations is the mirror of that falsely liberal mentality, fostered, de facto, by dictatorships, according to which defending one's self from terrorism has the sole effect of causing further desperation and, consequently, more terrorism.

To achieve peace, it is necessary to concede, to pull out, in other words, to surrender to terror. No credit is given to the facts, which indicate that September 11 was being prepared during the government of one of the most pacifist U.S. presidents ever, Bill Clinton. In the same way, Arafat, having prepared the intifada of terrorism when he could instead have received, in a short time, 97 percent of everything needed to create two states with definite boundaries, is the subject of derision. Ehud Barak and perhaps even Rabin (of whom no one dares to speak badly in public because he was assassinated by a right-wing Jewish extremist) were plotting, perhaps they were lying; perhaps what was clearly evident, i.e. the renouncement by then decided and the pacifist choice, was all a machination. The testimony of Clinton and of the many others present at the negotiations does not count. Terrorism's design to relaunch the game "from the river to the sea," its ideal link—also of the laical components of the war that was once territorial—with Islamist terrorism, which was becoming increasingly strong, all this was interpreted as being the consequence of bad Jewish behavior due, who knows, if not to history, to the Jewish disposition, to its nature.

And this factor of disposition and nature became even more evident when Sharon became Israel's prime minister. His military past together with his right-wing membership was sufficient to obliterate, without remittance, without question, the fact that he had immediately chosen, for the primaries against Netanyahu, the Palestinian state as his core political option; that he withstood terrorist massacres for a whole year without organizing a true defense against terror; and that he then chose unilateral withdrawal. His warmongering disposition had been fabled against all evidence to the contrary. In the face of an attack like those suffered by the Israelis in buses and pizzerias, any European state would have immediately mobilized the army, without the Israeli army's slowness and prudence. Furthermore, Israel was guilty, like the United States, of engaging in a war never seen before in which the enemy does not wear a uniform but is himself a civilian concealed among civilians. Israel has been criticized for eliminating potential human bombs, who would have perpetrated tomorrow's attack if they had not been stopped there and then. These cases were talked of as "illegal executions"; condemnations rained down from the United Nations and from all parts of Europe, as if the attempt simply to defend one's self were wrong. Who in an international court could state that a government is right only when it commits suicide? Rantisi was not eliminated in order to punish him without a trial, but to prevent the inevitable attacks that he was preparing. No article of international law requires a country not to defend itself from mortal peril.

At times, when I wake up in the morning in Jerusalem and see with my own eyes how moderately this country reacts to terrorism and how it daily demonstrates that it loves democracy beyond and above all expectations, it is very difficult to tolerate the wave of perversion pervading Europe. For us, in Europe, it is normal to go to a job or the cinema, to take the children swimming, or to attend a meeting against alcohol and drugs, or for the defense of single mothers, or for the rights of animals, immigrants, and cancer sufferers. For us it is easy, via our social behavior, to champion democracy and to point out to our children its practicality, versatility, and strength and even to teach how it should be used. In Israel, in the midst of the war, a prime minister is blood-libeled. The Upper Council of the Magistrature, the High Court, rules, with unwavering justice, now in favor of Arabs , now in favor of Jews on whether a house can be demolished or on whether a film full of lies about the Jenin refugee camp should be shown for the sake of freedom of expression. Mothers do not lie across doorways to prevent children going into a pub that might be blown up, or doing military service in Gaza, or going to university, or to the football or basketball game, or catching a bus, or going to street demonstrations.

Is that the beauty of democracy? If it is, why is it hated so much? Do we not understand that tyranny, for as long as it holds sway, will nurture terrorism? Many Palestinian terrorists received their training in Lebanon and Iraq. Millions of dollars in weapons and funds are transferred every year by dictatorships such as Iran or Saudi Arabia to the Hezbollahs and Hamas. Even countries such as Egypt—which in turn is under attack by the Muslim Brotherhood and permits publication in its national daily newspapers' front pages of caricatures worthy of Nazi newspapers and the broadcasting of praise of the suicide terrorists—do not combat terrorism; on the contrary, they offer terrorism ideological support and let popular excitement unfold in sanguinary ways against the West.

The natural product of underdevelopment and social neglect turns into incitement when the regime is totalitarian and, moreover, underpinned by a religion that does not exclude the use of violence. Poverty (take the cases of Thailand, Poland, or Peru) as such does not host or nurture terrorism. The Islamist dictatorship is its cradle and driver, and we are its victims. It is dictatorship that creates terror, not Islam. It is the venom prepared in Saudi Arabia and in Yemen that felled the Twin Towers and blew up the trains in Madrid. It is dictatorship that shoots at dissidents in the streets of Nablus, drives human rights activists to desperation in Palestine, and nurtures and funds terrorists. Hundreds of millions of oppressed people secretly dream of freedom—which also means our freedom from violence. Heroes of dissent write their samizdats in Egypt, in Jordan, in Saudi Arabia, in Syria, in Lebanon—and we abandon them, cloaking ourselves in the values of pluralism, rejection of ethnocentrism, and self-determination. In reality, by renouncing the democratic revolution in the Middle East and by accepting the violence of terrorism, we abandon the whole world to the worst version of Islam, to the totalitarian fantasies of bin Laden and Sheikh Yassin. We are scandalized by the dream of exporting democracy to a different civilization. And yet no one was scandalized by the Communist dream of taking the socialist revolution to all peoples, in all continents.

And is it not perhaps incredible that a democratic country stands up to the strategic threat of arrogance, totalitarianism, illiberal customs, and the arms cult? Zawahiri (bin Laden's deputy) has said that, as soon as he gets weapons of mass destruction, he will use them against Israel. Does anyone remember at the United Nations how Iran periodically shows off increasingly sophisticated Shihab 3 and 4 missiles in processions, publicly dedicating them to the destruction of the Jewish state, while its clerics condemn Israel to atomic death? And would it not be right for the plethora of NGOs, perceived as the shield of human rights, to ask themselves why they are ready to discriminate against Israel and to ignore all the dynamics—pleasant and unpleasant—that teach what a democracy is in the face of a terrorist attack? Does not the Israeli democracy in its struggle give hope to all of us? If it does, why is there a desire to see it dead? It is difficult to get used to the idea that demonstrations of hundreds of thousands of people march through the streets shouting that Hitler was right—people who care nothing about Middle Eastern dictatorships, the sufferings, the dead, the persecutions that those dictatorships inflict on their citizens; who do not want to know about Arafat's double speeches in Arabic and English; who march waving Palestinian flags, at times (as happened in front of the Rome ghetto) even dressed up as terrorists; who are totally ignorant of the Saudis' lethal maneuvers, of Bashar Assad's anti-Semitic and ferocious aggressions; who do not want to know that Syria colonially occupies Lebanon and infests it with Hezbollahs, weapons, and terrorist training camps. A public opinion that pretends to march for civil rights and does not want to know anything about the oppression in Sudan, or in Libya, of the suffering of women whom the imperialist project has turned into mere breeding machines, of the children used as human shields for fighters and as little terrorist robots.

It is unnerving to see the NGOs protest because Israeli soldiers stop ambulances at checkpoints, when it is known that they are in fact used to transport terrorists. It is exhausting to watch Amnesty International while it ignores the global television stations, watched throughout Europe, that find nothing better to do than broadcast dozens of hours of serials on *The Protocols of the Elders of Zion* and on the perverse idea that Jews use gentiles' blood in their Passover matzos, or video clips extolling children's suicide terrorism. It is impossible to see the degree of indifference evident in European left-wing movements today, to see so many falsehoods, without remaining dumfounded. I believe that many good people among the politicians and intellectuals have gagged and blinkered themselves; this, however, does not justify them in the face of history, nor will it save them.

A whole world dances with joy and distributes candies when a bus is blown to bits. The fact that some mothers are proud of their suicide-terrorist children and accept money in exchange for their death is normal social behavior. And we watch this spectacle as if it were a creative adventure film, at the end of which everyone calmly goes home.

It is true. I remember the fascination with blood of the totalitarian portion of the left wing. My friends in the Lotta Continua movement, and especially in the Potere Operaio movement, liked covering their faces with handkerchiefs, using their hands to mimic the P-38 firing position, and threatening their enemies with death. The totalitarian portion of the left wing has in fact never ceased to demonstrate and to take the form of terrorism. Now, however, seeing terrorism as a justifiable response, even going as far as complicity, is a mass phenomenon.

How many people with an astute air now aggressively state: "We have to seriously ask ourselves what *real* terrorism is"? This can be seen in all mass demonstrations against the United States and Israel, in all the falsehoods that hide or mask the facts. Terrorism has almost become politically correct. The biggest lie of all is that rejection of Israel is based on legitimate criticism of Sharon's policy. This is not true: It is not criticism but prejudice, the basis of which lies in the U.N. resolution that "Zionism equals racism." This prejudice goes well beyond this resolution by delegitimizing the state of Israel and by discriminating against all Jewish people, inasmuch as they are connected with Israel (as explicitly stated by the Hamas Charter and the various fatwas of bin Laden and Yassin, which make Israel the Rushdie of the nations, sentenced to death). This anti-Semitism uses human rights organizations as a mask to conceal discriminatory behavior toward Israel, the genocidal nature of the physical attacks (particularly by suicide terrorists), and the theories that conclude the world would be better off without Israelis. This conclusion is reached by portraying Israel as poisoning the springs of international goodwill and as a despicable object to be pointed out to the young as a violator of human rights. Conversely, the Palestinians are portrayed as victims of modern imperialism and colonialism. This falsehood—equal only to that which allowed the Holocaust to happen in the 1940s—has obscured the true story of Israel and that beautiful word *Zionism*, dressing them up as arrogance and despotism. The history of Jewish nationalism is certainly less violent and more morally motivated than any other national story, given the proven impossibility for the Jewish nation to survive unless it founded a state, a defense. Fortunately today, in the face of this new reawakening of the anti-Semitic hydra, the Jews, for the first time in history, have their own state, able to defend them, wherever they are in the world.

It is ridiculous to dress up the NGOs as organizations that express the liberal spirit of our times when instead they have turned into the long arm of a United Nations morally worn out by antidemocratic exploitation. It is horrible that there are people who say the veil is a refuge and who ignore that, at the very least, the veil is a symbol of sexual discrimination for Islamic women. Those who do not see the corruption of Arab dictatorships and their intrinsic bond with terror are blind—as are those who ignore Iran's role in fomenting terrorism in Iraq, the danger that we all run due to Iran's race for the atomic bomb and the link between its belligerent stance and the oppression of the noble Iranian people. Too many horrors, too many evident perversions, which are the antithesis of democracy and human rights, are ignored today by left-wing movements; too many truths about the history and internal dynamics of the intifada and its corrupt and violent leadership are intentionally forgotten. These perversions make it possible to be anti-Semitic as a new form of human rights practice. It is revolting to attribute Bush's policy to Jewish interests. It is a philo-totalitarian perversion, and what is worse, it is suicidal because, in reality, it denies the usefulness of the United States' democracy and its war on terrorism.

The new anti-Semitism is part of terrorism, just as the old type was part of Nazism and Fascism, and then also of Communism. Its distinguishing features are its acute, paranoid anti-Americanism, its anti-Western dimension, and its identification with Muslims. Anti-Semitism has become the cornerstone of extremist Islamism, which perceives the Judeo-Christian culture as an irreducible enemy (whence the choice of "crusaders and Jews" as the targets of the Islamist war), because this culture creates what Islamic societies cannot accept—freedom, equality, turnover of the ruling classes, and human rights.

But, like Fascism, Nazism, and Communism, terrorism, today's totalitarian ideology has found allies in the West, its apologists who believe they are serving their own cause, when instead they are serving just their own opportunism and also their own political power. Europe does not recognize the fascist and totalitarian dimension of the new anti-Semitism, in the same way as it does not see the imperialist and antiliberal design of terrorism. The Islamist origin of the two phenomena is the face of the Medusa: The hatred for Israel, inasmuch as it is the Jewish state, is identical to the hate for the West, inasmuch as it is the cradle of freedom. And the latter includes Europe, whether Europe likes it or not.

We will not win the war against terrorism if we do not win the war against anti-Semitism. We will not win if we do not defend everybody's democracy, headed by that of the Islamic world. These concepts, so tightly interlaced, will prevail only if the ideology that proclaims itself the guardian of democracy and of human progress manages to turn 360 degrees and embark on an authentic human rights policy against dictatorships and war, clearing the field of falsehoods, hypocrisies, and the fear that encrusts the religion of our times—the religion of human rights.

I was moved when I read a quotation from the report of the U.S. Agency for International Development, in turn quoted by Saul Singer in the *Jerusalem Post* of February 26, 2004: "The group was taken to the front of the bus, where they turned the headlights on them. They made them lie on the ground and then pulled them up one by one to execute them. He [the witness] does not recall them saying anything, except for the cries of three brothers who implored that at least one of them be spared. They were killed one at a time. Then the woman was killed in front of her 5-year-old son. The child clung to the legs of the executioner, who kicked him and shot him in the face." This part of the report refers to the killing of five of the 400,000 victims who ended up in Saddam Hussein's common graves. Another 290,000 Iraqi citizens were caused to disappear forever. In the survivors' stories, the horror is immense especially because—as in so many stories on the Holocaust—the victims were forced to watch the killing of their loved ones.

No report of Amnesty International or of Human Rights Watch exists on these subjects. On the contrary, Ken Roth, the director of Human Rights Watch, has published a long position paper on the war in Iraq called: "Not a Humanitarian Intervention."

The United Nations, nearly all the humanitarian groups, the NGOs, democratic journalism, and democratic parties now seem to believe that violations of human rights consist of the marginal consequences of the war on terrorism, rather than of the instigators of that terrorism and rather than the terrorist war that has been extended worldwide. And there seems to be no question that Saddam Hussein was extending a terrorist war to the world. Besides slaughtering his people—an indispensable ingredient for his policy of tyranny and gigantic personal enrichment—Saddam, by his own admission, had accumulated 8,500 liters of anthrax that, when powdered, fitted into a few suitcases and might be inside or outside Iraqi boundaries and in any corner of the Middle East. Before the eyes of the world, he donated $25,000 to each Palestinian terrorist and his family. His weapons of mass destruction have been seen by Richard Butler, who headed the inspectors expelled in 1998, and Wafiq Al Samurrai, ex-head of Saddam's intelligence department, who said during his get-away: "There are more than 200 barrels containing biological agents stowed away and hidden—and you will never find them—and at least forty-five missiles with a range of 600 km capable of transport-ing them."

The person who witnessed, without looking away, the killing of five thousand civilians in Halabja with mustard gas and nerve gas and honestly summarized this story, which also includes the invasion of Kuwait and the daily violence against Kuwait's people, should have rejoiced in the capture of this human monument to violence. Similarly, those who witnessed the Holocaust in Europe, have studied it, and even those who are only aware of it should seethe with rage and fight the reemergence of anti-Semitism. This has not happened, is not happening, and terrorism is gaining ground in our part of the world.

# Munich

The face of the boy seated in the third row at the Liceo Tasso, a secondary school in Rome, is with me nonstop. He was dark and thin and had light eyes. He was sitting next to his teacher, I think, and there was a delightful intimacy between the two of them. They were whispering, making ironic remarks about my complex explanations, nodding their heads enthusiastically in full agreement with one another and against me; there was a kind of electricity that ran between them. They chattered, not understanding, not knowing; happily they applauded whoever repeated their stereotypes. It was like a thorn in my flesh, perhaps because it reminded me of myself as a girl caught up in a web of lies resulting from an animalistic urge to follow the herd; it showed me the psychic harm caused by the lack of understanding toward Israel, which is not a question of ignorance but of denial. It made me angry, like when someone wounds you purely out of aggression, or wounds himself for the same reason, directing the aggression inward, maybe because he is a little crazy, or because he is imprisoned. And I felt an obligation to pause and solve the problems of that boy and his teacher, instead of those presented by reality: the mistakes of the past century still weigh so heavily upon us. It is both horrible and tiresome to know that they are still the same ghosts—totalitarianism, anti-Semitism, Third Worldism, sexism—our worst fellow travelers, our demented interlocutors.

To reason well about Israel and about the conflict with the Arab world is more than just a test of international politics: It is a test of one's relationship with democracy, of one's awareness of the conflicts that the Western world faces after having thought that it could take everything under the wing of its benevolent sovereignty; it is a test of character, because, faced with conflict, you must be strong to remain capable of reasoning without immediately siding with those who shout the loudest or weep openly. Who is really the victim? History is filled with treacherous tears. To reason well about Israel means being able to remain standing while confronting the anguish of having enemies opposed to our culture and our religions. It means having the courage not to give in to anti-Semitic refrains. It means not hiding behind ignorance and even at times appreciating the value of force, which our modern fable all of a sudden attributes only to those who are evil. Israel is for everyone a test of both reality and idealism, but an idealism that is truly willing to do justice rather than dispense rhetoric. Instead, these two things generally go together. To reason well about Israel means having the courage to say the words *war* and *border* when they must be said. To admit that when two parties are facing one another, one cannot speak of them as equals when one is authoritarian and the other democratic. It means admitting the limitations of media information, when you realize that live images on CNN can lie and that objective accounts can deceive. And finally it means having the terrible courage to say that the act of a child who goes to die is not in itself "good"; he may be the instrument of evil men, or he may even have fierce, reckless feelings because he is tragically overwhelmed by a culture that does not value life.

It was the early part of 2001 at Liceo Tasso, and the intifada had been going on since September of the prior year: September 28 to be exact. Or at least that is the official date when Ariel Sharon, solid and assertive, went up to the Temple Mount on the Plain of the Mosques. Actually, I had been writing for some days about Palestinian attacks, without understanding the situation very well. One of the attacks had particularly struck me: During a joint watch of Israeli and Palestinian police—an icon of the peace process, a pillar of the Oslo Accords—the Palestinians had fired on their Israeli colleagues who were part of the same watch and had killed one of the border guards. In the yellow dust, under the blue sky. How strange. At the time it was still only very odd.

Bewilderment set in when Arafat, after having said no to all Barak's proposals, climbed out of his helicopter and left everyone astonished by raising his hand and making a V for victory sign. Later it became known through numerous public statements by his ministers that he had already made his decision that he would not accept any accord, that his men should arm themselves, that he had entered into new agreements with Hamas, and that all sectors of the Palestinian world (police, Hamas, Islamic Jihad, Tanzim, and children with stones) should be ready. But at the time—in that same Gaza wind where Clinton had landed some months earlier, so kind, though a bit of a fraud, smiling a little too much, so full of goodwill, symbol of a most benevolent Pax Americana—no one understood it yet. The toboggan ride of peace is funny; the adrenaline rises while we all feel good. When during the same visit Hillary Clinton listened stunned but with no reaction to that simpleton Suha Arafat say that the Israelis deliberately polluted the air, water, and food of the Palestinian Authority, she made believe she didn't hear it. The whole world considered the matter a misunderstanding.

On October 11, following the first deaths, Sheik Ahmad Abu Halabiya, former rector of the University of Gaza, read his sermon in the mosque: "O faithful brothers, the terrorist criminals are Jews, they must be butchered and slain like Allah the Omnipotent tells us: fight them, Allah will torture them through your hands . . . O believers, do not take Jews and Christians as your allies, since they are allied with one another. Whoever takes them as allies, will be one of them . . . have no pity on Jews, wherever they are, in whatever city. Wherever you may be, kill the Jews, the Americans who are like them, and those who take their side." A small jolt was felt throughout the world and in Israel. Yet the world press continued to wonder if the peace process was still alive. Peace is essential, isn't it? A courageous peace, a good-natured peace. It seems like a theorem: How can Jews and Palestinians, as intertwined as they are, live together without peace?

Anything that did not favor the triumph of the peace process was automatically censured. Every sign was irrelevant. Truth obscured; evidence denied. That's why what I remember more than anything about the intifada—among thousands of atrocities, the dead, the wounded—is the face of the boy at the Liceo, a face that bore no sign of suffering. He was the very image of Western innocence, a pacifist, unscrupulous innocence that saves its soul by finding a scapegoat in Israel. If peace doesn't come, the fault must necessarily lie with us, but not really with us—with the Jews: the Jews who are almost us, the worst of ourselves, the best of ourselves, our guilt, our glory. Israel, the triumph of life, the descendants of those we have killed, and then saved, and then tolerated, and then vilified all over again.

For a long time I too didn't understand it. Peace is a wonderful thing; it's an essential element of our lives as Westerners born in the second half of the last century. The two wars of the twentieth century were the most sanguinary, the worst bloodbath in the history of humanity. Along with the failure of Communism, Nazism resulted in tens of millions of deaths. World War II, dominated by the extermination of the Jews, left psychological and moral traces that opened the way to a society of peace as a moral framework indispensable for civil rights, for democratic institutions, and for a constitutional state. How could it be otherwise? Peace is inherent in us. We do not believe, as Islam does, that the world is divided between Dar al-Islam, the house of Islam, submission to God, and Dar al-Harb, the house of war, and that the duty of every Muslim is to extend the house of Islam to embrace the other and direct it toward good, whether through peace or through war.

We do not have an acquisitive view of peace; without peace we simply do not exist. We are prepared to be Chamberlain to achieve it, and there is not always a Churchill waiting in the wings when it doesn't work out. Appeasement was not a dirty word prior to Munich, it just meant that we think that we can always pacify the other party with gifts and smiles, Nobel Prizes, checks, and tracts of land, that we can always cede something in exchange for the supreme good. So many times I heard it said—faced with the statements of the elder Assad, before he made Barak realize that, without that narrow beach on Lake Tiberiade, he would not accept the strategic extension of the Golan Heights—that war is no longer a territorial matter, since with the use of missiles the extent of a territory doesn't count. And Assad upset everything on account of ten meters. He preferred that his son Bashar inherit not the Golan but the possibility of saying that "Israel is a nation that is more racist than the Nazis."

We no longer know if land is important or not, but the Arabs know it so well that in the end they showed their clear-cut determination to make it the point-scoring, fundamental theme of the conflict, or at least its public standard. Peace for the sake of peace matters only to us: for them, instead, it's "land for peace." Peace is subordinate to territorial acquisition, which includes the land in all its mystical significance, not just a portion of it. Not 95 percent of the territories, the Jordan Valley, East Jerusalem and much of the Old City, Gaza without the settlements, the West Bank with peripheral tracts in exchange for which Israeli territory would be ceded, but the mystical Land of Dar al-Islam—all of it. We don't use the word *truce* as a synonym for possible peace, therefore establishing the right to withdraw and negate an agreement when the occasion to extend Dar al-Islam arises.

After having been so for several centuries, Western peace is no longer acquisitive. Peace is a song, a poem: it's beautiful, it's good. Only a few madmen think that war is tolerable. The Arabs, on the other hand, tolerate it quite well because they view it as a dutiful march toward the restitution of what was stolen from them: Jihad is one of their most deeply rooted duties. "You promised us a dove" mourns an Israeli song, whose imaginary voices are those of children who died in battle during the 1973 war, after so many other wars that Israel fought since 1948. There have been others after that, and each was supposed to be the last. Arafat's young children learn in school that to be a shahid, a martyr who blows himself up killing many Israelis, is a desirable and even wonderful thing, that the future still holds many wars.

During the years of the peace process, Israel altered its body and its soul. The sweeping change was indescribable, swift, dizzying. A society at war that is also a democratic society develops a system of values similar to a puzzle with millions of pieces in fragile equilibrium with one another. The army's special forces, the military elite, have always come from the more humanitarian kibbutzim of the left. The soldiers despair; they become debilitated if they strike children or women. Pacifist organizations demonstrate with Palestinians for relief from the imposed restrictions on their village on the same day the bus they take to go to work every day explodes in Tel Aviv.

A friend of mine, the director of a museum, telephones from Tel Aviv while they are shooting at Gilo, at the corner where my house is, and says to me: "I've been thinking about you a lot, each time the television shows more shooting there where you are. . . . How are you getting along? Most of all, how do you stand it when Israeli helicopters fire machine guns at the houses from which Palestinians are shooting?" In the *Ha'aretz*, the daily newspaper of the enlightened left, a long, sorrowful interview with the helicopter pilots attests to their anguish at having to strafe Ramallah from the air soon after the lynching of two Israeli soldiers in October 2000, even though the targets were strategic and surgical (the police headquarters where the unfortunate victims were killed) and even though people were warned first so that they could evacuate.

Along with half the world, I followed the peace process as a dramatic event that was also ethical, aesthetic, and in any case inevitable with respect to our inner selves as Westerners. It was my history: I supported it deep down in my most inner self. It was me, even though I never cared for the rhetoric that surrounded it, the ceremonies with green lawns and red velvet carpets, the Nobel Prizes, Arafat who became a champion of peace after having been the terrorist behind the killing of the Jewish athletes at the Munich Olympics and the slaughter of the children of Ma'alot, behind the Achille Lauro, the airplane hijackings, the bombings at Fiumicino. That Arafat is considered a national hero doesn't bother me. Israeli television, gaining the highest audience ratings, showed him again in 1993 in a documentary in which he became human, palatable to Western tastes: his house, his wife, his kaffiyeh—Arafat falling asleep on the plane that was carrying him from one place to another in the world to plead the Palestinian cause; Arafat in the living room of his house where in actuality he hardly ever stays, neither he nor Suha, who lives most of the year in Paris. People watched him, fascinated, astounded; there were those who continued to hate him in no uncertain terms, but even more astonishing was the fact that many were captivated by that figure.

So many times I've heard Shimon Peres say that peace is "the only possible choice." And what if it were the only impossible choice? I was wandering through the flourishing streets of Tel Aviv. The shops had new merchandise, dresses, sweaters, European shoes. Business was prospering; construction and high-tech ventures were going through the roof; restaurants were opening with Italian and nouvelle cuisine. I wondered if Israel would enjoy the fruits of peace for long without paying an excessive price. I sensed the hollow sound of what I saw as a process yet to be defined, a path that would perhaps rob Israel of its soul, but I didn't identify it as a mortal danger. To think that Arafat, after a lifetime of being a leader and terrorist for a single idea—that of giving his people a nation—would in 2000 at Camp David abandon the idea of drawing up the boundaries of his Palestinian state, that he would forego being Romulus and Remus all rolled into one now that Barak was offering him 95 percent of the territories occupied in 1967, plus an additional 5 percent from Israeli soil to meet his demand of 100 percent; that he would relinquish the Plain of the Mosques plus a large part of the Old City and East Jerusalem under his rule or under the protection of one of those international safeguarding forces that Arafat has always considered his property; in short, that he would decide to give up working, maybe to live on Salah al-Din, the main street with its buses, the sounds of car horns and Lebanese or Egyptian songs, the smell of wild thyme, newspaper, tobacco, carpet, and souvenir shops, monasteries and electricians, and to walk from there to the mosque of Al Aqsa to pray, from the house that was his home to the mosque that was also his home. No—no one had realized that he would say no, because the century just past designed us to deny reality, me and all those who were raised with the same democratic, pacifist upbringing. But reality is also Middle Eastern, drenched with Islamic revenge; it calls to mind the hamsin, the terrible, hot desert wind that parches and scalds with no remission. We Westerners have to feel it full in the face to understand what it is like. Otherwise we are left with a world that must be set right by imposing punishments on ourselves, swallowing lies, hiding our fear behind false moralizing, like the United Nations does, like France does.

At Liceo Tasso, observing the noisy student audience, I saw that boy in front of me and decided to address my explanation to him, to dedicate the efforts of so many years of work and study in the field to him, to explain to him how the devil we could have come to such a bloody, hopeless conflict. I especially had in mind the screeching of the ambulances, the shots that reach as far as my house in Gilo. The scenes of sahibs, child "martyrs" dead on stretchers, as grand funeral processions wind around displaying Palestinian flags or the green banners of Islam. The desperate embrace among eighteen-year-old soldiers who mourn the past and the future as they bury their friends. And the mothers: I lack the courage to look at their faces and see the horror of suicide terrorism gone berserk. In my shoes I have sand from Hebron, from Bethlehem, from Jericho, and I try to explain the dynamics of the clashes I have seen in person, the psyche of the children I have interviewed, the desperation of watching them go to die like that, the ambushes planned by the Tanzim against cars driven by Israelis, the strange yet real humanity of the settlers, the monstrous innocence of the Palestinian terrorists of Hamas, the instances in which a Jewish driver on his way to work is found killed in an ambush, leaning forward, riddled with bullets, his children killed or wounded in the backseat. I try to explain the anguish that makes you turn on the radio every half hour, the courage required to take the bus, the mechanic in Bethlehem who repaired my flat tire with a kind smile, while the smoke of other tires, burning, rose behind a wall, and the determination to die that we truly do not understand, the crucial question on the real objectives of the intifada.

I watched the Italian boy, but he didn't see me, he didn't hear me. His eyes were contemptuous, as if I were a stupid old woman typical of international imperialism, or one of its agents as they used to say: a miserable journalist who deludes herself that she is recounting something, but actually has nothing new to say about what is already perfectly well known concerning rights and wrongs. And he looked at me as if I shouldn't be allowed to speak, given the name I bear. I was upset at not being able to bridge the distance between me and the boy, so much so that I paused in the middle of my presentation, and since he was sniggering and whispering with his teacher, I asked him to stop. I asked him angrily. He knew, Europe already knows all the answers concerning the Palestinians and the Israelis: it knows everything that isn't true, and its distance from the truth is so pathological that it brings to mind the example of Fidel Castro's Cuba in the sixties and seventies. But in addition, there is a horrible secret here that has to do with fear and shame. Fear of Islam; shame with respect to what Europe has done to the Jews and a consequent need to justify past crimes by criminalizing the Jews.

For Israel peace has always been an ironic strategic objective. The social reason, so to speak, for Zionism is to go back home in peace, to put an end to that state of continuous confusion, of war without respite to which the Jews have always been subjected as a result of persecutions. Living in constant conflict with its 700 million Arab and Muslim neighbors has never suited it and has never been part of its ideology. It is certainly true that the history of the founding of the Israeli nation took place in war. But it was a war they were subjected to, bearing no relation to colonial wars. The Jews, unlike any colonialist country, had no other homeland. Their objectives were not to gain wealth and subjugate a population or its resources: They did not come from a rich world to a poor one to exploit it or even to educate it. They have nothing to do with the history of the "white man's burden." They had maintained a continual presence in the land that they had always considered their spiritual fatherland, the roots of an identity that, without Jerusalem, would never have survived throughout the centuries.

New historians have rightly debunked the national myth that asserts complete acceptance of close cohabitation with the Arabs: it is true, as they have shown, that in the war of 1948, soon after the nation was proclaimed, during the conflict that the Jews call a war of independence and the Palestinians call the Naqba, the disaster, various regions, for example, the one around Lod, were evacuated by force; it is true that Israel, being small and weak, was perhaps very angry and frightened at being drawn into war when six Arab countries (Egypt, Syria, Transjordan, Lebanon, Saudi Arabia, and Iraq), after rejecting the U.N. partition, asked local residents to leave before sending in their armies; it is true that there were crimes and forced evacuations, as there always are in war. But the Israelis certainly did not want that war. They did not declare it: even then they had neither an ideological nor a practical interest in doing so. Their antagonism was directed more at the British. They did not hate the Arabs, even though they had been attacked by them since the 1929 pogrom at Hebron, a city in which the Jewish presence has been uninterrupted since the time of the First Temple. Although Israel occupied the Sinai during the 1956 war, it returned it by March 1957, despite the fact that Egypt did not reopen the Suez Canal to Israeli ships and Gaza continued to be the departure point for numerous terrorist attacks.

In the years that followed there were countless attacks from all sides, including the Syrian border. When Egyptian radio announced on May 22, 1967, that Egypt was "resolutely determined to sweep Israel off the map," and Nasser stated "Our fundamental objective is the destruction of Israel," Israel found itself having to fight a war that today might be considered an offensive one given its results (Israel invaded the West Bank, Gaza, the Sinai, and the Golan Heights north of Syria and won), but which took place at the peak of the Cold War, with Egypt and Syria armed with massive, sophisticated equipment provided and supported by the USSR and fortified by the presence of a rousing leader like Nasser.

The result of Israel's victory was a policy of occupying the areas from which terrorist groups were spawned, but not annexing them, and it withdrew to the cease-fire lines. These were years of intense terrorism: the Munich attack, in which eleven athletes of the Israeli team were killed one by one, took place in 1972. Planes were hijacked (nine of them in the period 1969–1972); nursery schools and homes for the elderly were favorite places for slaughters. The surrounding countries were violently hostile, although Hussein of Jordan, concerned about the escalation of Palestinians' power within his country, killed them off and drove them as far as Syria and Lebanon. Assad of Syria declared in 1971: "Syria is the lung through which the body of terrorism breathes, and so it will remain."

The Yom Kippur war of 1973, which Golda Meir was unable to avert despite numerous signs, marked a concentric attack by Egypt and Syria that was particularly bloody and deleterious. Israel lost 2,378 soldiers in fifteen days. Golda Meir gave a famous speech that summarizes the thinking about the war at that time: "We will win because we must live. Our neighbors are not fighting for their lives, nor for their national sovereignty, but to destroy us. We will not be destroyed. We don't dare be destroyed. Therefore, the spirit of our men at the front, of our people in every house, in every city and village, is the spirit of a people who hate war but know that to survive they must win this war into which we have been forced." Israel won, and at the time of the cease-fire held Egyptian and Syrian territories beyond the Golan, all of which were given back to a point west of Quneitra, on the road to Damascus.

The conclusion of this war, like all the others, was accompanied by opposing positions. Moshe Dayan stated: "I don't think we will see peace with Egypt if in addition to controlling the port of Eilat, we do not also control the Suez gateway." Golda Meir talked about the "need for territorial compromises in order to have peace." "We will continue until all the land is liberated," Assad said. Sadat had made the famous statement that he was ready to pay the price of victory with "a million lives"; his general Gamassy, chief of staff, declared on March 4, 1974: "There is still a war ahead of us for which we must prepare," Arafat announced, as a series of attacks were taking place. "Just as the battle of Hattin [Saladin's victory against the crusaders in 1187] was only the beginning of the crusaders' defeat, the Ramadan campaign [a terrorist campaign] is only the beginning of the Arab nation's advance. This advance will stop only at Tel Aviv." And in fact the terrorist wave that followed was extensive, with recurrent bus explosions and invasions from the sea. In 1978 Anwar Sadat and Menachim Begin signed a peace agreement whereby Israel would return the Sinai and forcibly evacuate its settlements in the area (it was Sharon who cleared them out). In 1982, the Lebanon war, which subsequently had a long drawn-out, ill-fated continuation, followed in the wake of a terrorist uprising originating in what had become the land of Al-Fatah in southern Lebanon, Arafat's headquarters. Following repeated invasions of Lebanon, 39 civilians were killed in northern Israel and 375 wounded in the period from 1980 to 1982.

From the seventies on—reaching a peak in 1974 when the United Nations declared Israel a "racist state" in a resolution passed with a "nonaligned" (an ironic expression indeed) Soviet vote; the resolution was rescinded more than twenty years later, after the USSR and the Cold War had given way—an endless list of Israel's wrongs was gradually drawn: wrongs that transformed the original victory of the nation's birth following the Holocaust, one of the most vital conquests in the history of humanity, into an original sin against the Palestinian people. And not just against them—against the Arab countries, against the European nations who are friends of the Arabs, against the entire worldwide left. Slowly, from the politically correct view imposed on the world in 1948, when the USSR and the United States, aligned against the Nazi monster, voted for the partition, we have moved on to a different kind of politically correct stance, one that is utterly senseless. Israel is guilty; Israel is savage; Israel is intrinsically expansionist. And, above all, Israel does not want peace. This despite the fact that, even though Israelis are faced with Arab countries that adopt a belligerent posture, these attitudes are found only in rare, extreme cases, spoken by Hebron settlers (very few) and by a couple of radical individuals, such as the late Meir Kahane who was expelled by the Knesset.

The general conviction has always been that there would be peace at the end of the tunnel. Along with the fall of Communism, the beginning of the last decade of the twentieth century saw Israel's refusal to respond to Saddam Hussein's missiles and the conference at Madrid. After a thousand security checks, delegates walked through hospital white corridors into the imposing Madrid location designated the site of the first official meeting of Israel and the Arab nations. Jews and Muslims brushed by one another in the labyrinth without speaking. A plethora of journalists invaded large rooms dominated by immense screens. The new stars of the peace era appeared: Hanan Ashrawi came and went in luxurious limousines, followed by photographers; Farouk Al Shara, foreign minister for the elder Assad at the time and today for the younger Assad, gave an incredible speech in one of the red-and-gold assembly halls.

He waved a picture of Yitzhak Shamir, who was sitting not very far from him with his head in his hands, without raising an eyebrow; under the picture was written: "Wanted." It was the arrest warrant that the British, before packing their bags, had issued against him at the time he was performing acts of terrorism against the British army, while the Arabs were performing acts of terrorism against the kibbutzim and the Jewish populace, in addition to those against the British.

No one in Madrid reproached Arafat for the monstrous terrorist slaughter of the children of Lod and Ma'alot, no one raised the issue of how to deal with the instigator behind the killings at the Munich Olympics. No one raises it today, while Sharon is accused by the international press of being a criminal because "he was unable to prevent" (in the words of the U.N. commission who judged him following the tragedy of Sabra and Chatila) the massacre by Maronite Christians following orders from Elie Hobeika, a Syrian protégé, who until recently was a minister in the Lebanese government.

Shamir sat with his head in his hands; he was there to take the first steps toward peace, and he did, so that two years later, on the White House lawn, Rabin could shake Arafat's hand. But it is impossible to forget Shamir's expression, outraged and at the same time desperate, the way his hands, pressing his temples, held his thoughts in check and his gaze steady. Peace did not excite him: it compelled him. It did not crush him: it drove him. Once, at the end of an interview, he detained me for a moment: "Can you explain to me how a people that has produced Dante Alighieri, Giotto, Raphael can be so taken with Arafat?" It was a valid question that called for a reply. I thought I answered it by talking about oppressed peoples, the right to a national state, colonialism, the Third World, Catholics and Communists: today, after Barak went to offer Arafat all that he offered him only to meet with rejection, after Amnesty International gives no importance to the fact that the demand for the refugees' return can actually destroy Israel, the answer is not enough. At least not for me.

# Joseph's Tomb

The year of peace, 1993, was a year of ecstasy. Ecstasy can be a source of both illumination and obfuscation—it depends on the character of the person experiencing it. My friend Yigal, on the Golan Heights, was taking a walk one day while an eagle (there are many of them up there) circled in the sky. He was accompanied by a Syrian intellectual who had fought in the same armored tank battle in which Yigal had almost lost his life when he was a soldier in the war of 1973. Many of his fellow soldiers had been killed or maimed. The Syrians had attacked them by surprise. Yigal told me that never in his life, not even with those closest to him, had he felt a similar feeling of intimacy, of profound communication, as he had during that walk. Peace hovered over him, like the eagle. It hovered over all of Israel for a long time, creating a sensation of being in love: Yigal said he felt as if the individual who had almost killed him could be his best friend. In Syria, they hang people in the square without a trial; pictures of the dictator are on every available wall. The Jews fled in terror. Syria has never ceased to declare its existential aversion toward Israel, with whom it is at war. Yet Yigal felt as the majority of Israelis did: a man who, once the blockade that had been tightened around Israel since 1948 was lifted, could have taken his car and driven to Damascus. Free to visit with neighbors instead of fighting with enemies. Those who do not understand this basic feeling of the Israelis and imagine that they dream of territorial conquests cannot comprehend history. Many other intellectuals threw themselves into meetings, conferences, and debates with journalists and Arab writers who in general did not hesitate to accuse Israelis of every kind of crime. It didn't matter. Even Shimon Peres had the door slammed in his face, accused of hegemony, when at the economic conference of Casablanca he proposed his vision of a new Middle East in which computers and prosperity would triumph over fundamentalism and rejection. And yet today he still thinks that that's the right track. People were quickly convinced that their children would not have to go into the military; numerous espresso cafés appeared on the streets of Tel Aviv, and the opening of the first McDonald's in Ramat Gan had the feel of an epoch-making event. People, young people especially, would stand in line for hours in a state of ecstasy to seize the fruit of globalization, the hamburger. The speeches and even the resonant, bombastic tones of the politicians were unforgettable: their gaze focused on a distant horizon as they spoke, a fugitive tear always in the corner of the eye. Clinton specialized in compassion, Arafat in kisses. Rabin had a more restrained yet epic way about him, like an exhausted hero, and Peres wore a blue suit, emblematic of secular society and modernization. The sensation one got was that it was the best of revolutions, the kind that transforms a people's nature and culture, comparable to the Communist revolution for its depth and significance in Israel. Israel found a new epic destined to replace the old one, yet also to continue it. The epic of pacifist modernity after that of the new socialist man.

For fifty-year-old leaders, who had been young men at the end of the sixties and early seventies, and for the intellectuals who supported it, peace represented the natural end result of a evolutionary process that encompassed the creation of new states and governments at the conclusion of the Cold War. The children of the great pacifist revolution in America, which was later transmitted to the world, had rolled up into one the sexual revolution, a people's indisputable right to self-determination, as well as the struggle for "ethnocentrism," vital to the revolutionary repertoire of those years. This is the root of the surprising tendency to equate democratic societies with authoritarian ones, to define completely different concepts with the same words: a tendency established in American politics in its relationships with China and in Europe in its relationships with all the countries of the Middle East.

What does the word *parliament* mean? One would need a number of pages to explain the disparate versions that exist in various governments worldwide. Parliament has become, in the pacifist environment of Israel, the Knesset, in which every couple of days Arab parliamentarians declare their solidarity with Israel's enemies and parity laws are passed for homosexual families, while the major task of the parliament in Syria is to defend Alawite power. A leader: someone elected after fierce electoral campaigns among opposing coalitions in Israel, but also someone, in another context, whose power is based on dynasty and on the government's police organization. A school: a place where the foundations of a humanistic culture and an economic future are laid, but also a place where children with no hope for a future are incited to hatred by adults. Courts: those in which judicial power is fastidious to the point of exasperation and those that condemn a man to death after a twenty-minute trial.

In the very years when Bob Dylan sang "The times they are a-changing," peace became an intimate, dogmatic value, an essential element of a Western individual, of a democratic citizen. It did away with the idea that a legitimate defense could be a corollary to the commandment "thou shalt not kill." Two factors were transferred ideologically, one historical and one political: The historical factor was World War II, which had reduced human decency to a pulp in Europe, combining wartime butchery with Nazi and Communist massacres, in particular, of course, the Shoah.

The second factor, the political one, was the superimposition of the so-called peace campaigns, invented by the USSR at the time of the Cold War, on the idea that peace should be sought in itself. These campaigns spawned movements of women and citizens, with multicolored banners, who marched for peace against the U.S. nuclear threat or in defense of the national sovereignty of some African revolution; the USSR seemed like a lamb dedicated to the defense of oppressed peoples. Hundreds of thousands of Communist sympathizers marched under the peace standard, in Europe and in the United States, in actuality to defend the USSR's imperialist policy. Obviously, given what they had undergone in the war, the Jews were marshaled for this alignment. In view of what they had suffered at the hands of Nazism, they were generally enlisted in the ranks of the left. To become associated with the left was a question of identity and memory for the Jews.

Peace became an umbrella word, which went together with the imperialist and colonialist struggle, while the USSR recruited "non-aligned" countries and provided arms for all "liberation" movements (such as the Syrian army, in addition to the Vietcong or Che Guevara) and while young Americans burned their draft cards. Peace became an all-purpose word; Fidel Castro even used it during the U2 crisis. Its semantic value has been expanding out of all proportion as the years have gone by, incorporating the values of human and civil rights. Because it is logical that a nation at peace has a much greater opportunity for economic advancement than a nation at war, and since it is equally evident that traditional battles among tribes or ethnic groups are an offshoot of Third World indigence, the generalization emerged that peace is not only good because it allows men to be themselves (freedom, independence) but also because it allows them to have a full stomach (economic growth, development).

Now the Middle East, much more than any other part of the world, had every characteristic to become a triumphant demonstration of this ideological accretion: peace here could be a meeting of religions, an embrace after millennia of bloodshed, a multiethnic jubilation, a triumph of the postwar period's prevalent ideology, including Third Worldism.

Thus, peace in the Middle East became not only a source of rhetoric and lies, which even I myself admiring for the substantial promise that they contained (enough bloodshed, said Sadat, who for this was killed by his own people) if not ecstatically sympathizing with them (many of my somewhat perplexed writings attest to this, among them a long article in *Commentary* in 1995, others in the monthly *Liberal*, and finally a book published by Mulino, *Israele, una pace in guerra*—Israel, a peace in war); it also became the best training ground from which to launch a huge historical revision of the origins and history of Israel and the Arabs. It was here that the conflagration that led to the moral degradation of Israel took place, even before a face-to-face war.

Israel's great achievement, its inherent historical nature, over and above the marvelous vitality of Jewish survival after the Shoah, the fact that it had formed its own distinctive character and had aroused the respect and admiration of the entire world, was precisely its ability to remain in the conflict while being right, or rather to sustain a quantity of wars that were always defensive without losing its own democracy and without losing its faith in a constitutional state. Ultimately, Israel's wars were not fought by conquerors and colonialists to exploit territorial resources or geopolitical position or manpower. They were fought for defensive reasons by the David Ben Gurions, by the Moshe Dayans, by the Golda Meirs, by the poets and scientists, by the soldiers of the elite units, coming in large part from the kibbutzim, by a press that did not hesitate to attack the army and those in power, showing no mercy, while the community, according to the natural calling of democracies, subdivided and regrouped into the most diversified organizations, associations, sympathy groups and ethnic or cultural groups (Ethiopians, Russians, unions, Friends of the Israeli Philharmonic, feminists, Amnesty International, Peace Now, settlement organizations), something that hardly ever happens in war. And behind them was a judiciary that is sound and balanced, recognized as such both by religious nationalists and by Arabs. The war meanwhile also brought with it numerous episodes of military brutality, of abuses detrimental to the population, chiefly as a result of the intolerable territorial fragmentation in which the Palestinians live, due mainly to checkpoints and Jewish settlements. But it is also true that the hardship related particularly to the restriction of movement (which in and of itself involves a violation of human rights) developed in response to horrible terrorist attacks against schools, buses, and defenseless citizens.

In general, however, when one looks at Israeli society, what happened during a half century of wars contradicted every treatment of the subject. And so Israel, since 1948, has continued to be an impossible contradiction for other democracies, besides being a very tough opponent for its enemies. Its reduction to a country immersed in the peace process, on the other hand, far from leading to an expansion of democracy, a favorable image of itself, an unfolding of its own moral and intellectual powers, led instead to a shrinking of its sense of self, an avalanche of guilt feelings, an historical revision that turned its leading figures—among the most interesting and positive in the history of democracies—into cynics, idlers, and fools. David Ben-Gurion ceased being the genius who saw the crucial need to accomplish the founding of the nation, the humanist scholar of German philosophy and Oriental civilization who spent the years of his life in a two-room hut on a kibbutz in the Negev, the man who invited the Arabs not to leave Israel in 1948. He became, instead, an essentially cold, obsessed individual, cynical toward the Arabs, indifferent to the tragedy of Auschwitz.

The truth is that he understood with perfect certainty that Israel was the only way out of Auschwitz. Ben-Gurion wept like every other man, but he hid his tears in the interest of the task that awaited him. Moshe Dayan, a profoundly democratic and also, if you like, leftist intellectual, who could also be a great general, became a hardened warmonger, a thief of antiquities, a womanizer. Golda Meir, instead of the extraordinary woman and leader, human and courageous, that she was, was transformed into a "housewife" and a "fool" who refused to listen to the Arabs and because of this almost condemned the nation to defeat in the war of 1973.

The downfall of the memory of these people, brought about by a group of historians that emerged with the peace process, is parallel to the complete breakdown of Israel's historical memory. Thus a *yishuv*, settlement, relying on extremely weak armed forces when facing the invasion of Arab armies in 1948 (even according to historians like Anita Shapira who were certainly not of the right), became, in the writings of a group of self-proclaimed new historians, the core of a powerful armed nation that almost cold-bloodedly pushed the Arabs out of its borders, practically as a design for ethnic expulsion. As if the Arabs hadn't refused the division proposed by the United Nations in 1947 and invaded Israel in an attempt to eliminate it; as if the local inhabitants (who at the time were modest in number, not many more than the Jews, and who had never had a nation) had not specifically obeyed Arab demands to abandon their camps and go back to do battle; as if the expulsions had not occurred while war was raging and threatening the very existence of newly born Israel. Once the Jews themselves had renounced the fundamental moral value of the founding of Israel, burdening it instead with original sin toward the Palestinian people, every type of concession became possible, every kind of renunciation, every feeling of insufficiency, of guilt, every consternation regarding their conduct, and above all every loss of moral sentiment.

The search for peace got mixed up with a loss of identity and of a sense of their own motives. With the strength of a small world that was resolute and founded on values, Israel was able to stand up to a bigger world that lacked a sense of freedom and tolerance. It won because it was a small nation whose wealth lay in strong principles;

the others lost because they were weak, primarily as a result of the civil, economic, and political poverty into which their authoritarian regimes forced them. The entire world had no major problem in seeing Israel wage war, because it sensed its allegiance in fighting for principles that were shared: the Jewish nation, which had just been largely exterminated, Zionism as the undying will to return to one's own land, social solidarity, egalitarianism in many cases, and even the Bible, not so much as a religious work but as the foundation of modern ethical civilization. Israel was not ashamed to win. With its lack of resources, it had brought about development at magical speed. It was rich with human courage; it was able to make the desert flourish and construct modern cities and infrastructures. It did not complain about terrorist attacks; it did not weep for the butchery at Munich (the athletes) or Ma'alot (the schoolchildren slaughtered in their classrooms) but neither did it let the guilty parties escape. When the mortal danger of the Iraqi atomic bomb revealed itself, it destroyed the reactor. In defending itself, Israel has given the world a lesson in courage by keeping the structures of its democracy shining brightly. And the world has appreciated it.

The United States identified with the small frontier nation and affirmed its values and spiritual significance, namely, that war is justified when it is waged for principles of freedom and justice. For Europe, accustomed throughout the centuries to obeying, to reckoning with royal and ecclesiastical hierarchies, the projection was more complex: The somewhat mad brilliance of the Israeli victory aroused feelings of admiration but also some antagonism. Between Israel and Europe there was only the Jews' past subjugation on the old continent and therefore Europe's custom of not taking into consideration the idea of Jewish sovereignty. Europe still has what seems to be an insurmountable difficulty in accepting this concept. It might have succeeded in getting to that point by imagining Israel as a socialist nation. Instead, with the general collapse of socialism, Europe constructed for the Jews the limited sovereignty of the peace process. It has been the greatest instrument of interference interposed between Israel and its sovereignty, first with a simple denial of arms help (de Gaulle and his embargo in 1967) and later with progressively more extreme interferences, increasingly less positive, ever more forgetful of the basic principles of right, in the sense of being oblivious to who is right and who is wrong.

On the other hand, the Israelis themselves were irresponsible by undermining the idea of a Jewish nation, by lightly and indifferently making fun of religious tradition, making it seem more a matter of superstition, of sect, than the great cultural and spiritual tradition that it is. They have certainly been assisted in this by the irresponsible sectarian use of the Torah by religious politicians, but also by the concept of Zionism as purely a result of the Shoah. The Palestinian world is right when it asks: "What fault is it of ours if someone else made you suffer?" And Israel has no answer if it clings to the neo-Zionist idea of the right to asylum (of which A. B. Yehoshua is a great supporter).

There's much more to it than that. The Balfour Declaration, which recognized the Jews' right to a Jewish home in Israel, was born from a conviction that Lord Balfour arrived at during a meeting with Chaim Weizmann: faced with the need to establish a Jewish homeland because of the pogroms and anti-Semitic persecutions, the British statesman offered the Jews Kenya. Weizmann refused. It was then, Balfour wrote in a letter to his sister, that he became convinced of Great Britain's motives for supporting Zionism: a people so determined, so courageous, and so sincere could not help but win.

The motives of the Jews with respect to Palestine are based on fundamental values—on spiritual traditions, on history and memory. Once the Israelis accepted the breakdown of these starting points, they accepted not the path of international consensus as they believed, but that of blame. Their intentions appeared so weak as to be considered frivolous; their will to defend territorial principles and rationales lame to the point of appearing arbitrary: If Jerusalem is more Muslim than Jewish, what sense did it make to have unified it in 1967 unless the purpose was military conquest? David Ben-Gurion and Shimon Peres, who were never religious, traversed the land of Israel inch by inch with Bible in hand, emotionally moved at every spiritual-archaeological discovery. All territorial compromises were readily accepted (in 1948 and later with the restitution of the Sinai and the return of the Palestinian cities) within the framework of fundamental rules, which included receiving in exchange an assured recognition of Israel's own rights and integrity.

The peace process, even with its noble intent of saving human lives, shifted the boundaries within people's consciences: to justify its huge concessions, it promoted the idea that it is idiotic to die for piles of stones just because Joseph's Tomb or a three-thousand-year-old building stood nearby. Thus, and this is not an abstract tale, at the beginning of the Al Aqsa Intifada, Israeli soldiers abandoned Joseph's Tomb to the fury of the Palestinian crowd. Despite agreements made between the two parties for evacuation, a religious follower was killed as he fled trying to save a biblical scroll; a soldier bled to death because no unit arrived to save him from a siege that was surely not impossible to penetrate. They trusted the word of Jibril Rajoub, one of Arafat's deputies, who had led them to believe that the young man would come out alive, and in the end, the tomb along with the synagogue itself, one of the most ancient sacred shrines of Judaism, was destroyed stone by stone. The furious crowd that demolished this ancient religious monument was seen on all the televisions of the world, without any international entity officially responding. On the contrary, an Israeli journalist who visited it said to me: "The Muslims have now established a beautiful mosque there, much nicer than that horrible yeshiva that was so gloomy and hopeless." In a word, the contempt for tradition that became firmly established during these years led to Israel putting human lives and the defense of its own structures, not to mention the importance of its army, in second place.

Now, what happens when a democratic country conducts negotiations that are laden with a sense of guilt and therefore renounces its own historical identity, with an enemy that is part of a world immersed in unfortunate dialectics, or better still, conflict with the West? A demanding, assertive enemy dominated by principles that are completely different than ours, especially concerning the value of human life; an enemy totally taken by its own eschatological reasons for revenge? What happens when a threatened nation decides to forget the threat and immerse itself completely in a proposed solution put forth by democratic society: "peace"? This is exactly what happened to Israel. A process of treating of its own values, or rather democratic values, as relative with respect to those of its adversary. If the Palestinians are right (and they aren't) in saying that Israel cruelly and systematically expelled them, then the rationale for democracy and its values, the same values of Judaism as compared to Islam, are less valid than what the Israeli citizen had thought. Israel transformed the peace negotiations from an attempt to put an end to bloodshed to an excessive mea culpa. Played out before the Arabic world, the peace proposal became ideology, wound in a web of lies and exaggerations, of morally destructive accusations, that in the end destabilized the idea of self in the only democratic citizens living in the Middle East, while the autocratic Muslim citizen was reinforced.

Democracy gained nothing by the peace process; neither did Israel's cause, that of the only democracy in the Middle East. The paradox upset the situation: when it was at war, the Israeli sense of pride, the conviction that it was defending not only its own existence, but the values of democracy, the courage of its just causes, the vitality of its ancient culture, the moral revenge on Nazism, aroused respect and support in Israel's citizens, and to a large extent in the world's democracies (particularly in the United States because of the affinity noted above). For example, not only was discussion of the boundaries of the lands very important, but the idea that those desert lands, once arid and unpopulated, had been made fruitful through toil and technological innovation generated sympathy and a feeling of identification. In short, a sense that the Jews "had made the desert bloom" with their love. And now? Where did this ethic, sound though it was, get them? After the peace process, the new historians, and the ease with which territorial concessions were proposed, it was not difficult to get across the idea that the Israelis had colonized or robbed other people's lands. They themselves were the first to say it.

When all is said and done, a strong message of defense came from Israel, defense of liberty, of a constitutional state, of parliamentary democracy, of a humanist, popular army capable of anything for love of the values that informed it—for the world and for itself. To defend these values, Israel was capable of offering up human lives, of waging war and winning. Faced with a tough, unyielding enemy, only an active state of war seems to inspire the values of self-sacrifice that are necessary to defend and preserve a system designed for peace. A strange paradox. Those who delude themselves that it only applies to Israel should look ahead: the paradox awaits all of us just around the corner in Afghanistan, Iraq, Iran, China, Pakistan, and all the other antagonistic worlds that we paternalistically acknowledge.

# Sons of Monkeys and Swine

Islam is one of the world's great religions. As the greatest scholar on the subject, Bernard Lewis, says, it has brought comfort and dignity to countless men and women and has given meaning to so many lives in a world crushed by poverty, corrupt government, conflicts, and international exploitation at various times. It has encouraged different races and peoples to live together in brotherhood and has taught people of diverse creeds to live for several centuries in reasonable tolerance of the other. The civilization that had its origins in Islam has enriched the world. However, like all other civilizations, Islam's destiny has included periods of aggression accompanied by terrible internal and external wars. Christianity has experienced this, with its Crusades, its Reformation and Counter-Reformation, its persecutions. Unfortunately for us, a considerable part of Islam is now going through an extremist period in which rejection and condemnation of the West form a leitmotif with suicide terrorism as an operative corollary.

The key to a political understanding of Islamic fanaticism is the imperative to superimpose the order that comes from heaven, or from priests, over that which derives from political leaders and rulers. That is to say, in Islam there is no separation of church and state: the utopian element directly overlays the authoritarian one, though this is not to say that there have not been attempts, some more successful than others, to bring about democratic regimes in the Islamic world. Nonetheless, in general, the categorical imperative typical of a totalitarian utopia, which Europe has known all too well, is profoundly internalized, and secular nonbelievers in the society are considered by many to be blasphemous infidels.

Islam is neither superior nor inferior to any religion. There is not much difference between observance of Yom Kippur, of Lent, and of Ramadan. They are intense rituals of contrition, and I am certain that mine seems wonderful to me because as a child I went to the Florence synagogue with my grandmother, who would tell me profound, moving words about our faith. But Islam does not provide for separation of church and state, and this is what has given rise to bin Laden, along with transforming a war for a Palestinian state into a holy war of sweeping ambitions for all Muslim territories. Bin Laden associates the struggle for Palestine with chasing the infidels out of Islamic land and defeating them in general. Arafat, who rejects any exploitation of his battle on the part of bin Laden, indicates very clearly the ideological significance of the Israeli-Palestinian conflict when he calls the current conflict the Intifada of Al Aqsa.

It was not by chance that Israel became the epitome of all evils in the 2001 U.N. conference on racism in Durban, a racist nation in which apartheid prevails. The Palestinians became the army of good against imperialist and racist evil some time ago. The Al Aqsa Intifada doesn't mean the physical space of the Temple Mount: otherwise, since the Jews also have their point of origin there and the same attachment to their land, and since the Muslims' third-most important mosque is located there, any reasonable compromise would indicate that sharing should occur, like in the plan Clinton announced and that Israel accepted. When Arafat speaks of the Intifada of the Mosques, he embodies the aspiration of his people, as he has always been able to do to perfection; an aspiration that at the present time is nourished by a deep-seated desire to combat the Jewish usurpers.

Arafat has a profound identification with his people: Palestine is him, and he is Palestine. He epitomized in stages the ideological birth of the Palestinian people at arms. He rode the great Third World crest that allowed him to use terrorism without paying a forfeit, relying on the fact (still true today) that the Palestinian terrorist would become a freedom fighter for the left in the Cold War. Later he expressed feelings of reconciliation when the Palestinians lost their international foothold following the collapse of the USSR and the end of the Cold War and when a general atmosphere of aspiration toward prosperity prevailed. Now there is a new international foothold, and with it the intifada: Europe, which fears Islam, provides that foothold. The West, even as it wages war against terrorism, hastens to explain that the antiglobalist conflict is not a religious war, even though the Americans and their "coalition" knowingly play a slippery game with countries like Iran or Syria that sponsor terrorism to avoid confronting all of Islam.

The United States knows that Arafat could have stopped terrorism against Israel some time ago, that the death of all those young people on the pavement outside the Tel Aviv discothèque could have been avoided. In 1996, when bombing attacks on buses became paroxysmal and Arafat was not yet obsessed with the Islamic thrust, the rais (President Arafat) put a hundred men in jail in a single night and fifteen hundred more in the days that followed. But now the Palestinian people want to fight by any and all means; for Arafat the time has come to do so. On one side, a war without limits; on the other, the side that values international opinion, five cease-fires as the attacks continue. Arafat, in fact, stopped terrorism for several hours when America threatened not to make him a partner but an enemy. For a year, however, from October 2000 until the time the Twin Towers were destroyed, he preferred to maintain good relations with Hamas and the Islamic Jihad, an integral part of his people—organizations that in addition to their armed groups also nurture a large popular base in the great wave of Islam that is up in arms against the West and that since the time of the Iranian revolution has come crashing down on the shores of all Western countries.

American Islamic scholars say that approximately 80 percent of the mosques in the United States propagate the word or at least shelter groups whose religious message carries anti-Western and anti-Semitic sentiments. It is estimated that of the 1,200,000,000 Muslims worldwide, those directly engaged in fundamentalist organizations number more than 100,000,000, almost twice the population of Italy. It is evident to me that even those not directly moved by political motives, by obedience to a leader, or by an organization can still easily fall prey.

Near my house in Jerusalem there is a large fruit and dairy shop whose owners, the Pardos brothers, are natives of the village of Sharafat. Aside from not selling alcoholic beverages, they show no signs of being especially religious: They don't even have beards, although two of them sport moustaches. Their business does well even in times of intifada. The fact that their shop is on the street leading to the Gilo district means that they can boast an excellent Jewish clientele, which packs the store, poking through the crates of peppers, grapes, and figs. This happens on the Sabbath in particular, when the other stores are closed.

One of the brothers, let's call him Nadem, announced to me (we instinctively take to one another; Italians are well liked) that Hamas opened a school in the village and that everyone sends their children there because it is clean, the food is good, and the Koran is taught. That's how the infrastructures of terrorism are: kind, nurturing in a world that needs consolation, providing guidance and even subsidies. I told him that it seemed a shame to have Hamas organized right here under our noses, that it worried me, given that I live just above there. Beyond the number of charitable infrastructures it may establish, Hamas is intrinsically and above all a terrorist organization. But this truth is highly questionable from Nadem's point of view; to him, Hamas is a group that provides physical and moral assistance as well as political guidance. This conviction is in the air and in the weltanschauung of the Muslim world, just as it is in the air that the Hezbollah continues its attacks and abductions even after Israel's retreat from Lebanon. Arafat, no matter how many cease-fires he declares, does not stop the Islamic fundamentalist terrorists but, on the contrary, renews tacit alliances with them. And unfortunately it is also in the air that the world pretends not to notice, that it worries more, sometimes to a ridiculous extent, about possible feelings of discrimination or vendetta than of correctly identifying the enemy and the way to combat him.

There has been a significant effort to safeguard Islam's causes, to ease its social suffering, to extol, astonishingly, those things that at one time were called oppression, dictatorship, and sex discrimination and that now suddenly masquerade as "differences." Is it a "difference" to terrorize homosexuals to the point that they have to come to Israel to seek refuge from the Palestinian Authority? Is it a "difference" that trials last only an hour and conclude with a death sentence carried out in front of a satisfied crowd? Is it a "difference" that people in the square rejoice over the massive, unthinkable terrorist attack against the United States or show their satisfaction over the slaughter of young people at the Tel Aviv discothèque? And not just a minority, but everyone with whom you exchange a few words, even children wearing Nike shoes, even the young girls in blue jeans and chador, even the sixty-year-old laborer who has always been a member of Al-Fatah. Is it a "difference" that students of the University of Bir Zeit, Ramallah, put on a show in which the bombing attack against the Sbarro pizzeria, which left fifteen people dead, is reenacted to exalt the dismemberment, the blood, the destruction? Is it a "difference" that a man who should be one of the greatest religious authorities of the time, the Mufti of the Jerusalem mosque, continually extols suicide terrorism against Americans and Jews (not just Israelis, but all Jews—"sons of monkeys and swine"), that he urges that they be "killed wherever they are found," that he teaches the crowd of believers that the path of martyrdom or suicide terrorism is the path they should point out to their children?

Yet, this is the mood that prevails in present-day Islam, which is going through a terrible period, like Christianity at the time of the Crusades or the Counter-Reformation. Nadem knows well that what they teach the children of Sharafat, in Jerusalem, is the path of the shahid, the martyr—perhaps even his own children, so lighthearted and well-adjusted to modern life, their mouths always full of savory tidbits, destined to go on to university. He knows well that the school of Hamas at Sharafat could have disastrous consequences for his family, for his loved ones. Yet, he readily accepts this because this is politically correct in today's Islamic world.

We can get a milder sense of it, one less related to the masses, if we think about the time in which the winds of revolution were blowing in Europe and if we recall the ambiguous sentiment: "Neither with the State nor with the BR" (Red Brigades), while the hearts of the middle class left and the working classes were pounding for the courageous Communist sahibs of those days.

What television stations broadcast, what the newspapers continually write about, commenting shamelessly on it, is that the West poisons, impoverishes, robs, shackles, and is the origin of all evil. Let's not forget that Mohammed Atta, the terrorist behind one of the Boeing attacks in New York, had prescribed in his will that women should not be allowed to approach his grave. These are leitmotifs, recurring themes. Just as when Egyptian newspapers depict Jews with hooked noses, an American missile nearby and a bag of dollars in their hands; or when the Mufti tells a crowd of believers that a fourteen-year-old boy came to him and said that he would attain martyrdom in four years by killing many, many Jews, and he, the Mufti, was very moved by the heroism of this boy. And he explicitly incited young people to take up the path of martyrdom. He says this in public, in grand style, not in the closed setting of a strange Islamic sect, not in a basement where clandestine meetings are held.

Today Islam is plagued by fundamental extremism: It has spread in all Muslim countries, even the moderate ones, and its relations with the established authorities are a dance of precautions, reciprocal promises, and concealments, up until the time killings and massacres take place. Iraq, Syria, Lebanon, and Libya, which are by no means fundamentalist countries, finance, organize, and support it. It's in the air, it's the mood of the times: present-day expediency passes through Islamic extremism. This is the Islam that guarantees a hold on the masses, the one that provides transport, alibis, and restraint forces (like the Hezbollah, who are the real link of terror among Iran, Syria, and Lebanon—and in the end Lebanon is under its control). Even Arafat, who refuses to stop suicide terrorists, is part of present-day Islam whose hegemony is a mixture of anti-Western popular culture, control of the masses through an extremist press, armed troops, and finally the terrorists, semisavage and apparently autonomous, who in turn look after their own interests and signal their integration with society through a strong network of infrastructures. They are aided by a direct line to denominational countries, like Iran and the Sudan, the one being the ideological mover in addition to being an organizational force, the other being a training field; and also by Afghanistan, down to bin Laden and the Taliban, in whom the relationship among religion, terrorism, and financing from opium dealing is specialized to the maximum. One need only recall the supreme indifference with which the Taliban listened to the piercing laments of the West over the destruction of the Buddhas. That's where we made the mistake that we are again making today.

For extremist Islam, which as we said has many links to the world in which it operates, it is perfectly natural to take a fundamental principle like that of the overlapping of religious and temporal power and carry it to extremes. The locus of religion coincides with that in which trials are judged, orders given, the party line communicated. The iconoclasm that erases the symbols of other religions has no ethical, aesthetic, or psychological sense. The Cathedral of Santa Sophia became a mosque, the Temple of Herod and Solomon was trodden and effaced beneath the Muslim portion, the Temple of Rama at Ayodhya southeast of Delhi became the mosque of Babri Masjid. Bin Laden's hope is that a great mosque will soon rise on the site of the Twin Towers. The entire movement of Islamic revenge originated in the Wahhabi world two centuries ago. Now a rage has settled over this doctrinal conviction rendering faith explosive. It is the mood of the times: just as for us politically correct ideas have represented grave disorders, harmful exaggerations, nests of grave infection, so today Islamism has a lot of power over Islam. It creates victimism-triumphalism—a dual identity of being a victim ("after fourteen hundred years of conflict on an equal footing, they have defeated us by fraud," says the commonly held opinion in the Arab world; "by pure luck they broke through the Vienna blockade, and since then they've done nothing but exploit us, colonize us, corrupt us") and yet ultimately triumphing ("but now it's over, the West's excessive power is synonymous with anti-Arab violence; its real face is colonialism and imperialism, and we will defeat them and be triumphant Islam once again").

This is what Nadem tells me almost kindly, without a shadow of a doubt, as if anyone would automatically share his point of view, just as we at times repeat conformist litanies: that Palestine has seen many masters, the Turks have come and gone, the British have come and gone, the Jews too will be gone—forgetting not only the fact that the Jews were born there, but also that the Palestinians have never had an established homeland there, and that in any case the Palestinians never drove anyone out: one ruling master drove the other out, up until the time the United Nations divided the land between two indigenous peoples, one of whom has not accepted the partition. But herein lies the ideological sticking point that is unacceptable to the Palestinians, which is that one of the two parties is Western and therefore, according to the current cliché, colonialist and imperialist. This is understandable coming from the Arabs; but that such a large part of Western public opinion, which should be familiar with the history of the area, should accept this point of view is simply astonishing.

The Jews though, despite the cliché that holds that the United States has been guilty of being too pro-Israel (an assessment that in light of current events should be completely rethought, however, in the sense that the struggle against terrorism is important for all of us), have little to do with the current terrorist wave except as a possible lightning rod of anti-Western hatred. In any event, even the United States has only recently come to be viewed as the epitome of Western evil. Islam extremism has been more concerned with Europe: it is the origin of the world's corruption, the cause of the Muslims' affliction. It was Europe that defeated Islam in 1683, that has on occasion subjugated it after having been subjugated by it, Europe that initiated the perverse customs, which Islam thinks should disappear, Europe that colonizes and occupies. The thinking by which the West is Islam's enemy and jihad an obligatory duty originated around two centuries ago with Wahhabism, an extremely harsh ideology held since the beginning of what later became the Saudi dynasty: the infidels were certainly not Americans or Jews.

But contempt, a very specific form of hatred, which Islam much later on applied to the West along with fierce historical antagonism, derives from the grafting of ideologies that, bred within Europe it-self, hatefully criticized its history and culture. The long friendship between part of the Arab world and Nazism is well known. Equally well known is its relations of alignment and support with the USSR during the course of the Cold War. If anything, it is this that lies at the root of Arab anti-Americanism, certainly not America's support for Israel, which nevertheless has intensified it. (But so what? Should a just cause be abandoned perhaps out of opportunism?) Moreover, America showers the Middle East (Egypt and Jordan in particular) with economic and technological assistance and played a funda-mental role in forcing Israel into the territorial concessions that led to the accord that was later rejected at Camp David.

At Durban, a few days before the American tragedy, it was un-mistakably clear that the criminalization of America ranged from criminal consumerism in contrast to Third World poverty to slavery (of which the Arabs were masters) and globalization: jihad, perhaps unconsciously supported by all the antiglobal forces, was a presence.

The first great colossal act of jihad was the attack on the Twin Towers and the Pentagon: again I go back to what I've called "the mood of the times." The literal meaning of the term *jihad* is that of "striving, committing oneself," from the phrase in the Koran that speaks of "committing oneself to God's way." It may be interpreted as a moral obligation, related to self-awareness and perfection of the soul. This is what it is to the classic world of Islam. But by reading the newspapers, listening to the radio, and watching television in Muslim countries, one can affirm with certainty that the man in the street views the jihad the way it is described, that is, as a war against infidels and apostates. This interpretation is supported by the fact that since the jihad is a religious obligation, its particulars are dealt with in the sharia, the law of Islam, which details the specifics of war, captivity, treaties, and initiating and concluding hostilities. The mood of the times suggests that jihad today is understood to be an actual war, undertaken, as bin Laden says, to "kill Americans and their allies, civil and military, as the individual duty of every Mus-lim." While jihad is in the Koran and therefore extolled by the cur-rent, politically correct element of the Islam world, the same cannot be said for suicide, which is forbidden, though martyrdom is ex-alted. That is to say, the current offensive has brought with it a theo-logical invention, that of the sanctity of the suicide martyr; if someone chooses to use it within the Muslim world, this can be a picklock against commonly held beliefs because the question is: Can this ideological-terrorist spiral be broken without the use of force?

It could, if television, newspapers, school textbooks, sermons in the mosques, and speeches by leaders did not repeatedly demonize the enemy, a message that every authoritarian country (as are all the Islamic countries) is forced to convey to safeguard its power. Which is why Arafat's cease-fires are a sham, or why the Saudis do not to lend their bases to the Americans, as they did in 1991. Why, in short, the current antiterrorist coalition is a political fiction, perhaps useful at the moment, but destined to dissolve. Bernard Lewis brilliantly recaps the message, the summation of religious struggles, like this: "I'm right, you're wrong, go to hell."

# What Holocaust?

The unrestrained behavior, the lies, the abuses that the Arab world has employed in the course of this intifada are not only a soundtrack, a grim chant that serves as background to the action. They are the action itself. They represent a phenomenon without which the current conflict would not be what it is, namely, a war in which for the first time in many years, at least since 1991 (the meeting in Madrid), the countries surrounding Israel define it as an enemy to all intents and purposes, whose elimination is desirable.

The language of this last conflict has deprived Israel of its identity as a country; it has delegitimized and criminalized it to the point of stripping it of all human attributes, rendering it an outlaw nation. This operation has been performed with methods so unswerving and crude as to make those who use them appear ridiculous. And yet, the grotesque aspect of Arab excesses has never been pointed out by European and American leaders who have witnessed this process. The most glaring example was John Paul II's visit to Damascus, where the younger Bashar al-Assad, speaking alongside the Pope, literally said: "[The Jews and Israelis have] tried to kill the principles of all religions with the same mentality with which they betrayed Jesus Christ [and in] the same way they tried to betray and kill the prophet Muhammad." The Pope, the same Pope who had recognized Israel, said nothing at the time and continued his silence in the days that followed. The anti-Semitic criminalization of Israel is one of two focal points of the campaign that is underway. The second is the comparison between Zionism and Nazism, which has become incessant. In Egypt, in mid-March 2000, the Egyptian newspapers *Al Akbar* (government-owned) and *Al-Wafd* gave it front-page headlines, and a whole movement of intellectuals repeated it. As Abdullah Sinawi wrote in the May 13, 2000 issue of *Al-Arabi*: "Zionism is not just another face of Nazism, but rather a deceitful Nazism."

A respectable interlocutor always deserves to be corrected; only a foolish or hysterical one is met with a shrug when he rants in vain. This is the attitude the world has adopted: We hear people saying outrageous things, but never mind—what's important are the facts. But the diagnosis is incorrect: These words tossed around are the very backbone of the new intifada, of a rampant terrorism in which ontological hatred toward Israel takes the place of territorial demands for a Palestinian state and religion replaces the nationalistic component. These violent, senseless words are used in a variety of situations: by one Arab leader to another during summit meetings of the Arab League or of the Islamic countries; by leaders to their people during mass assemblies or conferences, in mosques and universities as well as in the public square; by intellectuals and journalists to their readers; by radio or television commentators to their listeners and viewers. No one in Europe or in America thinks anything of it, as if it were an ethnic and cultural characteristic of a culture that, on the contrary, originated as one of the most courteous and ceremonious in the world, the wellspring of vast sectors of world civilization.

The inflamed language used systematically and without regard for the facts, as well as the excitement and sense of cohesion based on the demonization of the Israeli-American enemy, are of crucial importance to the very structure of the power pyramid: the leader who attacks the most is the most assured, the most influential and approved. Saddam Hussein, for example, though he presented a continual risk for his people and for the countries of the Gulf, for Kuwait and Jordan, had gained great prestige through his language. He came into possession of a Pan-Arab and Islamic passe-partout from the time he first used the harshest, most violent words and expressions possible against Israel, for example, declaring his immediate willingness (as he did at the beginning of January 2001) to destroy "the criminal Zionist entity" provided that Jordan or Syria grant passage for his army, or repeating that he had a whole force armed to the teeth and ready to intervene in the Palestinian "war of liberation." At Arab summits, Saddam's envoys managed to earn the support (albeit unwilling) of even his Saudi enemies and others in the area who fear and oppose him, by dint of anti-Israeli curses and imprecations.

Bashar al-Assad makes the same use of increasingly violent rhetoric to assume the identity of a leader and consolidate his position. Young and ineffectual, he has based his immediate recognizability as a leader on the use of insane language at every public occasion (he has done so at all the summits, gaining immediate credit for his fragile leadership). In turn, the leaders of moderate countries, such as Egypt and Jordan, as soon as they have a microphone in hand, compete in lashing out against Sharon's "extremism," the Israeli "occupation," and Israel's "excessive use of force," "aggressiveness," "will to dominate," and its "policy of settlements and occupation," even if the facts show otherwise.

One of the problems of such incitement to hatred is that it comes from the leaders of totalitarian countries in which no one has the power to point out to the head of state that he is in error, in which no one can write an article or introduce a parliamentary investigation that demands explanations. Political criticism doesn't exist for dictators, whether they are absolute or moderate. On the other hand, another characteristic of incitement is to show its resonance among the people. In particular in Iran and Iraq, as in the Palestinian Authority, mass demonstrations are promptly organized around a leader's frenzied slogans. The crowds demonstrate by shouting their hatred for Israel and burn industrial amounts (literally—there is a flourishing industry for them) of Israeli and American flags, hoisting pictures of the heads of state. There are processions of youths dressed as suicide terrorists wearing white masks and fake explosives belts, shots fired in the air, "volunteer" divisions of children for the mosque of Al Aqsa. Such extreme behavior in the way the demonstrations are conducted is the result of their underlying assumption, which is expressed daily in the leaders' repeated references to "atrocities" and to "barbaric Zionist aggression against Palestinian civilians."

When incitement becomes an integral part of the discourse among Arab nations and their leadership and people, it precludes any hope for a policy of development and reform. Further, if Arab leaderships are based on incitement, the belligerent situation in the Middle East becomes not only natural and innate to their existence but an essential part of their survival policy. Incitement in the Middle East is intrinsic to the mechanism of power. No peace process can take place where one of the parties is dubbed "a deceitful Nazi." Yet, the great Western supporters of the peace process are wary of denouncing the continual, incendiary use of insults, lies, and exaggerations.

The Arab cycle of incitement leaves no vacuums anywhere, neither in the schools, nor in the public squares, nor on television. Its mechanism is simple: The leadership communicates the message to the crowds, the crowds transmit an amplified version back to the leaders as a demand for a harsh policy, and the leadership responds, their policies strengthened by the "sentiment of the masses."

The result of the continual use of inflammatory words and falsehoods creates situations that are first tragic and then also somewhat comical: for example, the remarkable news that an anonymous wedding singer in Cairo sold several million copies in three weeks of a song entitled: "I Hate Israel, I Love Amr Mussa" (head of the Arab League, and Egyptian ex-foreign minister). Now, this recording is sold under the eyes of the Israeli police in all the shops at the Port of Damascus as well as in music stores in East Jerusalem and the Old City. Several renowned Egyptian songwriters are claiming authorship of the lyrics.

Monstrosities are the order of the day. When in February 2001 a bus driven by a Gaza terrorist slammed into a group of young people at a bus stop, killing eight of them and wounding twenty-five, Arafat declared that, as far as he knew, it was simply an accident. The killing of a little girl, Shalhevet Pass, at the end of March 2001 by a Palestinian sniper at Hebron was reported by the Authority's official radio, Voice of Palestine, to be an Israeli lie. The commentator who manages the program explained that the little girl was actually a deficient, deformed child whose life was taken by her own mother—a shocking miscarriage, but not an isolated one, however. Arafat declared in front of an astonished audience of economists and politicians at Davos that Israel employs depleted uranium to kill people and pollute the environment and that the Israeli army uses nerve gas against opposing crowds. His television network showed scenes of convulsions and vomiting that experts easily debunked.

When foot-and-mouth disease erupted in Palestinian districts, the Palestinians accused Israel of having transmitted it, while in reality veterinary health-care organizations in Israel had already been mobilized to provide aid critical to combating the animal disease in the Authority. A few months earlier, when the peace process was still underway, Suha Arafat had deliberately said that Israel pollutes Palestinian water and air.

At various times news was also broadcast in Egypt and Jordan concerning poisoned chewing gum and drug-laced candy to kill children and make women perform sexually depraved acts. Even more surreal is the report, repeated constantly by the press of the entire Arab world, that the Temple Mount has nothing to do with the history of the Jews (the ruins of the First and Second Temple, although they were pickaxed Taliban style by the Waqf, the Islamic organization that oversees Muslim religious assets, without anyone lifting a finger, are among the most archeologically attested in the world), and that it was indeed a holy place for Islam even before Muslims existed.

What effect do all these ludicrous statements have since they are destined to fall apart when subjected to historical and factual verification? The scenario unfolds on two levels. The first is educational and concerns the cultural context of those to whom the propaganda is directed: the entire Arab population—citizens, students, women—in which what is family related and sound, acceptable and unacceptable, politically correct and decent evolves. The second level is political and has to do with the methods of communication among the leaders, the signs of their power alluded to earlier. These societies are, in some cases, apparently willing to grant intellectuals a certain amount of freedom in the press and television and are accustomed to letting them play the role of officious gadfly, promulgating a hard political line (this occurs particularly in Egypt and Jordan), which then makes them the source of indisputable, acclaimed "inspiration"—to which the politicians respond with a smile, paternalistically asking the bad little children to be a bit quieter while assuring them that they are still the darlings of the house.

This is how it went at the conference that took place in mid-May 2001 in Amman, at which the Holocaust was denied in the presence of two hundred intellectuals. Of course, King Abdullah wouldn't have been pleased, the dignitaries said; on the contrary, the conference planned around the same theme in Beirut a month earlier had been canceled because of Abdullah's visit. But then, those naughty intellectuals insisted that they, too, have the right to express themselves. And so it was that a number of immoderate anti-Semitic "scholars" were able to expound their thesis. As Hada Shahan wrote in the May 15, 2001 issue of the *Jordan Times*: "It is scientifically shown that the Jews suffered a Shoah of much smaller minor dimensions than what is believed. Their exaggerations served to raise support for creating the state of Israel." And then, with an interesting leap of logic: "The new form of Nazism is Zionism." Would King Abdullah repeat it? Of course not. Just as Mubarak would not reiterate what he lets his intellectuals say in the Egyptian press, perhaps the most satanic in recent times. Faced with a demand made by the United States that President Mubarak of Egypt tone down his anti-Semitic as well as anti-Israeli press, Mubarak replied that it must be understood that Egypt has a free press, which he cannot bottle up. When the Egyptian ambassador in Washington received a letter of protest from various intellectuals objecting to the anti-Semitic stance of the Egyptian press, one of the top columnists of Al-Ahram, Salama Ahmed Salama, wrote: "It is the right of the Arab and Egyptian press to intervene in the international battle of the media, showing the atrocities committed by the Israeli army so as to point out how the very ones who lament Nazi practices employ the same methods against the Palestinians."

In the Arab press, using the most atrocious words, the most shameful images to describe the enemy is not a practice applied only to the Israeli army: The press in Egypt shamelessly revived the story of using human blood in the Passover matzos, which a newspaper as widely read as *Al-Ahram* recounted in detail and in installments. It is pure anti-Semitism, whose modernization takes on various forms. For example, the attack on Colin Powell on the occasion of his visit some months ago: "The American Secretary of State did not hesitate to abase himself. He stood there humbly, a Jewish skullcap on his head, in front of the memorial to the Jews' spurious Holocaust during World War II . . . clearly this damned kippah causes whoever wears it to lose their sense of justice, as well as to set aside all logic" (Al-Ahram, February 17, 2001). And another columnist, Muhammad Abd al-Muni'm Murad, on March 11, 2001: "With Powell, the U.S. has become a joke . . . [W]e must teach him a lesson so that he will understand that the fact that he commanded the forces that opposed the invasion of Kuwait doesn't make him king of the Arab world and of the Gulf." As for Peres, Galal Duweidar attacked him on March 16, 2001, with an article entitled: "Is Peres, Master of Crime and Betrayal, a Dove?" Just one excerpt from a host of senseless remarks: "In reality Peres is a bird of prey, a master in killing innocents. This professional assassin, not much different from the gang that governs Israel, expressed his opposition to the Palestinians' request for international protection . . . [against acts that] make Israel worse than the Nazis. Peres peddles peace with betrayal and [says that if the Palestinians would stop attacking] the Israeli occupation would cease its barbaric, savage acts against humanity." Moreover, at the time of his two visits to Egypt in April, 2001, Peres was portrayed dressed as a Nazi on the front pages of Egyptian newspapers ("the Nazi Peres pollutes Cairo's air" was the idea expressed by the headlines). Twice in a row within the period of a month, without Egyptian authorities lifting a finger to defend their guest.

The tale of the Jew turned Nazi is one of the favorite stories used in the trivialization of the Arab-Israeli conflict. *Al Akbar* has no shame in printing a column that states "praise to Hitler" for having foreseen the need to wipe out the Jews, and that adds facetiously: "Too bad he didn't finish the job." Criticized for these remarks, the columnist repeated the identical statements a few days later. An article entitled "The Fable of the Holocaust," written by Hiri Manzour, appeared in the official Palestinian newspaper *Al-Hayat Al-Jadida* in April 13, 2001, following the Day of Remembrance in which all of Israel pauses to commemorate the victims of the Holocaust. The article states that "the theme of the Holocaust has been transformed by Zionist propaganda into a means of producing political and economic benefits and of strengthening the policy of occupation and settlement. . . . [T]he Jewish defenders of the Holocaust are on constant alert because they are afraid that attention will shift from the fable of the Holocaust to the specific historical Holocaust [that of the Palestinians]. . . . [T]he hen that laid the golden egg has reached its expiration date. . . . [T]he Jews' need to have a Holocaust is imperative. . . . [W]hat we see underway is an international marketing campaign. And isn't it plain by now that the victims of the Holocaust are the same individuals who created it? Indeed there is historical evidence that the Jews were active participants in marshalling

European sentiment against themselves, so as to prevent assimilation, which is the real enemy of the Jews. . . . Today the Jewish state is aware of historians' doubts concerning the actual validity of the Holocaust, and views them as an open door to the denunciation of all false claims made by the Jews."

The indecent tone of these declarations is widespread and recurring and has by now become an anti-Israeli standard. Even the Ayatollah Khomenei made it the leitmotif of his opening speech at the Islamic Conference held in Teheran on April 24, 2001, in the presence of thirty-four countries, the Hezbollah, Hamas, and the Islamic jihad. "There is proof," said Khomenei turned revisionist historian, "that shows how the Zionists had close ties with German Nazis, and how they inflated the numbers regarding Jewish killings . . . as an expedient for attracting the solidarity of public opinion and paving the way for the occupation of Palestine and the justification of Zionist crimes" and "for its satanic intentions and those of its Western supporters in general." Assad of Syria had already had his say, essentially: "The very ones who lament Nazism, are worse than the Nazis." On Palestinian television, Dr. Issam Sissalem of the Islamic University in Gaza declared: "Chelm, Dachau, Auschwitz were places of disinfection. . . . [T]hrough their propaganda [the Israelis] have said that the Jews were persecuted, murdered, exterminated. . . . [T]hey have portrayed themselves as victims and created a focus based on heroism and the Holocaust. What heroism, what Holocaust . . . ? Heroism belongs to our country, the Holocaust was committed against our people. . . . [W]e have been the victims, but we will not remain so forever . . ." The denial of the Holocaust is a strategic decision on the part of the Arab world: Bashar al-Assad paid out 2,500 pounds sterling to British historian David Irving, who was accused by Professor Deborah Lipstadt of denying the Holocaust for anti-Semitic reasons. Irving sued Lipstadt for defamation, but Lipstadt won.

The injudicious use of words and concepts leads to an injudicious use of arms. The idea of having a demon before you sets in motion an invitation to destroy him. Peace treaties cannot exist without an end to an ideological historical background that points only in one direction. The basis for peace is the recognition of the legitimate existence of the enemy and therefore of his rights. There is no respect for a give-and-take of opinion if you do not tell the other party the truth to his face. Following Khomenei's speech at the Islamic summit in Teheran, Sheik Hassan Nasrallah, head of the Hezbollah, said what anyone would have said given the view that suggests that Israel is a Nazi nation: "It must be destroyed."

"We are firmly opposed to any negotiating panel," Nasrallah explained. "We have no faith in any negotiations or compromise. . . . [T]he Jewish state should expect new attacks in places where they are expected and in places where they aren't expected." Assad repeated this idea quite frequently; and Saddam Hussein doesn't throw words to the wind, but to a wind of war. The word *Jews*, far from arousing a feeling of respect, an irrefutable *noli me tangere* after all that happened in World War II, has instead become almost a wink of the eye, in particular among Europeans. The Arab world is aware of it. After the attack at the Tel Aviv discothèque last June 2001, Joschka Fischer (German minister of defense) asked Arafat: "Didn't it bother you to see the bodies of those twenty young people killed by a suicide terrorist?" The reply he got was: "Why? Did it personally bother you Germans to kill Jews during the Shoah?" The denial of the Holocaust is not just a nervous outburst, yet another proof of cultural backwardness, it is also a sop thrown to anti-Semitism. The sop is never accepted by the Europeans or by the Christian world when it is thrown by other Europeans, other Christians. But if the Arabs are the ones to deny that the Jews underwent the Shoah and say that Israel's birth stemmed from this falsehood, which is to be added to Israel's other original sins, then one can pretend to consider it a forgivable lapse, a useless but ingenuous paragraph of the conflict.

But let's get back to the individual to whom the tone and inflammatory content of current propaganda, the work of editorialists who write about Arab politicians, is primarily directed. The Arab citizen in general, and the Palestinian in particular, is raised on incitement, naturally and innocently, like a child of ours may be shaped by Pinocchio or Cinderella. Israel is presented as an abstract, evil entity since it does not appear on the maps. In the popular imagination formed by leaders and intellectuals, Israel has no citizens, no houses, no hospitals or schools, but rather uniforms, rifles, and tanks. It is not a nation, but a satanic army. It does not enjoy the good breeding of the Arab scholar, reader, television viewer, or neighbor with whom it must coexist. The Israeli is described as a machine, not a person, a horrible, passing phenomenon, an evil fad; he is regarded as an object, depersonalized. He is assigned every possible negative connotation: aggressor, usurper, sinner, occupier, corrupter, infidel, killer, barbarian . . . A Palestinian video shows a theatrical reenactment of an assault (that never happened) by a group of Israeli soldiers in a Palestinian home: a little girl is raped by them under the eyes of her parents, who are then killed. In children's minds, instead of the image of Israel as a neighbor, the image of an implacable, repulsive enemy is formed, an enemy that encompasses all the negative connotations of the West: corrupt and exploitative, rich against poor. Its natural enemy is Islam, a predestined ex-victim that has now set out on the path to insurrection through this intifada. The Palestinian child knows from the time he is very little that the cause of all evil is Israel along with a predatory, imperialist America and to some extent Europe. He knows that he is a victim. He also knows, however, that the day is close at hand when he will win and win big. Victimism and triumphalism go together in his upbringing and education. If one asks where the child acquires the desire to become a suicide terrorist, or where he gets the information that will lead him to die young in some armed clash, the answer is very simple: in school and also from television. Praise for the shahid, the martyr who attains paradise in exchange for his sacrifice, is repeated in textbooks in all the classes.

The message maintaining the illegitimacy of the Jewish presence in the area recurs everywhere. Racism is an essential component of present-day Arab mentality: The Jews are not human beings like everyone else, they are the vehicle of all evil. By now, quantities of videos openly urge the child to sacrifice himself, without any international child protection agency intervening. In one of these videos, a little boy, Mohammed al-Dura (who was killed in armed conflict at the beginning of October 2000 and later became the symbol of the intifada), appears in a celestial landscape, with fountains and flowers all around, and invites his peers to set aside their playthings and follow him. The joy of having sacrificed himself and of now finding himself in the Garden of Eden is contagious to his young friends, who then follow after him. To put it bluntly, they go to seek death. In another film, the little boy who goes to battle and dies leaves a letter in which he asks that no one cry for him since he had decided to sacrifice himself for the intifada. A parent says that he will not weep for his fallen child, that his greatest joy is knowing that he was sacrificed for the cause. The music is compelling, the images very well produced: the children run, throw stones, one falls, the Arab world watches. A little boy drops his toy car and a little girl, her doll, they bend down and pick up stones.

We haven't seen any outraged educators write columns in the newspapers. And it is truly extraordinary how the Western nations, that go searching high and low for traces of the denial of the Holocaust in the European right and inflict political sanctions for it, completely ignore the phenomenon in the Arab world. Or how they don't utter a word of appeal for decent diplomatic behavior or the protection of children.

The spiral of verbal violence will not be curbed within its own world: Only the West can halt the verbal escalation. Without this, neither peace, nor any effective communication, is possible. We Westerners, who theorize about communication, treat the Arabs as if they were an autistic world, pathologically infantile, a desperate case. If this is so, a valid form of interdiction should be employed: international sanction for the use of violent, rude, senseless, inhuman words should produce results. Otherwise, if we believe that Arab civilization merits the respect demanded by its significant history, its ancient culture, and the courtesy of its people, then we should politely retort point by point, make our observations, and try to lead the other party to reasonableness. None of this is happening: the diplomats sit there stiff and awkward, and the intellectuals don't say a word. It is as if incitement were a necessary paragraph to the existence of the Arab world and Islam in general, as if the war itself, in truth, were a necessary paragraph. Perhaps this is the thought that lurks in our minds. Are we perhaps afraid? Or are we perhaps thankful for some quick, painless psychoanalytical therapy when, instead of us, someone else speaks badly of the Jews?

# The United Nations Motion of Shame    JULY 14, 1997

It seems like a bad dream: the phantom of the USSR, the ghost of Kurt Waldheim, the specter of the most extreme Pan-Arabism come back to plague the Glass Tower, to inhabit the United Nations. The facts are simple: tomorrow there will be a meeting of the General Assembly that Egypt has called for to expel Israel. The session is the continuation of April's "emergency meeting" concerning the Har

Homah neighborhood in Jerusalem (which resulted in a motion of censure) and the fifth session in less than five months on Jerusalem as a suitable place to build. It should be noted that the session in April was the first "emergency session" since 1982 and the tenth since the time of the Korean War.

In the period between April and the present time, there have indeed been two debates in the Security Council in which the United States did not support the building of the Har Homah neighborhood, understandably, but asserted that Palestinians and Israelis should settle this point among themselves. After all it is a typical border dispute that concerns an area south of Jerusalem situated in Israel, yet very close to Bethlehem in the Palestinian Authority: It's clear that both parties want it. Nothing to do with East Jerusalem, nor with the Old City, nor with areas sacred to religion. It's a totally political problem. Instead, the United Nations is once again making it an issue of total moral sanction against Israel and its perfidious, untrustworthy, detrimental way of life. For this reason, the agenda calls not only for censure, but for Israel's outright expulsion from the General Assembly, because, reads the draft submitted by Egyptians and Palestinians to the enthusiasm of the other Arabs, "The normal participation of a Member Nation cannot continue while international law is being systematically violated."

The United Nations has been a hotbed of real hatred since 1967. That year, during the debate at the "Convention on the Elimination of All Forms of Racial Discrimination," the United States proposed explicitly condemning anti-Semitism. The USSR, on the other hand, claimed that Zionism represented an example of racism. The compromise (evidently painful) that was reached was to not mention any kind of racism except for apartheid. (This laid the foundation to approve the notorious Resolution 3379 ten years later. Seventy-two countries voted in favor of it; thirty-two [among them, fortunately, Italy] voted against it.) From that time on, Israel became an unprincipled pariah in the eyes of its denigrators, and the Jews' civil and proper movement for national liberation was obscured by lies. Since then, the United Nations has not lost a single opportunity to link Zionism to all kinds of political perversion. Particularly monstrous was the deliberation of the World Conference on Women in Mexico City that, launching the United Nations' resolution, condemned "neo-Colonialism, foreign occupation, Zionism, racism, sexual discrimination and apartheid." In August 1975, the Arab states demanded Israel's expulsion, and only the United States' threat to leave the assembly foiled a vote that could have been dangerous. In 1991, the resolution was rescinded. A week later, another four anti-Israeli resolutions were added to the many documents already filed away.

Even in the Security Council, to which Israel has never been elected whereas fifteen members of the Arab League have been admitted, the United Nations has always played a partisan role; it has never adopted a critical resolution toward the Palestinian Authority, even when there have been suicide terrorist attacks, children slaughtered, and airplanes hijacked. And today the killings of the Palestinian land brokers remain suspended in a void. It is true that Netanyahu plays his peace game in a faulty way, never making up his mind whether to take one step forward or two steps back. But it is equally true that Arafat weaves a strange triangle with Syria, Iran, and even Iraq, and with Hamas, too, on the side, and that the words of hate now flying around the Middle East are among the bloodiest ever; blowing with feverish insubstantiality on the colored banners of the United Nations, they can lead to grave harm. We'll see if the United Nations will return to its grandiosity tomorrow.

## Western Media Join the Attack on the "Zionist Entity"

OCTOBER 22, 2000

Iran's representative at the Arab summit held yesterday in Cairo called Israel "the dirty Zionist entity" several times in his speech; the broad majority of the leaders who were there to represent their people, including Saudi Arabia, repeatedly called for a holy war, presenting the improbable image of an aggressive, genocidal Israel. After a peace process that went on for seven years, during which Israel put great concessions on the table, Rabin sacrificed his life, and Barak was prepared to give up half of Jerusalem, the Arab world tells the tale of a pitiless, occupying Israel that does not want peace. And essentially the world's press doesn't raise a fuss, just as it has generally accepted the repeated exclamation that the Jews shoot children for the enjoyment of it, or that the mobs that attack Israeli soldiers are unarmed—information that is taken as truth by the Italian schoolteacher, shopkeeper, lawyer. And yet the guns can be seen, the

Kalashnikov rifles can be heard, the complex dynamics of demonstrations in which children, Tanzim, and Palestinian police are intermingled are in full view of everyone. Nevertheless, there is an accepted "press release" in which the Palestinian crowd remains "unarmed." As for the children, only the Queen of Sweden has dared to say that they are used cynically. Why is this? Not only because, as we have seen, our journalistic culture has produced many individuals willing to let themselves be psychologically and morally overwhelmed by their sense of guilt toward the Third World or by a problematic relationship with the Jews. But also for an extremely cogent and very specific reason, to which we should all pay attention, partly because it does not only pertain to the Middle East.

Information is obtained from sources. These sources are more or less reliable according to their nature. An autocratic world, in which there is no government and opposition party like those found in the normal dynamics of a democracy and in which information is above all influenced by criteria favorable to a partisan cause as viewed by the most powerful leader, cannot generally be a reliable source. A democratic world, whose prime minister is constantly subjected to criticism (just look at poor Barak!) by an opposition party that uncovers his lie at eight in the evening, prime time, should he tell a story that isn't true, is a more reliable source. Moreover, a source of information like the Israeli media, which each day interviews Palestinian leaders, from Ziad Abu Ziad to Abdel Rabbo, no matter what they say, and tries to debate their terrible accusations in public, or that seeks out eloquent mea culpas by writers and intellectuals, is certainly a much more reliable source than Palestinian television, which expresses opinions that are all very similar and monotonous, all aimed at stigmatizing the enemy and which broadcasts propaganda videos in which Israeli actor-soldiers atrociously kill actor-children who shout out their desire to be martyrs.

# If the United Nations Were to Bring Israel and the United States to Trial    AUGUST 30, 2001

A big U.N. conference on racism was summoned in Durban, South Africa, the country of Nelson Mandela and defeated racism. A one-week meeting (from August 31 to September 7), accompanied by another big gathering of the NGOs (non-governmental organizations) in which all U.N. members will participate, is an extraordinary event. If this meeting were taking place with sincerity and purity of intentions, it would be truly a unique occasion.

But instead, the United Nations has succeeded in transforming the Durban conference on racism into a trial against Israel that goes back to the concept of a U.N. resolution annulled ten years ago: "Zionism equals racism." Indeed, it goes well beyond it and deals with a discussion of slavery that is entirely centered on the wrongs of the United States and therefore on the need for American reparations, as if the traffic in and use of black slaves were not also a historically established wrong for a large part of the Arab world, and beyond.

The formula "Zionism equals racism" seemed to have disappeared ten years ago with the annulment of the associated U.N. resolution. It was a celebration of freedom. The USSR had just fallen, and the formula that condemned Israel as an infamous pillar of an immoral, vile imperialism was swept away with it as well. The Iraq war was fought with U.N. approval, and a new era, that of the peace process, began. Who would ever have thought that the Arab countries caucus, which, today as then, can count on an "anti-imperialist" majority, would achieve the goal of focusing the entire discussion on Israel in the two preparatory documents, overturning the terms in those documents so that the rejected nation becomes a racist nation, the Jewish nation becomes an anti-Semitic nation? Indeed, not content with reintroducing the idea that Zionism is equivalent to racism, Israel is accused of "practices against the Semites," of "ethnic cleansing of the Arab population," and of "a new kind of apartheid." The documents also state that the ethnic cleansing perpetrated at the time of the founding of the state is on a par with the Holocaust.

According to the documents, the conference should talk about two holocausts: the period following the 1948 war when many Palestinians were driven from their homes, which the Palestinians call the Naqba,, and the period of slavery in America, when Africans were captured and brought across the Atlantic as slaves. Both were defined as periods of "extermination and genocide." The documents also say that anti-Semitism has been replaced by the stereotyping of Arabs, who are now oppressed by anti-Semitism in an etymological sense: therefore, wherever the old term was used, it should be replaced with Arabophobia.

This is just part of what was expressed during the preparatory phase of the conference. Reaction on the part of Israel, the Jewish NGOs, and the United States has been slow and uncertain. All are still undecided as to whether to boycott the conference by not attending, or whether to go and vote against a certain majority that will declare to the world that the first U.N. conference in the new millennium, the very significant conference against racism, is above all against Israel. Even the rank of the representatives is under discussion: Colin Powell, the black secretary of state, is much in demand. He might appear, greet the conference, and then leave as a sign of protest against the turn that events might take.

In many of the preparatory sessions, the United States and Israel have tried to set limits on the verbal violence, achieving ambiguous results. Even the South African government has said that there must be a limit on provocative language. But the final document will probably say that the Palestinians are suffering under a "discriminatory and colonialist military occupation" and that "other racist practices constitute a new form of apartheid and new racist crimes against humanity." The document calls upon the United Nations to "impose punitive measures against Israel." The organizations proposing this language belong to a world that has expelled the Jews and stolen what is theirs. And now, to attend or boycott? Let's hope that whatever steps are taken will serve to avoid the cultural horror of a debate that will poison the field of civil rights.

# The Return of an Old Fear    SEPTEMBER 14, 2001

We knew that the Durban conference against racism would be transformed for the most part into an opportunity to demonize Israel, that it would be snatched from the hands of the struggle against racism, from those in favor of civil rights, to become an occasion for anti-Semitism. That's indeed how it went. The fact that the language of the final document was less aggressive than the drafts they started out with only attests to European mediation efforts and the strong stance taken by America; this does not erase the climate, the propagandistic outcome, the political escalation, and the incredible content of the document of the NGOs that speak of Israel as a nation of apartheid (!), attributing the worst Nazi crimes to it. Nor does it erase the fact that "anti-Semitism" (in a conference on racism) and "Shoah" are mentioned in the official document only in the section on the Middle East (!), where they are compared to anti-Islamism, and that the document in fact views all of Arafat's designs not as political aims but as moral ones. The U.N. conference was an occasion of anti-Semitic hatred unprecedented in the postwar period: the idea that Israel and the Jews form a prominent part of the oppressor world that creates racism has paradoxically become a folk concept, shared by almost all so-called civilized society.

Africans, Asians, ethnic minorities, and native peoples, even as they heard their conference being snatched away by Arab activists, still had to repay their own legitimacy by adhering to the new type of Palestinian propaganda that, what's more, was supported by all the Arab nations, in the NGOs and in the official delegations. Anti-Semitism floated through the air like poisonous pollen and remained suspended there. During the days at Durban, delegates with a Jewish last name wore their name badges, required for security reasons, back to front; Jews wearing a kippah, or skullcap, were assaulted in the streets of Durban and also Johannesburg; during two demonstrations (at least) *The Protocols of the Elders of Zion*, the most classic work of anti-Semitism, was distributed; Jewish delegates to the NGOs were physically prevented from speaking and at times from attending the numerous sessions held to discuss the shameful document in which Zionism is compared to racism and Israel is defined as a "nation of apartheid."

The physical threat against Jews (not Israelis) was a constant at the conference against racism. The quarters of the Jewish Club of Durban, a white building where Jews could find a meal around dinnertime and above all friendly surroundings after the poisoned atmosphere that hung over the work sessions, was guarded by South African police forces the entire time. Not only was the physical threat a leitmotif that resounded even more loudly than the diverse, colorful claims of the slaves of Sudan and Mauritania, of the Mayas, of the Dalits, of the Tibetans; generally speaking, the anti-Semitism (ideological as well) that materialized from the conference was great, a black cloud that overshadowed every other demand and complaint. For this reason, the conference may be declared a failure. What emerged from it is the theoretical definition of a modern anti-Semitism that has been building in society since the time of the Cold War; a natural accessory actually to the Third World anti-Israeli ideology that accompanies the Israeli-Palestinian conflict. Its fundamental points are two: the delegitimization of Zionism and the denial of the Shoah.

With regard to the first, the Jews are the only people in the world who are denied the right to a nation in the land of their ancestors, as the United Nations, after the incontrovertible verdict of the Shoah, established through a partition that was rejected by the Arabs in 1947. The denial of Israel's fundamental international legitimacy is expressed through an escalation of terms in which "occupation," the "suffering" of the Palestinian people, Israel's "racist" attitude, the refugees' indisputable "right to return," and Israel's "criminal" aggression have all become a Greek chorus for denying Israel's right to exist in general—a demonstration of its criminal nature.

The second issue concerns the Shoah and anti-Semitism: the strenuous struggle on the part of the Arab delegations to include the subject only in the section of the official document that concerns the Middle East and not in the general recommendations for combating racism, legitimizes every anti-Semitic sentiment, every comparison (since this is the point) between the extermination of the Jews and Palestinian suffering during the conflict. Words such as genocide have passed into a lexicon that—reflected in a speech by Fidel Castro, worthy of Communism's darkest years, and now part of what is considered politically correct to say about the Israeli-Palestinian conflict—casts the Jews in a neurotic light as through they were international criminals, like the apartheid whites in South Africa. Never had such tones of unmindful anti-Semitism been heard.

And now let's be realistic. First, Jews who blindly believed in the idea of civilized society's support against dictatorships, of the left against a racist right, of a good Third World against a West harbinger of racism and anti-Semitism must now come to terms with their conscience. Second, after so many European lamentations concerning eternal memory betrayed by revisionist history and by comparisons of the Holocaust, here a document mediated by Europe to the point of anguish accepts the idea of not mentioning either anti-Semitism or the Shoah in the sections prescribing an antiracist struggle. Isn't it incredible? Only fifty years later, memory goes down the tubes, or better yet, to the Middle East. And finally, there is a series of dangerous little plays on the word *anti-Semitism* with the old excuse that Arabs can't be anti-Semites since they are Semites. But history speaks for itself: they can be, absolutely so. Moreover Martin Luther King used to say: "When people attack Zionism, they mean Jews. Let the truth ring forth from the high mountain tops."

# The Writing on the Walls at Durban    SEPTEMBER 20, 2001

After Islamic terrorists sowed death and destruction in the heart of the United States, I can't help but go back in my mind to events at Durban, where I experienced the anguish of the theoretical backdrop to what, in practice, later occurred in New York and Washington. In Africa I saw the fusion of Cold War and Arab-Islamic ideologies; I saw the breakdown of civilized society, whose non-governmental organizations (NGOs) exist, just as they did at the time of the USSR, only on condition that they pay their toll to the dominant U.N. ideology—notwithstanding weak opposition by the Western countries, counter to the actions of the United States, which along with Israel made the most reasonable choice: to leave the insane gathering.

A few days ago I returned to Tel Aviv from Durban: on the plane that was carrying me back to Israel overnight, I remained in a state of half-sleep that was steeped in anguish. I thought about the Jews walking around with their name tags turned back to front, taking off their kippah to avoid being assaulted; about the NGO meetings dominated by Palestinians, transformed into courts for alleged crimes against humanity from which Jews were frequently turned away and forcibly silenced. Like symptoms of a hangover or illness, the incredible contents of the preliminary documents flashed through my mind with their assertions that America is the cause of all the evil in the world and that Israel is a racist state, a nation of apartheid. The international assembly during the conference on racism was called upon to declare itself in favor of total condemnation of the Jews and of Israel, to declare Israel's existence illegitimate, and to heap upon the United States the fundamental sins of human oppression, slavery, and underdevelopment. And make no mistake: the NGOs, despite the strenuous struggle of some courageous members, produced the worst of all possible documents, calling upon the world's civilized societies, from the Mayans to the Tibetans and all those oppressed by racism, to make the battle against Israel their own, as if it were an ethical struggle for civil rights, to lash out against Israel and to condemn the United States.

True, many ethnic and cultural groups complained about the sequestration of the conference by the Palestinians, but those same groups (except for a very few), before talking about their own trampled rights, hastened to pay tribute to the suffering of the Palestinian people, terrible suffering inflicted relentlessly by the Jews, a horribly criminal, murderous, genocidal people, supported by the Americans: This was the price they had to pay to the politically correct globalized language of the left, which Fidel Castro and Arafat voiced in tones of hatred before the conference's assembly. Traces of this hatred could be found in almost every speech by African and Middle Eastern leaders. And the final document, the result of intense clashes with Third World countries, is not a decent document, as was repeatedly stated in an attempt at consolation and compromise: one need only recall that the Holocaust and anti-Semitism, far from being indicated as the worst expressions of racism, are mentioned only in the section concerning the Middle East. That the only section that talks about a political conflict is the one on the Middle East. And that Arafat's platform, namely the "right to return" and the "international commission," was included in the resolution of a conference on racism!

Back in Israel that same day there were four terrorist attacks, two of them suicide bombers, with five persons dead. And then, the enormous American tragedy. For those who witnessed Durban, the connection between the theoretical dimension of that event and the homicidal achievement of this catastrophe is evident. The anti-American hatred, which is distilled into hatred toward Israel, is nourished in fact not just by the Middle East territorial conflict but by the fundamental idea that there exist forces of good and forces of evil, in which evil is wholly identified with Western greed, corruption, and disgrace. The majority of Third World leaders enthusiastically applauded statements about America's sins and those of Israel—colonialism, imperialism, racism, exploitation, criminality—in which (and this is the point) the ideological pap of the Cold War was transformed and became equivalent to the victimism-triumphalism of extremist Islam (hoping that the moderate side will show up and speak or condemn, sooner or later). The anti-Americanism that is summed up in the idea that the West is the corrupter of man's decent nature, that it occupies what doesn't belong to it, that consumption makes it cruel, that it must reach the realm of prosperity by ruthlessly crushing the enemy, turned into the Islamic anti-imperialist battle that later led to the disaster in New York.

The key word Israel has been around since the time of the Cold War, specifically: the Zionist enemy, the colonialist aggressor, the persecuting racist. It's the small flag that marks the recent division of the world into blocs, and this is the source of the attacks on the Twin Towers and on the Pentagon. And the source, likewise, of terrorist attacks in discothéques, on roads, and in restaurants in Israel itself. What should a conference against racism in the seventies have done if not point out those to blame among the Americans and Israelis? And what should it do today? The same thing.

If you look at the collection of writings and statements regarding America and Israel well before the Bush administration and today's intifada, you realize that neither American politics nor the current confrontation are the cause of the uncontainable hatred that leads to suicide terrorism, whatever its dimension. On September 14, *Al-Hayat Al-Jadida*, the newspaper of the Palestinian Authority, wrote "history will not remember the United States, but will remember Iraq, the cradle of civilization, and Palestine, the cradle of religions. On the other hand, the murderers of humanity, creators of a barbarous culture and vampires of nations are destined to die." And in another newspaper we read that "the White House must become black."

# Yellow Star 2002   JANUARY 7, 2002

An evening affair in London, amidst aristocracy and silver, at the home of a woman by the name of Carla, the wife of an upper-class Englishman, who tells me she is Italian. Among the distinguished guests is the French ambassador to England, Daniel Bernard, who speaking of the Middle East refers to Israel in an unequivocal manner. "That shitty little country," he says in perfect English, "is not going to lead us all into a third world war." The elegant hostess, used to managing the conversation, is very animated: "I could never stand the Jews," she finally exclaims, "and everything that happens

to them is their own fault." In the *Daily Telegraph* the famous columnist Barbara Amiel recounts two or three other episodes of British
anti-Semitism. Then again Foreign Minister Straw stated that there's
no comparison between the terrorism that kills Israelis and that used
against the Americans. The news of a synagogue that was set afire
north of London received space only in a local Jewish newspaper. In
Europe, episodes of anti-Semitism involving physical threats are
multiplying. In 2001, in the area of Paris alone, three hundred assaults were recorded; this week a Jewish school in the Parisian suburbs was set on fire, and the adjacent synagogue pelted with stones.

"Since September 11," says Elan Steinberg, vice president of the
World Jewish Congress, "more synagogues were burned throughout
the world than in any other period since the time of Kristallnacht.
And they are events linked without a shadow of a doubt to Arab-
Palestinian violence, verbal and physical, against Israel and to an
anti-Jewish version of the conflict that has become a commonplace.
The right to criticize is understood, but here things have gone way
beyond that: Israel's every act, despite its being the evident victim
since the Oslo Accords of an ontological hatred that resulted in the
refusal at Camp David, has been demonized and covered with lies,
and now the corruption of anti-Semitism, accompanied also by terrorism, has returned."

In Italy, many intellectual and business circles wonder why there
were no Jews in the Twin Towers when they were brought down
(though naturally the information is disgustingly false). An indus-
trialist friend (not Jewish) relates that Jewish control over world
finance and the press is again being talked about, like in the good
old days. It's being repeated that the Jews have become like the
Nazis. Paolo Mieli wrote about the danger of the resurrection of anti-
Semitism. It has become difficult these days for a Jew in Europe to
meet with friends socially unless he shows that he is prepared to renounce Israel, unless he falls into line with not recognizing Israel's
peace offers or is ready to declare that Sharon is a criminal.

In the United States, a long, epoch-making article appeared in
the *New York Times Magazine*, November 2001, two months after the
Islamic extremists' attacks: "The Uncomfortable Question of Anti-
Semitism." The dismal subtitle: "Waking Up to My Father's World."
The author, Jonathan Rosen, an intellectual of the left, writes: "When
I was growing up, my father would go to bed with a transistor radio

set to an all-news station. Even without a radio, my father was attuned to the menace of history. A Jew born in Vienna in 1924, he fled his homeland in 1938; his parents were killed in the Holocaust . . . the grumbling static from the bedroom depressed me, and I vowed to replace it with music more cheerfully in tune with America. These days, however, I find myself on my father's frequency. I have awakened to anti-Semitism."

Rosen recounts what European intellectuals still won't say: How the criminalization of the Jews by the Arabs, a foul paradox that appears to be a kind of ethnic fecal discharge, not even worthy of consideration, has been willingly accepted at every social level, when all they're looking for is a scapegoat. "Only the Jews were capable of destroying the World Trade Center," Sheikh Muhammad Gemeha, representative in the United States of Cairo's Center of Islamic Learning and imam of New York's Islamic Cultural Center, said in interview that Rosen read. "If it became known to the American people, they would have done to the Jews what Hitler did." And the obscene rumors that the Jews withdrew their money from the stock market prior to September 11 are rehashed. Mossad, Israel's intelligence agency, is confidentially though cunningly cited, even in Italy, as being responsible for the terrorist attack.

Moreover, the groundwork had been prepared: at Durban, the Palestinian NGOs had distributed *The Protocols of the Elders of Zion* concerning the Jewish plot to conquer the world; a very modern slogan pertaining to human rights appeared like a charm (not by chance in South Africa) and was repeated by the French, Italians, British, and Danish: "Israel, a nation of apartheid," a logical and historical folly. Meanwhile, the propaganda machine repeated its lies (part of Arafat's speech in Oslo): The Israelis use depleted uranium and nerve gas; they poison the water supply; they give explosive toys to children; they employ nude female soldiers to confuse the Islamic soldiers. Israeli soldiers rape Palestinian girls to provoke the Palestinian family to a murder-vendetta against the rape victim herself. The Holocaust, in the words of Bashar al-Assad, in all the newspapers of the Middle East, in most of the Friday sermons in the mosques, on the screens of Al-Jazeera and Palestinian television, became a fairy tale, intended to aggrandize Israel and the Jews. Ten days ago Israel was described by Iran as a cancer to be eliminated, and the Hezbollah continue to promise the destruction of all Jews.

France presented the fact of having spared the Hezbollah from being included on the European list of terrorist organizations as a great victory and a sign of sympathy toward Lebanon (from which the Israeli army withdrew some time ago). It is heard around with great insistence that, if it wasn't for the Jews, bin Laden wouldn't have it in for the West as much as he does. Whereas, for anyone with a modicum of knowledge about the history of his interventions, the contrary is evident: Israel is a victim of Islamic fundamentalism because it is a sliver of the West in the Middle East. Israel represents the maximum concentration of Jews in the world, therefore it attracts the maximum amount of anti-Semitism, and that's that.

The Arabs, who are its great enemy, have worked it out according to classic standards: total demonization, denial of the right to exist, and a systematic buildup of obvious lies; for example, that the Temples of Solomon or Herod were never there, or that the Holocaust never occurred. This entire poisonous package has little to do with the Israeli-Palestinian question, with the territories, with peace. Here, too, the word *occupation* is by now devoid of any significance; it's part of the common vocabulary, like when they used to say—or rather, when they say, since it's appearing once again in Arab newspapers—that *azymes*, the unleavened cakes used for the Feast of Azymes, are mixed with blood. In a word, European anti-Semitism, fed by Arab inventions, is again at work. The idea that the Jews are an evil bloc destined to destroy the world, just as *Mein Kampf* would have it, is again part of the thinking about September 11, about Israel and about Jewish influence in the world, in the press, and in the realm of finances. The criminalization that led to the greatest slaughter in human history has revived.

Can it happen again? Israel has an impressive army, but a couple of missiles full of chemical and biological weapons can always hit the Azrieli Towers of Tel Aviv or the synagogue in Rome.

# Failure at Camp David    JULY 27, 2000

Barak had Ben-Gurion with him at the airport yesterday: the man for difficult moments. "We were not successful," he said and continued to speak about pain, sacrifice, and the will to go on at all costs. When Arafat climbed out of his helicopter amidst the rejoicing crowd, he made the sign of victory: He had not given in to the Israelis; rather, he had forced Barak to offer more and more, offers that cannot be withdrawn and that perhaps, Arafat certainly hopes, can be realized by September 13, the date of the proclamation of the Palestinian state.

There is reason for great disappointment, great satisfaction, and great concern in the failure of the Camp David summit. The disappointment is linked to the unrepeatable potential of the meeting. President Clinton made a cyclopean effort with regard to Middle East peace: His personal participation seems to have been inspired—more than by his desire to enter the annals of history in the final period of his term—by the real perception that what is at stake in Middle East peace is crucial peace between the advanced world and that of developing countries, between the Judeo-Christian world and the Islamic world. The other two participants were also the best: Ehud Barak is a modern leader, ready to take steps that are extremely courageous, yet reliable because of his military experience. After him, a return of Netanyahu is possible, however. As for Arafat, in spite of his old predilection for arms diplomacy and international coercion, he is still unquestionably the leader who has also shown a concrete willingness to negotiate in order to honor the promise of a lifetime: a Palestinian state. Despite the impressive protagonists, the summit didn't succeed, and this is very indicative of the depth of the conflict.

Nevertheless, and here we come to the reason for satisfaction, taboo subjects such as Jerusalem and the refugees came out of their futile hiding places, from their mystical-religious or propagandistic obscurity. Jerusalem, rather than being merely invoked, was finally referred to by the names of its specific neighborhoods, of the people who live there: from stones we advanced to people. And we'll start out again from there.

Still, the reasons for concern for the future are enormous. Arafat appeared at the summit as a leader whose hands are tied by three factors: First, his internal public image, always raising banners and rifles and always saying no, which even now does not conform to any peace mentality. From his school days on, he didn't intone, or write, or teach peace, and he hasn't learned it. On the contrary, he has grown fond of the horrible dream of the shahid, the martyr for Islam or for the national cause. In addition, Arafat has been conditioned by the maneuvers of the entire Arab world, first of all Egypt and then Saudi Arabia, which proclaim their moral sovereignty over

Jerusalem and are not really interested in a peace that can do away with their moral and economic hegemony. Beyond that, we saw that in the end the leader of a nondemocratic country could actually see to his own survival, first and foremost, by titillating the feelings of the masses, indifferent to higher principles. While Barak, having to account to his electors who elected him to bring about peace, had no choice but to go as far as possible with his concessions.

Despite Clinton's words of hope, the possibilities for peace in the Middle East are now undermined by the fundamental difference that exists between a democratic system that pursues peace as a value that cannot be given up and a nondemocratic world that views itself as oppressed and exploited and therefore values peace as an opportunity to recover land that it maintains was stolen from it. A vision that does not allow for sacrifices in the name of an abstract principle, valid in itself.

# A Theological Dispute with Political Consequences

AUGUST 7, 2000

There is a real poison apple rolling around among the Israeli people at this time and also bouncing around the Jewish diaspora throughout the world. It's that the disquisition of the old Sephardic rabbi Ovadia Yossef is not a purely theological one. Yossef is the spiritual leader of Shas, the party that ousted Shimon Peres from his role as president of the republic and decided that the government of Ehud Barak must fall by taking away the support of his seventeen votes. By tossing into the media and political arena his interpretation of the Shoah as a punishment meted out to souls guilty of sins in previous incarnations, Yossef seized a weapon that is extremely detrimental to the very foundation stones of the Israeli state, extremely aggressive toward the Ashkenazic component of society, and in general extremely disdainful of common sense and therefore of secular culture.

Let's talk about reincarnation, the Gilgul, or rebirth, of souls, as Yossef called it in his speech: it exists as part of a late Judaic tradition that originated in the Middle Ages in connection with messianism. It is in no way recognized by religious mainstreams. It was straining the facts quite a bit for the Sephardic rabbi to refer to it as though written in the Bible, as an article of faith that in reality does not exist. In fact, the head Ashkenazic rabbi, Israel Lau, stayed away from this tradition, declaring that he was completely agnostic concerning the reasons for the Shoah and stating that he was simply very struck personally by the memory of his dear ones lost in the camps—a rationalistic blow at the omnipotence of religion dealt by a counterpart of the Sephardic rabbi, who instead ventured to explain the Eternal Father's reasons.

And now we come to the Holocaust: Yossef's words did not only convey purely theological aggression, but also political aggression. In point of fact, the Holocaust is not only the Jews' greatest, most incomprehensible misfortune, but also the turning point from which the second part of their story begins—that of the building of Israel. To say that the victims of the Nazis may be guilty, though unknowingly, of who knows what sin, which justifies that horrible slaughter of the twentieth century, is to inflict two monstrous conceptual injuries: First, it makes the Nazis an irresponsible agent for a kind of act of divine justice, relieving them of their personal responsibility. Second, it endorses the insane idea of the Jews' responsibility for their own persecution, which is the idea the Catholic Church used when it maintained, for example, that the Jews were destined to atone for the murder of Christ, or which drove Stalin to believe that it was bourgeois, urbane behavior that led to the necessary steps of internment and elimination, and which even inspired the portions of *Mein Kampf* that explained how crucial it was to extirpate the cancer of Jewish conspiracy from the history of humanity. In short, the idea of the inevitability of the Jews' misfortune, the concept of an original sin—it doesn't matter whether historical or metaphysical—is a typical component of anti-Semitism, and the attempt to eradicate it once and for all is precisely the course taken by Zionism when it established Israel in 1948 as a nation among nations and cleansed Judaism of any original sin.

If one looks at the monuments to those who died in the Shoah that Israel has built since the time of its birth, one immediately perceives a conceptual turn: linking the Shoah with Gvurah or heroism—that is, destruction through heroism and therefore redemption. This new concept is found, for example, at the Holocaust Museum in Jerusalem, in the monument-manifesto to a young hero of the Warsaw ghetto, Mordechai Anielevitch, who died with rifle in hand aimed against the Nazis.

Now, Ovadia Yossef's version excludes any redemption, and thereby confines the Jews once again to a condition of guilt. The Jewish state will not save anyone from this, since only God, only religion, can do so—not Ben-Gurion's policies. In short, it is no accident that Yossef linked his theological diatribe with Barak's condemnation at a time when Shas again clutches all the weapons of the Sephardics' ethnic and traditionalist claims. In fact, the Holocaust, as much as it represents a tragedy for all Jews, was endured most of all by European and Ashkenazic Jews. To delegitimize it, even in part, is to delegitimize its historical subjects, Barak and the entire Ashkenazic leadership to be exact. Yesterday, a group of young people lit six candles in protest against the words of Ovadia Yossef and asked those responsible to avoid continuing to create a terrible abyss between religious and secular elements, between Ashkenazics and Sephardics. For now, there is no answer.

# The Influence of the Fundamentalists Grows

OCTOBER 16, 2000

And so with a smile on his lips, Sheikh Nasrallah gave the last rites to the desperate peace conference that opened today in Egypt at Sharm el-Sheikh. Not only did he announce in front of the whole "Islamic commission for the defense of Palestinians" and the television cameras of the entire world that he had abducted an Israeli colonel (yet another one, after the three abducted a few days ago and exactly six months from the day Barak pulled out of Lebanon), but it later came out that the abducted man, a reserve officer, was not on active duty and that the abduction did not take place in Israeli territory but rather in Switzerland: a blatant move to internationalize the conflict at a time when the leaders at Sharm el-Sheikh are trying instead to internationalize peace. Nasrallah declared that the operation was carried out in the name of the Al Aqsa Intifada, as those in the Arab world now officially call the outburst of violence in the Middle East. It was a heavy message to Arafat: Instead of speaking with the Israelis and the world, act, forget international legalities. Arafat is therefore going to the summit while being asked by some of his citizens, as well as by the radical Islamic world, to be the leader no longer of a secular struggle for a Palestinian state, but of a war to free Islam from the Western oppressor. The Lebanonization of the conflict, or the use of civilians and armed soldiers mixed together, as well as its religious formulation, know no national boundaries. And it is with violence—Nasrallah sends the word—that one wins. It remains to be seen if Arafat at this time will want to distance himself from the verbal and conceptual apocalypse that surrounds the current clashes and that has little to do with a political or territorial dispute.

An illuminating document on the subject is the text of a sermon delivered last Friday in a mosque in Gaza to a large public assembly, among whom sat Yasir Arafat. The sermon, broadcast live by Palestinian Authority television, was given by Dr. Ahmad Abu Halabiya, a member of the religious council of the Palestinian Authority and former rector of the Islamic University of Gaza. Here are some selected passages: " . . . O faithful brother, the terrorists are the Jews who have massacred our children, made them orphans, made our women widows, and profaned our holy places. . . . They are the terrorists. They must be massacred and killed, as the Almighty tells us: fight them; Allah will torture them by your hands, he will humiliate them and will help you defeat them, providing relief to the minds of believers. . . . Allah has accepted from the believer his person and his property in its entirety in exchange for the promise of heaven, so that he fights for the cause of God, they kill and they will be killed. . . . America and Europe are shocked by the abductions and the lynchings but they did not tremble at seeing the remains of the child Mohammed al-Dura, murdered. . . . This is the truth. . . . therefore Allah has ordered us not to form alliances with Jews and Christians, not to love them, not to become their partner, not to support them, not to sign pacts with them. And he who does so is one of them. . . . Even though an accord for Gaza has been signed, we will not forget Galilee, Jaffa, the Negev triangle, and the rest of our cities. . . . It is only a matter of time. . . . Don't have pity on the Jews, wherever they may be, in whatever country. Fight them wherever they are, wherever you find them, kill them. Kill the Jews and the Americans and those who support them and who are like them: they are all in the trenches against the Arabs and the Muslims because they are the ones who established Israel here, in the throbbing heart of the Arab world, Palestine. They created [Israel] so that it might be an outpost of their civilization and the vanguard of their armies, the sword of the West and of the Crusades. . . . Let us put ourselves in the hands of Allah, draw together and join swords, and the slogan will be jihad jihad for a Palestine Jerusalem and Al Aqsa. . . . Allah, take action against the Crusaders, against America, against Europe. . . ." Certainly not everyone in the Authority and in the Arab world shares this Gog and Magog perspective. But it's in the air. We can only hope that Arafat and his leadership, sitting down once again at the negotiating table, know how to do justice to it in the name of that rationality that distinguished their actions up until the failure of the Camp David summit. It would be enough, at this time, for them to simply order a cease-fire together with the Israelis and to begin negotiating again with territorial rather than eschatological demands.

# The Prayer of the Daughter of an Endless Shoah

JANUARY 27, 2002

A child born after the Shoah knows different things than other children: For example, she secretly looks at a forbidden book entitled *Der Gelbe Stern* (The Yellow Star), and there for the first time she sees the naked bodies of men and women, and her curiosity over their differences is overcome by her curiosity over a horrible death that jumbles the bodies together in an eternal tangle of pain. A child like that knows that her paternal grandfather, Joseph, born in Baranov, Poland, and his wife and four little girls, and Papa's adored little brother, Moshe, were all burned alive at Sobibor by jets of boiling water (this was the procedure at that extermination camp). The child looks at Moshe's photograph, stares into his pale eyes, and sees that he looks a lot like her. Countless other uncles and relatives of different kinds disappeared along with him.

The little girl knows from the time she is very little that her maternal family, on Grandma Rosina Volterra's side, is a family with many cheerful siblings. Later, she sees Angiolina and Gastone swallowed up by Auschwitz after years of hiding and fleeing, as a result of the betrayal of some acquaintances. Like the other brothers, two upper-middle-class boys, who were the first to arrive at Forte dei Marmi by car and who, like the antique dealers they were, arranged the traditional costumes for the football pageant for the *podestà* or mayor of Florence. Called "sweet darling" and "little treasure" by their mother when they were children, they later became so much meat for the slaughterhouse, Jewish meat. This Jewish child also knows that her grandfather, Giuseppe Lattes, at one time a bank manager, found himself out on the street one day in 1938 and had to devise boxes of colorful buttons, which he went around trying to sell from shop to shop on a motor scooter. These buttons remained in the house for us children to play with up until the sixties.

The daughter of the Shoah knows that overnight her mama Wanda and her aunt Rirì could no longer go to school, and neither the teachers nor their classmates even raised a voice in surprise. And that the Lattes family went around from house to house looking for a place to hide, and there were only a few who put themselves at risk for them; the majority did not. On the contrary, there were those who willingly denounced them. From her grandmother's stories, the little girl knows about a wonderful day—the day the British Brigade with the Star of David reached Florence along with the liberators. It came from Palestine, then a British Mandate. Among those soldiers was her father, Aaron, later called Alberto. The miracle of vitality and love for the life of the Jewish people, violated six million times over, shone in that soldier who was Jewish and an Israeli. This reporter experienced many memorable periods: The most beautiful was in Israel, when people could finally weep uninterruptedly for those who had been killed in the Shoah, when they could fully express their grief. Namely, during the time of the peace process. During the years of Rabin and the peace talks it seemed possible that the Jews had found safe harbor for their all too tempestuous history. No more deaths, no more terrorized children and mothers in despair. No more *The Protocols of the Elders of Zion*, Judeo-Masonic plots, Jewish plutocracy, caricatures of Jews with hooked noses and bags of gold in their claws. No more dirty Jew. Finally, after two thousand years of injustices, since the time of the Roman exile, after so many persecutions, peace would come for the Jews in the Jewish homeland, which had been recognized by the entire world.

But it wasn't to be: *The Protocols of the Elders of Zion* reappeared, distributed in the streets in Durban and made into a television series by Egyptian television: hooked-nosed Jews with bags of dollars reappeared in cartoons in Arabic newspapers, along with the notion of a worldwide conspiracy and even blood flowing from the hands and mouths of the Israelis. The call of Islamic fundamentalism reappeared, urging the killing of Jews, all Jews, wherever they might be. And the world didn't say stop!, not even when faced with the generalized denial of the Shoah as "merely an instrument to promote Zionism." Not a cry of indignation was heard! Nor was there indignation when accusations of deicide were made again, or when some vowed to destroy Israel in a single blow with the atomic bomb. And not even after September 11, when many loathsomely vomited the idea that only the Jews could have planned such a successful disaster. In the lightest of circumstances, in living rooms in France, England, and Italy as well, it was said that in any case the attacks had happened on account of the Jews.

How can it be? How is it possible that present-day man is still not wary when faced with the horrifying signs of anti-Semitism? The Shoah will not be over until this ceases. People may think whatever they like about the Middle East conflict, and on this solemn occasion we affirm that it is essential that the Palestinian people have a nation in mutual safety with the Israelis and that their severe suffering come to an end. But this has nothing to do with the issue at hand: To reach the point of protecting all minorities, of satisfying the demands of all those who are suffering, human conscience must be cleansed of the filth of anti-Semitism.

It is time, at last, for Jewish children, fifty years later, to be able to live in peace, wherever they are, without having to die in the streets, in a pizzeria, on a bus. And may it be so for every other child. May the sign of a real end to anti-Semitism be a sign of peace and well-being for everyone. But peace has yet to be achieved. This is the prayer of a daughter of the Shoah and of Liberation.

# Part II

## INTIFADA TWO:
## AN ANATOMY

# Israel Is Right    OCTOBER 19, 2000

In the current Israeli-Palestinian dispute, Israel is in the right. Briefly outlined, its reasons for being right all stem from its having chosen peace even at the cost of the most painful concessions, and from the wrongs of the Palestinians and the entire Arab world which now pursues a course of action that has a new name: Lebanonization, that is, the illusion that Israel can be driven out at gunpoint, as Islamic forces believe they were in Lebanon when Barak pulled out last May.

Israel's reasons with regard to this crisis are rooted in the Camp David meeting attended by Arafat, Barak, and Clinton. It was at this meeting that Israel offered Arafat everything it could, seven years after the Oslo Accords of 1993 by which 98 percent of the Palestinian population came under the rais's rule, the Palestinian economy vertically improved, and Arafat gained a police force and an armed security force. Barak proposed ceding more than 90 percent of the West Bank and sharing Jerusalem with sovereignty over a good part of the neighborhoods in the east and international apportionment of the Temple Mount (bordered by the Wailing Wall) on which the great Plain of the Mosques lies. It was at this point that Arafat, pushed by the Islamic countries, rejected the agreement under the astonished eyes of the world, thereby losing international approval.

Actions subsequent to Ariel Sharon's unexpected ascent to the Plain arose therefore from Arafat's need to solidify internal support, but also to restore his credibility on an international level. So much so that he later decided to sit down again at the negotiating table fortified by international opinion's apprehension over a new intifada.

But it is not an intifada: This time both Arafat's forces and guerrilla groups linked to Al-Fatah were equipped with firearms that were used profusely in all the attacks ostensibly led by children and youths throwing stones and Molotov cocktails. In conclusion, since the restitution of the Sinai in 1977 and later with Oslo and the unilateral pullout from Lebanon and the Camp David offers, Israel has always held out a hand to the Arab world, aware of the fact that the testing ground for relations between the West and Islam lies here. If we don't realize that, it would seem that we don't know our own priorities.

# Strategies of Terror    NOVEMBER 24, 2000

There is still something that can be done in the Middle East so that the two contenders may, as they now say dejectedly, sit down at the negotiating table once again. In theory, it is the easiest thing in the world, in practice, the most difficult. To allow peace to move forward again, thereby avoiding not only daily bloodshed, but also a likely, sizeable escalation in the area, Arafat must make a dramatic gesture of reconciliation by speaking in Arabic so that he may be understood by all his people. This does not at all mean that he must retract or diminish his demands: Arafat knows very well, for example, that the famous settlements in the Gaza strip, over which the cruelest of battles has now been rekindled (it is against one of them, Psagot, that the most recent attack on a school bus occurred), were the first pledge that Barak brought to him at Camp David, if only he had accepted them.

Arafat knows that he can obtain nearly everything he's demanding to establish his state; nevertheless he also knows that Israel is not a country to withdraw because of threats, but only through negotiation. At regular intervals, Arafat says he wants peace. Yet every disconsolate declaration of willingness to order a cease-fire, like the one made at Sharm el-Sheikh, or in words spoken to Shimon Peres or to Albright and the European emissaries, has been shown to be null and void, as is the case at present. The attacks have multiplied, and Arafat has not condemned them. If anything, he has distanced himself from them, declaring that he is not responsible, or saying as he did yesterday in Cairo that he does not approve of them, thereby implicitly assigning the blame to various segments of the Palestinian corps— uncontrollable according to him—whether they be Islamic Jihad, Hamas, or Tanzim. But it's not so: the attacks from Gaza against Israeli cities (shooting within Jerusalem, the terrorist attack at Hadera) have continued without pause, and the Israelis have never attacked first, not one single time. At every terrorist attack, it could be verified that all the various groups took part in the attacks, including individuals from Al-Fatah, and many times it was the police-soldiers of Arafat's army who did the shooting or set off the explosives.

The strategy is concentric and well aimed: On the one hand, the attack against the settlements to suggest to the Israeli left that there is strong internal opposition, then the escalation in Jerusalem, the contested capital. Finally, the assault on the heart of Israeli civilian life, as happened in Hadera. Arafat is hoping that the violence—understandably more intense as a result of the liberation of the extremist leaders—may provoke an Israeli reaction that, because of its force or by some error, might incite the Middle East, might allow him to call for the presence of an international force, might place Israel on the bench of those accused before the world, and might bring about territorial gains even greater than those that Barak already offered him at Camp David. It is a strategy that requires the sympathy of the world's peace arena, and it is for this reason that Arafat proclaims an inane, insincere cease-fire every so often. The end of this double-dealing situation will only come when the rais makes an unequivocal gesture like the one King Hussein made by going to embrace the parents of the Israeli children killed by his soldiers, or when he shows the emotion that Sadat showed when he said to his own people and to the Israelis: "Enough war."

# The Refugee Problem    DECEMBER 28, 2000

The greatest peace that the Palestinian people can hope to achieve is in danger of running aground on the issue of the refugees: their suffering and anger; the images of the hovels jumbled together in spaces where everything is lacking; their political force, a considerable presence in Arafat's political and military hierarchy as well; the points they've earned by paying for this intifada in human lives.

Beyond the humanitarian question, there is a logical hurdle in the issue of the Palestinian refugees that is fundamental, and Arafat cannot decide, cannot resolve it at this time when Clinton asks him to respond positively to the offer to accept a Palestinian state with Jerusalem as its capital, as he has always promised his people. The logical hurdle is this: Arafat knows that the moment he defines the borders of his state, all the Palestinians scattered throughout the world, all the refugees that still bear the wounds of the 1948 war along with their descendants, would yearn to live in their country, the Palestinian state, and not in Israel. But the moment a refugee has the right to go and live in Lod, where his house used to be, in the heart of Israel, and the moment Arafat includes this right, multiplied by millions, at the center of his struggle, then besides demanding a Palestinian state, he is also demanding that Israel become a country densely populated, given the demography, by his citizens. In short, it does not end the conflict, but creates a new one tendentiously aimed at replacing Israel.

For this reason, both the Jewish state and the Americans have asked that the rights of the refugees be met by allowing families to be reunited, but also by making substantial use of the tool of compensation: This was much spoken of in the Abu Mazen-Beilin accord, whose negotiation ran parallel to Peres's administration first and later Barak's, and then again at Camp David. Israel would not accept any "legal or moral" responsibility for refugees created during a war in which it had been attacked, but would nevertheless assist in their resettlement in a Palestinian state or any other part of the globe.

The issue of the refugees has gone through various phases, but it began in 1948, with the war of independence, after which the United Nations passed Resolution 194 on which the Palestinians today base their demand. The resolution does not assign responsibility however. Both the history and the document are controversial, if accurately read. Today there are some who talk about two million, some three, some four million refugees. They are the descendants of Palestinians whose number is estimated to be between four hundred thousand and eight hundred thousand, who left their homes during the war, desperate and impoverished. The Israelis emphasize that for the most part they left at the urging of the five Arab countries that attacked Israel soon after the U.N. partition and the declaration of independence.

But the Palestinians, supported by the new Israeli "revisionist" historians, maintain that in various situations the Israelis drove the population to leave with the force of arms. Israel also points out that soon afterwards the Arab countries drove out eight hundred thousand Jews by force and considers this tragic occurrence similar to other tragic population shifts following World War II. Journalist Dan Margalit cites the vicissitudes of the Sudeti, who live in a region of the same name in the former Czechoslovakia, or of the Pakistan-India population shift in support of this thesis; writer A. B. Yehoshua maintains that in either case the displacements were minimal in terms of geography, culture, and language.

Resolution 194 talks about the personal choice of refugees to return to Israel "in peace," or about compensation to be established—this, too, as a personal option. It is now brandished as a weapon by the refugee camps that not even the Oslo Accords has in any way disbanded, as well as by the organizations that have run such camps and that are still the lifeline that unites all the Palestinian refugees in the world. In fact, such camps have been maintained as sanctuaries of political extremism: the Arab countries have never wanted to naturalize the refugees, not even those of the third or fourth generation; Arafat has never wanted them to disperse. The desire to return is handed down from generation to generation, and given the number of refugees and the intensity of their feelings, they are the most disheartened group in the Palestinian world and the least hopeful about the prospect of peace. The issue becomes much more irresolvable for Israel than the question of Jerusalem. Where Jerusalem is concerned, feelings, history, and roots are at stake; when it comes to the refugees, the very possibility of Israel's continuing to exist as a Jewish state is in question.

The issue has always been handled with great delicacy even by Arafat, especially in his relations with the Arab countries. If it were to result in compensation, it has been estimated that Jordan would receive $40 billion: That's what the Hashemite regime demands for having accommodated the refugees since 1948. Generally speaking, the compensation allowance expected for the refugees would be $20,000 per person, $100 billion for a comprehensive resettlement. A very tempting plate for whoever manages it, yet one that does not offset the Arab countries' fear that a disgruntled Palestinian community, definitively settled in their midst, could cause serious problems.

## Bin Laden: The Billionaire Terrorist    APRIL 6, 2001

His eyes are moist and elongated, his face continually concentrated in an expression of mystic elevation, his beard black against a brown djellabah, the high spiritual forehead framed by a white turban. Since August 1998, Osama bin Laden has been the most hunted fugitive on the planet. In February of that year he called upon Muslims scattered throughout the world to kill Americans wherever they might be found, and on August 7, with an act of great consistency blew up two American embassies in Nairobi and Dar al-Salam, killing more than two hundred and twenty persons. It was the anniversary of U.N. sanctions against Iraq.

Osama is a name that is now given to many children in Pakistan, in Afghanistan, in the Middle East, because bin Laden, through his life, his culture, his diverse strategies for the glory of Islam, is a model for an ever greater number of Muslims. His contempt for the West and his conviction that within a hundred years Islam's flag will wave over the entire world make him an idol of the new Islamic fundamentalism. His ability to disappear and reappear causing tons of TNT to explode (the Americans are driven to frenzy without being able to catch him) makes him the banner for the plan to recover hegemony over the infidels: the dominion that the Islamic world has been chasing after in vain since the Middle Ages. Osama is the seventh of fifty-four children sired by Muhammad bin Laden, a Saudi construction tycoon and one of the richest men in the country. Before his death in an airplane accident, he had constructed the palaces of the reigning dynasty and restored the sanctuaries of Mecca and Medina. During the annual Hajj (the great pilgrimage), Muhammad bin Laden would receive hundreds of the faithful in his home. The boy Osama grew up as the idealized son of one of Muhammad's Palestinian wives. To save himself from temptations, Osama, a model child, married a Syrian girl when he was seventeen, and then another three women, with whom he had a total of fifteen children.

Osama studied theology and economy in Gidda and became an Islamic sage and expert businessman. Early on, imbued with the Islamic mythology that shaped his generation, Osama took up arms against the Soviets who had invaded Afghanistan in 1979. With his soothing though somewhat strident voice and nearly unlimited money to spend on weapons and influence, Osama quickly became a leader of the revolution that led the Taliban to power. His engineers used explosives to carve out tunnels in which the rebels were able to move about at will. Seated on a bulldozer, he laid out the route to Jalalabad and went into battle in the front ranks: "I saw a mortar land 120 millimeters in front of me. It did not explode. They unleashed four bombs from an airplane; they did not explode. We defeated the USSR. I do not fear death, however. To die for the cause of Allah is a very great honor, achieved only by those who are chosen. We love this death as much as you love life."

As the years passed, such a philosophy became more and more popular. At the beginning, bin Laden's organization mainly attacked Russians and Arab leaders who were "infidels," unfaithful to Islam. There was also a break with his native country, Saudi Arabia, especially after the Gulf War and the alliance with the United States. Bin Laden, who in the meantime also began to build chemical and biological weapons and was testing a way to make an atomic bomb (which he still pursues today), moved first to Sudan and then to Afghanistan, always in exchange for considerable cash. In 1995, he carried out a terrorist attack in Riyadh and in 1996 one in Dahran in which dozens of marines died. "The invincibility of the superpowers is a myth that ended for Islam, from the time we saw the USSR fall," bin Laden said, and launched his war against the United States, Israel, the "corrupt regimes" of Egypt and Jordan, against the entire West. Globalization is his battle: From Chechnya, where one of his important cells is based, he sends instructions and messages through the Internet (thanks to masked sites) to cells in Jordan, Kashmir, Indonesia, the Philippines, Algeria, Europe (London is very strong), and the United States. His organization, Al Qaeda, recruits anyone—and there are many—who wants to restore "Dar al-Islam" against "Dar al-Harb": the "house of Islam" against the "house of war." Smiling and serene, he seemed weakened by the arrests of many of his men in the United States, Canada, and Jordan. But in January, bin Laden went to his son Muhammad's wedding, in the Afghani city of Kandahar. Seated on a carpet with the new spouse and his father-in-law, he appeared very relaxed, which was encouraging to his followers who had imagined him in flight, in the mountains.

But bin Laden is not fleeing: He is on the offensive. He knows that the Middle East powder keg and Islamic fundamentalism are ideal for him. Italy is an ideal bridge between East and West for his activities.

# Arab Holocaust Denial    MAY 16, 2001

On April 20, in the Arab-Israeli newspaper *Kol al-Arab*, the editor Samil al-Kasim urged the citizens of Nazareth to stand at attention along with the Jews at the sound of the siren on the day of remembrance for the Shoah. A month earlier Elias Sanbar, a Palestinian historian who lives in Paris, had, upon the urging of friends in Beirut, gladly promoted an appeal to cancel a conference for the denial of the Holocaust that was due to be held in the Lebanese capital at that time. The appeal had been signed by various Arab intellectuals, among them Mahmoud Darwish.

Now, however, another group of intellectuals in Beirut has taken steps to organize that conference once again and to plan an almost identical conference in Amman. Internal opposition and an appeal to decency are unable to check the continuous insurgence of the blindest policy of denial in the Arab countries, a denial that has become a political flag during the recent intifada.

For the European right, the denial of the genocide of the Jews is cause for the most serious international sanctions; for the Arab world, it is not. They didn't bat an eyelid when, for example, Ayatollah Khomenei, the spiritual leader of Iran, in front of an assembly of thirty-seven nations, declared on April 24 that the Jews organized the extermination in accord with the Nazis to promote Zionism and that the Jews subsequently falsified events to "draw the sympathy of public opinion, establish the usurping Zionist state and justify Zionist crimes."

It doesn't matter that a leader like Bashar al-Assad at recent summits of the Arab League and Islamic countries employed the other leitmotif that is a companion to the policy of denial: Nazi crimes are nothing compared to the crimes of the Jews, the real Nazis are the Jews. At his next visit, neither the French nor the Italian foreign minister will remind him of it, and perhaps not even Colin Powell.

Similar positions have never been stated in public by the leaders of Egypt and Jordan, nor even by Yasir Arafat, though they have been expressed by the official press in these countries. An editorial by Hiri Mazouri, "At the Marketplace of Ashes," appeared on April 13 in *Al-Hayat Al-Jadida*, the official newspaper of the Palestinian Authority. The editorial maintained that the Holocaust "is a fable" invented to extort political and economic benefits.

And although Ahmad Tibi, an Israeli Arab elected deputy to the Knesset and at the same time an advisor to Arafat, said on Israeli television that the Arabs must strike down these positions, a few weeks ago at a conference in Nicosia, the chairman of the Palestinian

Legislative Council stated that "the Holocaust will not be taught in Palestinian schools. The Council must weigh what is contrary to Palestinian history or puts it at risk." And a renowned commentator from *Al Akbar*, the Egyptian government newspaper, twice (on April 18 and 25) managed to write in his column "Half a Word": "Thanks to Hitler, blessed be his memory, who in place of the Palestinians revenged in advance the crimes of the worse felons on earth."

It is a deeply rooted phenomenon that is pervading the mentality of millions of people. The basic idea is simple: The Shoah is a sham to perpetrate the true Holocaust, that of the Palestinians, which the Arabs call the Naqba, "the catastrophe." The Naqba, which is more and more used as a substitute for the Shoah, is the word Arabs use to characterize the establishment of the Israel state.

The result is a paradoxical demonization of the Jews, no longer victims but executioners, Nazis. It should be clear that several thousand illuminated Arab minds today believe what is commonly held opinion in Europe and America, namely that whatever one's own political opinions may be and whatever one's own interests, the extermination of the Jews was a tragedy for the history of all humanity.

The fact that some Arab intellectuals and politicians are trying to curb the policy of denial even at a time of intifada when the Islamic Middle East is solidly behind the Palestinians is a further indication of the importance of the issue. It is legitimate to debate whether the Cambodian extermination can be called a "holocaust," it is legitimate to question the numbers in reasonable terms, but to maintain, as Arafat's personal advisor, Issam Sissalem, did recently in a Palestinian Authority television broadcast that Auschwitz was a place of "disinfection of the Jews," leads to intellectual and moral corruption. And the corrupters are we ourselves who allow these statements to pass unsanctioned either culturally or morally.

# In the Mind of a Modern-Day Kamikaze   JUNE 7, 2001

It is not difficult, wandering around the somewhat Neapolitan-like confusion of Gaza, or the multistory buildings of Nablus in that suburb of Jerusalem that is Ramallah, to run into the next suicide bomber along the way. Too bad he can't be recognized, since he resembles any other present-day Palestinian boy. He might be that seventeen-year-old with the Nike T-shirt, gel in his hair, and a body sculpted in the gym; or that slight redheaded boy coming out of the computer store; or the electrician who greets his mother and his brothers affectionately when he gets home; or the guy standing in front of the window of the record store, listening to a song blaring at top volume and biting into a sandwich made with shawarma, a type of local ham. The kamikaze these days can be any boy. The standardization of hatred has made him so. The television era has made him a common figure. In a rural corner, in a house set amidst yellow flowers and gnarled olive trees that is a little reminiscent of Tuscany, two days after Mahmoud Ahmed Marmash blew himself up at the entrance to the Netanya shopping center, taking five lives with him and injuring more than one hundred, two hundred and fifty boys gathered to vow to become martyrs, shahid.

They are boys. They laugh, they joke around, they wear gym shoes. "By now they're waiting in line: a great many want to sacrifice themselves for their faith and for Palestine; many of them are university students, boys from good families," a Hebron municipal employee tells us. They are one of the most important phenomena not only of the Middle Eastern conflict, but of the epoch-making innovation represented by the onset of Islamic extremism that has spread like an oil stain. Today, they come with dynamite.

Tomorrow, experts say, they could reach any Western metropolis with an atomic device, or come carrying with them chemical and biological weapons. To stop them is nearly impossible: If you do it with physical force or a weapon, that is, by threatening them to stop, they can immediately activate the device and blow themselves up in the midst of other people. The suicide terrorist bomber has this characteristic that is feared by all the security forces in the world: He is practically invincible from the moment he sets out toward his objective.

His bomb costs very little, his training is minimal, and his goal will be achieved no matter what: once a young man is determined and indeed desirous of dying in the course of action, nothing except a technical error (the famous "on-the-job accidents" as Mossad, Israel's intelligence agency, calls them) can stop him. And terrorism experts now fear that Islamic extremism, guided by the example of the Middle East, might venture from Netanya or Tel Aviv to New York or Rome with more sophisticated means and a network that is presently distributed throughout the world. In short: Suicide terror-ism is a weapon with a high potential for destruction. For this rea-son, it is necessary to identify early on those two hundred and fifty, or those two thousand five hundred, who long to bring death upon themselves.

The identity of the terrorist suicide bomber is hopelessly generic. He is a young man between fifteen and twenty-five years of age, un-married, religious, from a large family that is generally poor, though nowadays it may also be well-off. If he is of a young age, he is not re-sponsible for the family's support. Very often he holds a diploma. He is a boy who has suffered personally at the hands of the Israelis (prison, violence at the checkpoints, losses in the family, destruction of homes, episodes of abuse) or who has witnessed events that have convinced him of his enemy's evilness. He is a young man who yearns for a role, who is somewhat depressed. At the mosque or at work, he does not take pleasure in conversation. He is not an extro-vert. He has few friends. His cultural background is nearly always religious: A boy who five times a day recites his prayers while fac-ing Mecca, observes Ramadan, and listens attentively to the sermons of his spiritual mentors, the imam at the mosque and the Koran study groups. He wants to assist divine justice by striking down the enemies of Islam, the Jews in particular.

"When they leave the house for their final journey," reports Boaz Ganor, director of the Inter-University Center for Terrorist Studies, a school of advanced antiterrorist analysis, "the kamikazes know that the attack will not be effective if it does not involve their own death. This simplifies matters greatly: There is no need for a getaway plan, nor does the organization have to worry that an eventual capture of its member might result in dangerous revelations. The boy must die; he knows it; his companions know it. In the end, a kind of raging de-sire for martyrdom is created in him. His friends envy him; a sup-port group (we'll call it that) exalts him hour after hour. The only possibility of defense is to find him before he leaves home to embark on his final journey. Afterwards, it's too late."

The boy, in any case, is not informed of his mission until one or two days before. During that time, if security conditions allow it, various purification rituals take place, along with prayers and read-ings. The family is not informed. The boy, as in the case of the Ne-tanya terrorist bomber, Mahmoud Marmash, is generally filmed as he leaves his final message to the world and writes a letter to his

mother or to his family in which he declares that he is proud of the
lofty mission for which he has been chosen. At the time of the great
leader of suicide terrorists, Iheia Ajash the "Engineer," whom Israelis were able to kill after hundreds of deaths on buses in the
nineties, complex rituals of dramatization were used that are used in
part today as well: For example, the boy would lie down in a hole
dug in the ground to try out being in a grave, while being praised
and comforted by his friends. In general, the suicide terrorist is not
outfitted with the explosives belt (approximately three to ten kilos
worth) until he enters Israeli territory, where, in most cases, he manages to get in via normal access entries used by Palestinian workers.
A network of assistance exists in Israel: Israeli Arabs have been discovered who accompany the suicides to their destination, as in the
case of the terrible explosion at the Dizengoff shopping center in Tel
Aviv. Often the "assistants" are blackmailed by the threat of death,
having spied for the Israelis at one time. But Israeli Arab suicide terrorists are also becoming increasingly common.

But what does the suicide terrorist gain from his mission? In the
first place, the honor of having served God and the community of
believers, in addition to having served the Palestinian cause. Afterwards, he will reap eternal life in paradise and will see the face of
Allah. Islamic paradise provides both spiritual and corporal satisfaction to the shahid, who will enjoy the attentions of seventy-two
young virgins ministering to him in heaven. The shahid also has the
privilege of being able to guarantee eternal life to seventy of his relatives. Moreover, Hamas provides the martyr's family with recom-
pense that is often divided into fixed monthly stipends of undefined
duration and apparent sociopolitical advancement.

The message the family receives from the shahid asks them not
to cry for him, since he is not dead but has merely gone to paradise.
After his death, the family receives visits of condolences and con-
gratulations, candies are offered to attest the joy of the sacrifice, the
mothers appear proud. The entire community exalts the terrorist.
His funeral is grandiose; the green banners of Hamas wave alongside the Palestinian flags. His picture is everywhere: in the shops, in
the schools, at the town hall, and in the mosque. He becomes a popular hero, loved and respected; there is not a trace of social sanction
or condemnation for his act.

"By this time," says a Palestinian intellectual whose profession
brings him into contact with the boys and who wishes to remain

anonymous, "there are those with university degrees and those who are disadvantaged, some who are poor and some who are well-off. They have a strong trait in common, which moreover is a social given that has grown in general in the Palestinian world: They attended Hamas schools since childhood. That is, they are religious boys, like Mahmoud, though they don't spend all their time at the mosque or with their teachers. The time when the shahid was a kind of young priest, an ascetic for death and for Allah, is over."

Since the second intifada has been raging, the young shahid is certainly a believer intent on establishing the kingdom of God at all costs, but he is also a modern young man who watches television, plays soccer, goes to the gym, and engages in many group activities. The voices that bombard him from the four corners of the Arab world, from television and from the radio, have an effect on his upbringing, over and above the influence of the mosque. But most of all his education is influenced by a kind of commonly held opinion created by the second intifada, one that demonizes Jews, portrays them as Nazis, or considers Israelis to be bloodthirsty beasts, as do the Hezbollah, the Lebanese Shiite guerrillas. The Jews, in short, not only politically but also by doctrine, are the quintessence of the evil that grips Islam. It is understood even from the messages of the suicides: "I will make my body a bomb," Mahmoud Ahmed Marmash—the Netanya suicide terrorist who killed five people and injured hundreds—says quietly in the video filmed just before he left for his final mission, "that will blow up the bodies of the Zionists, sons of monkeys and swine, to avenge every drop of blood spilled for Jerusalem, and to avenge the killing of Palestinians, women, the elderly and children, of Iman Hejjo, the four-month-old child killed in Gaza by a bullet during a retaliation, whose death has shaken my conscience and my existence."

A very political declaration, quite different from that of Ismail Abd al-Rahman Hamed who, seven years ago in November 1994, killed three people and wounded six in Netzarim: "Beloved family and friends, I write these words with tears and my heart is sad, but I want to tell you that I am going away, and I ask your forgiveness because I have decided to see Allah today, and this encounter is from every point of view much more important than remaining alive on this earth."

From these extreme messages one can understand why terrorism has intensified and embarked along a road of no return.

# The Two Minds of Mr. Palestine     AUGUST 6, 2001

In Gaza, Nablus, Ramallah, and Bethlehem, the possibility that Yasir Arafat might topple at any moment is openly discussed. The crisis of the current policy has been described in black and white by WAFA, the official Palestinian news agency, which on August 4 wrote that the violence in any case "will not lead to a victory over Israel."

The structural collapse to which the intifada has led the Palestinian Authority is in itself a political failure: only security and education are holding up. The legal and judiciary system has been wrecked. The search for spies and collaborators has reached a point of hysteria and reciprocal suspicion that undermines social relationships. Social services (for women, children, the sick, and the elderly) have come up against the voluntary structures of Hamas, well funded by Islamic groups and nations. The taxation system and the economic structure in general have gone to pieces.

The rais is going through a bad time, it's true, but it's asking for trouble to underestimate his abilities, to imagine him weak now that aches and pains and his age make him appear less assertive than when he walked into the United Nations with a rifle in his hand. Today, Arafat still has a rifle in his hand, and he has not given up the idea of being Palestine's man of destiny. He has previously encountered, in life, the atmosphere of mistrust and impatience that his people surround him with these days: Hamas terrorist leaders are tracked by Israeli missile launchers even in their own territory; the people side with the victims killed by Israel. Insistent, threatening criticisms accompany him even within his Gaza office.

Everyone wonders if Abu Ammar—Arafat's nickname or nom de guerre in the Arab world—is the man who can pilot his people into the port that will proclaim their nation, or if he has lost the way. If the latter theory is correct, the Palestinians will experience a dramatic shock, because for better or for worse, Arafat is Palestine. His birth in Cairo in 1929 was already a contradiction. From there he acquired a heavy Egyptian accent and the tendency to shroud his origins, since his Jerusalem mother and Gaza father were not refugees, but merely emigrants.

It was Haj Amin al-Husseini himself, Arafat's uncle, the Jerusalem Muftì who did not hesitate to seek the help of the Third Reich, who trained Arafat for battle, who taught him to be forever one with the Palestinian cause. It was he who forged the myths of his origins so that they might serve a battle to the death.

Arafat chooses weapons over diplomacy. The number of terrorist attacks credited to him is in the thousands: massacres of airline passengers and children in Israeli schools, colossal interventions, such as the slaughter at the Olympic Games in Munich, the carnage at Fiumicino and the Achille Lauro. The various Palestinian organizations, in fact, all act with his consent and under his strategic eye. He has no domestic or worldly pleasures: He has become Palestine, for better or for worse. The Oslo Accords is him, the choice of terrorism as a strategic weapon is him, the secular side that shows the West he is modern is him, the religious side that renders him charismatic in the Al Aqsa Intifada is him.

It is Arafat who accomplished the enormous political achievement of becoming an issue on the agenda of world stability—he who put Israel on the list of nations over which a perpetual shadow of disapproval hangs. It is Arafat who committed the enormous mistakes that led him to flee from Ramallah and from Lebanon and from Jordan, pursued by Israel, but also by King Hussein, by the Syrians, and by the Lebanese Christians. Arafat winks at Islamic movements; he supported and supports Saddam Hussein; and still, he obtains the support of the United States. Arafat outlawed Hamas at Oslo and stopped terrorism. But at Camp David, once it was clear that his people were against his leadership and that Hamas was waiting around the corner from any agreement that might not provide for the 1948 refugees' right to return, he chose to launch the intifada, liberate Hamas, and create a kind of national unity government.

But now that Israel is flushing out terrorists in their own territory and the crowds are joining forces with Hamas, demanding vengeance, Arafat is following the consensus that is moving more and more toward war. But the world is pulling from the opposite direction—toward a cease-fire that Arafat orders only reluctantly so that he can remain Mr. Palestine and continue being a guerrilla battling against Israel.

The old cat with nine lives, who in 1967 escaped the Israelis who were pursuing him in Ramallah (his bed was still warm) and who in 1982 survived an air disaster in the Libyan desert, is now at a crossroads: He can choose the people in the square and charge headlong until he provokes Israel, thereby triggering the arrival of an international force, or he can at last put the Hamas leaders in jail.

# America Learns What It Means to Suffer

SEPTEMBER 13, 2001

America vulnerable and exposed, wounded, arouses feelings of joy in the Arab world, as difficult as it may be to believe: in the Palestinian refugee camps in Lebanon, in Egypt, in the West Bank, territory of the Palestinian Authority, in Syria, as the leaders express their condolences, the people jump for joy in the streets. Children laugh contentedly, gripping the hands of their mothers who modulate the warbled song of happiness that is heard at weddings and birth celebrations. Sweets have been distributed in the streets. People congratulate one another. Arafat, who cancelled his visit to Syria, a country added to the list of those who aid terrorism, expresses condemnation and displeasure. Yesterday he even gave blood for those wounded in the terrorist attack. He says he is shocked, he declares his profound sympathy for the American people, he offers assistance while his camp rejoices. Hanan Ashrawi says the news of the Palestinians' joy is propaganda; he describes it as a marginal phenomenon magnified to damage the Palestinian cause.

According to a press agency report, the cameraman who filmed the joyful demonstrations in the Palestinian city of Nablus was detained for investigation and his films impounded. Along the streets of Bethlehem, where last night gunshots of joy and parades of cars with blaring horns could be heard, in the *suq*, the marketplace on narrow Madbassah Street in front of Manger Square, we are unable to find a trace of sympathy for the wounded Americans. On the contrary, the Palestinian people are filled with a profound anti-Western feeling that leaves no room for sorrow. It seems that rather than seeing men, women, and children who are dead and wounded, the Palestinians see the fall of the Great Satan, friend to Israel, who is responsible not only for the sufferings of the Palestinians but for all the evil in the world.

Dressed in jeans, with short, pomaded hair like a marine, fourteen-year-old Osama Ibrahim admits to being one of those who celebrated: "I'm happy about what happened. America is constantly picking on the Palestinians, Iraq, and Libya. It supports Israel in occupying lands and in its aggression toward our people."

Ibrahim takes a breath and goes on: "I don't care if Americans die, not even boys my age. Do they care maybe if my schoolmates die?" Osama's school is a few steps away from Rachel's Tomb, near the checkpoint, where all the protest demonstrations take place. He is always present at the demonstrations, he says. Several of his friends have been killed. And he doesn't care if he dies in this Al Aqsa Intifada.

Sanaa Moussa, thirteen years old, green eyes, wears the Muslim veil and blue jeans like so many of the female students: "It was time the bombs weren't only American bombs used against Iraq or Libya. Let a bomb be thrown at them! Finally, American kids will also not be able to go to school for a few days; I've had to stay home many times. I remember that when Clinton came to visit they brought us to welcome him with a demonstration of joy, for him and his wife Hillary. Then America went back to being a great enemy, the enemy of our entire world."

Near the mosque in front of the Church of the Manger, a man with shabby clothes, Mohammed Yunes, waits for the muezzin's call to prayer: "America? I don't see anything good about it. It kills us and it persecutes us. It seeks friends and finds nothing but ene-mies—Vietnam, Cuba, the atomic bombs against Nagasaki and Hi-roshima. For the Americans who have always been the strongest, the time has come to become the weakest, faced by an attack from a world that it has always despised. I am delighted. It's like a lion with a big insect in its ear: confused and upset, it is no longer good for anything."

# The Abayats: A Terror Family

Mint tea, photographs of Sheikh Jassin and many martyrs on the walls, a veil covering the face of the mistress of the house, children all over the place, tribal pride on the faces of the males, and the prayer room with a photograph of Mecca as a souvenir. The Abay-ats have at least eight members of their Bedouin family inside the church: the real story of Bethlehem lies not only in Manger Square nor in the Church of the Nativity itself, and not even in the tanks that for thirty-six days have been raising the dust of the city where Christ was born, as Palestinian soldiers occupy the church. To find the roots of the story, you must venture out during one of the curfew hours to a hillside district, rocky and dotted with houses, from which you can see the church beyond the olive trees and the goat pastures. We'll call it Abayatland, from the name of the Bedouin family Abayat, the most prominent family of the Ta'amra tribe, a tribe of shepherds, wheeler-dealers, and, above all, warriors. The family has eight members—fathers, children, uncles, and cousins—barricaded inside the Church of the Nativity. This reporter rubs her eyes in disbelief when she hears the number. Eight, all of them in your family? Yes, four probably on the list of thirteen confirmed who up until a few hours ago were to be deported to Italy and who instead are having difficulty finding a destination; and the others on the list of twenty-six who are to be released at any moment if an agreement is finalized.

We enter Bethlehem in the early afternoon, in the middle of curfew. Verifications and questions at the checkpoint. Various jeeps and an armored tank are stationed nearby; we know that there are two of them on the square and that the entire military apparatus was in the process of being disbanded until the order was revoked. Now, alone on the road, our car sets out along the right side of the church. A tank rolls up right behind us, and for a good stretch there are two of us: *La Stampa* and the tank behind us. Moving slowly, without any abrupt movements, with the Italian license plate that provides a certain security. Then the meeting with our capable Palestinian stringer and away we go, up and down the narrow streets. Children just outside the Old City don't observe the curfew: they play ball, and the old people play shesh besh, or backgammon, on the steps of the houses. You don't see any others.

But in Abbayatland, it's different. Here the rules that hold sway are those of the family, a wealthy family with many branches, made up of thousands of people. When we arrive, the Abayats are outside, in the fresh air, talking about their eight family members barricaded in the church, some of whom will perhaps be sent to Europe. "When they're in Italy, you will help them," they tell me. They speak very harshly of Arafat, who in their opinion has betrayed them; and they speak of the Israelis with hatred. The terrorist attacks truly seem to them to be the most natural response to the "occupiers, oppressors, who take our land." The terrain in front of the mosque is planted with olive trees; the goats are herded by the children in the family. Many children, many many goats. Many houses, a lot of land. They confirm this, proudly. In front of the mosque is a group of young men whose clothing and stance, moustaches, T-shirts, hair gel, and kaffiyeh give mixed signals of modernity and archaism. They are courteous and welcoming.

They show us a demolished car a few meters away: in November, an Israeli missile killed an Abayat, Hussein, thirty-seven years old, in that car. It happened in the Beit Sahur district. The car was brought home, and now it's like a monument. Hussein had been accused of being a Tanzim leader, with a lot of blood on his hands. All the Abbayat family members are Tanzims: his brother Ibrahim Mohammed Salem, forty years old (the master of the house we go to), his son Mohammed Ibrahim, nineteen years old, his cousin Naji, twenty-nine years old, his cousin Aziz Halil Mohammed Abayat Jubran, and another cousin Ibrahim Musa Abayat (Abu Galif), a prominent Tanzim operative accused of having killed an official, Yehuda Edri, in an ambush, and then a woman and of having later abducted and killed an American architect. All these men, almost certainly, are on the list of thirteen to be expelled from Gaza. According to the Israelis, Ibrahim, master of the house, has been involved (each time in an important role) with the cell said to have organized the Beit Jalla district, using it as an armed post against Gilo, and holding firm for more than a year.

He is accused of having planned Hamas terrorist attacks. The others are no less involved, but Ibrahim, who spent two years in an Israeli prison in the nineties, is a great, respected leader, with a great beard and a great physique. The family tells me he's lost twenty-five kilos in captivity in the church. The photos of Hussein as well as those of his relatives, Ibrahim in particular, show people who are strong, moustached, severe, and armed with Kalashnikovs. Their affiliation is part Al-Fatah, part Hamas.

In a photo his mother shows us as soon as we've gone up the steps to the house we see nineteen-year-old Mohammed: the face of an adolescent but with a record of various ambushes and terrorist attacks according to the Israelis. His mother is moved; all you can see of her are the eyes of a young woman, like dark green windows between the folds of the black veil. Her name is Aisha. Before I leave, she leads me away from the men to the prayer room in the house. She lifts up her veil. She has a small face that is two-dimensional like in a medieval portrait, a madonna who during the conversation with the men spoke as if she were at a protest meeting, though now she seems young, like the thirty-seven-year-old she is. Through gestures, since the interpreter cannot enter, she tells me that she no longer sleeps, that she weeps, that she wants to at least see her husband and her son again. She gestures to her eyes, she makes the sign for tears. Some of her children surround her: She has three boys and five girls, one of whom is pregnant.

Why did her husband go into the church with the rest of the family? She raises her shoulders: it seemed natural, they thought the tanks would go away very soon, perhaps after a couple of days. Who would have thought they would persist for so long? Maybe it really hadn't been such a good idea. Italy doesn't want them, she says, because the Israelis incite them, but instead they are decent men even if they are rightfully very militant, she explains with fervor, very religious, members of Iz ha Din al Kassam, the armed branch of Hamas. Together, we telephone her husband inside the church. Since yesterday they've been eating a little better; they are awaiting events, but no one knows anything, nothing is clear. It's cold inside the church; they don't sleep. Their son is well. No, no one knows when they'll come out. We have no information her husband tells her. They're talking about Greece, Spain, Italy.

From this house they seem like fantasy places, and this is surely how Aisha, who says "Italy" as one would say "the moon," sees them. Perhaps it is in their very nonexistence that she finds the consolation she needs at this time: If they are such distant places, perhaps no one can get there, perhaps her husband and son will come back home to all those children. At home they proclaimed a religious fast on Tuesdays and Thursdays, to spiritually keep those in captivity company. Meat was eliminated. There is much praying.

Among the children only one, a twelve-year-old named Doha who already wears a veil on her head, wants to study and be a doctor. Hanna, sixteen, wants to devote herself to the Koran, and little Sohai, ten, wants to be a teacher as well. Life is inconsequential yet imposing as the millenniums here. The younger children are dressed in Bedouin colors. I ask another cousin, Wahed, who holds the very important role of vice president of the Abayat family, if the entire family knows how to use weapons. The Bedouins are courageous, he replies. Aisha recounts that for them it is completely natural to be militants: "My husband has always been a fearless anti-Israeli militant, from the time they took away our freedom, since they stole our land. And as for the terrorist attacks, they're the ones who ask for them; Sharon is the one to blame. In fact, let him go into exile. And Arafat, he should defend his people instead of delivering them to the Israelis. Peace? The Koran never speaks of two nations for two peoples." Wahed is more of a possibilist: "When peace comes, we will partake in it willingly."

As she talks to her husband on the telephone, Aisha's tone is one of extreme intimacy. They talk at length; her husband describes the details of life there. Everything takes place in the church: no showers, no change of clothes, very little food, the bathroom on the other side of a courtyard that is very dangerous to cross. Then, too, a church is not a familiar place, "even though the priests have been like brothers." Aisha relates that they came to know each other many years ago when their parents betrothed them. They were neighbors. "I ran to the square when it seemed that they were about to be released. The soldiers didn't let us come near. But I want to see how my husband and my son at all costs, after thirty-six days in the church. This they should understand, in any case." Would she prefer an Israeli prison, nearby, or their being sent far away to Italy or Spain? Neither of these, of course, she replies.

Yet both Ibrahim's wife and Wahed are certain, perhaps because someone suggested it to them, that in Israeli hands their family members would surely be killed, and that in any case they would have no right to an attorney. There is in them a complete lack of trust in the idea of dialogue, a primary suffering, and also an evident cunning that is expressed quite well in the words of Aisha's reply when asked how she would be able to endure a long absence: "I will pray to Allah to give me patience. And anyway, the separation won't be so long. They will return shortly. They promised us."

# The Western Press

In the late sixties and in the seventies, those who ventured into the journalistic profession experienced a marvelous era: that of adjectives and liberty. Based on a journalism that was more informational and less investigational, a surge of literature arose throughout the world—colorful, eager to fascinate the reader—though the fact remains that the boom of the weeklies, while taking advantage of the situation, nevertheless prescribed the flow of adjectives with expressive rules. Television imposed new standards, as did the youth revolution. Lively writing served mainly to bring the reader the strong revolutionary sentiments of the generation that now dominates the media. On the wave of Watergate and Camilla Cederna, the Italian journalist who impeached a president, on the crest of investigations in southern Italy and the world, seeking out the vices and defects of the international and Italian bourgeoisie, an entire generation set to work tracking, scenting, attacking, and mocking for the good of mankind, distinguishing the good from the bad, the oppressors from the oppressed, with raised finger and a fine hand. As is still the case, the poor were described with emotional force, with Brechtian devotion. The generation that now covers the most important conflicts and provides commentary on them to forty- and fifty-year-olds, required—and to some degree still requires—justice more than truth. We were born and remain freedom fighters, combatants for liberty; and we've all remained more or less successful Hemingways.

This is how we got so many things wrong. Yet today, in modern times, it seems that we are once again setting out on a transformation or rather a journalism of justice that nevertheless is beginning to wonder which side it's on. If we consider the conflict in the Middle East, one of the most important topics in the newspapers and the one with which this reporter has the most familiarity, we find a rise and fall and a peak in this significant situation.

News coverage and commentary on the current intifada has certainly been better on the part of local commentators than on the part of foreign correspondents (not counting the habitué): in a situation so complex, they at least had elements of justice. And yet, the strenuous pursuit of emotion and the desire for what appeared to them to be justice for an impoverished people (considered oppressed more by Israel than by its leaders, however) overwhelmed the international press up until a short time ago.

There are three or four reasons for this, which can be quickly stated as follows. First, the word *intifada* echoed Pavlov-like in those who had perhaps covered it once before; that is, it pointed back to the 1987 scheme of things, before Oslo, when the Palestinian cities were occupied. Therefore, they liked to imagine that they were once again faced with a popular revolution, children with stones in hand against armored tanks that had actually been gone for two years. Second, in the cities now in Palestinian hands and armed with weapons that had been delivered to Arafat after Oslo, a strategic mix of militiamen and general population, plus a fringe group of terrorists (destined to grow enormously to the point of investing the very core of the society), gave rise to a very complicated war that was difficult to understand at first and one in which the age-old warfare distinction of army and civilians did not work. Above all, the religious-masochistic development (later revealed in the name of Al Aqsa and in the numerous suicide bombing attacks) was so new as to be difficult to recognize. Third, reporters flirted, insistently and futilely, with the idea that perhaps it wasn't really Arafat who had refused Barak's proposals, but vice versa. Finally, the enormous difficulty in accepting that newspapers, the speeches of Arab political figures, school textbooks, and television would become filled with horrifying classic anti-Semitism (the demonization of the Jews and an appeal to kill them wherever they are found, their identification with Jesus' assassins, the denial of the Shoah) created a moral blindness regarding the seriousness of the hatred that produced the wave of suicide terrorism.

This wave came crashing down on journalism, finding it completely unprepared. The writer-freedom fighter model shattered under the impossibility of reporting the causes, the history, the emotion of one of the most important contemporary phenomena of our time: terrorism. Only now is it beginning to be told. And the humanitarian organizations are also beginning to be aware of it more than two years after its inception, as can be seen in the last Amnesty International report that finally speaks of terrorism as a war crime.

And so we come to the present day. Many important signs indicate a turning point. A lengthy report by journalist Barbara Demick, "Martyrdom Dreams Take Root Early in the West Bank," published on July 20, 2002, in the *Los Angeles Times*, concerned the terrorist myth among children. Or the article "Arafat Bombs, Europe Pays" in the June 7, 2002, issue of *Die Zeit*, regarding the use of European money to finance terror. Or the July 8, 2002, article by Ian Fisher in the *New York Times*, "For Israelis Wounded in Bomb Attacks, Recovery Is a Battle." Or CNN's five-part series *Victims of Terror*. And in reportage on the Israeli attack in Gaza (in which thirteen civilians were killed by the Israeli air force, in addition to arch-terrorist Shehaidah, head of Hamas, who was planning six attacks and had been responsible for approximately two hundred Israeli deaths), Israel's apologies were taken into consideration, after it stated several times that it had received mistaken intelligence.

Several elements have led to this change. First, the rapid decline in the value of the Arafat myth when documents linking him to terrorism were discovered, when he continued to dispatch terrorists and praise suicide terrorism, when he was directly challenged by Palestinian and Arab intellectuals on the question of his sincerity and his willingness to combat terror. In the second place, journalistic remorse, despite the obvious legitimacy of criticizing Israel and sympathizing with the suffering of the Palestinian people, over two ongoing, towering news items: the anti-Semitism that gained a foothold in the world following the demonization of the Israelis by the United Nations, by organizations for the defense of human rights, and by the NGOs, starting in Durban and the enormous, tragic upsurge of children, women, and entire families torn to pieces on buses, at school, everywhere, of wounded young people maimed for life. News reports were unable to apply either literary pathos or the usual political emotion to this chain of events. On the wave of remorse came threats: the hatred of the Palestinians, of the Hezbollah, of Al Qaeda, of Syria, of Iran toward Israel ("just one of our future H-bombs will destroy it forever") began to be frightening.

And finally, perhaps the most important element of all: the assessment of the conflict in light of September 11. Bush declared in his speech that without democracy and reforms it is unlikely that the Palestinians will stop the terror and that it is therefore necessary to go back to the table. A definitive analysis of terrorism, that all of Europe also quickly took into consideration: Democracy and peace are bound together. Hadn't we known this since 1945? All of a sudden, everyone remembered it. A short time later, on Firday, the 26th, John Negroponte, American ambassador to the United Nations, said that the tidal flow of unilateral condemnations was over. Israel could be condemned, certainly, but only with the understanding that the terrorist attacks of Hamas, the Al Aqsa Martyrs Brigades (the armed wing of Al-Fatah) and the Islamic Jihad would also be condemned. This turning point was cognitive in nature even more than political; and journalism, no matter how much of an idealistic freedom fighter it is, is ontologically cognitive and deep down it knows it. Finally, the mistakes of Jenin and Bethlehem, where not only was there no massacre (in the first case) nor Israeli premeditation against the church but only open warfare against a tough, well-prepared nucleus of the Palestinian struggle, mixed wolves and sheep together. So that now we journalists are beginning to observe them, without trying hopelessly to transform the one into the other, with a fine hand.

# Arafat: The "Martyr"

Why, in the end, did war pop out of the hat? How many fatal contradictions led to the tanks' return to Ramallah in the last few days? Why did the Saudis' offers of peace and those of Arafat, long overdue, turn into shooting that even penetrated the offices of the rais? Why did the Saudi proposal emerge from the Beirut summit weakened and old before its time? Why did an Arab summit that should have supported Arafat not allow him to, in fact, speak? If we want to face the truth, the terrible answer is this: Terrorism has a momentous force, never before seen. It is a gangrenous defect that the Arab world does not want to or is unable to deal with, whose weight could drag the entire Middle East into a bonfire.

Arafat was to have appeared on screen in Beirut to give his speech. The reason he did not appear is that his Arab cohorts, moderates like Saudi Prince Abduallah as well as hard-liners like Bashar of Syria, did not feel like paying him what the Americans call "lip service," after having exalted the Palestinian cause and even, in the case of Bashar, terrorism. In short, so many fine words, but then better to keep a proper distance; better not to make Arafat the star of the party at a time when a suicide terrorist in Netanya had violated the religious solemnity of the ritual supper of the Jewish Passover by slaughtering entire families—children, parents, grandparents—as they sat down to recall: "We were slaves in Egypt." Three terrorist attacks with twenty-four dead and hundreds wounded within twenty-four hours are too many for even the Arab states not to realize that a U.S. war against terrorism might not exclude Mr. Palestine (Arafat) and might in some way include his friends.

On the other hand, the Arab peace proposal did not have a nullifying effect on Sharon's decision to attack. Why? That, too, because of the terror. Not only did Sharon have to respond to public opinion, to a society drowning in blood and desperate, but the Arab countries made counterproductive modifications to the peace proposal, substituting "natural relations" for "normalization" and returning the irresolvable issue of the refugees to the resolution. Above all, they did not utter a single official word on terrorism.

When Arafat, after all the attacks and Colin Powell's furious telephone call, stated that he was prepared "to accept the Tenet proposal" but avoided making any commitment against terrorism, Sharon certainly had no choice but to recall that the Netanya terrorist was on the list delivered to Arafat months ago. In short, that's the hitch; it's still the hitch: At this stage of the situation nothing can be credible any more unless there is a decisive move against terrorism. But Arafat, faced with the approaching tanks, again declared his willingness to be a martyr, a shahid, like my other shahid friends, he said, and the next million shahids of Jerusalem, whereas only an announcement that the shahids are going home can stop the war.

# The Ordnance for Terror

A large open space of cleared land at the military base of Ramle, near the district of Modiin, serves as a great open-air theater to accommodate a typical war spectacle assembled by Israeli soldiers between yesterday and today: Palestinian weapons seized in this time of war, an incredible ballistic caravansary where anything can be found. It attests to a determination to be armed at all costs by obtaining weapons from any and all sources or making them at home and equipping local factories.

The obliteration of the Oslo Accords is total and complete; also absolute is the obvious personal and subjective commitment on the part of the individuals who possessed or produced this cemetery of artillery now arranged in orderly rows, with explanatory signs and mannequins. Lined up on the ground and on benches are rows of light machine guns, mortar launchers, katyuskas, missiles, heavy antitank guns, automatic rifles, pistols, hand grenades, automatic magazines, cartridges of every caliber, uniforms and disguises, examples of suicide terrorist belts devoid of explosives, a mannequin in military uniform and kaffiyeh, Jewish skullcaps and wigs used as disguises, nighttime and daytime telescopic sights for snipers, mountains of bayonets and combat knives, and even scimitars and swords. It's not an enormous quantity. There are 1,500 pieces more or less, as Colonel Gilad Ras explains, representing approximately 10 to 15 percent of the weapons seized. The others have been destroyed or cannot be displayed because they are dangerous (the ones composed of explosives). Fifty percent are illegal, that is, procured in various ways that violate the Oslo Accords. The other 50 percent are legal: Rabin and Peres delivered to Arafat 30,000 Kalashnikov automatic rifles and M-16 rifles for his police, who were to maintain internal public order and strike down extremist forces.

Things turned out differently. With the continual broadening of the conflict, the Palestinian Authority greatly increased its firepower, including heavy weapons. The best-known episode is surely the purchase of fifty tons of Iranian arms that were about to arrive on the ship *Karine A*; the arms were discovered and the ship was halted at sea. Zeev Schnerson, an officer who is a ballistics expert, explains that all explosive devices have been excluded from this display for obvious reasons. The belt is merely an example. Some of the weapons were purchased abroad, some stolen from the Israeli army (along with the uniforms), some made at home.

The supermarket of Palestinian arms is professional but also domestic: Many pistols and light machine guns bear the name of the combatant or a maxim incised in Arabic characters, very decorative and colorful, at times fluorescent. We see five submachine guns from the Lebanese army (their origin and even a cedar are engraved on the stock) that probably passed from the Hezbollah to the Palestinians; some thirty Russian antitank grenade launchers (RPGs) of various kinds, one of which looks just like a trombone. In all there are probably about fifty cannons capable of launching large missiles from a distance of four and a half kilometers. There is a row of Turkish Cobra rifles, very efficient and modern according to what they tell me; new Heckler and Koch MPS light machine guns of the kind used by the American Delta Forces. Many Kalashnikovs, which in contrast to the other weapons are legal, except for those purchased (there is an Egyptian one) or self-manufactured in excess. There are some manufactured in the West Bank by secret factories, with gold coins inserted in the stock. The M-16s equipped with telescopic sniper sights (they can fire up to a distance of 600 to 1,000 meters) are illegal. There are guns manufactured by the Chinese and the Russians, the AK-47 or Kalashnikov in particular, on which a bayonet can be mounted.

The weapons made at home, automatic rifles with gilded or silver plated stocks and triggers, pistols, personalized knives, speak of
mysterious personal stories; who knows how they ended up here.
Close by lie legendary scimitars and a huge, well-used machete.
There are hundreds of knives, big ones. They are mostly the bayonet
kind, or equipped with a device capable of cutting metal fencing as
well. There are many personalized pistols: Colts with the shiny
gilded horse, a Beretta made in Egypt, a Helwan, gilded and silver-
plated Smith and Wessons, Rugers, Belgian FNHBs, some with
mother-of-pearl or wooden stocks. There is also a Lady Lock 26,
plastic and therefore lightweight, "very beautiful" says the officer.
There are also German HK pistols with silencers, the kind that the
FBI, for example, uses in certain operations. Many of the pistol and
rifle stocks are engraved, decorated; they show particular care, a
precise aesthetic. On display is a sniper's nocturnal telescopic sight
that is absolutely prohibited as are all other sniper devices. Magazines in great quantity, manufactured at home and abroad. Cartridges of every caliber, some of them red. One submachine gun "can
pass through a Peugeot from side to side, even from a distance
away" the officer explains. "Almost all these weapons," he says, "are
suitable for ambushes along the roads." Numerous MAG machine
guns; a quantity of Scorpios made by the Palestinians—it's the light
submachine gun that Arafat always carries with him. Very significant, so it seems, are some Iraqi Al Nasirah RPG antitank grenade
launchers, 40-millimeter caliber, clearly stamped "Made in Iraq."

Each of the illegal weapons has its own specific path, across the
Egyptian border, via the waters of the Red Sea, from the Lebanon
border by way of emissaries of the Hezbollah or of Iran. We're not
talking about enormous quantities, but of a complex, reliable mosaic
that has been pieced together with much time, much patience, and
much determination.

# Shabbat Shalom

It was already dark in Jerusalem, late Saturday, a holy day for the
Jews, when at the entrance to a synagogue in a religious quarter, Beit
Israel, the crowd was attacked by a human bomb, a suicide terrorist.
The impact was enormous—as of now nine deaths have been

recorded and thirty-seven wounded, eight of them seriously. Among the dead are at least two children, one of them a year and a half old. In the quarter, and especially in front of the Mahanei Israel Synagogue where the bomb exploded, numbers of religious men with side locks, black or white suits, high hats with fur, began running in all directions, covered with blood; meanwhile thirty Red Star of David ambulances blocked a narrow lane at the end of which burned intense flames that firemen were trying to put out. As a crowd gathered, looking for family members and friends, the police checked that there were no other human bombs or car bombs in the vicinity.

There have been three suicide terrorist attacks and car bombings in Beit Israel in the last few months. Up to now residents described them as if talking about a miracle in which the population had been spared. This time there was no miracle. The primary road, a wide street that connects Jerusalem with Ramallah starting at the center of Israel's capital, skirts this religious Israeli district on one side and the Old City and the eastern section, namely, the Arab neighborhoods, on the other side. Not too difficult to cross the street on foot with a load of TNT. Some residents of Beit Israel reported seeing a man disguised as a religious figure enter the neighborhood, a kippah on his head and a large knapsack in his hand, and actually ask for street directions. According to the accounts of witnesses, the man lit a cigarette. He is said to be the suicide terrorist, a militant of Al-Fatah, and from what we know at this point, was a resident of the Deheishe refugee camp that borders Bethlehem.

Yesterday's terrorist attack, the most recent of a long series in Jerusalem, claiming hundreds of victims, was a retaliation that immediately followed the harsh action of the Israeli army in Balata and Jenin (from which the army withdrew). In these two refugee camps, several important representatives of the Palestinian organizations claiming responsibility for terrorist attacks were shot to death over the course of the last three days, and the civilian population, including women and children, was also involved (the Palestinians talk of a total of thirty dead, militants and civilians, since the beginning of the operation). The reason for the action, as stated more than once by Israeli authorities, which several hours ago withdrew its troops from Jenin, was to deny refuge to organizations involved in terrorist attacks and take away their ammunition magazines. In fact, stores of explosive were dismantled, and missiles and ammunition reserves destroyed; five explosive belts used by suicide terrorists were also found ready for use. But the soldiers created a great deal of shock by searching house to house and knocking down walls between buildings to avoid exposing themselves to snipers.

An Israeli soldier, Jaacov Avni, twenty years old, was killed yesterday; another the day before. The Palestinian Authority requested and obtained a show of solidarity from various European countries, such as France, Sweden, and Denmark, in addition to the demand that Israel withdraw its army. Even the United States asked that Sharon attempt to soothe the waters, though recognizing Israel's right to defend itself against terrorism. Arafat condemned last night's attack at the synagogue, while Al-Fatah nevertheless claimed responsibility for it. In the streets of the Palestinian Authority, where the past days saw promises of random attacks in addition to protest and mourning, there were demonstrations of joy. Arafat's condemnation is probably related to the fact that the attacks are again striking at Israelis within the Green Line.

# "Kill the Jews"

As I write these lines, on June 19, 2002, I hear dozens of ambulances wailing: three hundred meters from my house, on the descent toward the intersection with Pat road, a bus exploded ten minutes ago in front of the shop of my Arab friends, the Pardos brothers, where I do my shopping, near the florist where I buy roses on Friday, down the wide street where I walk ten times a day. In the midst of my life and, to a much greater extent, in the lives of all those individuals who will no longer be the same persons after today. Again, they are talking about forty wounded and at least ten killed. Among them the kids who go to school in the city, the workers who crowd onto the buses at eight in the morning. Shattered families in which parents bury their children; people of all ages who will be crippled forever. By now the praxis has a ritualistic character about it: Television and radio begin to add up the numbers almost immediately after the explosion, the dozens of wounded, many *cashè* (serious), many *cashè meod* (very serious), many *anush* (critical). According to the bulletins, these wounded will soon be revealed as actually having died. Just now, as I write, the ten deaths have already become fourteen. After a little while, seventeen. How many mothers crazed with fear are running down the sloping street to look for their children? How many wives and husbands have left their jobs to hasten to Sharei Tzedek or Hadassa Ein Karem Hospitals in search of their loved ones among the wounded?

The customary practice continues: helicopters in the sky, police checking to make sure that there is not another terrorist in the vicinity, and within minutes dozens of wailing ambulances move into the area. There are volunteers of all ages, young people who have taken continual refresher courses since they were fifteen. They know exactly what to do when faced with injuries and inhuman amputations. Nothing frightens them: Under the direction of doctors and paramedics they clear the wounded from the area in just a few minutes, sorting them according to their injuries/traumas, finding the time for a kind word. The first thing they learn in the courses is this: "Remember that you are dealing with human beings." Once the area has been cleared of the wounded, the Zaka volunteers with their yellow smocks begin their patient work of reassembling the dead. Yet tonight the streets of Jerusalem will once again be full of people, the restaurants and bars will be doing business, even if at a reduced pace. Cars are already beginning to move again. Yossi Olmert, mayor of Jerusalem, says with tears in his eyes: "The citizens of Jerusalem are the bravest in the world. No one is as courageous as they are."

The other side also has a praxis: Early in the morning a driver preselected by the Tanzim or by Hamas goes to pick up the suicide terrorist. He himself has chosen the most suitable place for the terrorist attack. According to the words of one of them, a certain Sarahna whom I interviewed in an Israeli prison, it must be "quiet, as crowded as possible, preferably unsuspected so that it will be understood that we are capable of striking anywhere." The trip by car avoids the checkpoints, or else the car passes through them while the terrorist with his belt or knapsack enters from a secondary street. Terrorists, whom I have interviewed a number of times, talk about their decision as if it were part of them, "built in," something essential in order to "liberate their land," "take revenge against Sharon," "kill the Jews." During the interview, the cultural basis for their decision, strange as it may seem, appears to be mired in conformist mud, I might almost say conventional. The social classes to which the terrorists belong are at this point quite varied and their culture a religious-nationalist mix. The suicide terrorist knows for certain that his society wholeheartedly approves of his action, that his picture will be posted on all the walls, his farewell video applauded, and his family compensated. His society plans to emulate his choice, intends its sons to emulate it, and teaches it to them in school and through radio and television. The demonization of the Jews even more than that of Israel is circumstantiated by evidence. It starts with the denial of the Holocaust, and goes as far as "sons of monkeys and swine." It touches on the idea that their very existence as a nation is illegitimate, and even more so the territorial dimension of that nation; a nation that, according to this mindset, is plainly devoid of any historical foundation and whose origins are stained by horrible moral culpability.

The terrorist, or suicide terrorist, reflects a central fact of this socalled intifada, namely that it is not an intifada like the one before: On the contrary, the earlier one was much more respectable and judicious in its secular and territorial demands. The suicide bomber, and perhaps this is not sufficiently understood by us, is not viewed as an extremist, but is instead recognized as a hero of this war. Arafat and the Palestinian Authority, in all its components and expressions, have exalted him unendingly; any condemnation has been weak and above all never followed up by any action.

Terrorism is the mainstream, the commonly held belief in this conflict. To every hint of a proposed accord, such as that originating with the United States or Saudi Arabia, the response is a volley of attacks, all aimed at Israel's womb, at its vulnerable progeny. These attacks convey a very plain rejections, precisely because they are always related to the opening of new talks. It is therefore our duty to ask ourselves conscientiously and firmly: What help can each Jew give to his nation of brothers, assailed on a daily basis by the unprecedented phenomenon of suicide terrorism, the new lethal weapon of our era? And secondly, we must ask ourselves the most painful, difficult question of all: What if Arafat isn't interested in any kind of agreement? What if a Palestinian state isn't in his plans now but only an expansion of the conflict?

# Bethlehem: Terrorists and Tanks

Since yesterday Bethlehem the Holy City has once again become a battlefield. Manger Square, in the city that was to be the pearl of the Jubilee, the uncontested high point of every pilgrimage (beautiful hotels had been constructed for visiting pilgrims, almost to the doorway of the Church of the Nativity), is instead a desert of silence, lifeless except for the Israeli tanks and the Tanzim and Hamas who are on the move trying to escape the assault of the military operation currently underway. Our Italian journalist colleagues, who entered the city that morning with Israeli permission, find themselves in the heat of battle right in the square; the Israelis do not want them there, and the shots come very close. The carved olive wood shops are closed, the restaurants and hotels are closed. Only the Town Hall is partially open, along with the well-remembered Peace Center, financed with funds from the now defunct Oslo Accords. And the Church of Nativity, where the Italian journalists take shelter unaware that in a short time a large group of armed Palestinians, perhaps more than a hundred of them, will also decide to barricade themselves at the site of the Grotto of the Ox and Donkey, as was done in the Middle Ages. There the journalists' adventure begins, caught between the devil and the deep blue sea: They don't want Israeli help; there could be a bloodbath. Instead, they seek the Italian consulate's assistance and that of the international community. The Tanzim make them go down to the Holy Land's kitchens with the nuns and the Franciscans. A terrible adventure in the silence of the church's arched passages broken only by sporadic gunshots after the Israelis, during the course of that morning in Bethlehem, begin to put Operation Defense Wall into action, taking possession of several apartments that overlook the Old City, searching through the mosque in front of the church, roaming through the narrow streets that surround the center like a casbah.

What to do about the churches and mosques? The world is concerned, yet at times that's exactly where the conflict unfolds. Even the Palestinians know that Israel is afraid of the world's judgment. The city is dead, but the men the Israelis are searching for know how to move about through the narrow back streets. During the last intifada, Bethlehem was a stronghold for Tanzim forces and for the toughest Hamas as well. In the past month, three suicide terrorists, two boys and a girl, all very young, actually came from Deheishe, the refugee camp alongside the city. The religious leader of the mosque in front of the church is Sheikh Abdel Majid, a thin, pale forty-year-old with a black beard, very powerful both theologically and politically. In the room next to the prayer room, on the first floor, he often sits on low sofas or on carpets with his followers, awaiting prayer. On the wall is a small map of Palestine that includes Israel as well, in its entirety. Yesterday at a certain point flames burst out in the mosque but were quickly extinguished. Majid will certainly keep his distance. The Israelis know that Bethlehem underwent a number of changes in the time of the intifada, that an important group of Tanzim and Al Aqsa Martyrs Brigades have their headquarters there: The gunshots and mortar rounds fired at the Gilo district from Beit Jalla, a Christian zone that was formerly unfamiliar with violence, are directed from Bethlehem.

Most of the shooting in Bethlehem took place that morning, starting at dawn when the tanks reached the city; an elderly Palestinian woman and her thirty-five-year-old son were killed. The tanks are unable to enter the narrow streets; one of them tried and crushed a car, climbing over it.

In the early afternoon there is shooting also in Deheishe, the refugee camp of the suicide terrorists, where Hamas and the Tanzim are strong: a heap of shanties in one of the most hardened strongholds of the 1948 refugees and their children and grandchildren. On the perimeter walls that were opened at the time of the Oslo Accords, and everywhere along the deserted narrow streets, are hung pictures of the three suicide terrorists, who by this time are in the paradise of the shahids, the martyrs that Arafat always refers to in his speeches. Inscriptions alongside the pictures call them heroes and saints. Their faces are the smooth, handsome faces of young boys of our time.

Children come out of the camp to throw stones at the tanks; at the beginning, armed men also came out to shoot at the tanks, but then they withdrew. You don't dare think what would happen if a battle were to break out in those abject, tangled alleyways where poverty reigns and where guerrilla organizations now commonly prevail. Deheishe, a world of indigence and unemployment, has had sixteen deaths since the start of the intifada. All the families know one other, and often they are related; the children go to school to-gether. Mohammed el Dararmeh, who blew himself up killing ten people when he exploded in Meah Shearim, the religious quarter, on March 5, had been recruited a short time earlier by the Al Aqsa Martyrs Brigades, or Al-Fatah: Everyone adores him, everyone would like to emulate him, everyone recalls how he changed when his best friend was killed in a confrontation at the checkpoints. The children that come out to throw stones make you tremble with pain and fear: They repeat that Sharon hates them, that Sharon is thirsty for Palestinian blood, that being a martyr is a splendid thing.

Perhaps Israeli soldiers will soon search through the camp, as they've begun to do in Bethlehem; they will go from house to house arousing fear and hatred. They will find documents proving connections between suicide terrorism and Al-Fatah's official structures; they will look for men who have killed and who have sent others to kill; they will give the Palestinian population an impression of horrific might, of intolerable oppression. At the entrance to Bethlehem, the wives of reservists, people thirty-five, forty years old, desperately kiss their husbands who are about to set out for the territories. The soldiers tell us: "What a senseless war. The Palestinians could have had everything without a fight if they had wanted to. Of course, we don't like it, but what we are going to do is necessary now. We must be strong." When the wives turn the car around to go home, they go back to a society where people are shut up in their houses, assailed by fear of terrorist attacks, a society that is constantly burying its dead.

## Demographics of Terrorism

It is often said that the Israeli-Palestinian conflict is very imbalanced with respect to the number of those lost: 1,450 Palestinians and 525 Israelis. Unfortunately, the statistics must be constantly updated. From these numbers one gets the impression of a Palestinian David against an Israeli Goliath with a quick trigger finger. But one of the specialized institutes most esteemed by terrorism experts, the International Policy Institute for Counter-Terrorism (ICT)—a research institute and think tank dedicated to developing innovative public policy solutions to international terrorism—yesterday provided an interpretation of the numbers and of their significance, which, though it does not overturn their import, nonetheless modifies it dramatically. As Ely Karmon, professor and researcher at the ICT, reports, the facts are these: among the Palestinians killed, more than 50 percent were directly involved in combat actions. Karmon clarifies that this does not mean children with stones or a rudimentary Molotov cocktail, but combatants who died in terrorist actions—in suicide bombings, ambushes, gun battles—or while using explosive materials. In a very general sense, we might view them as combatants, as the research calls them, in an extensive Palestinian army. Israeli combatants, on the other hand, that is soldiers or policemen killed in action, are much fewer in number compared to civilians, namely 25 percent. This makes the difference between civilian lives lost in the intifada equal to 25 percent.

Another very important fact is the data concerning the female gender: Palestinian women of all ages killed in the conflict amount to half the number of Israeli women; less than 5 percent of Palestinians killed are female. Among noncombatants, deaths among Israeli persons over forty years of age are more than double that of Palestinian deaths in the same age bracket. These data show that the Israeli civilian population has been struck more than the Palestinian civilian population—an obvious result of the use of suicide terrorism, which intentionally strikes crowds indiscriminately. The number of children killed is more or less identical: Palestinian terrorism has never targeted a nursery or a school. But in the youth bracket we find a (relatively) high number of young Palestinians, among the noncombatants as well. In short, while the Israelis belong to all age brackets and both genders, since terrorism strikes randomly, the Palestinians who have died, on the other hand, are concentrated in the thirteen- to thirty-year-old age bracket. Professor Don Radlauer, research coordinator, tells us that these results, obtained through lengthy, patient work, are drawn from press sources and documents furnished by humanitarian organizations in the Palestinian camp (while in the Israeli camp the work was simpler because of the availability of incontrovertible documents).

The results reveal a tragic trend: The participation of young Palestinians in confrontational situations in which they expose themselves to death. Why does this happen? The researchers' response is very distressing: Palestinian society indoctrinates its young people by reiterating its approval of the idea of "martyrdom" on television and on every public and private occasion. The tendency is fed by a religion whose message is spread by extremist voices. Thus a culture is created in which the decision to die for an idea is glorified. Young Palestinians feel motivated to face Israeli forces by seeking death, even in situations in which they will not obtain results. Naturally, the researchers say, the greatest responsibility for this falls on the leaders who promote this culture of death.

In conclusion, say the ICT experts, what the research clearly shows is that the commonplace endlessly repeated by Palestinian spokesmen, namely that the Israelis deliberately attack their civilian population, is incorrect. And a great many of the losses have causes that are more ideological than military.

# Durban Revisited

On July 29 in Johannesburg, they will again celebrate another divorce between the institutions that should safeguard human and civil rights in the world and Israel. It is the huge Conference for Sustainable Development summoned by the United Nations, with more than six thousand attendees including delegates and NGO volunteers. From the way it's being presented, we will probably witness another Durban, where instead of holding a conference on racism, the United Nations held a racist conference against Israel. This divorce, underway for years at this point, between institutions for civil and human rights and the only democratic nation in the Middle East is a high price to pay for international political correctness: in the long run, for men of goodwill at least, it undermines the credibility of these institutions at their very foundations. From the meetings of the Geneva Convention to those for the defense of children, peace, education to a U.N. Security Council presided over by Syria.

Last July 1, 2001, for example, the world sacrificed much to the usual international majorities maniacally committed to resolutions against the Jewish state. Israel, together with the Americans, did not ratify the Rome Statute of the International Tribunal for war crimes and crimes against humanity, although both had originally signed it. Why? Not only out of concern that soldiers involved in the war of defense against terrorism might be incriminated, but also because of what the charter of association stated. Far from adequately treating the issue of terrorism as a crime against humanity and therefore eligible for submission to the judgment of the court of Aja, where the tribunal was to be based, the charter (after the Arab countries' lengthy intrigue on this point) declared the transfer of a population into occupied territories to be a war crime, thus rendering all the inhabitants of the West Bank and Gaza settlements potential war criminals.

Now, their continued residence in a territory that will be within the borders of a Palestinian state, once political conditions permit it, is certainly not desirable. Barak had proposed that they be removed almost entirely, and to this day there is hope that new developments brought about by Bush's speech will allow the renewal of negotiations. Yet, what is needed for the colonists to be in a position to leave is precisely a political agreement that is satisfactory to both sides, not the threat of another international assembly that, under pressure from the Arab League States assisted by Third World countries of ex-Soviet persuasion, will devote itself to describing the Jews as criminals, wanted men, dead men walking.

# Daniel Pearl

Moments before they slit his throat, journalist Daniel Pearl, clearly under pressure, declared to his Pakistani torturers' telecameras: "I am a Jew. My parents are Jews." He was not forced to declare that he was an American, another great crime, but that he was a Jew, an enormous sin with many centuries of tradition.

Among us journalists in the Middle East there are a number of Jews. At times, seated on a carpet in a mosque, barefoot, facing a representative of Hamas, for example, I've wondered what mechanisms, if only psychological and, in more extreme cases, concrete, would come into play if he were to ask me what my religion is. Several times the identity, the name, might have made a difference, for me and for many colleagues who nevertheless perform their work without fear, as I do, for that matter.

Besides being accused of being an American, Pearl had been accused in his abductors' e-mails of also being "a spy for Mossad,"

Israel's Intelligence agency. His distressed father had begged the Israeli journalist who interviewed him in the United States not to mention that the family had any connections to Israel (scientists born in Israel; Pearl had only an American passport) because otherwise "not even his body will ever be recovered." During the entire period of the abduction, Pearl's religion was downplayed.

The fact that Pearl was forced to provide his murderers with a good reason to kill him by stating "I am a Jew" is a new phenomenon, and it is urgent that it be loudly denounced and stopped at once: It represents the unchecked anti-Semitic hatred that pervades the schools, newspapers, and television in the Islamic world. Jews are designated with negative stereotypes, both ancient and modern. Egyptian newspapers publish *The Protocols of the Elders of Zion* in installments, and television makes a series out of it. In every part of the Middle East, Jews are portrayed as hooked-nosed caricatures with sacks of dollars in their bloody claws, mouths flowing with Palestinian blood, as colonialist-imperialists thirsty for Arab blood, foul beings whose right to be part of the world of nations is disputed. It is against this backdrop that journalist Daniel Pearl was murdered: an American, a Jew, he deserved everything he got.

If at Auschwitz, before entering the gas chamber, a Nazi had filmed a Jew in utter physical and moral agony as Pearl was and had made him say "I am a Jew and my parents are Jews" before sending him to his death, this video would now be shown in our schools to explain what racism is, to explain the horror of anti-Semitism. The world community of journalists owes it to him today to publicly denounce the anti-Semitism of Islamic extremist organizations and the vast public opinion they control or influence, so that all journalists may continue to perform their jobs in blessed peace.

# The Israeli Public

All of Israel at this time is a stage on which a vast tragedy of elemental feelings is being played out: bereavement, war, a desperate clash of views while dancing at the edge of an abyss. There is astonishment that the suicide terrorists have managed to go so far, and indeed a great uncertainty about what to do about it. Yesterday, while Sharon in a public speech told about what he had seen at the bus stop of the number 32 bus, his voice faltered, his words became flustered in a very unmilitary-like way: "In so many years of warfare, I have never seen such bloody carnage." Yesterday, after the funerals of dozens of people, another three youths of twenty, seventeen, and nineteen were mourned in addition to a grandmother buried with her five-year-old granddaughter. And adding to the sense of desperation, a boy of seventeen, Avraham Nehmad, died after four months in the hospital following a terrorist attack in the Beit El district; his fifteen-year-old brother had been killed instantly.

The mood as never before is one of war. Telephones have been ringing in every house: The army is recalling its reservists through an emergency procedure. While the army repeats scenes very similar to that of Operation Defense Wall, with arrests and weapons seizures, one wonders how effective the operation will be this time. Meanwhile, Sharon announces that this time the army will stay until the terror stops, and this provokes much debate. Peres is more and more gloomy: "They are killing our citizens, the economy is ruined, war and the wall will not do any good!" he was heard to exclaim. The deputy of the left, Chaim Ramon, cries out: "You, the colleagues of my party who are in the government, only know how to occupy more land. Get out of the government once and for all." But Defense Minister Fuad Ben Eliezer explains that the most urgent thing at this time is to take action against the killing, that there is no policy of occupation. But it is known that he and Sharon are on bad terms.

Meanwhile, Chief of Staff Shaul Mofaz is not at all favorable to a long-term occupation: he fears the high cost of human lives. And well-known commentator Zeev Shiff says that an occupation is impossible in any case: Israel would find itself responsible for a debilitated community intent on suicide terrorism and would provoke international hatred and dissent, including that of the Americans. One who thinks that Israel should remain in the West Bank is Minister of the Interior Uzi Landau, who recalls how the extreme onslaught of terrorists had stopped during Operation Defense Wall. The Israeli public is opposed, however: the peace index, a monthly survey by the University of Tel Aviv, shows that 59 percent of Israelis are prepared for a unilateral evacuation of the settlements. The results are from May 6, 2004.

Given all this, what will be the role of the physical barrier that is being built to separate the suicide terrorists from their objectives, at least at the most vulnerable points? The consensus is broad enough, but opponents are very concerned. Yesterday at the Beit El settlement, the mayor, speaking on behalf of all its citizens, said: "We don't even know if we will be on this side or that side of the wall: and Arafat's urging not to strike civilians within the Green Line appears to make us targets fated for slaughter."

Finally, there is an unprecedented, hopeless sense of horror toward the culture of death emanating from Palestinian society. Amnon Dankner, editor of the daily paper *Maariv*, wrote yesterday: "What kind of people are you, you Palestinians, that you support and express joy over these inhuman, brutal acts? What kind of society is it that produces this phenomenon? . . . You are a society crazed with animosity . . . and you are destroying both yourselves and us by your suicide attacks. You have a choice between hope and desperation: and you have chosen desperation, trying to drag us with you."

# The Face of "Moderate" Araby

The peace between Egypt and Israel has lasted more than twenty years; Hosni Mubarak uses the word *stability* like a mantra. And yet analysts doggedly debate whether the land of the pharaohs is part of the problem of the eternal Middle East crisis or part of its solution. A book written by three eminent American strategists, Joseph Cirincione, John Wolfsthal, and Miriam Rajkumar (*Deadly Arsenals: Tracking Weapons of Mass Destruction*), presents proof that Egypt has accumulated a "deadly arsenal" of biological weapons since the sixties and that at this point they are available in great quantities. Moreover, in the twenty years following the Camp David peace of 1978, Egypt increased its military spending to the point of using $25 billion of the $35 billion given to it by the United States up until 1999 to purchase Western arms, which now make it a formidable power.

The most recent move was to order the new generation of Harpoon missiles, the Block II, and the warships on which to mount them for $400 million from the United States. If the U.S. Congress, which is now examining the case, decides in favor of delivery, the military balance between Israel and Egypt will be seriously modified. The new missiles in fact are not only sea-to-sea but also sea-to-land, like the Israeli navy's Tomahawks, but with a much greater range that will enable them to strike any strategic objective within

Israel. This, after the United States these past years has already provided Egypt with very powerful F-16 airplanes, M-1 Abrams tanks, and new warships. And demands are on the table for long-range air-to-air and sea-to-air missiles, which will keep Israel in their sights from a long distance away—in addition to F-15 airplanes, combat helicopters, and submarines. This, while peace with Israel remains more than cold. In the army's intermediate and lower ranks, training exercises, including incitement to hatred, simulate war only against Israel. Professional organizations forbid contact with Israelis. And the national press prints recurring pieces of pure anti-Semitism: On April 29, 2002. *Al Akhbar* came out with an editorial in which Fatma Abdullah Mahmoud, after again denying the Shoah and accusing the Jews of being "a model of cruelty, disgrace, degeneracy," addresses Hitler, exclaiming: "If only you had succeeded, brother . . . the world could then breathe in peace without their evilness and their sins."

# Euros for Terror

This is the limit! Chirac meets with Shimon Peres and explains to him that Europe does not want to put the Hezbollah on the list of terrorist organizations because it has an important social and cultural function in Lebanon! Oh really? The fundamentalist inventors of suicide terrorism (hundreds dead in America, and—such a short memory, Chirac—France), the agitated abhorrers of the West armed by Syria and Iran? Moreover, Foreign Minister Dominique de Villepin promised during a recent tour of the Middle East that "the [European] Community would not yield to pressure." American pressure, naturally. Europe, at a time when ideas to resolve the Middle East conflict are being sought, seems to lack the courage to hoist up its anchor, preferring to adhere to the old anti-American line of conduct.

Bush is striving to create a premise for war against terrorism based on the promotion of democracy and reform of the Palestinian Authority; the European Union (EU) renews Arafat's financing and guarantees his control over the funds. During the intifada, the EU handed over approximately 10 million euros to the Palestinian Authority. It did so with good intentions certainly, to alleviate poverty. In May 2002, however, given the enormous terrorist wave, the funds were suspended; but later on June 20, 2002, Chris Patten, head of external relations, said that there was no evidence of connivance and that "if there is to be a Palestinian state, there must be a Palestinian Authority." Right. But don't those who distribute the money also have a responsibility to promote peace by promoting new leadership, rather than financing the old one and ignoring what the entire world can see?

Examples: Palestinian national television, which depends on EU funds, is used by the intellectual, religious, and political elite for continual programming that propagates indiscriminate hatred and killing of Jews in general and that makes appeals to emulate the shahids or martyrs (suicide terrorists). All of it, from trucks equipped cafeteria-style, is financed by the EU. There's more: new textbooks issued on September 2, 2000, which, according to a report by Die Zeit cost 330 million euros, praise the "martyrs," eliminate Israel from the map, and consider the Jews an archaeological relic. Since June 2001, that is from the time the EU began paying out monies directly to Arafat, the Authority soon began financing illegal arms and terrorism: The *Karine A* (costing $10 million) was carrying heavy weapons and 220 kilos of TNT toward the Gaza coast. Also found were many documents signed by Arafat in which he authorized the payment of terrorists. Does this mean that the Authority should not be helped, even when people are suffering from hunger and unemployment? Not at all. But it is time to open a public debate, in Europe and in Italy, on the issue of aid. In general, if Europe wants to promote peace, it should fund the fight against terrorism and its promotion and instigation.

# Partners

At this point American analysts at the Pentagon and the White House put the word *partner* in quotation marks when it is used in reference to a "European partner." Whose partner is it? When it comes to crucial topics such as the Middle East and terrorism, it's not clear. When President Bush speaks about the "axis of evil" (a fundamental, strategic definition nowadays), the French and Italians sneer: "How primitive he is!" The elegant Danes, Finns, and Belgians widen their pale blue eyes, wondering if they heard right. The war against terrorism appears futile; it's much more important to stalk Israel. Thus, the Europeans on the U.N. Human Rights Commission, aside from Germany, England, and the Czech Republic, voted to issue a strong condemnation against Israel and actually exhorted the Palestinians to drive out "foreign occupation by any and all means including armed conflict," namely, terrorism. Don't the Europeans wonder whether terrorism isn't an immense violation of human rights? And whether the eliminations, the lynchings by Palestinian "collaborators," shouldn't also be condemned? No. On the contrary, the Council of Europe (forty-four member nations) is so virtuous that, while Israelis are grappling with terrorism, it urges the European Union to suspend all commercial agreements with Israel. "How can it be?" a source who does not wish to be quoted asks with curiosity in a telephone call from Washington. The U.S. administration wonders if, with all this desire to please the Arabic world, Europe will not pull back the moment Saddam Hussein, with all his biological and chemical weaponry, is attacked. And if the war against terrorism were to expand? Where will Europe stand then? With the pacifists, with whom it will accuse us of war crimes, and with whom it will offer, even if only apathetically, rearguard protection to the enemy? The "partner," therefore, could become an indifferent friend, an acquaintance to whom one addresses a hurried greeting. A useless "partner." Israel feels it: In the end it was Bush who forced the Israelis to set Arafat free. Israel trusts the United States because the United States knows what terrorism is and does not accept it. Europe, so virtuous, could never have pulled it off. Therefore, if Europe wants to test its strength on a different Middle East policy than that of the Americans, it might even be helpful; but as regards terrorism, now is not the right time. It runs the risk of finding itself in an embrace with the number one enemy of the United States.

## Appeasement Still Fashionable in Europe

There are many things that aren't working right regarding how events in the Middle East are perceived and reported. For one thing, the obvious corrosion of the idea that the Jewish people truly have a right to a nation in their own land, whatever rights the Palestinian people may also have. Then, too, the complete eradication of the results of the Camp David meeting, as if Arafat had not rejected an agreement that would have given him and his people legitimate territorial borders for their state. And yet the idea that the territorial dimension, the occupation (even after restitution of the cities, which have been under Arafat for some time now), is by far the most important dimension of the current conflict remains intact: It is the bible of every politician and essentially of any line of reasoning concerning the conflict.

The phenomenon, unique in the world, of a democratic country that day after day must deal with an impressive number of terrorist attacks is not the story that interests us, despite the fact that it could become our story, the story of any of us in any democratic country. But the crucial point I would like to focus on is the "cycle of violence," a formula over which someone involved in providing information cannot stop despairing. It happens every day: on the one side there are Palestinian deaths, on the other Israeli deaths. On the one side a pregnant Palestinian woman gives birth to a baby girl after her husband was killed at a checkpoint, on the other an Israeli woman gives birth to her child after her father, along with another man, was killed in an ambush as he was traveling in a car with her. These two events appear completely symmetrical in newspapers and television accounts; in the collective European mind even soldiers who killed a terrorist who was trying to stab an Israeli at a checkpoint and a terrorist who injured many Israelis as they waited for a bus can be seen as equivalents. With my own ears I heard a BBC journalist ask a representative of the Israeli government why the Jewish state did not think about extraditing the soldiers who had killed the pregnant woman's husband at the checkpoint, inasmuch as Israel felt that the murderers of Minister Rehavam Ze'evi should be extradited: a question that equates two situations—an unintentional act versus one of intentionality—that neither common sense nor the law considers equivalent. There is quite a difference between a mistake, though it may be tragic, even unforgivable, though it may reveal a tendency to be quick on the trigger, and the Tanzim's lying in wait to ambush a car full of civilians (described almost always as "colonists," not as men or women, as if this took away their right to exist). There is quite a difference between aiming at empty buildings purposely cleared out so that as few people as possible might be hit and the plot of a Hamas band or its agents to kill a specific person, or to educate, arm, and lead a designated suicide terrorist to his destination, one where there are as many Jews as possible.

It's true that reprisals and targeted eliminations also exist. But as much as these reprisals might be censured, the intention, motivated by the omnipresent, obsessively persecutory terrorism, is to prevent further attacks on the road, to stop the human bombs. The feelings that every Palestinian victim generates are painful and tragic; mistakes are to be condemned. Israelis, exasperated by the situation, view with horror and condemn the deaths of both Israelis and Palestinians. The generous sense of equidistance that the world shows toward the dead and wounded of both sides is sacrosanct when it responds to the human condition. But we commit a real injustice if we consider two injuries inflicted under completely different circumstances to be equivalent.

From some quarters in the heart of Italy, though it might be better to say from all of Europe, there is the insidious, malignant belief that the Jews deserve to suffer. This was expressed by the hostess at a dinner party in which Daniel Bernard, the French ambassador to England, called Israel "that shitty little country." "Oh come on," the woman said, after a moment of embarrassed silence on the part of the onlookers, "we all know that everything that happens to them [the Jews] is their own fault." In our case therefore, not only are those who strike by mistake equally as responsible as the Palestinians who plan indiscriminate attacks on civilians for political ends, but when all is said and done, they bear responsibility (and the "colonists," doubly so) for their own death. The tangle of mutual hatred is presented as though it too were equal, as though children in Jewish schools were taught to adore and emulate the shahids, just as schoolchildren are in Palestinian schools; or as though sermons on the Sabbath preached that the Arabs are sons of monkeys and swine and urged that they be killed wherever they are found, as is preached in the mosques on Friday when speaking about the Jews; or as though a recording entitled "I Hate Palestine" were sold in the shops of Jerusalem and Tel Aviv, just as a song called "I Hate Israel" is currently sold in the streets of the entire Arabic world, including Palestine, where it has become a big hit.

In short, the equidistance that we often see in our political figures, as well as those in government and those in the opposition party, is a ruse, an illusion, that distances us from reality. It merely indicates once again how little justice interests Europe and, on the contrary, how important it is for Europe to demonstrate its inane sympathy for a vague humanitarian policy in the Middle East, which, in any case, might appear contrary to that of the Americans. This attitude becomes more and more dangerous and irresponsible: before Islamic extremism reached the heights whose signs we are beginning to see here as well, Europe and Italy flirted with policies of gratification and appeasement, hoping to tame terrorism, to declare themselves a safe zone. But there is no such thing as a safe zone; its boundaries—its psychological borders as well—are destined to shrink more and more. Complacency over our superb spirit leads nowhere and obstructs the view of the enormous, uncontainable dimension that terrorism has assumed in this situation. This, with the understood hope that the Palestinians may establish a peaceful nation of their own, under safe circumstances for Israel, once terrorism is defeated.

# The War of the Heroic Shahids

Ilona Sportova, fifteen years old, has a picture of herself before the June 2001 terrorist attack in Tel Aviv hanging over her bed. Her hospital room is in the Lowenstein Center for Rehabilitation. Ilona wanted to be a model, and you can tell that from the photo. But the fact that she is tall meant that her head was higher up than that of her friend who was struck squarely and killed. Ilona now has part of her head destroyed, and the nails discharged from the suicide terrorist's bomb driven into the part that remains. Now the rehabilitation staff is teaching her how to walk and talk: she has learned thirty words. She understands nearly everything, however, and is able to paint with one hand during art class, where she has completed the spots on a giraffe that she began before the explosion. The doctors never would have thought that she would survive, and they feel she is recovering nicely.

She shares the hospital room with Maya Damari, seventeen years old, who was approached by a boy with bleached hair while she was eating at the Karmei Shomron pizzeria with a friend; the boy stared at her and said: "Good-bye, never to see you again" and blew himself up. Maya now has a long nail in her brain; the right side of her body is paralyzed. Avraham, her father, forty-six years old, is very proud of his daughter's progress, who resumed fighting for her life after coming out of an eleven-day coma. But Maya lives in terror of amputation and is ashamed of her visible wounds. She refuses to be taken to the beach and says that she would like to die because she is only seventeen years old and she can't stand the thought of remaining this way all her life.

At Wednesday's terrorist attack at the university, besides the seven dead, there are about a hundred wounded as well. In addition to the almost six hundred deaths reported in the headlines, a host of more than 4,000 injured weighs upon Israel (one-thousandth of the population, that here at home in Italy would be equivalent to 60,000 wounded), along with tens of thousands of family members whose lives have been totally changed; not to mention the doctors, psychologists, nurses, volunteers. Israel is one big wound: Its streets, schools, houses.

Dr. Avi Rivkind, gray haired, not yet fifty years old, explains that wounds resulting from terror are immense and frightening and roughly of two types: Those resulting from lacerations that amputate or damage limbs or from a blow whose force fractures the bones. And a new type, resulting from bits of metal mixed in with the explosive in the suicide terrorists' belts or knapsacks. Steel nuts and nails of all sizes. Often the terrorist puts some poison into the bomb as well, rendering his act even more deadly because the poison makes the hemorrhaging occur more swiftly.

Israeli doctors are now perfecting new techniques, which they are passing on to doctors in other hospitals and other countries: On August 15, 2002, a group of New York doctors will come to study these techniques at the Soroka Medical Center in Beersheba, which performed 180,000 emergency operations in the year 2001 alone. In every hospital, they are constantly making critical decisions. When fifteen-year-old Adi Huya was brought in after the explosion on Ben Yehudah Street (two hundred people wounded) on December 1, 2001, in Jerusalem, both her legs were practically torn off. Her mother, Mali, ran to Hadassa, a Hospital/Trauma Center, facing the prospect of immediate amputation. Instead Rivkind made a quick assessment: They would use a treatment, which would cost the state $10,000, and try to reattach the limbs. Mali weeps as she recalls how the doctor told her daughter: "Now don't worry, we will dance together at your wedding." After eight months, Adi took her first hesitant steps. In the case of Ronit Elchani, on the other hand, a thirty-eight-year-old mother of four who three weeks ago found herself on bus number 18, the doctors had to accept the fact that the pieces of metal that had penetrated her body and her brain were in places that were too dangerous to reach. Neurosurgeon Ricardo Segal decided that nothing could be touched; now Ronit, who doesn't remember anything, spends her days at the rehabilitation center. It is unlikely that she will be a normal mother again.

Sometimes what appears to be a successful rehabilitation actually barely mitigates permanent suffering. Four months ago Motti Mizrahi was wounded at the Moment Café in Jerusalem. The nuts and nails smashed into his chest and the nape of his neck, and something almost tore his hand off leaving it attached at only one point. Now, he is able to move the fingers of the reattached hand. But he weeps and moans when the nurse makes him use an arm in which nine holes the size of coins can be seen. His life has changed forever; he tries to keep up his work as a software engineer, but his concentration is not what it was. Those he interacts with no longer have the same rapport with him. The nails cause him terrible pain, as they do to all the others. His local soccer team where he used to play center forward, plummeted from second to fifth place.

The family, too, becomes a mutual aid society. Mothers, fathers, brothers, wives, fiancés plunge into a life they never imagined. Paulina Valis and Emma Kuleshevsky, two secondary school students, put on their pretty dresses more than a year ago and went to the Dolphinarium discothèque on the beach in Tel Aviv, where twenty-two teenagers were killed and more than one hundred wounded. Emma has two nails in her head and one in her abdomen; Paulina has so many iron fragments in her flesh that they emerge from under the skin all over her nineteen-year-old body. Once she was a dancer; now she is learning to walk. "They say I should thank God that I'm alive; but he took too many of my friends, and I don't know why."

There are also many children with burned faces, unusable hands, sight permanently destroyed; and elderly people, who have become tremulous and totally dependent; and those out of their head, who continue to hear the boom of the explosion and shut themselves up in their homes. All this while local and state organizations, scientific exchanges, and reciprocal aid groups are being set up so the victims will be able to live.

# The Moral Collapse of the West

There is no guarantee that we will win the war against terrorism. Our difficulty in defining it has ancient and powerful roots, and therefore detecting it and fighting it is an obstacle course punctuated by the most radical stylistic features of our culture, our politics, and, even more important, our fears.

Europe in particular suffers from this inability, and therefore it will probably find itself in greater difficulty when terrorism becomes a more widespread reality. Yet, even the United States is not immune to it. Not only that, the very structures that the Western world created after World War II to guarantee the realization of the new principles of democracy and the safeguarding of human rights, peace and security, are infected at their roots by our psychological difficulties with terrorism: the United Nations, the European Union, and the institutional and volunteer organizations (the NGOs) that protect against abuse and poverty are in fact sacrificing their credibility to the moral blindness behind which they have hidden.

Our difficulty in dealing with terrorism is linked to our failure to recognize the phenomenon as a constant danger, present in and produced by cultural, national, and religious groups that are basically Islamic. September 11, it's true, drew us into a frenzied vortex of mournful commemoration and expressions of collective grief, since the magnitude of the event and the fact that it had struck squarely at the heart and mind of our world, the New York World Trade Center, compelled us to several months of contrition.

But during the course of the months that followed, as Israel became the center of the attack in mounting geometric progression, a very strange phenomenon and one worthy of note could be witnessed, one that writer Cynthia Ozick in her essay "Three Meditations on Cruelty" calls "a gargantuan cruelty." That is: "[T]he malevolent frenzy of fanatical spite that undertakes to turn young men and women, some barely past childhood, into self-detonating bombs . . . [and that] two societies appear to accept this. On the one hand, the Palestinian Arabs, and Muslim nations generally. . . . And on the other hand, the West, the civilized, humanitarian, psychoanalytical West, which by giving false answers to spurious questions effectively ratifies, with scarcely a murmur, the radical reinvention of savagery in our time." Indeed, it is very strange that Western

reactions are so weak when faced with the most unacceptable distortion of human nature: Namely, the sight of a mother who, con-
senting and even content, places a hand on the head of her young
son as he goes off to commit suicide and randomly kill innocent
people and who hopes that her other little boys who are still children
will follow his fate in the name of Allah and the power of Islam.

And it is even more bizarre that the depraved morbid socializa-
tion of an entire society, sanctioned by its intellectuals, psychologists, media, and textbooks, is read by the West as the consequence
of social desperation (as Cheryl Blair, wife of British Prime Minister
Tony Blair, has asserted), as an indispensable political strategy ("this
is the only weapon they have" British Foreign Minister Straw,
among others, has said; like so many others he believes that one
should feel pity for the suicide terrorists as well as their victims). In
the case of the Palestinians, European statesmen such as Italian Minister Urbani say that there is a difference between bin Laden's terrorism and that of the Palestinian suicide bombers, the latter being a
consequence of Israeli occupation—lines of reasoning that appear
morally astounding and that are also easily challenged.

In actuality, the sociology of the terrorists shows only rare signs
of social desperation. The arms with which the Islamic world has by
now equipped itself are numerous, expensive, and horrific; the
Palestinians have many of them as well and have tried to purchase
others or produce them on their own in violation of the Oslo Accords. Terrorism existed well before the 1967 occupation, though it
continued in a more strengthened form following Ehud Barak's offer
to Arafat of 97 percent of the territories and half of Jerusalem. The
other falsehood dictated by good political manners concerns the nature of Islam, which articles, essays, and political speeches throughout the Western world continue to describe, against all evidence, as
a philosophy in which the word *jihad* expresses a kind of spiritual
contrition. The orders that resound in the mosques to "kill the Jews"
and "fight the Americans to the death" wherever they are found, are
metaphysical parables and essentially irrelevant.

In fact, the phenomenon of terrorism is huge, its origin certain,
and its violation of every and any human right evident. As a result,
the apathy and negation that surround it end up being all the more
fraught with consequences, especially when they emanate from the
very organizations committed to the defense of those same human

rights. Indeed, that negation dramatically thwarts the culture that defends children, animals, women, minorities, indebted nations, and the sick. Not only that, but a tragic stake has been driven into the heart of the discussion of terrorism: When it comes to the inhabitants of Israel, the international assemblies, the above-mentioned organizations, apply parameters relative to terrorism that set the Israelis apart from the international community, as if they were a different species. This phenomenon took shape definitively acquiring a theoretical basis in February 2001, when four regional conferences of the United Nations, one of which was held in Tehran, gathered to prepare preliminary documents for the U.N. conference on racism, later held in Durban. But let's take things in order.

In Israel, in the space of a few months, more than six hundred Jews were killed in terrorist attacks, for the most part young people, children and women. Explosions and ambushes at gunpoint resulted in thousands of cripples, amputees, and mentally imbalanced people—thousands of people lost, individuals deprived of mother and son, wife or husband, children, or both parents at the same time. The six hundred deaths, in a society of approximately five million Jews and little more than a million Israeli Arabs, often strike the same family and the same neighborhood two, three, five times–or that someone who escaped a bus explosion is later killed in a coffee bar, someone who adopted the children of a sister killed in a supermarket is then, in turn, killed along the street. The more than 600 deaths in Israel correspond to what would be approximately 35,000 deaths in the United States, 6,000 in England, 10,000 in Germany, and around 7,500 in Italy. A recent, very thorough study done on Palestinian sources by the Interdisciplinary Center for Antiterrorist Studies in Herzliya verifies that even if 600 Israeli deaths correspond to approximately 1,400 Palestinian deaths, only 25 percent of Israelis are soldiers, while 75 percent are civilians. The proportion of military combatants killed with respect to civilians is exactly the opposite among Palestinians (in absolute numbers, women killed amount to half of those killed in Israel), which demonstrates that the explicit targets of Palestinian terrorism are innocent civilians.

"The intentional attacking of innocent civilians for ideological, religious or political reasons" is precisely the definition generally attributed to terrorism: a definition that scholars throughout the world have labored on to clear away the old theory that had its origins in the Cold War, namely, that your terrorist may be my freedom fighter. The definition seemed ascertained when, on September 28, the United Nations, in the wake of September 11, adopted Security Council Resolution 1373, an extremely tough and absolutely promising measure prescribing an unrelenting war against terrorism. The resolution linked an individual's basic right to security and peace to the fight against terrorism, appealing to the right of self-defense related to the Charter of Association of the United Nations itself; it urged that life be made impossible for those who shelter, fund, and ideologically support any terrorist cells, and it spoke of an international conference against terrorism (the conference was instead boycotted by the majority of U.N. nations; and the state entrusted with the presidency of the Security Council, Syria, continues to protect and shelter more than a dozen terrorist organizations, including the Hezbollah). Terrorism, as a "threat to international peace and security," was designated by the United Nations as an entity extraneous to a given culture and to the constitution that legitimizes it, and therefore to be fought on national and international ground under the principle of universal jurisdiction.

And yet, soon after this statement, which followed the attack on the Twin Towers, and in fact after Bush's June 2002 speech, which changed the general worldview by linking dictatorship to terrorism (and therefore demanding democratization as a preventive condition for any peace process in so far as democracy is a guarantee against terror), the Palestinians and the Arabs in general attempted to legitimize the killing of civilians in conflict, which delegitimized, in the name of cultural and political relativism, a fundamental mainstay of international law. This principle was enunciated in 1582 by Balthazar Ayala, a lawyer for the King of Spain, who wrote in the Netherlands: "The intentional killing of innocent persons in war (for example, women and children) is not admissible (unless unintentional, as when a city is attacked with catapults or other weapons of war; such a case is different, since these things are inevitable)."

The wave of "legitimate" terrorism against Israel (Arafat and all the Arab leaders, with their chorus of news media and Arab intellectuals, publicly sanctified it a number of times) began, therefore, when Durban deliberately laid its theoretical foundations. The conference, which symbolically took place in South Africa and which was to have laid the basis for a new, imposing, and even conclusive fight against racism, in actuality transferred onto Israel and its supporters (who indeed either left the conference in outrage, like the United States, or fought tooth and nail, like Canada) all the historical-political traits that turn an entire nation into an international outlaw, an enemy of mankind, in short, itself a terrorist, which another terrorism may justifiably attack. From the first document in Tehran, Israel was the only topic of discussion at Durban. In the NGO sessions and in the conference hall, it was the principal if not the only center of the malicious interest of the thousands of conference participants; there was no place for any discussion of the discriminated minorities, mistreated indigenous peoples, and groups oppressed or discriminated against based on race who were in attendance. I heard someone say to a Dalit (an Indian untouchable) and to some slaves from Sudan that the Palestinian problem was the most serious in the world because it was the result of one of the greatest crimes against humanity, the creation of the state of Israel. An impressive number of Third World nations sided with their leaders (among them Fidel Castro and Mugabe), who were especially applauded when, in plenary session, they called Israel "a country of apartheid, racist, a mega-violation of human rights since its birth in November 1947." The rejection of Israel's right to exist had been transformed into a legitimate blueprint for the conference from the time Iran had excluded Israel from preliminary meetings with the other Asian countries, and the United Nations had not objected, incredibly deeming this gesture part of a possible basis for the first worldwide conference against discrimination and racism!

The main accusation against Israel that accompanied its delegitimization in Durban, and one that was repeated thousands of times, was that of being "a threat to peace and international security," just as terrorism was according to the U.N. resolution. In Durban the occupation of the territories (though they were never annexed) following the war of 1967, and the struggle against a bitter Arab resistance that spread to vast geographical areas throughout the years, were pegged to the idea that Israel was an enemy on a par with those identified in U.N. Resolution 1373.

Despite some diplomatic accommodation (mainly due to the Americans' leaving the conference) whose mark could be seen in the final resolution, Durban consequently became the epitome of the legitimization of every act of aggression against Israel while Israel remained a pariah excluded from the international assembly. From that time on, the terrorist upsurge on the part of the Palestinians may have changed public opinion somewhat, but not the attitude of institutions. In March 2001, when the Commission for the Convention on Human Rights, meeting in Geneva, condemned Israel as a state in violation of the convention—an unprecedented gesture—Israel was already shattered by its losses and by the surprise of finding an unwilling, hostile Arafat contrary to the expectations of Oslo. Never before had a nation as such been condemned, despite so many that violated human rights through countless ethnic and religious massacres, made indiscriminate use of capital punishment and torture, and repressed all freedom of expression. Considering that the United Nations has dedicated volumes of anti-Israeli resolutions to the Middle East conflict, this is perhaps only a little surprising, but it certainly raises legitimate doubts concerning the ability of the greatest international institution, the United Nations and its adjuncts, to understand the significance of the problems of our time.

If we look at Amnesty International's report for 2001, we see that the disease is contagious: Despite all that had happened in the area of terrorism, Amnesty stubbornly devoted itself, according to its tradition, to the issue of capital punishment in the United States and to the possibility that antiterrorist measures might create civil rights problems for Islamic minorities. Regarding terrorism, Amnesty concerns itself with advocating the idea that terrorists "be tried in accordance with international standards for human rights and not be condemned to death." A justifiable concern, though it lacks advice on how to safeguard populations that are condemned to death by terrorists. Nor does Amnesty attempt a theoretical discussion and firm line of reasoning on the global violation of human rights by terrorism itself. Israel, criticized because "it detains 2,200 prisoners held on political charges," is regarded as a country in which the above-mentioned political causes have nothing to do with a phenomenon that, on the contrary, gives it every right to defend itself, according to the resolution of the Security Council and according to common sense.

The International Court of Justice for Crimes against Humanity, established by the Rome statute ratified on July 1, 2002, without using the word *terrorism* for the crimes over which it has jurisdiction, speaks instead of "systematic attack against civilians" and doesn't always attach much importance to the subject. Isn't it a little too tri-fling, given the times we're living in?

The organizations that protect children, such as UNESCO and its offshoots, and in particular the movements that protect children from war, have still not uttered a word of censure for the use of young suicide terrorists. The organizations involved with education are not concerned about the fact that not only Palestinian textbooks but those in the majority of the Arab world do not show Israel on the map, while they extol suicide terrorists as heroes to be admired and imitated and hold them up as models for children. Women's organizations that have frequently devoted sessions to the Palestinian cause at international conferences, don't raise a word of protest when they read twisted texts of approval, poems, songs, and public praise (by now there is a whole library of it) for young female suicide terrorists, seen as authentic women liberated by Islam from the Western model. The pacifist NGOs never go and sit in Israeli restaurants to act as human shields for the people of Jerusalem. The journalists' associations, even the Italian ones, or the associations of psychologists, writers, university professors, or researchers do not get publicly outraged when members of their groups appear thrilled and enraptured at the sight of Israeli blood. Instead, Israeli university professors are excluded from academic institutions without a word of explanation, as occurred in England at the University of Manchester.

No international organization devoted to public education, no teachers' union has decried a scandalous curriculum that incites Palestinian children to hatred or complained about a year-end per-formance in a Gaza school in which children in the early grades staged smeared their hands with red to simulate the lynching in Ra-mallah. Nor did student organizations flinch when their colleagues at the university of Bir Zeit held an exhibit eulogizing the the Sbarro pizzeria explosion, replicating the dozens of dead torn to pieces, the tables and chairs smashed to bits. And the European Union has con-tinued to distribute tens of millions of euros to the Palestinian Au-thority, despite the fact that the world is by now inundated with proof that Arafat is the direct signer of orders for payment and pro-visioning of terrorist attacks carried out by the Tanzim and the Al Aqsa Martyrs Brigades, which head the list of suicide terrorism in recent months.

Even the U.S. State Department in its annual report "Patterns of Global Terrorism," published in May 2002, employs parameters defining terrorism that mislead the reader, leading him to believe that Middle East terrorism is a secondary phenomenon, or at least not one of paramount importance. It does so by counting damages to property in the same way it counts attacks against individuals, so that, for example, the 178 attacks on the oil pipeline in Colombia become, in the report, equally as important as the 178 terrorist attacks that have left hundreds dead in the Middle East; they are counted in the same way, thereby diminishing the importance of Islamic terror. Moreover, the origin of the terrorists is ignored: The attack on the Twin Towers, for example, is grouped under American terrorism, along with, for example, the Oklahoma bombing, and not specifically identified as Middle East terrorism.

The constant attempt by human rights institutions to diminish the Islamic impact on terrorism and to ignore that the terrorism that has befallen Israel is a primary phenomenon of worldwide and not just local significance runs the risk of prompting analysts and all judicious individuals to reject those institutions. Of what use is the United Nations if it is so intellectually corrupt? Of what use is Amnesty International, or the U.N. International Court of Justice, or the NGOs, or the environmental organizations that replicated the Durban farce in Johannesburg on July 29, 2002, in a huge conference on sustainable development, in which an anti-Israeli element predominated? Who will be able to believe in their sincerity, their effectiveness? Who will be able to trust their good faith anymore when in one single move they discriminate against Israel and relegate terrorism, the most dangerous threat to peace and international security, to a position of minor importance? As the plain truth of terror becomes increasingly evident, a shadow is cast on those who do not recognize that the terrorism directed against Israel is identical to that of the Twin Towers, when it is obviously so according to all the most significant factors and according to the declarations of the terrorists and their ideologists. An example: Europe puts off inviting Arafat to the negotiating table because it refuses to see him as the instigator of terrorism and insists on treating him as "an elected leader" instead of as an autocrat who uses his people for a backward, disastrous war; the United States, on the other hand, from the time it saw the glaringly obvious truth, pronounced that truth, perhaps opening the door to the possibility of a truce, if not of peace.

At the end of the 1967 war, I returned to Florence from Kibbutz Neot Mordechai, where I had been living as a rash Jewish Communist young woman. My parents had sent me there to get me off their hands for a while, with those yellow miniskirts and a head full of freedom, self-determination, feminism, socialism, and therefore also kibbutzim. At night, when Syrian tanks tried to enter the Golan Heights, which towered over my kibbutz below the hills, the other volunteers and I and our Neot companions huddled as a group to watch the lights of *shelanu,* our own, our armored tanks, which ascended a little way. Then, driven off, they turned back, chased away by the Syrian tanks. The shooting echoed far off in the distance. Nasser of Egypt had promised to "push the Jews into the sea" and had driven out the U.N. peace forces stationed in the Sinai, while deploying his army along the Israeli border. The Syrians, then the Jordanians followed. The war cry of the Arab world filled the air. When, for a short time, Galilee was cut off by Syrian forces near Roshpina, in the narrow passage that marks Israeli geography in the north, for several hours my parents thought I was dead, and the entire world imagined that the Jews trapped in that region were lost. There was no occupation at that time, there were no Israeli "colonies" to condemn, and when the confrontation began, they told me on the phone from Italy that people were flaunting big stickers on their utilitarian cars: "I defend Israel."

In the kibbutz, where the Syrians appeared from the Golan and machine-gunned the vineyards from their airplanes, I learned to tread like a leopard with a gun at night. I dug the trenches. They entrusted me with the task of taking the children to the bunker when the siren sounded an alarm; by the second or third time, I was already used to it. The children would wait a few minutes while I went on taking my shower until I had rinsed myself off; we no longer ran to the shelter with our hair full of shampoo like we did at first. Trucks and Nagmash (light tanks) passed along the road bordered by eucalyptus and tanks loaded with young soldiers heading for the Lebanese and Syrian border shook the ground. I felt no sense of contradiction with my Communist, pacifist spirit: Israel was defending itself, without swagger; frightened yet courageous. My kibbutz allocated one day's produce a week from its fields to the Vietcong. It was only when I said I was Communist that the boys who were my friends, Uri, Tirtza, and even Michael, who never teased me, started to laugh and asked me if I knew that those Syrian

MiGs up there in the sky, the ones that wanted to kill me, had been supplied to the Arabs by my Russian friends.

When General Motta Gur announced: "The Temple Mount is in our hands" everyone knew that Dayan, before entering the Old City had, exclaimed: "What do we need it for, this Vatican?" And when he gave a speech on the radio and I asked what the words of the great general meant, my friends answered: "Shtuiot," nonsense. My leftist conscience was in order: The war was a defensive one, and Israel did not have any expansionist urge. As we girls sympathetically offered water and fruit to a soldier leaning out of a tank that was pulverizing the dust on the Syrian road, he made that sign with his middle finger that meant: "Get lost, you and the war." In short, by the time I returned to Florence I had not experienced, as my Italian friends thought, the great war in which Israel occupied the Jordanian West Bank, that is, Judea and Samaria (Israel had asked Jordan thousands of times not to enter the conflict, without result). Instead I had seen what the Six Day War had actually been: a victorious, successful defense of one's homeland, ending in a territorial expansion that had not been sought. Later on, Israeli religious nationalists and the settlements would result from it; but also the demarcation of former Jordanian territory where the PLO (Palestine Liberation Organization) soon designated the boundaries of the nucleus of a future Palestinian state.

By the time I returned to my Communist, revolutionary companions in Florence, I had experienced an adventure that I could never have imagined, an experience that they would transform into a virulent, incongruous intolerance toward the Jewish state, which did not know its place, which had dared to be decidedly victorious by making better use of its weapons and strategy. The reaction that greeted me was hysterical. No one any longer used the categories that up till then had been the basis of a rational postwar culture; democracy and freedom were no longer important, and the USSR suggested using the word *self-determination* as a comprehensive key to understanding international dynamics. Europe was approaching an identity crisis, which later on turned into anti-Americanism.

It was at that time, after the war of 1967, when de Gaulle declared an embargo against Israel, that categories began to be overturned. Institutions that should have formed the foundation for a large-scale, courageous war against that greatest violator of human rights, terrorism, were transformed into organizations that have in the end sacrificed their credibility on the altar of anti-Israeli hatred. From the time the French position toward Israel changed as a result of the Six Day War (followed then by all of Europe), the attitude toward the Jewish state has become a testing ground in which moral suicide is possible and, through a significant historical parabola, physical suicide as well, if terrorism takes advantage of the instrumental removal that we have described.

In 1967, during the early part of the conflict, when it seemed that little Israel would be defeated and there was no "occupation to justify the hatred or colonies to serve as an example of Jewish imperialism, journalists all over the world spoke about the danger Israel was facing. But the moment Israel demonstrated its ability to defend its land, the sympathy immediately turned into hostility. Equating all military force with a blind instinct of aggression and immorality began to gain ground in Europe. The Six Day War soon became an object of condemnation like the Vietnam War, their names pronounced in the same breath. The Vietcong and the Arabs became a single victim oppressed by imperialism and, naturally, protégés of the USSR. This is where "the tanks with the Star of David" became immoral in the eyes of the collective imagination, like the American helicopters, while the explosives, the bombs in the streets, terrorism against civilians began to be thought of as resistance.

It was in those years that a trend began in which every discussion of a historical, personal, or group nature (women, blacks, the blind, the paralyzed, the insane, ) was turned over and over a thousand times. The very structure of social thought was revisited and, though many errors were made, generally speaking good safeguard mechanisms were instituted. But in international politics, the Cold War's obligation to view the themes of self-determination and freedom in accordance with Soviet parameters limited the discussion somewhat. It became forbidden to speak reasonably about Israel's wars and Arab rejection, and this provided immediate justification for the massive use of terror that the PLO began in those years. The world let it happen from the beginning: The airplane hijackings, Munich, Entebbe, Maalot. The horrible crimes against civilians and children were never the object of genuine scandal; the scandal was imperialism, which created the conditions for these acts. The political correctness that was exerted over everything gagged Israel. From that time on there was no more freedom of speech, neither on university campuses, nor in young intellectual circles.

The party officials, journalists, teachers, society figures, academics, and diplomats in the world and in its institutions, who today are dealing with terrorism and the conflict of cultures, were born in that bed of intimidation, and it is very difficult to imagine that something good might come of it, something that will be effective in the battle that faces us, like it or not. Viewing the Israelis as aggressors and the Palestinians as victims in the Israeli-Palestinian conflict has over the years led an organization such as the United Nations to devote an absurd amount of time and energy to anti-Israeli resolutions—considering all that needs to be done in the world to alleviate hunger, to curb human rights abuse against women, children, homosexuals, and dissidents in the majority of countries in the world that are totalitarian, and to check the proliferation of unconventional weapons. The United Nations supports, as though it were completely logical and consistent, the idea that the Israeli-Palestinian conflict can be resolved through a "land for peace" principle, uncommon in conflict resolution. It continually and unhesitatingly puts Israel in the defendant's seat on every institutional occasion, questions its basic right to existence, and considers the defense measures of a nation that is relentlessly under attack to be war crimes. All this while terrorists make Israel their testing ground, their extensive platform, ideologically and physically. The entire world will pay dearly for our hypnosis, for our moral turnaround, if we are not able to achieve a quick cultural revolution. Or maybe only Europe will pay, since the United States seems to have the courage to turn the page.

## Shiri Doesn't Live Here Anymore

The road flowing with heavy traffic leading to Gilo is as clean as it ever has been, disinfected: the skeleton of the bus that flew through the air like a football when a suicide terrorist blew himself up on Tuesday, June 18, 2002, has been cleared away, the implausible carpet of human remains expunged. After the mass murder of nineteen of its residents, the neighborhood shows its usual grit: "The citizens of Jerusalem," says Mayor Ehud Olmert, "are the bravest in the world. No city would hold up like this faced with such devastation

of daily life," he adds, his eyes moist. The day after the terrorist attack, while the quarter, one single quarter, buries nineteen people of
every age and circumstance, the young people and the elderly jog in
sweat suits on the tree-lined streets; in the public park full of pink
rhododendron and jasmine, at the shesh besh and chess tables, an
old Russian plays with a Chinese man known for his greyhound
dog. The children go to school; bus number 32 is running. On the
day of the attack, after the explosion, parents ran down the slope
crazy with fear, looking for their children. The supermarket in the
amphitheater-like building, the bank, the shopping center with the
Burger Ranch and playground, everything returns quickly to life.

And yet, never again will you meet Shiri Nagari, twenty-one
years old, at the children's low wall, noticed by everyone for her
long blond hair that came almost to her knees, "She was beautiful
even in the morgue," says her sister, "regardless of her injuries. Our
tears are inappropriate for her. She was so cheerful." Shiri had returned two months ago from the United States, she was about to
enter university to study biology. We will not see tiny, dark-skinned
Galila Bukara any more, an eleven-year -old Ethiopian and Christian
girl who was on her way to school, excited about planning the year-
end party. Nor Shani Avitzedek, fifteen years old: he spoke of nothing but his upcoming departure for Berlin as part of a delegation of
young people; his body was identified only by the new swimsuit he
was wearing for the school swim meets.

Gilo is a tormented neighborhood. For a year and a half it has
been under fire from the Tanzim organized in Bethlehem and stationed every night with Kalashnikovs in Beit Jalla, the Christian zone,
in a specious appeal to past history meant to involve the entire Christian world. The quarter is partially in what was formerly a Jordanian
zone. For this reason, its residents have been called colonists, despite
their total aversion to this ideological connotation they've been sad-
dled with by Palestinian propaganda. The issue of Gilo, five minutes
away from the center, was never raised in the peace talks. And yet in
one year, it has had two people killed and many wounded while simply in their homes. And in any case, the bus number 32 was blown
up within the Green Line that crosses the quarter, leaving only part
of it on the other side. Nevertheless, Gilo has been criminalized, enduring fire attacks until a brief interval afforded by Operation Defense Wall. To their astonishment, an absolutely peaceful and largely
pacifist people (one of their most esteemed leaders, Eli Amir, lives

here) found bullets whistling through their kitchens and nurseries, especially on Anafà Street and Margalit Street, now all protected by massive walls. They were streets whose beauty, an open view of vast pastoral landscapes of olive trees and white houses, was transformed into an unexpected hell.

For more than a year, psychiatric offices have been treating children who can no longer sleep. You risk your life in every store you go to; you're a sitting duck, a target. Someone hates you down there. At the social center, a psychologist by the name of Idit tells us that the most common nightmare children have is that of total destruction: losing their mother, losing their way, being in the dark, not finding their way any more. Gilo is the most desperate quarter in Israel, at the center of a conflict in which the dark minds of terrorists hold sway. Shiri with the long hair doesn't live here anymore.

# A New Game for Sharon

As the funerals of the youth of his nation continue to multiply, Ariel Sharon is playing a new game: the screams of the wounded at Moment Café, the weeping, the daylong procession (young men and women in tears over their eleven friends, all killed by a suicide terrorist), the subdued, televised criticism from the blond waiter who said: "Even in Lebanon it was better. Now we have really hit bottom, and yet they will go on hating us if we don't put an end to it" reached Sharon's windows, thirty meters further on, even if he wasn't at home. And so, even as the army remains active in the Palestinian territories, even as storehouses and hideouts of terrorist organizations are freely targeted in the refugee camps, still a new phase, barely outlined, is being planned in the Israeli world. Sharon seems to feel the blame for both his own people's deaths and those of the enemy. His society doesn't tolerate one or the other.

The signs begin Friday evening when Sharon announces that he has decided to cancel the precise condition he had set—seven days cessation of all terrorist attacks—before he would sit down at the peace table with the Palestinians. Therefore the Tenet agreement for a cease-fire must be enacted quickly, and then a discussion on reliability measures and Israeli relinquishments based on the Mitchell accord will begin. At a meeting of the cabinet, in which two ministers of the nationalist right, Benny Elon and Ivet Lieberman, announced their resignations, Sharon defended his decision with determination: "At the time the decision was the right one. I reflected upon it, I opened my eyes," he said verbatim. "No one feels the national interest more strongly than I do, and for me reaching a cease-fire is in the greatest national interest. And therefore I have told the Americans that I am prepared to give up the seven days cessation of terrorism before beginning talks."

Later on, he went further, provoking additional anger from the right. Asked if he intended to put an end to Arafat's detainment at Ramallah, he spoke words that were unusual. "I set Arafat the condition of arresting the killers of Rehavam Ze'evi. He arrested them. It's true that what happened later, happened [Sharon here was referring to the recent terrorist attacks], but we made a promise." That is: it is expected that with the imminent arrival of Anthony Zinni, the American envoy, Sharon is preparing himself and the Israeli public to allow Arafat to leave Ramallah, perhaps even in time for the Arab summit in Beirut on March 27, 2002. He wants to take advantage of the visit of Bush's representative to at least seek a pause to the intolerable situation that exists and probably also to divest himself of a kind of tragic aura that has surrounded him since the start of the intifada. Therefore he is getting the red carpet ready for the guest who will come in concert with Vice President Cheney. Cheney will visit the entire Middle East exhaustively, in a strategic mission that requires a peaceful setting: the war against terrorism, a clear account of the subject with the Arab countries, a possible attack against Iraq.

In this scenario, whose stage is full of blood, devastation, and death, even the United States is in earnest. Just last night it announced that Zinni is coming to establish a kind of permanent office, and that he has no plans to go home until matters are resolved. But here's where the great unknown, Arafat, comes in—the unpredictable rais who continually changes face. The Palestinian president continues to wave an olive branch from afar to the international community, thereby gaining European consensus and also vague American support, but then his organizations, namely Al-Fatah and the Tanzim, claim responsibility for almost all terrorist actions. Arafat, they say in the Palestinian Authority, is far from being confused or debilitated while in exile in Ramallah. On the contrary, this circumstance has taken him back to his days of fame in Karama and the Beirut siege; he feels spiritually elevated, connected to the suffering of his people. Possibly he even sees himself as a potential shahid. Arafat feels he is the leader at another great historical moment for the Palestinian people.

Though painful to him, still the number of victims probably seems to him like a doorway to independence, a doorway to a destiny on its way to glory. Sharon's current renunciation of the seven days cessation appears to Arafat as a victory. Every missile that falls on one of his offices in Gaza or Ramallah elevates his status in the eyes of the Palestinians, who in the past had often argued about him, even in a very harsh, critical way. Every terrorist attack claimed by Al-Fatah also assures him a more decisive place in the belligerent heart of his nation. Will Arafat in this situation want to accept the American cease-fire proposals? It's not easy to predict. His people are in a state of great need: water, gasoline, hospitals, infrastructures, the economy—everything is suffering and in need of peace. In addition, the Peres-Abu Ala plan would constitute a good point of departure for him since it establishes that the U.N. resolutions are the basis for any accord. But will Arafat want to negotiate, when the present situation guarantees him such enormous internal consensus and international approval as well, especially from Europe?

## Profile of a Terrorist: Ibrahim Ahmad Salem Sarahna

Ibrahim Ahmad Salem Sarahna, thirty-three years old, is sitting with us in a room in the preventive detention prison in the Russian Compound in Jerusalem. "They will give me two hundred, three hundred years, and since it is clear that I will not be able to serve the term, I am hoping to get a defender who will send me out of the country with my family, like the family of the nativity." He smiles, content at the thought. He smiles a lot during the entire interview. Sarahna was the driver for at least three successful suicide terrorist missions. Once he was arrested, his entire cell was captured, and his wife Irena, a Ukrainian woman, is in jail because she was with him in the car, with their one-year-old baby girl, on one of his deadly trips. For the three attacks, he transported four suicide terrorists who were prepared to blow themselves up, among them a young girl who in the end returned home.

The first attack took place on March 29, 2002: A young girl of sixteen, Ayat al Akrash from the Deheishe refugee camp near Bethlehem, blew herself up at the Jerusalem supermarket in the Kiriat Yovel quarter, leaving three dead, among them a seventeen-year-old girl and dozens of wounded. The second attack, three days later, cost the life of an eighteen-year-old guard on Ha Neviim Street in the center of Jerusalem and caused a dozen injuries, The third goes back to Wednesday, May 22, 2002: At Rishon Le Tzion, in a park where people play chess, a seventeen-year-old suicide terrorist, Issa Badir with bleached blond hair, killed two people and wounded forty. Arin Ahmed, on the other hand, a twenty-year-old who was to blow herself up shortly thereafter, decided to return home to Beit Umar in Bethlehem. When Sarahna was arrested, he had boldly gone to bring Arin back home, with his wife Irena and their baby daughter still in the car.

Questioning Ibrahim Sarahna, the onetime Deheishe camp car thief seated in front of us, wearing shorts and smiling, you realize that questions concerning suicide terrorism have only just begun, and that the measure by which we judge this horrendous crime are entirely foreign to a vast world represented by that man with the wide-eyed stare, hardly any teeth, and a self-satisfied look. Why did Sarahna become part of the terrorist network? We will keep strictly to his story: one day he gets a visit from "a guy I've known for four or five years, Mohammed Said, also from Deheisha, one of the Tanzim in the Church of Bethlehem. He's in exile now. He asked me if I wanted to transport a terrorist to the site of the attack. I decided it was OK." Why? "An inspiration, just like that."

Why does a well-off car thief decide to turn to terrorism when he has a local wife with five children and on top of that recently acquired another wife, blond Irena the Ukrainian, whom he met (though he doesn't tell us this) while she was working as a prostitute along Ha Masgher Street in Tel Aviv and who bore him a baby girl, Rasali, a year and a half ago?

"Said came to me because Ibrahim [he often refers to himself in the third person] is clean; he's not a collaborator. He knows that if Sharon did Sabra and Chatila, if the occupation is killing us, we have a duty to fight. I realized right away that I could change things. I have an Israeli identification card. I've always worked in Jerusalem, which I know like the back of my hand. I speak Hebrew well. I pass through the checkpoints easily. I can recognize a policeman from a mile away. Deheishe was primary during the old intifada, and now it doesn't know anything about it anymore, I said to myself. Everyone is planning attacks, they come out of Ramallah, Jenin. And us? I also quickly realized what might be a good site: the Kiriat Yovel supermarket, where I worked three years ago. And when. On a Friday, when it's full of people. A peaceful place, where a bomb had never exploded, easy to reach, crowded with people."

Ibrahim is very pleased with his story. Asked whether he had thought about the fact that he would be killing children, he replied that there are few children at the supermarket on Friday (which makes absolutely no sense) and that Palestinian children also die. In fact, he adds, "this is a war between Arafat and Sharon in which the little fish are destined to die." So then, the first attack: The girl he picks up that morning carries the knapsack with the explosives between her legs. At the Betar Illit checkpoint they are allowed to pass through. "Yes, we talked, we said we knew each other for a long time, but she didn't recognize me with short hair. I told her, 'Are you sure you want to do this? If not, we'll throw away the knapsack.' She answered that she was ready to die, so, no! I'm not sorry about her. I asked her. I explained where she had to go; she got out. I took off. Soon afterwards I heard the ambulances; it was done. Now the Jews would know that we could appear anywhere at all, that they have no place to hide. The day after they assigned 1,500 policemen to guard duty in Jerusalem. At the second attack, the boy, he must have been seventeen, was in a car behind me with my brother; I was driving in front with my own car. Said had told me: We have one who was in jail for a local crime. He says that since he will be killed anyway; he wants to die a martyr. On the way, when we were already in the city center, the police stopped me. I showed my identification card. My brother put the car in reverse; the boy jumped halfway out and exploded. I thought my brother had died, too, but instead he escaped." The police report that Sarahna, in all the chaos, did not forget to make the policeman give him back his identification card.

Finally, the height of glory, Rishon le Tzion: This time a new Tanzim agent comes looking for him since Said is inside the church. "I very quickly found a suitable place, on a side street, without checkpoints. We went in two cars: me, my wife, the baby, and behind us the two terrorists, a male and a female. My wife thought we were going for a drive; she didn't see the two of them." Hard to believe. He speaks to the terrorists by cell phone: "Put on the belt, turn right." Once they get to Rishon, the story becomes complicated, and Sarahna gives us a different version from that of the police: The two young people go off at three o'clock, "one to the right and one to the left," then both call again (somehow they are together again) to say that the girl has a problem; she wants to go home. Mughrabi, the boss, talks to her on the telephone, and perhaps with the boy as well. Sarahna gives the two money to take two taxis back. But only the girl goes back. It isn't until nine o'clock that night that the boy blows himself up, killing and wounding. The boy "told me he wanted to go ahead with it." But did he really want to? Or was he forced to? And was Sarahna also perhaps blackmailed or paid off? And what role did his Ukrainian wife play, having been a party to the whole episode? "She got nervous," he says. "I didn't tell her anything. She realized it only when we picked up the frightened girl and she got in the car."

Now Sarahna is pleased: He has brought Deheishe back to its former glory. "I never saw the leaders face to face, only a very low-ranking agent, but now they consider me important in Deheishe. I terrorized Jews a long distance from there, as far as Rishon, and I passed on the name of Deheishe."

# Moment Café

Up until an instant before the explosion, the Moment Café, where eleven people were killed and dozens wounded last night and which has been reduced to a mound of bloody rubble, was like an island of oblivion in the midst of the conflict. It was situated like the prow of a ship on a thirty-degree angle at the corner of Aza Street and Ben Maimon Boulevard, right in the downtown area, just in front of the sentry box of the guards who watch over Ariel Sharon's residence on Smolanskin Lane. The Jerusalem of journalists and attorneys, beautiful young women and cameramen, filled the café from the early hours of the morning till late at night, a Jerusalem exposed and relaxed, right there on such an accessible corner, against all good sense and with an unshakable will to live.

Up to a little more than a year ago, Moment Café was at 30 Aza Street, a little more hidden. But then the city's worldly sanctuary moved to that larger location because of its great success. Its three partners, two Israelis and a Palestinian from East Jerusalem, made it a place of almost European tranquility in the midst of the intifada, with a little music in the background, with new, all-wood interiors. The strong Italian coffee, the spaghetti al dente, the huge salads had multiplied the number of regular customers, some of whom sat in the sun in the garden in full view, others in a triangle-shaped glass enclosure. Madness when you consider what is happening in the city. Even the mayor, Ehud Olmert, was a regular patron. Early in the morning the journalists would read the news together from a bunch of daily papers and exchange ideas, and the attorneys would compare their documents. Toward noon the beautiful young women of the television world would make their appearance. Returning from some disturbance with their television cameras always close at hand, the cameramen would stop for coffee. With the mocking style typical of the media world, they would exchange a couple of quips each time the prime minister left his house with his big car and his escort, as the police stopped traffic.

Two days ago a waiter very courageously stopped a suicide terrorist at the door of another famous place downtown, the Caffit Café. Proudly, quickly, the people of Jerusalem had gone back to sitting at the tables of the various cafés with challenging words. And despite the fact that last Saturday at a religious feast a suicide terrorist from the Deheishe refugee camp killed ten persons; despite the fact that Saturday has become an occasion for slaughter in Jerusalem, both for those coming out of the temple and for young people out for a walk or at a pub, even last evening Moment Café was full of people who didn't want to give up living, who wanted to believe that it is still possible to tell a few jokes and have a beer with a friend.

But this time the suicide terrorist struck right at the heart of an Israeli society that wants to persist in living a normal life. Shabby Simantov, a television producer and one of the most devoted customers, who the journalists laughingly say has his office at the Moment Café, looks around in astonishment as the ambulances still wail, carrying away the last of the wounded: "I can't believe it. Now for the first time I feel that there is really no place left to go, nowhere to find a moment of peace. I feel like it's all over. Our life is being continually destroyed, devoured." Another regular customer who arrived soon after the explosion is weeping in despair: "My friends. I got here late. I won't ever see them again. I can't forgive myself. No, I can't describe what was on the ground when I stuck my head in. I can't believe that my eyes saw what they saw." Other customers, having run to help their friends, fainted from grief and horror and had to be treated in turn.

What Jerusalem has gotten from the suicide terrorist attack at Moment Café is a kind of definitive prohibition against trying to live a normal life. Who would have the courage now to sit down in a café or take a bus? Almost every day Jerusalem has either been struck by a terrorist attack, or an attack has been foiled at the last minute. This time it grazed the door of the prime minister, and at the same time, or perhaps above all, it broke the very heart of his society.

# Shavuah Tov

For the Jews, secular and religious, Saturday is a feast day, a ritual, a family and social tradition that is untouchable, fundamental. On Saturday, people stay home quietly or go on family outings. They forget about habits and banalities. At the end of the day on Saturday, they all go out together; the young people go to a pub, the adults to a restaurant, the religious come out of the temple and linger awhile to chat or wish themselves Shavuah tov, have a good week. Even yesterday in the midst of that pool of blood some, all splattered, would automatically say Shavuah tov to the journalists. Saturdays were an opportunity to forget the fear and blood that have devastated Israel since the start of the intifada, seventeen months ago.

Now Saturday is no longer what it was, it has been radically altered. Indeed, it has become a strategic occasion for suicide terrorism. People gather together, they form relaxed groups along the street, and the terrorist finds grist for his mill. In addition, he symbolically destroys the abstract, invincible point where the Jews have always met throughout the centuries, their paradise on earth. This is how it was last evening in the religious quarter of Beit Israel, where people live as though in eighteenth-century Poland, no cinema, no television, no amusements, no army, no cafés. Only stone houses in narrow alleyways, full of children and old people, and the synagogues with the yeshiva, the religious schools, where men and women flock, separately, seemingly having just disembarked from another world. Blood, screams, death have wiped out Saturday. The Shabbes, as the religious say in Yiddish, has been profaned.

Another terrible Saturday occurred in the village of Karnei Shomron in the territories, always the target of gunfire and mortar rounds, but not of suicide terrorist attacks. On Saturday, February 16, 2002, at the end of the Sabbath, the reopened shopping center was particularly reanimated because the birthday of a sixteen-year-old girl was being celebrated in a pizzeria—a good occasion for young people to meet after twenty-four hours that were much too quiet for teenagers. The suicide terrorist blew himself up right in the entranceway: Four people were killed, the last being a young girl who died in the hospital just two days ago, after a lengthy struggle.

On Saturday, February 9, 2002, a woman driving her car in Cisjordan was killed by gunfire as she was driving home. She threw herself on top of her children to protect them with her body. Ambushes at the end of the day on Saturday, when religious people are once again driving their cars or secular people are returning from outings, are particularly attractive to the terrorists.

Perhaps the worst Saturday of terror among so many occurred on December 1, 2001, when a double suicide terrorist attack in Jerusalem's pedestrian zone killed thirteen youths and wounded forty-two. The choice this Saturday evening was the young people of Jerusalem, who were trying to go on living, to meet with friends, despite the fact that on that very day eight other people had been killed in terrorist attacks within twenty-four hours. The young people meet in Zion Square, on Ben Yehuda Street, at the corner of Rav Cook, to go to Apple Pizza or to the Blue Hole Café together—a way of affirming their own right to live. There is also a café where Israeli and Palestinian youths always meet. Religious youths from the Mea Shearim quarter, bordering the one in which a bomb exploded yesterday, live opposite it, and on Saturday evening they, too, perhaps without their families knowing it, come to watch their contemporaries who live a life so different from theirs, a life of music and beer. The two human bombs created much carnage by exploding twenty minutes apart, the first time attacking by surprise, the second striking the rescuers as well.

The entire period of Saturday (which according to tradition begins on Friday evening) is a target, precisely because it is a time of quiet and sociality, in which the illusion that a long, enjoyable life is possible awakens once more. The Tel Aviv bombing at the Dolphinarium discothèque on the seaside promenade on June 2, 2001, in which twenty teenagers waiting in line to go in and dance were killed, and so many other terrorist attacks, in Netanya, in Hedera, took place on Friday, when people were getting ready for Saturday or going out to have a good time. It shouldn't surprise us: Terrorism is the negation of all human rights, the worst of all such violations because it obstructs every single move, every indispensable step of daily life, every civil gathering. Saturday, theologian Abraham Heschel tells us, enables man to leave behind the tyranny of things or events and become attuned with the sanctity of time, that is, with eternity and therefore with God. But at this point, all this seems to pertain to another world.

## School Days, School Days . . .

It was no accident that while the "Quartet" in Washington—the international mediators from the United States, Russia, the EU, and the United Nations charged with drafting a "road map" to peace in the Middle East—laboriously began to talk about peace again, in Immanuel, a settlement in Sharon near Nablus, an inferno of fire and dynamite was unleashed, costing seven lives and wounding twenty-six—almost all young people and one pregnant woman.

It is around three in the afternoon when armored school bus number 189 completes its route from Bnei Brak, the orthodox quarter of Tel Aviv, to the entrance to Immanuel, a religious settlement in the West Bank. Last December on the day of Hanukkah, the Feast of Lights, right at the exact same point, another attack on another bus had left ten dead. And now an incredible replay: two bombs, each weighing twenty kilos, explode near the bus full of schoolchildren who had gone to spend the morning in Tel Aviv and were now returning home. The bus was hit when it was almost at the entrance to Immanuel.

As the driver continued to drive, trying to get a little further away from the site of the explosion, the bus was already filled with

screams, with dead and wounded. That's when a group of three terrorists disguised as Israeli soldiers began shooting from above, the
roof being the only unprotected part of the bus: more injuries, more
deaths, more screams. The doors of the bus were locked, no one
could get out, no one could get in to try and save the innocent victims trapped inside in a sea of blood. Heroic attempts were made by
rescuers, who arrived within minutes, and still the shooting did not
stop. A small line of cars and ambulances that had formed behind
the bus in turn became a target for the terrorists; the drivers of the
cars were also hit. Yitzhak Kaufman, of the Red Star of David, recounts with horror the lengthy attempt to open the doors: "They
were locked and very heavy, and when we were finally able to open
them, we were faced with a spectacle that I will never in my life forget, no matter how many I've seen. Children on the floor were crying for help on a carpet of dead and gravely wounded." Helicopters
transported the most seriously injured to three different hospitals.
Some of the wounded, the hospitals' doctors told us, are from the
same families that had had members killed and injured in December's attack. And since the wounded were assigned according to the
seriousness and type of injury, some parents had to go looking for
their children in different hospitals.

The three terrorists had awaited the bus without even hiding,
since they were wearing Israeli army uniforms and were armed with
M-16s. Hamas and later the Al Aqsa Martyrs Brigades of Arafat's Al-
Fatah declared that the three were in safety in Nablus. As for the Israelis, for now no specific response is anticipated. Today's meeting
between Peres and his task force and a group of Palestinian representatives was called off, however. A signal to Washington from
Sharon's office: Since you are there to talk about the reform of the
Palestinian Authority, be aware that reforms should start with those
related to safety. The Israeli government has no intention of partici-
pating in talks under fire.

# Andrea Koppel: Massacre at Jenin

The battle of Jenin represented a very tough challenge to the idea
that is plainly and truly a trump card for Palestinian propaganda
throughout the entire world, namely, that the Israelis are Goliath, the

Palestinians a poor, weak David crushed by tanks, but fortified by a just cause. Even suicide terrorism has not completely demolished this idea, which is still largely accepted by the media (except a few hours after every bombing). The persistent comment it generates among people is this: "What else can those poor people do if not use their bodies as a weapon against the Israeli army?"

Well then, Jenin is another story, or at least it would have been if its truth had been understood. It is the story of a terrible battle lasting two weeks, a life-and-death struggle in which one of the two contenders (Israel) made a tactical error: it underestimated its adversary and had to correct itself as events were under way, trying clumsily to continue respecting its own principles. It is the story of the use of suicide terrorist tactics on a large scale, when it is no longer a single individual who kills himself but an entire country that self-destructs and is prepared to explode, indifferent to its own life, as long as it can defeat its adversary. And it is also the story of how the information media, just to avoid this psychological and cognitive turning point, took the dangerous route of describing a massacre, which it then had to recant, a little at a time, without damaging itself. Jenin is a tragic case study of a new war in which people suffered, it's true, not just because of the Israelis, however, but as the result of a series of mechanisms.

"I simply spoke with my colleagues and they told me that there had been a massacre." That's what the blond journalist from CNN, Andrea Koppel, said in the hall of a Tel Aviv hotel, explaining to someone why she had used that term when speaking of the battle of Jenin. "Did you see the shooting, the bodies?" "The Palestinians reported the massacre to us." "And you believed it without any proof? They often lie and distort the facts." "Oh, so therefore they are all liars?" Andrea replied. It has a certain philosophical significance that, a little later on in the same conversation full of prejudice and vanity, this diplomatic correspondent of the great American network confided an eschatological prediction to the person she was speaking with. He was saying disconsolately, speaking of the wave of terrorist attacks: "We could lose our lives, even lose our country." And Andrea replied: "Yes, I think you might lose your country. I think, today, the beginning of the end of Israel is in sight."

Andrea Koppel denies it all, but it is hard to believe her. What she said merely makes her a normal journalist. Janine di Giovanni of the *Times* of London writes: "The refugees . . . were not lying. If anything, they underestimated the massacre that occurred and its horror. In more than a decade of wars reported on from Bosnia, Chechnya, Sierra Leone, and Kosovo, rarely have I seen such deliberate destruction, such disdain for human life." And the Washington Post: "Some of the most severe urban attacks and aerial bombings and some of the most devastating land operations have been carried out here in more than two weeks of Israeli assaults against Palestinian cities and communities throughout the West Bank." And The Independent: "A monstrous war crime that they tried to cover up for two weeks has finally been exposed."

The story of Jenin is a milestone in the history of how the current Israeli-Palestinian conflict is perceived. Jenin epitomizes the oversimplification of the conflict and of the total obliteration of Israel's justifications, whatever the results of the U.N. fact-finding commission accepted by Israel may be. Koppel sums up in two sentences what has been transmitted to her and what she is prepared to transmit to world opinion: passive acceptance of the version that the Palestinians and their friends furnish her; the perception of the Palestinians as pitiable victims, without exception; an absence of feeling toward Israel and the catastrophic terrorism that assails it day after day, with the consequent loss of freedom and life, resulting in approximately five hundred deaths and thousands of wounded; total ignorance of the firepower and organizational strength that has nonetheless been demonstrated by the terrorist and paramilitary groups of Al-Fatah, Hamas, and the Islamic Jihad during eighteen months of war; the unconscious desire that Israel—alas!—might finally disappear from the scene inasmuch as it is the fomenter of a hatred that in the end overwhelms all of us, Americans and Europeans; and a conviction that Israel is a temporary phenomenon besides.

And primarily that Israel is evil, evil, evil, in any case, so much so that it picks on innocent civilians and uselessly slaughters them. This message, which in September 2000 issued from the description of battles in which bare-handed Palestinians and even children fought the superarmored and superarmed Israeli Goliath, was later fortified by photos of poor Arafat by candlelight in the rooms of his Mukhata compound. The armed Palestinians who occupied the Church of the Nativity were portrayed as medieval asylum seekers sheltered by religious men of goodwill. But Jenin contains all the symbols that confirm Israel's treachery, and for this reason it soon became a media battlefield, in addition to a real battlefield, in which the Palestinian Authority fired its heaviest weapon: "a new Sabra and Chatila, a massacre with five hundred people dead." Nothing could seem more fitting: Israel enters a refugee camp, a true symbol of Palestinian oppression, and who does it kill? Above all civilians— families, women, and children; indeed, it massacres them, it slaughters them.

If later it is shown that it was war, not a massacre, the stain of an attack against civilians will nevertheless remain upon the army. If afterwards it is shown that the refugee camp had been transformed into an organizational center for terrorism and guerrilla warfare and if in the end the battle there resulted in twenty-three Israeli deaths and seventy wounded, it's of little importance. International opinion seems to specialize in setting aside factors necessary for evaluating this conflict to clear the way for prejudice and a virtuous judgmental attitude. It doesn't matter that Arafat refuses to grant Colin Powell even a miserable cease-fire from terrorist attacks; that documents prove that the Palestinian rais's office was an active headquarters for financing and coordinating the Al Aqsa Martyrs Brigades and the Tanzim; that the Israelis attempted to arrest dangerous terrorists in Bethlehem. In the, end only accusations count. The information media have completely obliterated the fact that the entire origin of the conflict lies in Arafat's Camp David rejection, shifting responsibility for the conflict to Sharon, because of his visit to the Plain of the Mosques. In like manner, they have confused, simplified, and mistaken consequences for causes in regard to the battle of Jenin.

Jenin was the battlefield on which the Palestinian forces decided to put all their military skills to the test. On a strategic level, none of the experience accumulated during these months of intifada was set aside. Over time Al-Fatah along with the Al Aqsa Martyrs Brigades, Hamas, and the Islamic Jihad have learned to work hand in glove. Arafat and Barghuty have managed most of suicide terrorism, more or less directly, without depriving Hamas and the Islamic Jihad of the honor of their own suicide terrorist attacks. Suicide terrorism and the consequent use of explosives is a distinctive mark of this war, and Jenin is a prominent center of it; 50 percent of the attacks in the last wave, even one claiming eight victims after the army had surrounded the town, originated in Jenin. In all, twenty-four terrorist attacks came from the refugee camp, which, before the conflict, numbered around 13,000 people. In addition, the civilian population (which in the end has suffered horribly nonetheless, because a child is still a child, an old man is still an old man) is strategically a fundamental pawn in this war, from elementary school to the grave. Some soldiers recount that when the guerrillas came out with their hands up, they were followed closely by two elderly people, one to the right and one to the left. Every Palestinian is a combatant; the walls of the houses inside and out are covered with colored pictures of the shahids. A reservist soldier told me about having stopped a six-year-old child with a satchel in his hand. "What do you have in there?" he asked him. The child dropped the satchel and ran away: it contained two and a half kilos of explosive.

I saw a tailor's shop among the ruins that was gutted—two Singer sewing machines, spools of colored thread, a big box of tea near a gas burner—and the torment of the people who were looking into the shop from the devastated streets. Women were weeping; a little boy spoke quickly to me in Arabic pointing beneath the ruins—down there, down there. On the wall of the shop an enlarged photo of a horrible terrorist stood out, Ra'ed Karmi, one of those responsible for the massacre at the Dolphinarium.

Amira Haas, one of the more determined champions of the Palestinians' cause, writing for the Israeli newspaper *Ha'aretz* reported: "Al-Haija was killed on one of the first days of the IDF (Israeli Defense Forces) attack, hit by a rocket. Al-Haija was an activist in Hamas, who together with members of other armed groups had sworn to defend the camp to the death. J.Z. . . . estimates that they numbered no more than 70. But everyone who helped them saw himself as active in the resistance: those who signaled from afar that soldiers were approaching, those who hid them, those who made tea for them. . . . According to him," Haas writes, "no door in the camp was closed to them when they fled from the soldiers who were looking for them, the people of the camp, he said, decided not to abandon them, not to leave the fighters to their own devices. . . . This was the decision of the majority, taken individually by each person."

"Rather than emphasizing their role as victims," James Bennet and David Rhode wrote in the April 21, 2002, issue of the *New York Times*, "Palestinians could have presented this fight as a brave but losing struggle." Instead, even though it appeared more and more clear as time went by that there had been no massacre, the press did not go that route. It preferred to stick with individual episodes that showed the victimization of the civilian population. While this certainly occurred as it does in every war, it increasingly appeared that it was not particularly widespread, much less intentional, and that the so-called massacre was instead caused by the use of urban guerrillas and ordinary residents. But the Third World, anti-imperialist vision of the world, which characterizes the information media's view of the Middle East, loves guerrilla forces and regrets the arrest of Marwan Barghuty and prefers to underscore the suffering of the poor at the hands of the rich, the abuse of the wretched by the powerful tyrant. It is the memory of that kaffiyeh worn around the neck in universities in the seventies and eighties that arouses this Manichean dualistic vision of an imperialist Israel and a downtrodden Palestine. It is this viewpoint that dominates more than concealed, anti-Semitic disgust.

The aforementioned article from the *New York Times* clearly states that "What precisely happened will not be known at least until the debris is sifted and the residents . . . return home. . . . But dozens of interviews with residents of the camp, hospital officials, Israeli soldiers and officials, and Palestinian fighters produced no solid evidence of large-scale, deliberate killing of civilians in the camp." Today it is known that the number of civilians killed was seven.

But further on, even though we are informed in the background that militants were involved, still the article points to a number of examples that bring to mind inhuman cruelties, a tragic indifference on the part of Israeli soldiers: "The morning the fighting started, Fadwa al-Jammal, 27, from Tulkarm, was here visiting her sister, Rufaida. Fadwa, a nurse wearing a white head scarf and lab coat, stepped outside with Rufaida to ask where the Palestinian field hospital was, so she could offer her services, her sister said. The two women were talking to a group of fighters when Rufaida was shot in the leg. As Fadwa ran to help her, she was shot and collapsed over her sister's legs. 'She breathed three breaths and was dead,' Rufaida said. Hani Abu Ramaileh, a 20-year-old fighter, tried to come to the women's assistance and was shot in the chest and stomach. A 13-year-old boy was also shot dead that day . . ."

The succession of civilian deaths as described in many other articles following the outbreak in Jenin is such that it continues to suggest terrible aggression on the part of the Israelis against the civilian population, a hopeless thirst for blood. These are the opening lines of Haas's article: "Leaning on a cane, the man stood on a huge pile of ruins: a jumble of crushed concrete, twisted iron rods, shreds of mattresses, electric cables, fragments of ceramic tiles, bits of water pipes. . . . 'This is my home,' he said, 'and my son is inside.' His name is Abu Rashid; his son is Jamal . . . confined to a wheelchair."

The day I arrived on an armored bus and then in a Nagmash (an armored vehicle similar to a tank), there was a terrible hot desert wind in the Jenin camp and it was 35 degrees centigrade in the shade. It was Tuesday, April 15, 2002, thirteen days since the start of the operation. I saw for myself the desperation of the residents of Jenin, women and young children, and in the background, far away, behind a veil of fine white dust, men who were moving about as though behind the scenes. A tragedy had occurred, it's true, and it was certainly and above all a tragedy for the Palestinians who had been killed: militants, women, civilians. As of that day the total was thirty-nine. It was also a tragedy for the twenty-three Israeli reservists killed in the camp: doctors, farmers from the kibbutz, lawyers, shopkeepers. It's true, as U.N. envoy Terje Larsen said, that "it looks like an earthquake." Toward the square situated in the low part of the city, along the street where the battle raged most fiercely, the rubble has accumulated to the point of forming a horrible, high white hill. The scenes in the destroyed part of Jenin—the residents who have fled or who are in the hospital, the civilians who have been killed, their wretched lives shattered in a vortex, the pompous red couch left suspended in a house that has been broken in half, the screams of women who point beneath the ground explaining that they have no food or water and telling tragic personal stories—all of this wrings your heart.

Still, that devastated zone, the area that is shown on television, covers only 8 to 10 percent of the refugee camp; the rest is still standing. Trees in the parks continue to color the April days with their flowers. They say there are approximately 13,000 residents in the refugee camp. But the Israelis maintain that at the time the battle got underway (between Tuesday, April 2, and Wednesday, April 3), a great number of families had fled or had been placed in safety in nearby villages, so that in fact there were only a few thousand people in the camp, militants and civilians, with whom the army came into contact.

Even before the soldiers told about having fought "one of the most difficult battles in the history of Israel," I walked along the streets, noting that the amount of rubble grew as you approached the square. At the beginning, in fact, the fighting went from door to door; the destruction was very minor, the victims few. But the Israelis continued to die suddenly and unexpectedly, amid many explosions of mines, ambushed in courtyards and behind doors, and approached by daring individuals strapped with TNT or with a bomb in their hands. The risk was enormous; the helicopters attempted to wipe out nests of snipers with shots directed at crucial windows, but in fact the usual techniques were not helpful against a compact, well-protected band of men who had planned a new type of battle. When the Israelis lost thirteen men all together a week from the start of the battle, they realized that their expectations had been mistaken: The Jenin refugee camp was not a refugee camp; it was a stronghold in which efforts had been focused for some time to equip all Palestinian groups for war, to offer a remote area for terrorist attacks.

The thing that was most unusual to me in my experience as a journalist was the enormous quantity of booby traps I saw, within the space of a few meters, a trail of explosions ready for the enemy's attack in the middle of the streets, in the walls of the houses, and in the adjacent sewers. Many of these mined holes were linked by various white, plastic wires, which climbed up into the houses or went into the yards and connected to an electrical device that detonated the mines one after another. I almost stepped on one of these, a metallic bottle covered with white dust but was held back at the last moment by a soldier who then warned the other journalists not to go near it. "Now do you see why we didn't let the rescue workers come in right away?" he asked, defending himself against accusations of having caused a humanitarian tragedy by prohibiting entry to ambulances, UNRWA (United Nations Relief and Works Agency) and the United Nations, for a long time.

He also added that the army had nevertheless offered medical aid, which was refused. That when the soldiers brought cans of water into the alleyways, they were fired at, and so they had to toss the bottles of water into the houses by rolling them to their destination. But some sick and elderly people allowed themselves to be treated and transported, an official tells me, adding that it was difficult for him, just after the death of his companions, to take care of a twenty-year-old who had the symbol of the Jihad tattooed on her arm and who looked at him with eyes "flaming with hatred."

Asked if the rumor of mass graves was true, the soldiers' response was always one of shock and outrage, just as the tone of the reservists was generally shocked when they were asked to account for an alleged massacre: "We fought the battle with one hand tied behind our backs; we could have won it in a few hours, especially if we had used airplanes, like the Americans. Instead, fear of hitting the civilian population led us to decide on house-to-house combat. We covered one hundred yards a day, risking our lives at every door. What we found was incredible. A suicide terrorist pretended to surrender and threw himself at us, arms outspread, as he exploded."

The soldiers weren't prepared for it: there were explosives in the refrigerators, in the bathrooms, in the water pipes, under the bed. A great deal of it was manufactured at home, from chemical materials used for agricultural purposes. From the very beginning, the idea was to round up the terrorists by working from the outskirts to the center, to assemble them in the square and arrest them. In part it succeeded: three dozen of them gave themselves up on the eleventh day.

Before that, however, Israel changed its strategy, and this is what triggered international suspicion. When the thirteen reservists were killed all together on Tuesday, April 9, bulldozers began to be used. They knocked down houses in which heavy ambushes were suspected. Yet Amira Hass writes that a Palestinian family told her that when a bulldozer struck a house forcefully, its owner came out to protest and the destruction ceased. "We always allowed plenty of time for people to get out of the houses," the soldiers said. "No house was knocked down without many warnings being given. We detained males between fifteen and fifty years of age, but we let the others go."

In total seven hundred were detained; among them was Tabah Mardawi, one of the three dozen who surrendered on April 11, an Islamic Jihad activist who dispatched eleven suicide terrorists and who, according to Israeli sources, is responsible for having killed twenty Israelis and wounding one hundred fifty. He began his terrorist activities in 1994 and has already spent four years in prison. At his deposition, he stated that he had exploded gas cylinders in Jenin, causing the destruction of various houses. It is still not known how many houses blew up as a result of being booby trapped. General

Eyal Shlein on duty at the scene says: "A rational person does not mine his house with the intent of going back there." Shimon Peres added: "There wasn't a single house that wasn't mined. And there was no way to neutralize the danger without demolishing the structures. We also encountered men wearing explosives belts who put their hands up in a sign of surrender while attempting to go and detonate themselves among the soldiers."

Jenin has always had a tragic destiny even though the pleasant zone in which it is situated, amid the greenery of Galilee, might have promised something quite different. I can't help remembering a spring day (like this one, when I went there on a Nagmash, wearing a blue, bulletproof jacket) at the time of the Oslo Accords. To the joy of all Palestinians, the Israelis were going away; the Palestinian Authority was coming. I interviewed an attorney among others: a modern type, with a moustache, wearing a blue T-shirt with an alligator over his heart. I asked him about his plans for the future, and after some light, hopeful conversation, he turned thoughtful: "My wife," he confided, "doesn't agree with me. Recently, she's been devoting herself to doing good works with Hamas. She's involved with widows and children. She's wearing the veil again and long dresses . . ." Just now? I asked him. He replied that her decision filled him with admiration, that he was seeking the courage to follow her in her religion and in caring for the poor instead of setting out along the fleeting road to success and peace of mind.

There among the devastation, I thought about that episode a lot. At that moment, all the people of Jenin were in the square with the group; they were beginning to construct new buildings, banks, shops. And yet its destiny was sealed; the influence of its political extremist affiliation could be seen engraved in the anti-modernist choice made by the attorney's wife. Alongside the town, in fact, stood the refugee camp created in 1953, in which a number of qualified agencies, coordinated by UNRWA, were to have furnished not only relief aid and physical assistance, but hope, an impetus to rehabilitation and a life of freedom. Instead, the people and the international humanitarian organizations that looked after the refugees all these years, rather than trying to solve the problem, became an integral part of it. Jenin became a terrorist stronghold in part because of them. In the name of the widely accepted concept of self-determination, the officials of UNRWA and all the others who deal with the refugees in the camps accept the directives of the rank-and-file; that is, they accept the directives of the current leadership.

Thus it is that in the Jenin refugee camp the school textbooks have always been full of words of hatred against the Jews. The shahids are adored and emulated; public morality is based on war rather than on a dream for peace, on lies that can only define the Jews as hateful occupiers determined to remain such forever. In the Deheishe refugee camp, for example, where I was able to verify it personally, no one knows that Arafat rejected Barak's very generous proposals. They think the rais was fooled and betrayed by the Israelis.

Jenin has suffered an unjust fate: for fifty years, its resident refugees, similar to those in other refugee camps but with greater militarization due to specific circumstances, have remained prisoners of the organizations that should have led them out of there. There are twenty-seven refugee camps in the West Bank and Gaza, and another thirty-two in Jordan, Lebanon and Syria. In the year 2001 alone, UNRWA spent $310 million in the camps. Now, in accordance with respected international agreements, UNRWA is demanding damages to compensate the tragedy in Jenin. But what about the structural inadequacies of the UNRWA, which have enabled this human tragedy? Instead of making that camp and all the others into communities, the UNRWA allowed the camp to be transformed into a base for organized battle and suicide terrorism. Who will pay damages for that? Who will pay damages for the wasted lives in Jenin's refugee camp, those spent sitting hopelessly in the dust, those lost in a never-ending conflict over an objective that Arafat could have obtained without war?

## The *Times* and the *Independent*: Massacre at Jenin

It was the *New York Times* that wondered, a few days ago, if it wouldn't have been better for the Palestinians to describe the battle of Jenin as a proud decision to fight to the death, as the strategic acquisition of a tough, determined stance in a head-to-head war in which the Palestinians have instead often been described as David facing Goliath, with their stones and their children, victims of one of the most powerful armies in the world.

Instead, the media's choice was very different: Massacre, the Palestinians said, and for days and days the media echoed the desperate message. "If anything," wrote the *Times* of London when the Palestinians spoke of five hundred deaths, "the refugees underestimated the massacre and the horror. . . ." The same thing applies to Bethlehem: This lengthy as yet unresolved confrontation was not described by the Palestinians as the bold, strategic decision of a strong group of men from Al-Fatah (that is, Tanzim and the Al Aqsa Martyrs Brigades) and Hamas, but as a merciless siege by Israeli tanks against a group of people who barricaded themselves in the church in self-defense, as they did in the Middle Ages.

In actuality, the next U.N. inquiry commission, with all the possible prejudices it may bring with it regarding Israel, will be a turning point in the analysis and understanding of the war between Israel and the Palestinians—that and public feeling, once the facts show that Bethlehem involved the occupation of sacred walls by armed men, even though they were besieged by other armed men. Up until now, the description of suicide terrorists provided by special correspondents from throughout the world, namely that they are desperate misfits, essentially freaks, instead of people from a poor but sound society, has not contradicted the media's portrayal of Arafat as a victim.

Despite suicide terrorism, the idea that the Palestinians are mere victims has been left standing in Europe (and this is astounding). But the battle of Jenin, which lasted two weeks, will change the media's perception of the war just by virtue of the inquiry commission, which the Palestinians wanted so much. Even if the commission establishes that Israel behaved wrongly, reprehensibly, and callously from a humanitarian point of view, the enquiry will likely reveal a real, bona fide war between two sides that were both strong. First, along with the twenty-three Israeli soldiers killed, approximately double that number of Palestinians were killed, among them few civilians—this is what has emerged so far from the work of the excavators. Even the newspaper *Ha'aretz* and its correspondent Amira Haas have had to exclaim that "there was no massacre." Instead, testimonies gathered after the fact, both from direct experience and from many journalists from all over the world, reveal a very fierce, sophisticated, well-planned resistance in which the entire town, a real blockhouse, had been wired with mines; in a word, a town in which individual terrorist suicide, seen as an act of extreme heroism, spread throughout the entire refugee camp.

One might wonder why the UNRWA, an organization entrusted with the well-being and safety of the population, wasn't aware of it and why it did not sound a social alarm. The population that had remained in the refugee camp, together with the Palestinian organizations that had joined forces (Hamas, Jihad, Al-Fatah), offered to supply the combatants with all the necessary logistics, and that's what happened. The sentries, the bearers of food, water, weapons, and even explosives, were women, young boys and girls, and even small children. Every house, water pipe, manhole, even refrigerators and beds, became booby traps. The Israelis tell of guerrillas who came out of the houses when they issued a warning, their hands up and wearing dynamite belts, or else accompanied by two civilians, one on the right and one on the left.

The fact remains that Tzahal, the Israeli army, lost in one single blow more than half of all the soldiers that fell in this war; the units on duty say that it was the toughest battle of any that they can remember. They say that the bulldozers began to destroy the walls only after they saw that it was impossible to fight door to door because it was too costly in human life; and that in any case they had asked the residents to leave well before that (according to them, the combatants had evacuated many of the residents to nearby villages, within sight of the battle). The soldiers also insist on repeating that the inquiry commission will verify how many houses were demolished by the bulldozers and how many as a result of the booby traps. Tzahal adds that perhaps it was slow in allowing ambulances and journalists to enter, but according to its version, it was nearly impossible to let them enter, with all that TNT around. The commission will verify it. But what it will surely discover in the end, despite the fact that at the time the *Independent* of London wrote of "a monstrous war crime," is the remnants of a huge, genuine battle in a city which produced 29 terrorists, not by accident, and that was known for its rigid, unified militancy. In any case, there are some very important leaders among the 790 individuals detained by Israel.

In Bethlehem, too, once the confrontation is over, once the men wanted by the Israelis will have perhaps departed for a place of exile agreed upon between Arafat and Israel, or will have been left in Israeli hands, we will be able to measure the boldness of a plan that nearly caused a belligerent clash between the Christian world and that of the Jews. Under orders to fight to the end or even let themselves possibly be killed, a group of armed men has held the Church of the Nativity, convinced that the Israeli soldiers in the square would attempt to enter the church at all costs to take them prisoner. A battle for life and death, a very risky strategic wager.

This great strategic resolve, culminating in suicide terrorism, has yet to be understood: norms are not easily overturned. There is nothing of the freak in the Palestinian combatant, nor does the suicide terrorist act out of existential desperation. Arafat at this time, before going back to being the rais in Gaza, had them call him simply "General." And that is what he is today: The general of a unified, close-knit army, who knows how to handle dynamite and strategy and who turns the war of images, the media image of himself as victim, into one of the most salient points of the conflict, so that we hope he will return to the political table as soon as possible.

# Jenin: Town of Terror

Inasmuch as it was an epitome of the Israeli-Palestinian war, Jenin was an extremely harsh battlefield for the information media. A battle was played out here that left twenty-three Israeli soldiers dead in two weeks. Those wounded numbered seventy. On the Palestinian, side the number of deaths tallied as of now are around forty; it is expected that more will emerge, unfortunately, from beneath the ruins of the refugee camp, where this reporter went as the battle was still winding down. While I was at the camp, they were still shooting, and a small, homemade bomb almost exploded under my feet. A soldier yanked me away by the arm and told me that explosions were the norm in Jenin. Everything exploded during the battle, everything was mined, the soldier said. It was like one big collective suicide terrorist, he said, and I will not forget it.

The spectacle before my eyes was horrible: In an area of approximately two hundred square meters, the ruins of houses were piled up one on top of the other. Groups of Palestinian women came toward us journalists in desperation, explaining that their dead and their possessions remained buried beneath the rubble. Many had fled to nearby villages. The demolished zone encompasses about 10 percent of the refugee camp in which 12,000 people live, and it is the only area that was shown on television.

Yet the houses still standing outnumber by far those that have been leveled. It seems that from the first signs of battle, and even quite a bit earlier—that is, from the time Jenin had become a chosen center for suicide terrorism and for this intifada in general—many families had moved elsewhere. Jenin was a very well equipped stronghold. In the quarters near the square that lay in ruins, I saw with my own eyes dozens of explosive traps placed in the middle of the street, in the interior and exterior walls of houses, in water pipes, in refrigerators, in garbage cans—wherever an explosives charge could be placed. And the charges were connected to white wires that were detonated from inside the houses. The militants had put them there beforehand to prepare for an Israeli attack, at the cost of blowing themselves up along with their houses.

The U.N. inquiry commission will establish how many houses were destroyed because of the booby traps and how many as a result of Israeli bulldozers. The bulldozers were put into use when, after fighting house to house in search of terrorists, the Israelis realized that they were paying an enormous price in bloodshed. Aerial forces that would have followed the American scorched-earth technique against the enemy were rejected at the start. But after thirteen Israeli soldiers were killed all together, the strategy changed, and bulldozers began to be used. The Israelis say that they always repeatedly asked the remaining residents to leave and that they did leave; Shimon Peres said that having them surrender one by one meant that at times they would rush toward the soldiers with their hands up, wearing explosives belts.

Amira Haas, a journalist from *Ha'aretz*, who is certainly not fond of Israel, recounts that when a bulldozer struck a house from which a resident appeared, the equipment was quickly stopped. Haas, in addition to portraying the sufferings of individual Palestinian citizens, describes an unprecedented battle, as well as the total support of those who remained in the camp for this war of the Tanzim, Hamas, and the Islamic Jihad, who had turned Jenin into a very significant stronghold representative of their clout. Fifty percent of the recent wave of terrorist attacks originated in Jenin, approximately two dozen suicide terrorists came from there. Even during the recent fighting a human bomb was dispatched, killing eight people on a bus. One captured terrorist among the 700 detained in the last several days is responsible for the death of 22 Israelis. The battle that took place there is worthy of the importance that Jenin has assumed, particularly since suicide terrorism became the crucial strategic weapon of all factions of the intifada; these factions found an enviable situation of unity, almost unique, there. The entire town was a stronghold equipped for the Israeli attack.

The accusation that the Palestinians made against Israel was, as everyone knows, that of having perpetrated the massacre of civilians. The U.N. commission, which Israel accepted, will verify the number of deaths and the causes of the terrible battle. Meanwhile, the word *massacre* no longer appears in the reports of press correspondents and foreign and local television commentators. The number of Palestinian deaths seems to be very limited.

But Jenin, if viewed in the proper terms, which naturally entails compassion for human losses (all human losses), also poses the problem of these refugee camps, which UNRWA has retained as enclosures of a culture of aggression, strongholds of suffering particularly impregnable to hope and welfare. Refugee camps in areas that before the war had begun to experience a situation of greater prosperity and hope—such as Deheishe, in the formerly thriving zone of Bethlehem—were never opened up. Life in the Palestinian Authority has not at all replaced the hope of returning to Haifa or Jaffa, that is, of exercising the right to return, which destroyed the peace process. Moreover, children in the refugee camps are raised in the cult of the shahid and study textbooks filled with prejudices and in which the map of Israel does not exist.

An Israeli soldier told me that a little child, six years old, came toward him with a satchel that was bigger than he was. When he was asked, "What do you have in the satchel?," he ran off, leaving it on the ground. It contained a device with two and a half kilos of explosives. We can only hope that all of this will end, that in addition to the truth about what happened in Jenin, the will for peace will also finally emerge from beneath the rubble. Israeli reservists who fought in the zone expressed astonishment and regret over what they found. They continued to repeat that they—doctors, farmers from the kibbutz, bank clerks—fight for their homes and country only because they cannot do otherwise, that they dream of peace, that their children await them, that their only desire is for terrorism to end so that talks can begin again. From the destruction and rubble of the Palestinian camp, murmurs begin to be heard, secretly wondering where the tragic wind blowing from Mukata, around Arafat, will lead them. Even in Ramallah and Shkem, they are perhaps beginning to dream again about a future for their children.

# Shahid

You have to see these suicide terrorist attackers for what they are. Like the one Wednesday morning at the intersection of Meghiddo, between Hedera and Afula, they continue to slaughter dozens of innocent people (all the more innocent if they are conscripted soldiers who at age eighteen find themselves on their way to the base at dawn to defend their homeland instead of being able to enjoy their youth) on regular, scheduled buses. You have to set aside superficial theories regarding desperation, or the eccentric psyche of a fanatic, a savage individual, or a mentally deficient one. You have to look further to fight better: The terrorist who leaves home with a belt or a car packed with TNT and tries to kill as many people as possible is normal in today's Palestinian environment. He does not act on behalf of a war for the territories, because he too knows that that war is much better fought at the negotiating table where full results can be obtained (like at Camp David, when Arafat rejected 97 percent of the territories and part of Jerusalem). Nor does he act in the name of God, since a very high percentage of suicide terrorists now come from Al-Fatah, Arafat's organization, which is not Islamic fundamentalist but secular. He acts with the conviction of becoming the hero of a global war of liberation. He has seen pictures of the other shahids on city walls and in houses, he has heard them exalted in Arafat's speeches and in those of all the Arab leaders in the area. Starting in school, and then with today's television and radio, he has felt himself driven to what an Egyptian psychoanalyst publicly called "a moment of ultimate joy, of total ecstasy."

The suicide terrorist has also been motivated by offers of money for his family: Saddam Hussein sends $25,000 to each family of shahid. And the organization that sends the terrorist stays close with him up until the last moment, arranging for the trip, the farewell video, the bomb filled with nails so as to do as much harm as possible. Women, children—as long as they are Israeli, they must die. And the ensuing scene is always the same: Arafat condemns, but does nothing to stop the terror; he remains passive. And at the earliest opportunity he will say that the real terror is that of the Israelis and that Sharon bears responsibility for everything. George Tenet, in the area, powerlessly watches the taunts of Palestinian terrorism. Perhaps he is beginning to realize that to continue to propose the traditional negotiating table, at which Arafat would sit across from the Israelis, is a losing proposition. Terrorism is the real protagonist of this Middle East conflict, and also its unwelcome guest.

# The Milium

"How old am I?" he asks, a bit scornfully because of the pointless question. A very strong, upright gentleman, with a full handlebar mustache, straightens his pistol in the belt of his military uniform and rises to his full height: "I'm seventy-eight, why? I got here yesterday; my unit signed up for two weeks. What am I doing here? I'm serving as a volunteer: I'm a sharpshooter. What do you mean, still? Put an apple on your head if you want to, you'll go back to Italy safe and sound after I split it in two." Not very enticed by the invitation, I step back a little from Levi Goldberg, born in Petah Tikva, the first Jewish town, four generations of Russian Socialist pioneering and wars. His cell phone rings, it's his wife, Yael: "Everything's fine, the usual group. I found a uniform. Now we're going to eat; two days of training and we leave." He explains: "Fifty-seven years together. Why should she complain if I go off to the army? I've been going off to the army all my life. I never betrayed her; she's a wonderful woman She's concerned, but our two children and eight young grandchildren are there to keep her company."

Around here, there is an abundance of white hair. The grandfathers (without quotation marks) are out in the cold in their shirtsleeves, stomachs sucked in, enviable physiques, cell phones ringing: a lot of business deals were left hanging, a lot of people at home are worried about Papa or Grandpa. We are in the volunteers enlistment area of the Lahish recruitment camp, one of the largest in Israel, fully operational since Operation Defense Wall began.

On a suburban street amid yellow flowers and olive trees, near Kiriat Gat, an Israeli town not far from Hebron, a huge gate slides open. Without pause it swallows up buses and cars full of young reservists, called up these past few days; volunteers arrive as well, over forty-five for combat units (though they are often called up even older than that for compulsory service involving non-front-line duties), over fifty-five for other units. Part of the 20,000 soldiers called up at this time have arrived here: the Miluim, the army reserves of the Israel Defense, is the real secret weapon of the Israeli army—approximately 500,000 men and women added to the 200,000 conscripted soldiers. When the famous concentric attack of the Kippur War took place in 1973, the nation reacted to the shock only when the reserves were finally able to be mobilized regardless of the religious holy day.

But Miluim this old had never been seen until the inauguration of a project in 2001 that presently has 4,500 candidates. Now, every day between 70 and 200 volunteers set out. After two days of running or drills in which they take up arms again, they generally go to Kav ha Tefer, along the Green Line. The idea is that a fatherly face helps the soldiers and that they can bring a bit of good sense to delicate situations and relieve tired, rattled young men at the checkpoints and even on patrol rounds. This is how Colonel Betzalel Triber explains it to us: he sends them left and right, to get rifles and canteens. In a couple of hours, he makes soldiers out of courteous gentlemen sixty-ish and much, much older. They all hop to it; they form a line to collect their equipment and uniforms. They recognize and greet one another; they recount their recent news: many were together six months ago, during another stint, two weeks like this one.

"It's not right to keep them for a longer time. There's no age limit, it depends solely on their condition," Triber explains. "Once they are here, they get exactly the same treatment as all the other soldiers. Nights in tents on a cold dirt floor, plain food, continual danger, many hours on their feet, risking their lives. Even six months ago it was less dangerous. We can't keep up with sending off all those who apply. There, that was a fifty-eight-year-old woman on the telephone; she's leaving tomorrow."

In front of a shed, the men wait in line for their military outfits, shoes (it's hard finding a right shoe that matches a left one), rifle, knapsack, kit bag. Haviv Yehuda, a sixty-three-year-old aeronautics engineer, explains his reason for enlisting: "It's certainly a lot better if a bullet hits me rather than hitting my son." Understood? And does he have sons? Yes, both of them volunteers: one is an attorney, the other does the same work as his father.

"I am absolutely capable of carrying out combat duties. I am in very good health; I exercise at the gym. My wife says to me: you may have a sound body, but you're touched in the head. I'm a leftist; I have an instinctive sympathy for the Palestinian people. Now, however, our lives are in danger. My wife goes to the supermarket, and she is at risk; my son goes to work, goes to a bar to have a coffee, and he can be blown up. We can't go on this way. Occupation is something else; but if it's a question of defeating terrorism, I want to do my part. Now, please excuse me, I have to phone my clients to cancel some meetings."

Benny Pinkas, age sixty-five, divorced with two young grandchildren, is on his second round of service. He is the owner and manager of a cystic fibrosis treatment center on the Dead Sea: "Before the war we had many Italian clients. I have a patient from Bolzano. I came because I feel that we must put an end to this insane situation: terrorism will end when the brainwashing that drives people to explosives belts stops."

Only one of the people we talk with, a tour guide, speaks of a "Jewish right to all of our lands" and maintains "it's not clear who's occupying whom"; he is grandfather to eight grandchildren, and lives in Tel Aviv. The others have left their affairs without being influenced by ideology, as if driven by a natural impulse to defend their homes and also by a nationwide, collective Spartan spirit.

Yacov Ritov, a mango grower from a kibbutz on the Sea of Galilee is going because he couldn't stand the anxiety anymore: His son Dan is in the same unit in which Oded Kornfait, another boy from the kibbutz, was killed two days ago. "I think now they need every one of us. We have to get back to living, not barely surviving in terror. Let's get back to talking about two nations, enough raving about mosques and Islamic lands. The mangoes are fine for now; the difficult season doesn't begin until July."

# Panorama of Terror

A solution. We beg you, give us a solution, any solution. Don't you see that you are making us look bad, that you are making us seem like a pack of incompetents? It's what the world is demanding of the Israelis and Palestinians gripped in a riveting man-to-man struggle: here within, the sounds are muffled, the appeals pointless. As the funerals follow one upon the other, the international assembly, outraged by so much insistence on death, in its enlightened way expects to see a solution to the tragedy handed to it but gets nothing but war. It is not prepared to play on the chessboard, much too vast, of Jewish history, of the Arab world, of terrorism as an absolute weapon, and of the power of the army in a time of democracy. Journalist Tom Friedman visits Abdullah, the Saudi prince, and everyone gets fired up at the feeble peace proposal, which for now hasn't even come out of the royal coffers. Egypt's President Mubarak on a visit to Bush proposes the pharaonic idea that Arafat and Sharon should perform a triple somersault by meeting at Sharm el Sheich under his auspices. Again there is applause. Every minute the Europeans coercibly condemn Israel; every so often they urge Arafat to contain terrorism, as if it were a secondary phenomenon caused by the ongoing conflict.

Israel has less and less faith in its elected prime minister, Ariel Sharon: He was chosen to stop the Al Aqsa Intifada, which had contemptuously erupted after the failure at Camp David. And instead he was not successful. His policy of punishing Arafat's military structures—the F-16s that bombarded Al-Fatah's evacuated offices from above, the hunt for terrorists and storehouses even within Balata and Jenin, and his decision to detain the rais in Ramallah—also brought about widespread killing of civilians, which aroused international protest as well as horror among a great many Israelis. Sociologist Ehud Shprinzack states: "This is a war that cannot be won, ever. Democracies can only make peace; the opposition, internal and external, thwarts them with regard to the moral significance of war."

The Palestinians are a much more determined society, though suffering. They insist that the heart of the problem is the occupation, yet they regard as heroes the suicide terrorists who presently blow themselves up any time, any place, dragging women and children with them. The moral objective of their war is independence, but the underlying vein, equally as strong, is to affirm the Jews' extraneousness in the land of Israel—their illegitimacy. What should Israel do? Give up demanding an end to terror and go back to the route that failed, that of negotiating over the territories? And should Arafat have a role in this? And is Sharon the right man under the circumstances, given that he appears so harsh in the eyes of the Palestinians and is so disliked? Or should Israel engage in a battle to destroy terrorism using the strength of its army?

Bush says nothing, but contrary to the Europeans, he shows signs of understanding what it means to be besieged by terror. It is not easy to understand: The destruction of daily life for those who live through it is inconceivable. Just as one cannot imagine the suffering and absence of life that is not war in the Palestinian Authority, impoverished, restricted, completely taken with the myth of the shahid and the feeling of having reached the final shore of its war of independence against a people of hateful invaders. And Israel questions itself and lies on a Procrustean bed of war that has also become contemporary society's psychoanalyst's couch.

The late night party on Monday, March 5, 2002, at the Sea Market restaurant and night club in Tel Aviv, with music and wine in abundance, is high spirited and untroubled. Accompanied by her friends, Irit Rahamim, a young woman with a mane of black curls, is celebrating a farewell to being single. It's a lovely party, with celebrities and sports figures (her husband-to-be is soccer player Liron Basis). When a terrorist begins shooting and lobbing grenades into the crowd, Irit, by now face down on the ground, says she wasn't thinking of an attack. That's really strange if you think about it, given that in the preceding twenty-four hours, twenty-one Israelis had been killed. Instead, Irit calls her future husband from beneath the table, and through her tears, like in a television serial, tells him that she loves him amid the shots. Three people are killed, but Irit gets married all the same.

In the hours that follow, a bus explodes in Afula and a man dies; the mother of two small children is shot to death on a heavily traveled road between Jerusalem and Bethlehem; a nineteen-year-old soldier, Sergeant Steven Kenigsberg, is buried (a young man whom everyone recalls as being too good and too good-looking, who brought his whole family with him from South Africa because he wanted to defend Israel), as well as a thirty-three-year-old Druse sergeant from Kissufim, a fifty-three-year-old gentleman from Lod, and a fifty-two-year-old from Herzlja. The day before there had been approximately twenty funerals for Israelis and seventeen Palestinian funerals. Yet, Irit didn't realize that she could die. She thought it was a prank, like those of Purim, the Jewish carnival.

On Sunday, Hannah Nehmad buried five grandchildren, a son and a daughter-in-law in Reishon le Tzion. In front of the seven bodies wrapped in tallith, she continued to repeat: "I want them all here beside me, like always, near me." They had gone to celebrate the bar mitzvah of another one of Hannah's grandchildren in Jerusalem. Shauli, a fifteen-year-old, one of the grandchildren killed when suicide terrorist Muhammed Darameh blew himself up in the doorway to the ceremony, was going to get wine for the guests in a building next door to the party. His brother, Eli, who was behind him lost an arm. A woman had gone into the building to change her clothes, and meanwhile the suicide terrorist killed Lidor, her twelve-year-old son, and Oriah, age eighteen. The father, Shimon, was embracing the remains of his son when the rescue workers arrived. He was murmuring: "Don't die, don't die. your father loves you so much." When Darameh blew up, Sofia Ya'arit happened to be passing by; she was taking her seven-month-old baby out for some air. Both of them were killed. A religious woman who had come to Jerusalem to celebrate the bar mitzvah against her family's wishes later went on television with her twelve-year-old son who had been with her. The child begged his grandparents not to think that what had happened was his mother's fault, only the suicide terrorist was to blame. Both of them wept in despair.

A woman telephones the radio station: she is the mother of one of the soldiers on guard duty at the checkpoints, who have recently become the favorite target of a new type of guerrilla warfare, which the Tanzim conducts at checkpoints and settlements. Several days ago on Sunday at Ein Arik, near Ofra, a sniper, shooting from above, killed ten persons, one by one, seven of them soldiers. He was able to fade away amidst the rocks and shrubbery. The woman on the telephone is the mother of a soldier: "My son called me on Friday and said to me, 'Mama, we're like sitting ducks. The checkpoints are located in the wrong places. We have no helmets; the armored cars are absolutely inadequate.' He also told me that he had asked his wife to look after their child, because he was sure that he would be killed. He's still alive, but his companions are gone." A wave of controversy follows this phone call, in particular over the fact that the army hasn't equipped itself as though it were fighting a real war; it doesn't realize what the checkpoints have become: besides being points where possible terrorists are filtered out as they try to pass, the checkpoints have turned into traffic jams, slowdowns, immovable, exposed stations, which make soldiers targets rather than active ground forces.

The Palestinians denounce the checkpoints as points of harassment and humiliation. In the past few weeks, two pregnant women underwent unexpected inspections: the husband of one of them was killed; the other lost her baby. Several months ago a photo of three Palestinians appeared: They had been made to undress at a checkpoint till they were almost naked, standing in the cold, to verify that they were not carrying explosives or arms on their persons. Israeli military radio itself frequently denounces episodes of abuse by soldiers who act cruelly with bureaucratic, obtuse, and at times senseless persistence, even in cases where it is clear that the person trying to pass through the checkpoint is not a terrorist. Israel torments itself over this; there are articles, debates, open confrontations among political powers. Things have become even more complicated since women also entered into service with suicide terrorist groups. Then, too, in the past few days, the army fired at a Red Crescent ambulance killing a doctor: The soldiers had fired at the ambulance because, they said, it was coming toward them at top speed and they were afraid. But ambulances have to speed, the Palestinians responded. Still, the Israelis say that the soldiers' fear is justified because ambulances have been used many times by the Palestinians to carry munitions or transport combatants or terrorists to their destination. Female suicide terrorist Wafa Idris, for example, is said to have reached the center of town by ambulance. The fact remains, however, that that unfortunate doctor, sixty years of age, was killed. Israel apologized, just as it apologized for having fired a tank missile at a car carrying a woman and three children, the family of a Hamas leader. It was a tragedy that aroused terrible anger and desperation in Ramallah, along with Sheikh Yassin's promise of severe reprisals.

Everyone wants to be a *shahid* like Muhammed Darameh, a seventeen-year-old suicide terrorist from the Deheishe refugee camp in Bethlehem who killed ten Jews last Saturday. His picture is idealized by young girls, mothers, and Tanzim militants, who uniformly see him as a sensitive boy, extremely afflicted by the death of his closest friend at a checkpoint, a good boy, heroic: "The finest young man in the world." Asked if the fact that he killed so many children doesn't upset them, they reply that Palestinian children die as well. Asked if they don't think that there's a difference in intentionally killing innocent victims, they respond that Sharon intends to exterminate the Palestinians.

The shops are all closed, and often the schools as well, but young people and children are moving about the streets. They wander around in the midst of aerial attacks, the satisfied echo of a suicide bombing that just took place, get-togethers and gatherings, funerals full of despair and rage, waiting, shooting. Life is desolate and monotonous. Almost no one, in Bethlehem as in Ramallah or Gaza, is concerned with anything anymore except the war. Radio and television continuously provide a version of events that demonizes the Israelis; only rare voices, like that of Sarin Nusseibah, recall the possibility of coexisting side by side. Sharon is viewed as clouded by his thirst for blood. Abu Ammar, Arafat, is seen as a leader to be debated only in private, and who in any case would like to make peace, though the Israelis don't want to. The Israelis are seen as a unified whole that resembles an evil cloud. The leader who has the firmest hold on the field is certainly Marwan Barghuty, who has led Al-Fatah with its Tanzim to the relentless guerrilla warfare that is the Palestinians' new weapon and that gives them an illusion of victory: They feel like the Vietnamese, like the Algerians. Even the Israelis begin to speak of them in these terms.

Israel is depressed. It doesn't want to kill; it doesn't want to hate; it doesn't want to believe it's at war; it can't make up its mind to awaken from the peace process. Two reservist soldiers, Shimshon Barina and Avraham Tkuma, rather elderly men, put on their uniforms in the middle of the night and on their own initiative, to try to rouse the nation, went to the Ein Arik checkpoint where seven soldiers and three civilians had been killed three days earlier. They told the soldiers on guard duty: "We've come to help out." They said they were given an enthusiastic welcome and found much courage and cheer, along with a clear awareness of defending one's homeland. "The soldiers are much calmer than our politicians and intellectuals, who seem somewhat panicky."

Sonya Shistik, fifteen years of age, awoke from a coma a week after a suicide terrorist had almost killed her in front of Tel Aviv's Dolphinarium discothèque. Disfigured, her bones broken in several places, including her back and limbs, everyone expected that the first thing she would ask about would be her best friend. They dreaded that moment because Karen was dead. Instead, Sonya asked her mother, "Let me see the baby." Her mother took out a photograph of her sister as a newborn. "It's not my baby," Sonya said. "It's my little sister." From that time on, she has had to learn slowly, very slowly, that she herself is her baby, that it is she herself she must give birth to once again. With her are thousands of young people who have been left without limbs, without eyes, without self-love. Many adults, or even elderly people, must also give birth to themselves again—such as the parents of soldiers who have perhaps come to Israel from countries that are comfortable and content like Italy. Like Amichai Porat (from Porto), the young Italian who was killed last week, who always had a smile on his face and who had so impressed Hillary Clinton.

# RMA: A New Response

"O sister Wafa, oh pulsing pride, bud that bloomed on earth and is now in heaven, sister. . . . Allah Akbar, oh Palestine of the Arabs, oh Wafa, you have chosen martyrdom, in death you have brought hope to our struggle." Thus sang an elegant singer to the Palestinian public in a concert hall, accompanied by an orchestra; it was shown at least twice on Palestinian television. The singer was celebrating the new heroine of the popular epic, suicide terrorist Wafa Idris, the twenty-six-year-old nurse who blew herself up in the center of Jerusalem, killing one person and injuring dozens.

Terrorism still dances on the stage of history, a great, macabre protagonist. "The available manpower is just about infinite," says an exponent of Shin Bet, the Internal Security Services, "even though in the last month explosives have become more expensive, skilled experts are lacking, and the price of belts has increased." And yet the terrorist attacks continue: more people maimed, more people blinded, more funerals at which mothers throw themselves on the clods of earth that cover their children. Operation Defense Wall hoped to put an end to this situation by entering the cities in Area A, the area under the control of the Palestinian Authority, destroying terrorist infrastructures, killing dozens of men in combat, and taking, as it did, two thousand prisoners. Instead, after the operation came to an end a month ago, Israel counted another eight successful suicide terrorist attacks; one of them, a particularly sizeable one at Rishon Le Tzion, with fifteen people killed and dozens injured, was followed a week later, as though contemptuously, by another explosion in the same place, which killed two persons. And an incredible number of attacks have been thwarted, between thirty-two and thirty-seven depending on the sources. "During Defense Shield," says Eli Cohen, an attorney from Netanya who, after the Easter massacre, again found himself in the midst of an attack, that of a few days ago, "we had the grief of the news of soldiers killed, the shock of the controversies over Jenin and Bethlehem, but life had become almost normal again: we dropped the children off at school almost without concern. We had timidly returned to the shopping centers and restaurants. The roads could almost be traveled. The violence continued, but at a less traumatic level. But now, are we back to square one again?"

The experts and secret service agents, the Shin Bet, the Mossad, and Aman (the military forces) flatly deny this. Instead, they talk about something absolutely new, RMA, or Revolution in Military Affairs, which could only be put into effect after Operation Defense Shield, and that, according to General Uzi Dayan, vice chief of staff, allows for a situation of containment in which an Israeli victory may also be discerned: ". . . because our objective is not to crush the enemy, but to defeat terrorism which is the enemy of the entire free world: therefore, we look to specific actions against the organizations and exponents of terror and the great solidity of our society. Which by no means went to pieces as Arafat anticipated, and which is quite capable of resisting, knowing what it has to lose if 'they' were to win: its civil rights, its well-being."

What is RMA? It is the application of superior knowledge of the field and of technologies combined with "domination of the battlefield." The Americans tested it in Afghanistan; Israel is doing so in much more familiar territory, the West Bank, because that is where the most active terrorist centers are located. RMA strikes the enemy and clears out once the objective has been met, after having broadened its informational bases. It can be applied when knowledge of terrorist infrastructures is very extensive. And such knowledge was expanded enormously by Operation Defense Shield, reveals Israeli terrorist expert Boaz Ganor, director of the International Policy Institute on Counter-Terrorism and adviser to the prime minister.

Now that Tzahal, the Israeli army, knows the structure of the Palestinian Authority's international ties with funds and weapons supplies and Arafat's personal involvement, now that it has destroyed or controls the location of munitions factories and arms deposits and the stationing of terrorist units, now that it has become easier to put in place the courageous spies that furnish intelligence from various towns, once word is given, it is possible for the army to quickly penetrate the zones from which warnings are received and perform preventive operations like those that have enabled terrorist attacks to be thwarted. "This system," says Weran Lerman, a former officer of the services, "enables us to conduct operations that are not pure, blind retributions: at this point, only an extreme right-wing hawk would invoke retributions."

But as effective as RMA is, it has an obvious limitation, namely, the great influence ideology has on Palestinian society and the cult of the suicide terrorist. Professor Ariel Merari, a well-known psychoanalyst who takes part in all the peace negotiations and all the war councils and who has conducted dozens of studies on the psychic and social structure of suicide terrorism, points to social approval of and social pressures on the suicide as a fundamental factor of the terrorist upsurge, although there are certainly those opposed to it (a phenomenon that surveys indicate is on the rise) and who reject it. The terrorist is neither insane nor depressed and therefore not predisposed to dying; nor is he an ignorant individual or a religious fanatic. He is a man, a boy, a young woman steeped in youthful ardor, whether patriotic or religious doesn't matter, but above all enamored of approval and fame. He has soaked up ideological coercion from school textbooks, from Arafat's speeches and those of other charismatic leaders, and from incessant television programs, like the one cited earlier. The Arab world sends back a grandiose echo, which further drives the shahid to prepare himself for "martyrdom": Bashar al-Assad exalts them, the Iranians adore them, the Hezbollah actually threaten them if they stop committing suicide.

Their act is not suicide, but an act of war, the most exalted and morally most rewarding—not to mention Saddam Hussein's payment of $25,000 to the family of the *shahid* and the assistance of the Saudis, always ready to help those who survive the suicide terrorists. The walls in every city are plastered with their pictures and the eulogies. By this time, Merari explains, once Al-Fatah, Arafat's secular organization, assumed leadership for the attacks with its Al Aqsa Martyrs Brigades, the fusion is complete. Recent attacks have not been claimed by one single organization, not just to avoid reprisals but because there is a great deal of blending by now. The territorial-Islamic appeal operates on the basis that the more Jews that are killed, the more successful the action has been.

"Most likely the sixteen-year-old boy already wearing his belt who was stopped by soldiers yesterday, fortunately before he could touch the detonator, had been observed, then enlisted, then filled with worldly promises for his family and otherworldly promises (paradise) for himself. Then once he was ready, he was probably filmed in a typical video in which, dressed in martyr's clothing, Koran and submachine gun in hand, he declared himself one of the living dead for Al Quds, for his own people, for the mosque. This way, the boy can't pull back; the people responsible for him who accompany him to his death are always with him. In fact, there are also those who, in addition to patriotic words, write to their mothers: 'I'm sorry, but I have no choice.'"

Suicide terrorism loses weight, however, to the extent that it does not attain its political outcome, namely that of provoking rash reactions so that the enemy society falls apart while at the same time launching its army in violent operations, which call forth international intervention and give Arafat what he wants. It has not happened: Arafat wanted international pressure also brought upon Israel, and Europe satisfied him, but the same pressure was brought upon him by the United States. Terrorism is too big a risk after September 11. We are no longer in the Munich years when Abu Jiiad remarked on the massacre of the Israeli athletes: "I don't give a damn what they say about us Palestinians, as long as they talk about our cause." Today, using terrorism, you can always attract a big audience, but you can also lose your life.

# Arafat's Government Ledger

Sheets of paper bearing the letterhead of the Office of the President of the PLO and of the Palestinian Authority, topped by the little royal eagle with outstretched wings, were found in drawers in Arafat's office and that of his chief administrator, Fuad Shoubaki, with lists of illegal weapons and explosive devices. Ariel Sharon waved the papers in front of the Knesset assembly, evidence gathered during ten days of war in Ramallah, Tulkarem, Jenin, Nablus; ten days during which, as the battle raged, no office remained inviolate, numerous houses were searched, hundreds of pounds of arms and explosives were seized (with many belts already prepared), two thousand Palestinians were stopped, and about a third were detained on suspicion of being members of suicide terrorist organizations. The three documents that Sharon held in his hand weren't the only ones found: we receive them along with others from a female official of the army's secret services (Aman), and as might logically be expected, Palestinian sources describe them as an Israeli falsification.

The most important of the documents is a brief letter: "To Brother Abu Amar, may God protect you, greetings"; a request for $2,500 each for three militants follows. The first of them is the most significant. He is Ra'ed el Karmi, commander of the Tanzim of Tulkarem, responsible for the deaths of twenty-three Israelis. Killed by his hand were two Tel Aviv restaurateurs who had entered Tulkarem; he was arrested and then released by Jibril Rajoub. He became the local boss of the Al Aqsa Martyrs Brigades, specializing in car ambushes and subsequently in organizing suicide terrorists. The Authority had never wanted to arrest him. His elimination by the Israelis provoked a chain of attacks by way of reaction. Below the request for payment, Arafat writes in his own hand: "give each one $600" and, having discounted the price, signs his signature. The second one to be collected on is Ziad Muhammed Das, commander of a group of Tanzim who planned and carried out the bar mitzvah attack in Hedera. Six victims because of him. The last one, Amar Qadam, is without further details, an official of Force 17, Arafat's personal security guards. Perhaps he is not a terrorist.

The second document, this time bearing the insignia of the Al Aqsa Mosque and the crossed rifles found in the offices of Arafat's administrator, is a bill presented to the president signed by the suicide terrorist group of the Al Aqsa Martyrs Brigades, responsible for almost all of the most important terrorist attacks in recent times. Listed are the expenses they incurred. One item reads: "Cost of various electrical and chemical components for preparation of bomb charges. This was the biggest expense. Every bomb prepared costs at least 700 shekels. We need from 5 to 9 bombs a week for our cells in various areas. 5,000 shekels for 4 weeks = 20,000 shekels." A shekel equals about ten cents. Other items request various funding, for example, to produce the martyrs' pictures on wood for the funerals. The names of the martyrs are then listed. There is also a request for a great quantity of ammunition: 22,500 shekels for Kalashnikovs and 60,000 for M-16s.

Sharon's third document is a list of illegal weapons, that is, in violation of the Oslo Accords, accumulated by the Authority. There are all types: from seven RPG-7 antitank rocket launchers with their projectiles. These weapons were accrued and distributed in various areas of the Authority. There are documents, related to these, in which the Al Aqsa Martyrs Brigades ask Shubaki to finance an ambitious plan to construct a factory for heavy weapons such as artillery missiles and mortars, similar to the Qassam-Two, long-range artillery rockets (all weapons prohibited by the Oslo Accords). The sum requested is $100,000 plus $15,000 for outstanding expenses. Shubaki is involved in the *Karine A* affair, the ship that was transporting fifty tons of arms made in Iran to the Palestinian Authority.

Another document to which the Israelis attribute great importance is a report by Hamdi Al Darduch, head of the intelligence department in Tulkarem, for one of the most powerful men closest to Arafat: Rafik Tirawi. It describes the situation of the armed militants of Fatah in Tulkarem. It tells about their various terrorist operations, and says that funding comes from President Arafat. It describes their terrorist attacks within Area A (in Israel) and outside. It then describes the three squads in depth, their level of militancy and how the factions were left to their own initiative and then, instead, "developed the concept that the armed militants of Al-Fatah constitute first and foremost the main corps and support of the Palestinian Authority and its security apparatus."

# The Psychology of Terror

Children and their mothers in a pastry shop. From behind the glass window, Shiri Cohen, eleven years old (now in the hospital), notices a particularly odd motorcyclist, and from the hospital she later tells how he got off his motorcycle to come closer and scrutinize the children: "And then he exploded with us . . . that's it, and the very little children died." Shiri is silent. Her truth has now been told, the black knight came on horseback and brought death to the pastry shop. The children are really dead, but Shiri is hallucinating about the motorcyclist: it seems the terrorist came in a yellow Subaru. Or . . . who knows: everyone sees his own specter.

One of the primary consequences of the continuous sequence of terrorism in a modern society, besides the horrible grief and loss of freedom, is the psychological and social confusion. Death strikes young and old the same way; even if you don't do anything dangerous, you won't be spared, not even in a café or at school. The death of children precedes that of parents and grandparents in an era of assured longevity. People remain blind, deaf, lame in an age of obligatory well-being. Night does not bring repose; Saturday is no longer a day of rest. One's own wedding can be an occasion for death.

Two famous psychologists, Professors Ronnie Berger and Muli Lahad, conducted an extensive inquiry during this year and a half of catastrophic, uninterrupted terrorism to understand what has happened to people. The report speaks of "PTSD disease," post-traumatic stress disorder, which is quite widespread. It has both short-term and long-term results. In the short term, people lose their appetite and the ability to sleep. They regard their loved ones with infinite anxiety. Their own life seems devastated, and they may fall into clinical depression. Those who react with strength and courage (and they are the majority in Israel), continuing to do the things they always do, may experience delayed symptoms: frequent heart attacks, failed immunological systems, cancer.

Social expectations have changed: if you were a schoolteacher, you are transformed into a guardian who must above all defend the children; if you are a parent, instead of focusing on your children's upbringing, you must devote yourself to their safety; if earlier you thought that a public park was a place for playing or that the cinema represented a well-deserved moment of relaxation, now you have to be on the highest state of alert in all these places. Every person dressed in a loose-fitting garment is regarded as a possible terrorist; suspicion is essential. Even your home is no longer a refuge after children have been killed in their beds.

What is broken, Lahad explains, is that precious bridge between yesterday and tomorrow, which allows a life plan. Children are impacted the most; their eyes are wide open on a reality that contradicts the loving upbringing that Israeli society offers them. They are afraid; they don't know what to think. And the adults are in a bind. "When my son was little," Lahad says, "he told me once, 'I don't want to be a soldier, because I'm afraid of dying.' I answered him as everyone does: 'When you grow up, it won't be necessary to serve in the military any more.' Now I hear parents respond: 'Don't worry, there are many different kinds of duties in the army.'"

Is Israeli society therefore in despair? On the contrary, the psychologists reply, it's strong, closely knit. It resorts to the traditional endurance of the Jewish people, survivors even of the Shoah, and is determined to defend its nation. It conducts itself based on the idea that if you are defeated, too many wonderful things are lost—culture, wealth, democracy. For this reason, the scientists suggest that we create islands of endurance, "islands of resiliency"—a hobby, a love affair, a book—to stand up to the cyclopean wave.

## The Targets

They get on the bus with a sandwich from home, their mother or a brother accompanies them to the final hour of their life. Many are returning to the base. They are often conscripted soldiers obliged to a long period of service. Their pictures that are now in all the newspapers, in color, seem like photos of kids in the third year of secondary school. Instead, they represent a phenomenon that is unparalleled in Western society: in this terrorist paroxysm, in fact, fathers and mothers bury their children. The fourteen young people (plus two adults) killed yesterday in Megiddo have fair and dusky faces, light and dark eyes: from Morocco, Russia, Iran, the Ukraine, Sabra. All the faces are smooth, however, unblemished; these are sons and daughters who are still children in a society where life, holidays, unfold in the maternal nest.

Irena, the mother of David Stanislavsky, twenty-three years old, had only this one son. A widow, she immigrated from the Ukraine with him a year and a half ago. David had been a big help to his mother on the path to integration "with his sense of humor," Irena says, "his optimism." David had just bought an airline ticket: he was going to pick up his fiancée Victoria. In the Ukraine, a feast was ready and waiting. Irena, in her abysmal solitude, murmurs: "I can't bring myself to call Victoria to cancel it."

Adi Dahan, shoulder-length curls, blue eyes, was seventeen years old; they buried her next to her brother Shlomi, twenty-five, who two months ago fell from a peak in the Arava desert. Her family is from Afula, Eastern women with scarves on their heads. Her mother paces back and forth unceasingly calling her "my beautiful girl, my intelligent girl." Her brother had accompanied her to the bus a half hour earlier than usual because their older sister had no place to leave the children: Adi wanted to baby sit for her.

Violetta Hizgayev, nineteen years old, a soldier, was very excited about being a teacher to the soldiers. Both her mother and father were dead, and therefore she lived with her aunt in Hedera. Her brother was supposed to take the bus with her, but a medical appointment detained him. She was meticulous, quiet; every once in a while she complained about not having a boyfriend. She never got to have one. The girlfriend with whom she spent the night in Tel Aviv said good-bye for the last time as Violetta pulled the covers up over her.

Lior Avitan, nineteen years old, from Hedera, with very dark hair and eyes, from a poor, Eastern family, seemed already to be a woman. That morning before going out she cleaned the kitchen, did the shopping: "She was like a mother to her sisters and little brothers." She was always looking after a little brother who had difficulty moving. The army was her joy.

In the photo, Sivan Viner appears beautiful and childlike, with a radiant face; she turned nineteen two days ago. She had celebrated her birthday with her family and later with friends at a Tel Aviv discothèque. She was tops in athletics at her high school. She was a member of the popular corps de ballet at the Ort Leibowitz School in Netanya. Her father is returning from Prague for the funeral. Her brother Dudu who had accompanied her to the bus, had phoned her half an hour later to see if everything was all right; she had reassured him. After an hour, the cell phone rang in vain.

Sariel Katz, twenty-one years old, was skilled with the computer, his specialty in the army. Extremely thin, not very talkative, he was a sports lover and a volunteer. Ygal Nedipur, twenty-two, worked as a waiter in Netanya when he was on leave from the army because his family was in chronic difficulty. His little sister says that now that he is dead, she is afraid, because he protected all of them. Zvika Gelberd, twenty years old, his hair standing straight up with brilliantine, is laughing in the photo like so many of the others who were killed: "No one ever saw him sad. He was a great soccer player; he was crazy about the world championships." He leaves behind his parents, Tamar and Yehuda.

## Sharon: The Statesman

Maybe Ariel Sharon dreams that Arafat will flee the country making a victory sign, like in the days of Lebanon, when Sharon made him take flight. But Sharon doesn't say so: and he didn't look at all pleased yesterday when he declared Arafat an enemy and announced yet another war for the state of Israel (a defensive war, he explained, against terrorism and no more); when he repeated—after a sleepless night spent in head-to-head combat with his ministers, tormented by news of still more terrorist attacks—that given the strategy that Arafat had chosen (he said it four times—terror, terror, terror, terror—as though to explain the enormity of the bloodbath) there was no room for negotiations. For the first time his foreign minister, Shimon Peres, eluded him by abstaining, though he spoke very harsh words against the massacres of the past few days. Defense Minister "Fuad" Ben Eliezer said it loud and clear: "We'll go, but only if you promise me not to touch Arafat." And throughout the night, the right had hammered him with exclamations: Enough, we have to put an end to Arafat who tricks us, who talks of peace and sends terrorists. We have to force him to flee; he must be eliminated somehow from the political scene. Yvette Liebermann had even talked of physical elimination. Sharon's body had become a defensive shield.

That terrible session of the entire government, with death bulletins that continued to come from the hospitals and from the police, that went on from eleven o'clock at night until morning when Sharon, accompanied by his band of ministers appeared before the press, gave no pleasure to the man who is called a hawk and whose name, in Europe, is always written with that epithet. In reality, Sharon would have preferred a fate like de Gaulle's: a tough general who brings about peace. And he tried to show it in every way, receiving a thankless fate in exchange. From the start of his term of office, when the intifada had already begun, stirred up but not caused by his walk among the mosques (in fact, it had already been underway since the time of Arafat's refusal at Camp David, three months earlier), Sharon had promised to bring back peace and security, even if it meant making "painful concessions." He wasn't able to do it. And yet during seventeen months of unremitting terrorist attacks he tried (in part because he was restrained by Peres and the Americans) to contain his responses within limits that would allow him, on the one hand, not to lose key government players on the left and, on the other hand, to show signs that he understood the desperation of his injured people. He insisted that he had chosen to strike terrorist structures, even though the Palestinian population was often caught up in the strikes. The number of deaths was very high, but Sharon maintains that it was never intentional, and that they always tried to strike just the terrorists, though the latter hid among the crowds. He confined Arafat, but he always left the door open to his possible rehabilitation regarding the struggle against terrorism. He continued the occupation, but he always said he wanted to reopen the question, limiting the number of settlements.

He came on the scene as the general who was able to win the war of 1973, who considered it proper to build in the territories, who in 1948, in Latrun, was wounded in the stomach while winning the siege of Jerusalem, but also as the man accused by the Palestinians of being responsible for the massacre of Sabra and Chatila, in which Maronite Christians executed a horrible vendetta in the refugee camp and he was unable to stop them (this was the judgment in two trials). The Palestinians have always portrayed him as a man who hates their people and Arafat in particular. They have demonized him, achieving a chorus of consent in Europe.

In reality, Sharon has never shown any signs of feelings of hatred. If anything, he's shown determination to break terrorism with force, on the one hand never going beyond a day-to-day strategy, while keeping the door to negotiations open on the other. This is why, for example, he declared a cease-fire three times, without reciprocation; why he didn't react after the massacre at the Dolphinarium discothèque, nor after the recent horrible massacres in Jerusalem or even Netanya. But he never wanted to leave the settlements without there being a halt to the terror first. He came down hard on the refugee camps in search of a way to eradicate terrorism, which in fact turned out to be impossible. Perhaps his greatest sin in the eyes of the world was that of having embodied a return to harsh reality, one without Nobel Peace prizes, after Arafat's refusal of Barak's offer of 97 percent of the territories and after the magnificent dream of Rabin and Peres.

Sharon has always considered Arafat an enemy, and certainly in recent months, his aversion has increased. But the man remained even-tempered until March 2002 yielded 103 Israeli deaths from terrorism and 845 injured. Yesterday, he appeared before the press and the entire world with a heaviness that he would have liked to avoid despite his long-term lack of trust, his considerable contempt for Yasir Arafat, whom he has always considered a terrorist rather than a statesman. His frustration in the last few days must have been enormous and must have brought him insults and ridicule. After the arrival of Zinni, the American envoy, Sharon made a number of moves that should and could have led to a cease-fire. He cleared out Area A as soon as Zinni got there; then he retracted the famous seven-days-with-no-attacks he had required before going on to the measures contained in the Tenet document. He declared a cease-fire; he told Arafat he could leave for Beirut if he too would declare a cease-fire, and that he would let him return in peace if there were no terrorist attacks during the days of the summit. Again and again he asked the rais for a statement against terrorism, for some move on his part indicating that the Tenet and Mitchell talks could go forward.

But by this time, the distrust was enormous. Arafat did not want to disarm his men before being given a signal of clear, immediate gain. Here, perhaps, Sharon might have made a more inspired gesture, created a better incentive. He didn't do so; it seemed to him that he had done enough given the great number of attacks. His bitterness grew when he realized that international opinion seemed only aware of Arafat's confinement, not of the catastrophic terrorist acts in Israel. And then, in the last few hours, how astounding that no one in the world took into account the ambulance that, in addition to a mother and three children, carried an explosives belt to its destination, or that the killing of two international observers of the TIPH (Temporary International Presence in Hebron), an intervention force, was met with silence.

Even Sharon can feel alone in the sea of blood flowing from his people who were killed at the Easter celebration; he too can feel helpless even though he must insist that he is strong. Sharon was so shocked and angered in recent days as a result of the contempt Arafat seemed to show him that he refused Zinni's demands. What! Is it possible, Sharon repeated to himself many times in recent weeks, that I have to yield while Arafat doesn't give an inch? Though maintaining his usual determined demeanor, Sharon was worn and tired when he declared war after twenty-four deaths had occurred in twenty-four hours. He would have liked to go down in history as the prime minister who had restored peace and security, showing the world that he is not a hawk, but a lion, as his first name, Ariel, tells us, whose strength, he always says, lies in even-tempered composure. But the fate of being a tough aggressor plagues him, along with Arafat's shadow, which has always been behind him, for his entire life.

# Netanyahu

While it seemed obvious to the entire world that Bibi Netanyahu was renewing his reputation as a hawk by having the Likud Central Committee vote on a motion stating that they did not want a Palestinian state, no one raised an eyebrow, and this is quite surprising, when Sharon crossed over from the hawks to the doves. And yet in theory, Sharon should have been an avowed enemy of both the Palestinian state and peace in general, according to the stereotype that accompanies him. Therefore, it might be worthwhile to venture into some considerations about what happened in the central committee.

Sharon: The prime minister paid a heavy price, that of being in the minority although he leads a nation in a state of extreme emergency, choosing the logic of political overture to the world over partisan logic. Actually, he has remained loyal to his policy since the beginning of the intifada: no yielding to terrorism, but a readiness to make "painful concessions"—the compromises he has always said he was prepared to negotiate as soon as the suicide terrorist attacks stopped. Sharon has also declared many times that he is prepared for the birth of a Palestinian state, with the guarantee that it would not be a base for launching persistent operations against Israel. His statement six months ago caused a stir: "We Israelis will be the ones to give the Palestinians what they have never had, namely, a state." He recently made this promise to Bush, as well, and has given his word to Shimon Peres and Fuad Ben Eliezer, his ministers of foreign affairs and defense, both Labor Party members. And Sharon has remained faithful to his word.

Netanyahu: as is known, the former prime minister is in the race for the next term of office, and he thinks that yesterday's move gives him an advantage. It's a risk, because Likud's view, contrary to that of the central committee, is not favorable to his policy, and the "peace index" always shows those prepared to abandon the territories at almost 70 percent. In addition, Netanyahu is a little out of phase: Sharon has fought but without committing massacres; he entered Area A, but did not remain there; he has been implacable regarding Arafat but hasn't harmed him; he has lashed out against terrorism but without disrupting the nation's structure. By doing so, he has set up a chapter that has yet to be played out in which, for the first time, Arafat is truly called into question. The price the Authority paid to Operation Defense Shield is truly enormous, and new leadership is cautiously arising. Furthermore, Netanyahu disturbs Bush a lot. In short, he had a motion passed that might turn out to be irrelevant because if things go forward with the various peace conferences, the Saudis, and Palestinian reform, the Likud motion will be just an outdated piece of paper, and Sharon will be pleased to initiate a new peace process, just as Begin did with Sadat. If this were to happen within a year and a half, that is by the time of the next elections, Sharon would defeat Netanyahu. But as usual, the terrorists have the last word: Just as Sharon rose to Barak's position because of them, so Netanyahu could be elected instead of Sharon— by the Palestinians much more so than by the Israelis.

# Sharon: The "Hawk"?

Perhaps it is really time to take another look at the stereotype of the perfidious Sharon, Sharon the hawk, the man who has always dreamed of killing Arafat and who compulsively pursues his dream. It is an unfortunate, trite image, which Sharon has tried in vain to disprove since the beginning of his term of office—an image burdened by recurrent accusations regarding the Sabra and Chatila massacre, though it's true that two courts found him guilty of not having been able to prevent it. A serious accusation for a defense minister, but certainly a lot less serious than the one that might have fallen upon (it never happened!) the now-defunct Eli Hobeika, leader of the Maronite Christian militants, who planned the savage operation and carried it out.

Sharon has led the government in a situation in which his mission has been literally impossible, since it takes two sides to bring about peace: He has been faced with a wall of extremism that is unprecedented, an incitement to hatred that has anti-Semitic overtones. And above all, the gigantic, strategic barrier of suicide terrorism, the real Islamic atomic bomb. Arafat had simply rejected the territorial agreement. He could not accept a Jewish state alongside Palestine and continued pointing to the three Khartoum "no's" of 1967—no peace, no recognition, no negotiation. This is the platter Sharon found served up to him. Could he have withdrawn from the territories unilaterally? No. A Palestinian state, though necessary to bring an end to the conflict, must not become a reserve of Iranian and Iraqi weapons (long-range missiles as well) for the Tanzim, Hamas, and the Hezbollah. Sharon must sit down and negotiate. But while it is true that it is necessary to negotiate to bring about peace, Arafat simply did not want to. Terror has occupied the political scene. An ideological terrorism, intent on driving out the state of Israel—prey to a lulling territorial perspective—or else dictated outright by Islamic extremism.

What Sharon is reproached for today is also his policy of returning blow for blow. In reality, faced with one of the bloodiest terrorist attacks ever, the Tel Aviv discothèque with twenty-five teenagers killed as they sought some enjoyment on the beach, Sharon did not react. Nor did he retaliate after the wave of attacks in Jerusalem. On his first day in office, he sent a personal letter to Arafat proposing an

agreement to spare civilians and begin talks. Nothing. Upon the urging of the European Union and the Americans, Sharon has declared
a cease-fire approximately ten times; at every truce, the checkpoints,
finally eased (since it is tragic to impose limits on the Palestinians'
freedom), were then used by terrorists to enter. The Tenet plan, the
Mitchell plan—both were accepted. Is it all just a trick, as Arafat
says? Let him put it to the test by ordering an end to terrorism.

Meanwhile, we can see that Sharon has renounced the seven-
days-with-no-attacks required before talks could begin; that he has
sent his son Omri to Arafat a number of times; and that he adheres
at least in part to a plan for peace that Shimon Peres was able to define with Abu Allah. Now he has declared himself ready to meet
with the Arab countries, praising the Saudis' plan that proposes a
withdrawal from all the 1967 Territories in exchange for peace.
Those who want to view the war of the past few weeks as an extreme
action, do not realize that Israeli society is on the edge of collapse,
what with 150 people killed and 800 injured in cafés, buses, and religious ceremonies during the month of March. What could any nation have done but defend its citizens? And while it is terrible to add
up the number of Palestinians and Israelis killed, to see the humanitarian disasters created by the situation, nevertheless to attribute
them to a kind of madness that emanates from Sharon and is transmitted to the army is a form of pure prejudice that would not be applied to any other state but Israel.


# Israel Day, Rome     APRIL 15, 2002

Let us welcome, then, Israel Day—organized by *Il Foglio* newspaper—which enables us to establish general and specific principles on
which we believe men of sound judgment and feelings of decency
should come together. Israel, during the course of these twenty
months of the intifada, has endured what the United States also experienced on September 11: catastrophic terrorism that decimates
your loved ones and your friends, that suddenly stuns you and
makes you see the impossibility of living your everyday life. The impossibility of going nonchalantly to a restaurant or to work or of
bringing the children to school without feeling the constant breath of
death around you; the relentless, irrational hatred that wants noth-

ing to do with peace talks or practical solutions, that is prepared to sacrifice its own life just to see yours destroyed. This cannot be: Italy, and the world, are well aware that suicide terrorism has immense potential, that it threatens all of us. It has little to do with issues of a territorial nature, which we hope can be quickly resolved to the satisfaction of both parties, once the wave of hatred has passed, by the creation of a Palestinian state with Israel's security assured.

But for the time being, something else has come into play: the huge dark cloud of suicide terrorism that has borne down on Jewish women, old people, children while they were eating a pizza, or playing, or traveling, that has left five hundred innocent people dead. We cannot accept this, we must defend the right to not have to endure terrorism; it is the worst of all human rights violations since it violates all of them.

In addition, this celebration in Italy will be an opportunity to reassert the fact that we disagree with, and intend to combat, the questioning of Israel's very existence by the Palestinians and by a large part of the Arab world, with the insinuation that Jews have an evil, colonialist, imperialist, scheming nature. Israel is the triumph of life over the appalling tragedy of the Holocaust, the landfall of the mortally wounded Jews, approved by the U.N. decision of 1967. As Martin Luther King says, those who are anti-Zionist today are in fact anti-Semitic. They hate the fact that the Jews are alive.

Finally, we go to this march to demand that media coverage about the conflict, so clearly one-sided, beginning with RAI television news, at long last becomes, if not balanced, at least reasonable, at least not propagandistic, at least not ignorant as it was, shamefully, with regard to the Bethlehem situation, for example. *Il Foglio* and *Panorama* magazine will continue to do their best.

# Interview with a Shahid

The suicide terrorist can't be recognized by sight; he doesn't have Satan's fangs or cloven hooves. He's a little shy, he wants to be cited as "Muhammad." He sits in the car with us (outside the temperature is 42 degrees centigrade) after a number of disorienting turns, which take us to the outskirts of a West Bank city. He doesn't ask for any compensation for speaking. His impending specific objective: to blow himself up with a belt or a satchel full of TNT and nails, thereby killing as many Jews as possible. He's thirty-five years old, with a striped T-shirt; he has a moustache and dark eyes. In his expression and in his words, we look for signs of the immense cruelty and destructive impact that this man's plan entails. Aside from some moments of extreme despondency in his gaze, we find mainly a dull lack of awareness, a repetitive, conformist mentality, a complete ignorance of events. The man has three brothers and three sisters; he speaks affectionately of his mother who is a widow. He's poor; he has not suffered losses from the intifada, but he knows people who have. He has a simple job and supports a large family. Although he has a positive recollection of the time of the peace process, Israeli occupation is a pervasive theme for him. In his view, the Israelis are an all-absorbing, absolute font of all evil—as though their very presence prevented him from thinking of any other subject, any other plan. He is religious. He doesn't appear to be insane, and certainly he is not a person who is suffering for the most part. He is the exponent of a new, widespread type of individual who considers terrorism a normal way to liberate his land, as well as to aspire to social excellence.

**FN:** Did you nominate yourself to become a suicide terrorist? (I use the expression "suicide bomber," which he understands even without a translation.)

**M:** Yes, I let it be known that I am prepared to sacrifice myself to give my people a nation, since they have nothing while the Israelis have everything: a nation, an army, houses, cars, wealth . . . Their oppression drives us to what you call terrorism, but the fault is totally Sharon's and the suffering that he inflicts on us.

**FN:** After you nominated yourself, what happened?

**M:** At this point, I know that they are assessing me. There are organizations that investigate, inquire . . .

**FN:** All the organizations, Hamas, Jihad, Tanzim, together?

**M:** No, each one on its own.

**FN:** Did they actually ask you to blow yourself up in Israel? Will you be trained?

**M:** I can say that there is a process underway, that things are moving ahead.

**FN:** Are you expecting the order to come at any moment?

**M:** Those in charge will decide when. I can choose the place.

**FN:** And where do you want to carry out your attack? In Jerusalem? In Tel Aviv?

**M:** For me the Israelis are all soldiers, and therefore every city is a military barracks.

**FN:** Are the children soldiers, too? Even the newborns that have been killed in the attacks?

**M:** The shahids never killed a child.

**FN:** Well, actually, that's not true. Many children have been killed in terrorist attacks.

**M:** Never, not even one. Those are propaganda lies. Palestinian television gives accurate information about the martyrs, and a child has never been killed, nor even wounded.

**FN:** Believe me, there are many children among those who have died in the bombing attacks and a great many among the wounded as well.

**M:** That's not true. [Mohammed shows signs of impatience, his escorts signal to me to stop.] Go and look in the Israeli hospitals; there are no children there.

**FN:** That's not so.

**M:** It is so.

**FN:** So then, if you saw children around, you wouldn't activate the device?

**M:** It won't happen. There are no children around. Things are always well organized.

**FN:** Do you have a family?

**M:** A wife and three children. The oldest is twelve.

**FN:** And what will become of them?

**M:** You see up there, on that hill? If an Israeli wants to shoot me now out of hatred, or just for fun, I could die right this minute. That's how the Israelis are. So it's better that I choose my death to give my people a nation.

**FN:** Don't you think that your house might be destroyed after your death? Aren't you afraid of the instant when you will have to activate the belt? Don't you think about your mother?

**M:** My house could be destroyed in any case. As for being afraid, of course a martyr is afraid, but above all he is happy to help liberate his land. As for my mother, she doesn't know anything about it, and neither does my wife. My mother would try to stop me. But afterwards, they will be happy to have given their country a hero.

**FN:** Do you know that Saddam Hussein sends a monetary reward of $25,000 to the families of the suicides?

**M:** I know that, just as I know that he sends $10,000 to the families of those killed in battle. But I am not doing it for the money.

**FN:** Your wife will be overcome with grief, and perhaps your oldest son will follow you.

**M:** If he does, it will mean that he is proud of his father and that he is still enduring the occupation. If my loved ones weep, that makes me sad and happy at the same time. We Palestinians suffer in any case: and martyrdom renders our suffering useful.

**FN:** And if the opposite were true? Perhaps it is terrorism itself that keeps your state out of reach.

**M:** With Sharon and Bush no peace is possible. Earlier, it might have been.

**FN:** But if peace should come, and your Palestinian state as well, you will not be able to enjoy them if you kill yourself. Not only that, the Koran forbids suicide.

**M:** Martyrdom is not suicide, it is part of the jihad to liberate our land. It is the jihad for Al Aqsa and therefore for God. I will be in Paradise when Palestine is liberated.

**FN:** And will you enjoy the liberation of your land in Paradise?

**M:** I don't know. Only the angels see for sure. What is certain is that I will enjoy paradise.

**FN:** Do you believe that a paradise of pleasures will open its doors to you?

**M:** Yes, and very soon: I will see God up close, in a place where you can satisfy every desire, where everything is beautiful, where a river of yogurt and honey flows . . .

**FN:** Do you believe that you will be surrounded by seventy virgins?

**M:** Of course, why not? The Koran promises it.

**FN:** Were you able to study as a child?

**M:** Yes, I attended school through the first year of high school, I stopped going on account of the Israeli occupation.

**FN:** In what sense?

**M:** I went to prison for two years, I was already a militant.

**FN:** Do you enjoy life? What gives you satisfaction in your daily life?

**M:** I enjoy life, of course, my children and my wife more than anything, but the most important thing is a liberated Palestine.

**FN:** Are you pleased by the attack on the Twin Towers?

**M:** Not particularly. Americans should be attacked only when they are soldiers. Otherwise, I am only interested in our right to our land that is here.

**FN:** How many Israelis would you like to kill with your explosion to make it worthwhile?

**M:** Even one would make it worthwhile as long as we make the Israelis realize that we will attack everywhere until we achieve liberation.

**FN:** If Arafat were to say "stop suicide terrorism," would you obey him?

**M:** If they were to give us everything that is due to us, Arafat as well as Yassin would order us to stop. But would the people want to? Imagine if my wife wanted to avenge me after my death by becoming a shahid, who would be able to stop her? Who could have stopped Ayjat el Akrash, the sixteen-year-old martyr from Bethlehem?

**FN:** Why do you admire her especially? Doesn't it bother you that she died so young, ripping apart three innocent people at a supermarket, among them a seventeen-year-old Israeli girl?

**M:** I only hope that I will soon be called upon to follow her, to vanquish the Israelis and liberate suffering Palestine.

# Terrorism: A New Religion I

The idea put forth by those who want to try to help resolve the Middle East crisis, namely, that it might be useful to others and to ourselves to accept the thirteen Palestinians from the Church of the Nativity as guests here in Italy, perhaps with clear terms to avoid eventual misunderstandings, is undoubtedly a meritorious, humanitarian one. Those who imagine that this has anything to do with safeguarding the peace, however, and in particular that it may be of some practical use to our country (as former head of state Francesco Cossiga seems to think when he affirms "it would mean having Arafat and the Palestinian terrorist organizations sign a certificate of guarantee against terrorist attacks in Italy") are forgetting what has occurred over the past ten years. Both the Hezbollah and Al Qaeda, have in fact supplied terrorism with an international theoretical and practical structure that has a very strong hold: it is not concerned with irredentist or territorial issues, but inflames other organizations, even those not genetically religious, with the intent of going back to fundamentalist Islam and its ancient power.

Up until a few years ago Middle East terrorism had a dimension that was chiefly territorial: It exported confiscated arms and bombs in an appeal to public opinion to support territorial causes. Today, even those who undoubtedly have a territorial claim, like the Palestinian groups, from Al-Fatah's Al Aqsa Martyrs Brigades to Hamas, feel a great attraction to a cause that is much greater. Italy is a country that much as it may make an effort to appear friendly, will never be so deep down because it is a fundamentally Western nation, Atlantic-oriented, democratic, critical, if you wish, but essentially a friend or, better yet, a relative, of both the United States and Israel. Terrorism has acquired a substantial ideological dimension that is self-sufficient and self-serving; it is an act of affirmation, delusion, and revenge that knows no bounds. As various ideologists (whether Egyptian, Lebanese, or Palestinian) write, terrorism is now a great force worldwide that has its own intrinsic ethics and aesthetics, a force that links itself with other fundamentalist groups such as the antiglobal factions or those of the old Communist persuasion. We have already seen many instances of terrorism in Italy, from the hijacking of the Achille Lauro to the carnage at Fiumicino, and the fact that the Munich massacre partially originated in Italy. Terrorists in the seventies and eighties often made it clear that they were fighting for the Palestinian and Arab cause. Later on, in the nineties, the horizon broadened. Now all the countries from which terrorism fans out have ties that bind them together and link them to other terrorist branches in the name of vast ideals. We Italians would really be deluding ourselves if we thought we could find a license to slip out of the enormous conflict that is underway.

# Terrorism: A New Religion II

The dynamics of Palestinian terrorism is at this point twisted and mysterious. This time, following several weeks of respite, a very great effort was made to massacre young people. Instead of the usual suicide terrorist, we saw a real, unified commando operation in the style of (and probably with the help of) the Hezbollah. From Al-Fatah to Hamas, with mines, weapons, stolen uniforms, and escape routes, all the organizations put forth the best they had, breaking through the Israeli army's siege, which nonetheless has prevented so many terrorist attacks during this period.

If you look at it from a standpoint of political justification, the matter is totally incomprehensible. Terrorism, suicidal or not, has never worked except within a logic totally internal to the world of the jihad. In that world the battle for good, which is religious, against an enemy who is also God's enemy has a value in and of itself; the martyr and the warrior are saints. For a long time Arafat was seen as a political man who was tough but reasonable, and Palestinian society was viewed as more modern than many other Eastern societies. The terrorist attacks changed the world's viewpoint and run the risk of reducing the Palestinian cause to minimum terms. Now the attacks are again occurring coercively, after the strategy of bringing Israel to its knees and forcing the world to support the Palestinian cause failed.

Arafat's power is in its death throes over Bush's demand that he create the only Arab democracy in the world. As for the hypothetical elections of 2003, announced by the rais, it is not even known whether he will be a candidate or if instead he will be retired to an honorary role. Saleh Abdul Jaawad, head of the political science and history department of the University of Bir Zeit, clearly states that never before has the rais been in such serious difficulty: "You Westerners are satisfied with 50.1 percent, but Arafat, who is the symbol of our struggle for liberation, wants much more." But the condition, for him as well, was to let Bush push Sharon into giving him economic relief, so that people might forget the corruption of the ruling class for a time and settle down comfortably with hope. Given that there were no further attacks for more than three weeks after June 20, 2002, a fact that tragically is a considerable record for Israel by now, Arafat could have obtained some results at this time: The "Quartet"—the United States, Russian, the EU, and the United Nations—these days talks of him and him alone, about his future, about his reforms.

Yet the explosion of bombs is heard again from the Palestinian side, photos of children armed to the teeth are back in the newspapers. For hours, television airs clips with songs that praise the martyrs. Can all this be stopped? Why is it happening? Where does the great desire for death that invests an entire society come from? A few days ago, Noah Salameh, a Palestinian activist who favors dialogue and the director of the Center for Conflict Resolution and Reconciliation, was talking with his twelve-year-old daughter who was returning from a basketball game in Bethlehem: the girl told him that she wanted to become a suicide terrorist. She explained to Salameh that "at school everyone is talking about Ayyat Ahras, the seventeen-year-old suicide who killed two Israelis and injured twenty-eight at the Jerusalem supermarket. She is the heroine of all my friends. Her organization, the Al Aqsa Martyrs Brigades, often comes to speak to us, and she is my heroine."

Revenge, patriotism, and anger at the base of a culture that, as an exponent of Hamas told an Israeli journalist, "loves death as much as you love life, and this makes us strong." That plus scant motivation toward the future and backward social relations and dealings between the sexes. A culture stifled by religion, and juvenile psychosis nourished by a maximalist, autocratic leadership cause 51.1 percent of Palestinians to see the goal of the intifada as "the liberation of all of Palestine," while 42.8 percent view it as "the end of Israeli occupation." Ali Jarbawi, a political scientist from the West Bank, says that if this 42 percent also feels disappointed in its expectations "then one moves toward extremism." But extremism is something quite different from the spasmodic killing of women and children (the count is at six hundred victims) from serial terrorism.

The explanation the Palestinians give is simple yet complex: S.H., a psychologist who lives in Rafah, says, "At the beginning of the intifada, when families began to suffer losses or someone lost a friend, people sought relief in revenge. A strong religious inspiration was then added; more and more women cover their heads; more men pray five times a day; very many people adore the Shahid. Religion, as always throughout history, became the defense of the poor."

But in this case, more than a defense, religion seems to have become an offensive tool. "This is because," says another psychologist, Dr. Mzeini, who once belonged to Hamas, "young people imagine that they are fated to die in any case, from the moment they experience death among their friends or family members. Therefore they decide on a predetermined death." Many say that the Palestinians undertake terrorist actions out of desperation. Hamas militants in particular respond to this with a resolute no, stating that it is purely a political and religious choice, not connected in any way to social or sociological conditions. Of course, we might add, the tens of thousands of dollars that both the Saudi Arabians and Saddam Hussein's regime ($25,000 per family) pay out to the terrorists' families tell a different story. Also important, according to Mzeini, is the promise of the seventy-two virgins and other delights related to paradise, given the condition of sexual apartheid that exists in Middle East societies. Women are promised one single man in eternal life. In actual fact, whether for reasons of revenge, religion, juvenile psychosis, hatred resulting from the occupation, a lack of other models or for reward, terrorism is now so popular in Palestinian society that even the intellectuals who signed the appeal against terrorism (among them Sari Nusseibah and Hanan Ashrawi) have not dared to state their reasons other than to say that it damages the Palestinian cause. Even the quasi-opposition that is now demanding reform does not mention terrorism but remains anchored to the themes of corruption and inability to govern. As Salameh puts it: "Stop the corruption, I say. But not stop the struggle against Israel." The Al Aqsa Martyrs Brigades are still there, even as Bush talks about the need for Arafat to reform the Authority.

# Terrorism: A New Religion III

The signal that the Americans are sending Arafat by considering the Al Aqsa Martyrs Brigades (the Brigades that belong to Al-Fatah itself, and that at this point claim responsibility for the majority of suicide attacks along with the Tanzim, another organization close to Arafat) a terrorist organization is a firm warning. But who knows if it will be enough. Arafat seems to have made a strategic decision: skip the Tenet accords that require him to disband his armed groups and force the Israelis and the Americans to discuss territorial concessions at once.

The weakness of this plan is that the suicide terrorist bombings of yesterday and the day before—one on a bus, the other in

Jerusalem—smack too intensely of barbarism. These attacks, which incredibly bring the number to nearly twelve thousand in eighteen months (not counting Molotov cocktails and stones), took place while a tenuous glimmer of hope was lit as a result of Dick Cheney's promise to meet with Arafat, and as a result of Sharon's repeated public declarations that he would accept both the Tenet accord with its cease-fire and other conditions and the Mitchell proposal in which "painful concessions" would be made. Indeed, crucial "cease-fire" meetings were underway. But Arafat, who has said more than once that he accepts the international documents and accords and that he condemns the attacks, in fact does not show the least sign of stopping his strongest strategic weapon. In part this is because it is capable of provoking Israeli reactions that are then condemned by the entire world. He is pushing the game, or letting it be pushed, to the point where the Israelis, he believes, will have to get on their knees and beg him for peace or else run away in fear. On the one hand, condemnation, on the other, the official radio station, the Voice of Palestine, to which he weakly explains that it is not the time for terror, while continuing to call the suicide terrorists "heroic martyrs": those who attacked civilians Tuesday night in the village of Aviezer in the Eilah valley and the one who blew up a bus in front of Uhm el Fahem ("a young Arab who became a heroic martyr"). Marwan Barghuty and other leaders called them terrorist acts: "a response to Israel as well as to the American position." A well-thought-out posture of defiance.

Suicide terrorism has become an irrepressible chapter of this conflict, a vicious strategic weapon, for the simple reason that it enjoys mass consensus (87 percent according to the University of Nablus) and is easily fueled by the dream of "liberating all of Palestine" (87.5 percent). An Arab television network recently broadcast a video of a suicide terrorist making a premortem claim with Koran and submachine gun in hand. The innovation consisted of his mother's presence in the video: In a calm tone, she thanks God for having given her a son destined to be a shahid and begs other mothers to emulate her by sending their sons and daughters to kill as many Israelis as possible. Another clip, with a joyful musical background, shows the training of young girls to become suicide terrorists. A photo portraying a nursery school shows a small child (perhaps five years old), very handsome in his TNT belt, a bandanna on his head; standing next to him are five real terrorist pretenders, masked and wearing belts. How can peace agreements be made when suicide terrorism, the most repellent and monstrous of weapons, becomes common practice, a game, something young people aspire to? Don't they understand, doesn't Europe understand, that this perversion can become a common model for exportation?

# Terrorism: A New Religion IV

In Israel on Wednesday a great many parents, brothers and sisters, boyfriends and girlfriends accompanied their deceased loved ones to the cemetery: all young people, between seventeen and twenty-two years of age. It was a massacre of innocents who were traveling from one part of the country to another on a regularly scheduled bus. At that age you have your whole life before you, you are full of dreams and love, even if you are serving in the army as a conscripted soldier, as happens in Israel. Each and every one of those young people were all torn from life in one single blow by the worst phenomenon of our time: suicide terrorism. An extremely potent weapon, which we saw at work on a grand scale on September 11 and which has left approximately five hundred people dead in Israel. A weapon that costs very little, that relies on the most powerful of incentives—fanaticism—and that is by far the most repellent of all forms of aggression.

Why the most repellent, given that so many people are killed by violence in other ways as well, for example, in the Israeli-Palestinian conflict during military incursions? First, because in contrast to a soldier in battle or even in the midst of a difficult mopping-up operation, the terrorist's deliberate objective is civilians. It is not by accident that he kills women and children; those are his preselected victims. The more of them he kills, the more successful is his operation. If an Israeli soldier happens to kill civilians, he does not do so intentionally, despite the fact that he may subsequently be censured for committing a grave error and penalized by his own superiors or government officials.

Second, the suicide terrorist violates all civil rights, each and every one of them, by hampering every manifestation of life. When schools and pizzerias, buses and parks, supermarkets and heavily traveled streets are threatened, life becomes a prison: adults and children live in a prison of fear, and essential rights like those of getting together, of teaching, of taking delight in living, are denied.

There are those who tend to justify, or in any case try to understand the terrorists, citing two main reasons: the first is the Israeli occupation of the territories, the second is a subjective justification that views suicide terrorists as young men who commit this act because they are desperate, without hope for the future. Neither of the two is completely accurate, although it should quickly be stated that it is essential that the two parties reach a peaceful solution that provides for two peoples and two nations existing safely side by side and that allows the Palestinians to invest in their children's future with the help of all of us. But this does not entail any justification for terrorism.

The occupation: up until September 2000, negotiations were underway that continued those that had formerly resulted in the Oslo Accords. Palestinian cities had already come under (and are still under) the Palestinian Authority, governed by Arafat. When Arafat refused the Camp David accord proposed to him by Ehud Barak and President Clinton for 97 percent of the territories and part of Jerusalem, a confrontation was unleashed that could have been avoided. Negotiations were broken off, and the Palestinian side thought it could obtain more by fighting. This is the point at which the terrorist attacks started. As for the subjective justification, the Palestinians are indeed impoverished and suffering: but during the years of the Oslo Accords they had begun to develop a growth economy, interrupted by the conflict. Their suffering has been enormously increased by the state of war; foreign investments ceased for that reason.

Nonetheless, the young people who choose the TNT belts belong to various social groups: they are students, farmers, builders, nurses, policemen, as well as unemployed. What they have in common is the experience of this war, which has made them suffer and endure the painful loss of family members and friends and above all a relentless indoctrination, from schools to television, from the photos of the martyrs on the walls of their cities and homes to the speeches of their leaders. They all exalt the suicide terrorist, especially if he is young, as the hero of their world, their times, and criminalize the enemy as a bloodthirsty monster, an inhuman nation. The desire to emulate the martyrs has extended to all young people, who are attracted to the glory and at times are responding to social and economic pressures as well: their families will be honored as well as compensated. Thus, their own lives, and those of so many young Israelis like them, are merely a chess game in which as many pawns as possible must be taken. The mother of a martyr, when he dies, even though her heart is broken, will maintain before the television cameras that she would like her other children to all become shahids, martyrs; the mother of the recent young Israeli victim will throw herself on the clods of earth that cover him, weeping for her son, her little prince.

# A Terrorist Traitor

This is an ugly story of terrorism, love, mental confusion, manipulative fanatics, and, in the end, healthy fear. It is the story, told to us yesterday in prison, of Sarin Ahmad, twenty years old, who on April 22 returned home after leaving her knapsack of ten kilos of TNT and nails in an old car in the center of Rishon le Tzion. This act saved only a few lives because Sarin's young male companion, sixteen-year-old Issa Badir, unlike her did the job thoroughly, killing three innocent victims in a little park. Courteous, well-mannered to the point of being affected, the repentant terrorist sits with her legs slightly apart, at ease, in the preventive detention prison at the end of the Russian Compound (the central police station) in Jerusalem; she's wearing a two-toned T-shirt and dark pants. Well-shaped eyebrows over oriental eyes highlight a round, rather common face; her gestures are midway between Eastern modesty and a certain brazenness. Ibrahim Sarahna, the suicide terrorist driver from Bethlehem whom we interviewed in these pages, brought her back home from Rishon le Tzion after she refused to blow herself up at the last minute. Sarahna's Ukrainian wife was cross about it: "My wife doesn't want me to see other women." "That day," Sarin tells us, "I was wearing a T-shirt that was too tight and very brief, like the Israeli girls." On the eve of the trial, the girl launches a message from the columns of La Stampa: "I want to tell other young people who go to blow themselves up among the Jews: think twice about it. It's time that the two peoples, Palestinians and Israelis, stop killing one another. There's a way to find agreement, if they want to."

Is she sincere? Here's how the story goes: The girl was born in a very well-off family in Bethlehem. "We have three houses, all beautiful, with a garden. I've always profited from my studies, now I'm in my second year at the school of economy and business, and I received a grant as a computer specialist. But I've always been somewhat different, an only child while everyone else has so many brothers and sisters. My father died when I was six months old, and my mother went to live in Jordan with her new husband. My grandmother, even though she too changed husbands, created a family for me with my two aunts: one of them takes care of the house and the other has a master's in mathematics."

Sarin hasn't experienced any of the Third World kind of economic problems typical of the Palestinian world: "I've always felt the oppression suffered by my people; many friends have endured losses. I've participated in their pain and in their discussions." Every day she went to the University of Bethlehem where she fell in love with Jad Salem, a twenty-six-year-old member of the Tanzim. According to Israeli police files, Salem is responsible for a number of terrorist attacks planned in Bethlehem, one of the terrorist centers, among them the Beit Israel explosion, with nine dead, and a car bombing near Male Adumim, in which a guard was killed.

"He was brave. At night he was always on the move. No, he didn't tell me anything, but he told me that I was his whole life. I understood; I begged him not to go, to be careful. God, no, we were never alone together. But we spent hours and hours together at the university, and then on the telephone. He wasn't a student at the university. He came there for me and because of politics. I knew he killed people, but only soldiers, and to me this is right. If my objectives had been military, I too . . . In any case, my boyfriend was killed by the Israelis." How? "Murdered," Sarin says. But the files speak clearly: Salem died by one of his many bombs in an "on-the-job accident." But for her, he is a martyr: friends congratulate her, she sees his pictures on the wall, she praises him on television.

So then, she seeks out a common friend. "It was a Tuesday. I told Ali Moughrabi, a friend of Jad whose brother, head of a Tanzim cell, had been killed by the Israelis that I wanted to help." Her account differs some from Ali's, who states that the girl had declared to him that she was prepared to be a martyr.

"We met at the university on Friday," Sarin reports bitterly. "He told me they would let me know. On Tuesday, he showed up again and told me 'OK, we accept you. May Allah's will be done.'" No, the word *explosion* was never uttered. "And Wednesday, at eight o'clock, during class, Sarahna appeared: he had already come to pick me up." So soon? Yes, right away, let's go. What do you mean you're not ready? Pray to Allah.

He brings the girl to a house where she meets the boy, Issa Badir, who is also ready to blow himself up. "They told me 'we must pray.' And we prayed to ask God to honor me as a brave girl." But do you pray often? "Five times a day, but I don't believe in Paradise the way they describe it. For me, it means being in God's hands. And instead, I wondered if I was about to go to Hell. But I was especially shaken, scared, when I saw the satchel with the bomb. It was enormous, heavy. They told me: It's for Palestine, for God. It weighed thirty-five kilos." In actuality, it was ten kilos.

The girl and Issa were taken to Rishon in two cars, that of Sarahna, with his wife sitting in front. "The boy was taught to drive in half an hour. He didn't have a license. The car had no brakes and the headlights were broken. We called Sarahna on the cell phone to complain; the boy wasn't able to drive. But Sarahna told him not to make such a fuss."

In Rishon, Sarin got out of the car and went in the opposite direction from her companion. She was supposed to blow herself up five minutes after his suicide. But she decided she didn't want to: "They, too, were human beings. I thought about some old friends from a kibbutz who I might maybe kill by accident. I thought that they had sent me hastily, without preparing me. And I thought that it was 90 percent certain that I would go to Hell. The boy also wanted to call it off. I phoned Sarahna. He said no: We had to die. I told him I was going home anyway. Meanwhile, I had put the explosives back in the car. In the end, the boy decided to do it." But he was a sixteen-year-old, she a young woman whose family owns three houses.

Her aunts welcomed her, and that night she saw on television the results of the terrorist attack. She went to sleep. "My friends would have made a cross and a question mark over me," that is killed her as a collaborator. She remained in hiding for six days until the Israeli police found her: "Now I'll be in prison for five or six years, then I'll go to live in Jordan with my aunt, and I'll continue studying." She repeats that the martyrdoms should not continue, that other political solutions should be found. The truth is that the web of terror, which in this case involved a girl from a good family, unscrupulous terrorists, and an ex-criminal like Sarahna, is so vast, so avid, so efficient as to preclude any solution.

## The "Liberated" Palestinian Woman

Female suicide terrorists, lives that explode in bloody tatters taking innocent victims with them, are the new horrifying phenomenon that has sadly shocked the Israelis. A large part of the entire Arab world, not just the Palestinians, has discovered a new type of Joan of Arc. Three women have committed as many suicide attacks in the past month. On January 27, 2002, Wafa Idris went to blow herself up in Jaffa Street, among people who were shopping in the stores in the center of Jerusalem; she killed one person and injured approximately a hundred. By now she has become a symbol and object of emulation, immortalized in colored pictures with a kaffiyeh wrapped around her forehead, found in offices of organizations and in homes in the Palestinian Authority. She appears coquettish; one searches her round face in vain for a sign of the terrible determination that led her to put the TNT belt around her hips. She was a twenty-eight-year-old nurse, divorced, associated with Al-Fatah and therefore with the secular, not the Islamic fundamentalist, wing of the Palestinian movement. Her mother recalls that she was very sensitive and pained by the fate of those injured in the intifada, whom she was continually treating. Israeli police confirm that she actually had her companions bring her to the site of the bombing in an ambulance, the tool of her trade.

Then on February 25 there was Moura Shaloub, at fifteen years of age the youngest of the three: she tried to stab the soldiers at a checkpoint. She left two messages: one for her family, in which she said she had decided "to attack those arrogant men at the damned checkpoint, by God's will, and to kill them to show them that they will never be secure in our land" and one for her companions urging them to "love the holy war and pray to God that He will accept me as a martyr." And finally, on Wednesday night, Darin Abu Aishe, a twenty-one-year-old English literature student, blew herself up at a checkpoint along Modiin Road between Jerusalem and Tel Aviv, wounding two policemen and a soldier. Two sinister guardian angels accompanied her in a car, bringing her to her death. The girl left one of those vindicating videotapes that the world is familiar with by now, but with a feminine slant. The Arab satellite network ANN (Arab News Network) broadcast it to affirm that the girl, originally from the village of Beit Wazan, was associated with the Al Aqsa Martyrs Brigades, the armed wing of Al-Fatah.

Female suicide terrorists, the new shahids of this Al Aqsa Intifada, are equal to yet different from their male counterparts. First of all equal, because their social and political origins are suited to a confrontation in which all social strata of the Palestinian world are involved, in which it is no longer necessary to be a poor, ultra-religious young man to be sent along the path of suicide terrorism. On the contrary, students, middle class and quasi-intellectual, secular or religious stand in line to become martyrs, as Palestinian leader Mahmoud Dahlan once said. The battle with Israel dominates the horizon; the idea, constantly repeated by television and the press, that there is no other hope than to fight, that the enemy is a monster who must die, and that the war has all the qualities of authentic sanctity is the prevailing culture at this time. Today's young women, students on the threshold of emancipation, are also part of a mass culture that is omnipresent as a result of the diffusion of education and communication media: they share commonly held beliefs and in fact find a great emancipatory outlet, so to speak, in the confirmation of prestige and glory that are very difficult, otherwise, for a woman to achieve.

As a result, the difference in the female terrorist's experience lies precisely in the extraordinary, glorious prominence given to her role. Color videos in which women with their faces covered, just like the men, parade with their weapons, wear explosives belts (display belts, for the occasion), and learn the arts of war are repeatedly shown on television: The women march, fight, and declare themselves eager to become martyrs as quickly as possible. After Wafa Idris, all the Arab newspapers, not just the Palestinian press, published dozens of pieces praising the female terrorist. "She is a woman . . . who shocked the enemy with her fragile body, who blew herself up shattering the myth of feminine weakness into a thousand pieces . . . a woman who teaches all of you the meaning of liberation that female rights activists tempted you with." Thus read a significant editorial in the weekly *Al Sha'ab*. And among thousands of other commentaries, this one in the Jordanian newspaper *Al Doustur* was even more pointed: "Wafa Idris never dreamed of owning a BMW or having a cell phone. . . . She carried no makeup in her purse but enough explosives to terrorize the enemy. Wasn't it the West that asked Eastern women to become the equals of men? Fine, this is the way we understand equality."

# The Roots of Betrayal

The panorama in which the heart ventured at a time when Third Worldism was young and the United States was just beginning to be hated was above all agricultural. Nothing much happened after the United States liberated Europe from Hitler, winning the war in a way that left no doubt about the need for a democratic future for Europe. This elemental truth, that democracy had won, wasn't much appreciated right away, at the start of the Cold War, which again pitted the two systems against one another: democracy and totalitarianism.

Strange as it may seem, Europe did not yearn for democracy following the totalitarian storm. On the contrary, vast groups of youthful intellectuals envisioned—to the point of violence—worlds in which one social issue, namely, the redemption of the poor, held prominence, though it wasn't at all a liberal choice. On the one hand, the *vitelloni*, handsome, but poor, unemployed young men, increased in the rural communities, while other young people born after World War II (when in the sixties the landscape began to become urban, the suburbs began to grow, and prosperity bought all Italians a Fiat Seicento and envisioned industrial gains for everyone) enlisted in various armies: in postcolonial Africa, in antiapartheid Africa, in Cuba and Latin America, in Vietnam, in China, even with the Soviet army (though with little emotional adhesion), and finally with Arab-Muslim forces. I would have said that these young people became Third World supporters and anti-Western (in particular anti-American) proponents in the wake of, and by orders of, the USSR, but there was a lot more to the turn of events. From all sides, there was concealed advice on how to dress, what music to listen to, how to speak, and above all morality. All this forged and changed our lives to the point of marking our very identity and creating a strange, hybrid beast that, while declaring itself the staunchest defender of human rights, developed a profound indifference for human life itself, a moral blindness, which today might actually prevent us from facing up to the battle against terrorism.

Deliberately, and with some regret as a human rights advocate from way back, I am leaving aside the solid, factual reasons, the list of unforgivable misdeeds, for which we could despise and blame Fulgencio Batista y Zaldivar for human rights violations in Cuba, or Shah Reza Pahlavi for Iran. Their bullying arrogance, their craving for power, their cruelty—the savage vulgarity of the former and the pretentious totalitarian modernization of the latter—go along with the many intolerable abuses of power inflicted upon their rebellious people. We'll take as a given the implications of all anti-imperialist, antitotalitarian revolutions, though with gradations (certainly Batista was worse than the Shah). What interests me instead is the specific outcome of each situation leading up to the moral blindness, which I mentioned. It was from each of these situations that we extracted the essence of the last century's culture: generally speaking, a sense of solidarity for oppressed peoples, a desire to help the weak, a people's right to self-determination, and anti-imperialism. Excellent things. But we also developed some specific capital sins that are now in danger of making us into victims and fools, sins whose origins I recall in my own biography.

Latin Americans: In general they cost us a sense of order and decorum, of manners and distinction. Gabriel Garcia Marquez, in Macondo, Marquez's fictional town, threw us into a convulsive, intricate samba, full of people who shoot, who go to bed with this one or that one, a world of savage women, filthy men, and peasant overtones. To the rhythm of a samba, he threw us into a system of moral equivalences, in which color replaced chiaroscuro, and the flatness of southern light on dust and brushwood, the whiteness of the lime, obliterated the serene building stone and ashlar. *Cuba che linda es cuba* and Comandante Che Guevara together with Nordeste, Virgolino, and the Certao combined to make a thick soup, and while we were swimming in it, we did not wonder (or only very distractedly) about certain things. Like what was happening in the Cuban prisons. Or how much craving for media power there was in Che Guevara's decision to abandon his power for the jungle, not to mention a passion for shooting and using machetes for improper ends. Or how hateful a *lider maximo* who speaks ten hours to an immobilized crowd in the square could be, who does away with homosexuals, who keeps dissidents in jail, who shoots his minister when he tries to put a stop to coke dealing, who like Mussolini leads the sugarcane harvest wielding a scythe bare-chested. Handsome, sexy young men like Fidel and Che led the hit parade of crooners, competed with Eros and Priapus, made us dress in violent colors with ugly imitations of Indian shirts, and so we watched provocative groups (the Shining Path in Peru, the guerrillas in Uruguay, and FARC, the Revolutionary Armed Forces of Colombia) with a sense of admiration. "Guantanamela" and "Comandante Che Guevara" were sung at every opportunity. Latin American songs were especially popular because their rhythm was catchy to the point of obsession. The Inti Illimani, a Chilean group, hopelessly repeated them at every unity festival: "El pueblo unido jamas sera vencido" and also, however, "El condor pasa." In the background, American imperialism stood against the peace of the Andes, Cuban women's legs, Fidel's beret, the farmers' toil, hoes, machetes, and rifles. We didn't see the USSR in the wings; we didn't see the horror of terrorism. We were only interested in defeating the imperialist. We had read Lenin.

China concerned another important aspect of our ethical upbringing, namely, the silence of conscience when faced with a systematic, savage, destructive totalitarianism concealed beneath an appearance of spontaneity (what is found today in many terrorist organizations). The reading of Mao Tze Tung by young Italian radicals, though less common than the romantic, Latin American, Leninist passion, was linked to the suggestion of continual revolution. They were times in which we sat day and night in smoke-filled gatherings and meetings. Life had to be one and the same with politics, persistent revolution again and again. Spontaneity, the breakdown of the university and of traditional knowledge, as we called it, carried as its standard, in part unconsciously, Mao's broad face. If the USSR represented bureaucracy, China, in our superficial view, seemed instead spontaneous. The little red book, the cultural revolution, intellectuals who were dying in pigsties, the assault (once again) of the rural poor against corrupt townsmen—we did not hesitate to adore the mass murderer.

Che Guevara, Fidel—the Latin Americans had added the anorak to our wardrobe. The Chinese gave us wide, comfortable pants but shirts with high, tight-fitting collars, like a noose. Anticonsumerist red monks, like the young men of Serve the People, lived in communes and were ascetic in imitation of the Chinese. They did not practice the sexual revolution, but forbade it on their own unless they married within the revolutionary rite. Others from Tuscany to Sicily rented farmhouses to cultivate the land with their own two hands, communes flourished, and the sexual revolution recruited many tramps from ideology, even if it was not really possible to make Mao into a sexy hero. We forced ourselves to admire some of his pictures as a young man, during the first long march. The bath in the Yan Tze was a little ridiculous, however, flat. The little red book, on the other hand, the tragic symbol of millions of persons killed during the Cultural Revolution, became a banner to wave during the demonstrations. We made various shorter or longer marches in town centers, despite the risk of being tried in half an hour and shot in a minute, before mass demonstrations against capital punishment ever dreamed of taking to the streets. Another capital sin was created around the myth of Maoist collectivism: an insensitivity toward dictatorship, toward geriatric hierarchies, toward political killing.

I was in China a couple of times for my work and it was enough for me: anyone who saw that immense prison quickly understood what it was all about. I had the opportunity to speak at length with a homosexual intellectual actor from Bertolucci's film *The Last Emperor*. He had lived through the cultural revolution. His knowledge of Italian, of Dante and Boccaccio, was judged by the Red Guards to be an antirevolutionary crime; for ten years he was "reeducated" in the country. While I was in China, I saw the fear of children in the street who, looking around, refused the piece of chocolate I offered them. I met Deng Tziao Ping; he was old and extremely diminutive. His immense power put him in a good mood. When his car passed by, with the Italian guests' motorcade, his motorized guards preceded him, making the bicyclists literally dart away, ending up on the ground. It was easy to understand that we were dealing with a brutal, fascist dictatorship. It is not easy to understand how frequently the Italian visitors didn't notice it.

A few words about Russia and the surrounding area: A love for the USSR cannot be listed among the capital sins of immoralist Third

Worldism. There was no love there, except among the old members of the PCI, the Italian Communist Party. Instead there was omertà, a conspiracy of silence. Unless we belonged to "Chinese" groups, we felt a sense of fearful respect: Russia was a formidable mistress to be obeyed, particularly with regard to her anti-imperialist and anti-colonialist policy, even if we didn't like her. She was an annoying but respectable aunt, bureaucratic and verbose, even obtuse and full of distasteful demands, and many people who had traveled to the East had seen her face to face. But when a young man we met casually on a trip to Rumania asked the person traveling with me to give him his blue jeans, my companion, a Communist, asked him: "Do you prefer blue jeans or Communism?" Faced with such a crazy question, the young man wisely replied, "Blue jeans." At that point, my companion exclaimed: "So then you'll get nothing." The situation changed in 1968 when the Soviet tanks rolled into Prague, crushing the Czechoslovakian experiment in social and political reforms that became known as the "Prague Spring." But by that time, although we criticized the USSR, we had absorbed a cynicism toward refuseniks and the idea of history as a plot on the part of the bad guys (the United States and capitalist countries in general). We passively accepted hierarchies, parades and demonstrations, the corruption and alignment of the intellectuals, and militarization disguised as revolution.

The Vietnamese: They seemed like tiny, battered angels. The photos of the big bad Americans were the only images we were determined to watch, the Americans who for the most part did not support their own reasons for the war but devoured themselves with criticism. With the film *The Deer Hunter*, the public was astonished that the little angels were also vicious torturers. But by then we had digested the idea of the physical treachery of the Americans (My Lai), and we were also hypnotized by the insane notion that self-determination and socialism must be one and the same (in Africa and in the Middle East, every self-determined nation whose borders had been drawn with a ruler by a former colonialist master was a "socialist democracy" or an example of "democratic socialism"), and that an exotic, tired face like that of Ho Chi Min must be synonymous with good. We would have to write pages and pages about the Vietnam War, which, along with the Six Day War, represents the turning point at which anti-Westernism became one and the same with defectionist neopacifism. It was at this point that prohibiting democracies to win became decisive. Israel only won because its life was at stake, although all the world was asking it to lose as always, as the Jews have always done, to remain legitimized by the left. The Americans, on the other hand, since they could afford to do so, accepted the dictates of world opinion. And from this we internalized another idea that has disastrous effects today: that the poor, the underdogs, win in the end.

So as not to omit another very important topic, that of negritude, I will limit myself to recalling the parallelism between antiapartheid fighting in South Africa, the American civil rights movements, and anticolonialist movements. The latter later resulted in an Africa that is the desperation of all well-intentioned people because of its social and political problems, its wars between ethnic groups, and the implacable dictators who, with rare exceptions, have infested the continent. Besides the songs of Miriam Makeba and an enthusiasm for Martin Luther King and Nelson Mandela (by whom the unrestrained, savage use of terror and common crime was nonetheless ignored and continues to be so today), a number of evil shoots began to sprout from this hotbed: the black Muslims, accusations that the United States was responsible for all the horrors of slavery (whereas there is no civilization, nor religion, that has not used, bought, sold, and killed slaves; the Arabs still use them in Mauritania and Sudan), anti-Semitic hatred, and the extremist, anti-Western attitudes of many leaders of intolerable dictatorships. But for us, black remained the most lucid, pure color; black rhythms seemed more pleasing than ours. The innocent cruelty of fratricidal wars in which dictators became real killers and sent armies of children to fight and be mutilated seemed like secondary issues. The capital sin we internalized from that world is a paralyzing sense of guilt that simplifies everything, settling for "hunger in the world" and "debt" as slogans to protect us from the duty of condemning erratic, corrupt regimes that appropriate relief funds to buy arms and pad accounts in Switzerland.

From the time of Rosi's "Battle of Algiers," the Muslim revolt that began as a struggle against colonization acquired a justly positive character; though not in France, the war of Arab liberation became a *lied*, a trumpet call like other revolutions, except with a kaffiyeh. This large black-and-white scarf, which replaced the anorak as a revolutionary signal, evolved from being the head covering of the fellahin—the Arab peasants—to the scarf of the fedayeen, who, vowing the liberation of Palestine (well before 1967, the time the territories were occupied), massacred the athletes in Munich or killed Jews in cold blood on hijacked airplanes. The kaffiyeh eventually became the all-concealing mask, except for the eyes, which suicide terrorists, dead men walking, wear at demonstrations, shooting in the air and shouting their hatred for Israel and for the Americans as well.

I will not linger on the historical aspects of the Middle East situation except to repeat that 1967 initiated the most out-and-out distortion of the truth: a country under attack, which was legitimately victorious against forces greater than its own and which resisted an entire world surrounding it, was said to be guilty of the most shameful violations of civil rights and came to be viewed as a violent culture. The Cold War contributed its best here in a Goebbels-like misrepresentation of the truth: The Middle East was redefined and reportrayed in the Western mind as a region in which the Arabs, who at the time were forming various dictatorial groups connected to Moscow, were weak, despite their oil and despite their rejection of the 1948 U.N. partition. While the only existing democracy in the region, which had been attacked many times and which, on top of it, had already practiced "peace for land" (the totally unheard of formula created just for it) and would do so again, was accused of imperialism and fascism, and its popular army regarded as a kind of bloodthirsty war machine.

The distortion of values, which began in those years, is the reason why we are unable to face realistically today the terrorist attacks rooted in Islamic extremism that are taking place and that will probably become more widespread in the following months and years. The blindness was already evident when the Munich terrorists murdered one Israeli athlete every hour until the final one was killed. Dressed like those who participated in the 1968 French student uprising, with long hair and kaffiyeh around their necks, the terrorists appeared in crowded press conferences while the Israelis were held captive in the athletes' barracks. The journalists who were there had more or less the same look, the same clothing: The Palestinian leaders had established that the moral aspect of the matter was not at all relevant, only its media significance.

The media impact was enormous; and on top of everything the games were not suspended. Germany denied Israel the right to intervene to save its young athletes. The power of the media contributed to Islam's first great victory since it was vanquished in 1683 beneath Vienna's walls. The media has helped to foment anti-Christian persecutions, rampant anti-Semitism, which is more offensive than ever, the indiscriminate use of violence as a preferred weapon, and finally the horror of suicide terrorism. Many justifications have been sought for the Twin Towers attack; dozens have been found for the equally catastrophic assault against Israel. The worst violations of human rights have been buried under mountains of U.N. resolutions critical of Israel. The process by which our Third World culture was transformed into complete moral indifference came to a head during the years of the intifada.

But while up till then we had not paid a price for our stupidity, while Cubans, South Africans, and the Chinese (for now) remain distant, the day of reckoning with our acquiescence is not far off: To insist on being liberal with an enemy that is possessed by suicidal fever is a risky approach.

# Denial

Speaking with our young people is a delight. They are better than we parents in so many ways, much more informed, more level-headed, little inclined toward political extremism. Democracy has permeated them, fear of anti-Semitism has left them or is slight and concealed in any case, and there is an evident desire for justice in the sense of bringing about civil rights for all. But there's something else we see in them: a desire, indeed a certainty, of being able to live in peace, a search for compromise at all costs that is tender and a bit futile at the same time.

Many times, in reference to the Middle East conflict, but also in reference to terrorism, to Islamic contempt for our democracy, to repeated declarations of open aggression against us, I hear, offered with some anxiety: "When will it end? What can we do?" And it is sad to have to answer: What if it isn't going to end? What if we don't hold all the cards, since it takes two to make peace, in every sense, cultural and practical? What if we have to hold out a long time, and maybe even face a battle? What if terrorism is an endemic problem in contemporary society, that no magic charm but only a conscientious, intensified struggle can defeat, or at least diminish its impact? Many adults as well as our young people do not want to hear this sad hypothesis. Everyone wants to be reassured, to believe that the Middle East conflict is about to end, that the limits of terrorism are defined, that they will not cross the borders of Jerusalem or New York.

As a result, we have witnessed two strange phenomena in this period: Comments on America's alarm over a possible series of upcoming attacks and comments on the fate of the thirteen alleged terrorists in the Church of the Nativity. In the first case, instead of delving into the possible truth of the hypothesis, the Europeans have preferred to fiddle around with the reasons for Bush's declarations: Perhaps he wants to divert attention away from other political problems, perhaps he wants to cover up the tragic error he made when he underestimated the information that was already in his possession before September 11, perhaps he is simply laying the groundwork for an attack against Iraq (God forbid! said several editorial writers, followed by acclamations of appeasement, forgetting the real chemical-biological and even atomic threat posed by Saddam).

As if terrorism were a mythological element, as if the Twin Towers had never happened, as if Iran with the help of Syria and others did not furnish arms to all the existing terrorist movements, as if Libya were not also heading toward atomic weapons, as if Israel were not being blown up at every corner, as if the Hezbollah were not in control of much of Lebanese politics. As if. But there must be something that can be done, those who are hopeful keep repeating. They don't realize that in Israel, for example, the number of terrorist attacks increased during the very periods in which the prospects for peace were greatest; that Islamic terrorism is not a matter of action-reaction, but a continuous line that has a predetermined ideological nature; that it is not we who cause it, but rather that it is self-generating in its all-encompassing rejection.

The same hopeful attitude can be noted in media information concerning the men in the basilica, thirteen men whom everyone is in fact contriving to call "militants," "soldiers," "refugees," "exiles," or what have you. Fabulous tales are being told about them, as if they were individuals in distress, nostalgic for their homes, exiles whose destiny might perhaps have been to return to the shelter of their families (often powerful political clans) and enjoy the status of ex-servicemen of a legitimate, fairly waged war. The tales describe their letters from home, the tedium of the long wait, their fear of being scattered abroad.

Here, too, the magic charm is clear: a refusal to recognize that our new guests (in particular one of the three who fall to us) have a detailed, precisely stated curriculum; that some of them are principals behind the suicide terrorists of the Al Aqsa Martyrs Brigades and Hamas; that they have ambushed and fired at innocent civilians; and that they are men who play an organizational role in studying potential targets for the massacres, occasions that encompass religious feasts, civilian dwellings, roads traveled by cars carrying clerks, professionals, and mothers with children to work or school. In short, they are part of a strong, powerful network of ideological terrorism, generated by geopolitical situations unlikely to be eliminated and are driven by extremely deep-seated, self-validating ideological and religious motives. They have contempt for human life, both their own and those of their enemies, and a profound faith in victory, because they believe that they are in the right. We refuse to recognize that they won't love us any more or spare us further attacks if we are kind to them. On the contrary, they consider us part of an exploitative, repressive machine that hates and suppresses them, a corrupt, weakened system: the corrupt West run by a lobby of Jews and Americans.

# Yom Ha Shoah

The true story of the Shoah and Israel, over and above the many specific versions, is that of an incredible mass rehabilitation of lives scorched in horror, lost in the unspeakable. It is the story, not found in the archives, of the tenacity of the human being when he finds something to cling to, of the slow resumption of affairs, of the ties of family and friends in safeguarding the new Jewish state, the promise of security, home. Yesterday, the Day of the Holocaust, Yom Ha Shoah, in Israel, could not be like the others. "It was my first Holocaust Day as a soldier," said Ofer on the radio, from Netanya, where the Passover massacre took place, "and when the siren sounded in remembrance of the six million, the dead of our times were there to look at us questioningly with them. It is difficult for a young man to explain to himself why the Jews, after so much suffering, after so many struggles, have not yet reached the point of being able to live in peace in their own homeland, why we still have to see so many children, old people, Jewish women killed intentionally in the streets."

In appearance, the Day of the Holocaust proceeded according to the ritual. Monday evening, in the cold Jerusalem night, at the museum of the Shoah on Mount Hertzl, the generation of survivors along with young people took part in lighting the great brazier of life with torches. Not far from the Children's Museum, where one by one the names of children killed in the camps were being recited as a candle reflected millions of faces in the dark, the wind was blowing over the tombs of Yitzhak Rabin, Golda Meir, and Moshe Dayan, Zionist heroes who restored life to a people who seemed to have perished forever in horror and death. So many ceremonies since yesterday morning: a big conference on the moral and cultural legacy of memory and twenty-four-hour television and radio coverage broadcasting the subdued voices of survivors: miracles, unspeakable horrors, journeys across Europe on foot to reach the land of Israel. And the central focus of the day, the siren that sounds at ten along the highways and in the cities, with everyone standing motionless at attention, forming an ideal chain of hope and continuity with those slaughtered fifty years ago. But the siren had a more hollow voice this year. In the times of the peace process, the amplification of grief caused limpid tears to flow freely. You could cry in peace. The singer Yehuda Polliker sang a song about the Shoah that shocked people at the time: "It hurts, though less so; less so, yet it still hurts," he would sing.

Today things are different. At the supper of the Passover massacre, at least five of the victims were survivors who through a painful, daily application of will had effected an astounding recovery: children and grandchildren, work, various interests, sports, attachments, and social commitment. But George and Hana Yacobovich, for example, are exceptions to this happy story, as is Marianne Leman. The first two, husband and wife, were both born in Rumania in 1923. They were at school together, and later on the same train to Auschwitz, George jumped from the train and was able to escape. Hana reached the infamous ramp with her father, mother, and siblings. Her family was chosen and gassed upon arrival; Hana went through hell and came out of it alive. The paths of the two converged again in Israel, where it was possible to imagine life going on, and in 1979, each after a marriage that had ended and each with two children, George and Hana finally combined memory and hope: The two schoolmates married. The evening of the Pesach supper, the Seder, the couple invited Hana's son André with his wife and two daughters to Netanya. The suicide bomber, in a sea of blood (twenty-seven dead), killed George instantly; Hana struggled between life and death. Andrè was killed as was his wife; the granddaughters were injured and are still in the hospital.

Another story: For four years during the war, during the nightmare of Nazis who periodically stormed in to hunt down Jews, Marianne Leman, now seventy-six years old, had gone in and out of a closet in an old house in a village between France and Germany. Her dream of recovery, of life was none other than Israel, with its promise that even the most persecuted human being can find shelter, a home. This year Israel feels that its home is not secure, that those who have come here have not really found safe landing. What's more, yesterday, right at the moment of remembrance, Syrian television broadcast a documentary entitled "Zionism and Nazism," which revived the contemptible comparison that is frequently heard in Palestinian media reports as well these days and that even European intellectuals like José Saramago have no scruples about embracing. A comparison that greatly disrupts the crucial debate, totally different, concerning the moral responsibilities of a people who have suffered so much and who must nevertheless continue to ask themselves the questions that are lost, at times, in battle: that is, questions about the eternal, constant, and, in any event, indispensable humanity of its adversary, even when he is a terrorist.

# Zaka

The worst time is at night, before being able to fall asleep: a cigarette, a cup of coffee, a glance at the lights of Jerusalem from the balcony of his house. In the bedrooms his wife Friedel and their nine children are breathing slowly, they moan a little in their sleep, and Bentzi Oiring, a stout man with a beard and side locks, wearing black knickerbockers and a white shirt from which the tzitzit (the little tassels) of a small prayer shawl slip out, isn't even able to sit down. Did I do all right? he wonders, when the mother of that little boy, unrecognizable because of his wounds, came to the morgue. Did I say the right words? Had I arranged his face in such a way that she could at least look at him one last time? When I removed the child's body from the carriage at the Sbarro pizzeria, did I do so with enough tenderness and gentleness? In the smoke, the flames, among the dismembered bodies, as I was putting the shreds of that woman back together, did I resist letting myself be overwhelmed with disgust, did I remember that man is made in God's image?

Not far away, another man has similar thoughts, in this case regarding the living wounded, and he, too, never sleeps, or else he falls asleep exhausted and is sometimes wakened by dreams. He is originally from Turin, rather from Asti, and has a distinguished last name: Artom. In fact, Elia, fifty-two years old, is the grandson of the biblical commentator and rabbi, Elia Samuele Artom. At night he makes his coffee with an espresso maker and thinks to himself: "When I and my volunteers of Mogen David Adom, the Red Star of David, got to the site of the bombing attack, in that inferno of screams and blood, did I assign the volunteers correctly? Did I evacuate those with the most serious injuries first? Did I save as many lives as possible? The one who was shouting in the corner, and the one who instead didn't respond . . . Were we quick enough in carrying away that girl with the chest injury, in suturing the wound of that boy whose leg had been blown off? Could we have saved one more? Could I have prevented that fatal heart attack? Could I have acted more quickly, more quickly than I did?"

You see them all the time on television because they are the good protagonists of the era of terrorism. Soon after a bomb has exploded, two groups arrive in ambulances, sirens wailing. One group wears the white coats with the red star symbol, and they are Elia's volunteers. The other, a vast group, wears the white coats as long as there is a need to and then transforms itself into Zaka teams with the yellow vests. Zaka is an acronym for Zihui Korbanot Ason, which means "identification of disaster victims." It is also called Hessed ha emet, Kindness of Truth; the Torah reserves the phrase "kindness of truth," or ultimate, eternal kindness, for burial of the dead.

Jewish law considers respectful treatment of the dead important, and Zaka members, 99 percent of whom are Orthodox, see them-

selves as fulfilling this role. Its men collect and reassemble the remains of the dead, even the tiniest fragments. Elia's men arrive first
in the white ambulances ("with bulletproof vests, because we enter
before the police, and everything could still flare up"); he subdivides
the areas of the attack by number and assigns every ambulance crew
a stretch of sidewalk, or rubble, or chaos. All the injured call to them,
"but we have to look for those who are gravely wounded because
they don't have the strength to cry out." The police shout that they
should leave the scene. The volunteers finish clearing out the
wounded as soon as they can, and in general they do it in record
time. Then everyone is moved off so the area can be checked. Soon
afterwards, Bentzi begins his work: nothing, absolutely nothing,
must remain unburied, every man must return to Heaven as whole
as possible, everyone is sacred even at the end of their days. No matter what the cost.

Mogen David Adom: Elia is the chief instructor of both the
young volunteers and the veterans: in Israel there are 6,500 volunteers aged fifteen and up, 800 of them in Jerusalem. The young people in school vie with one another. Permanent employees, including
doctors and the paramedics who drive the ambulances, number
1,500, 150 of them in Jerusalem. In 2001 there were 409,000 calls,
compared with 344,000 in 1998. There are three types of ambulances,
depending on the gravity of the disaster. Lately all of them have
been put to use. In one of them, as a call is underway, Elia shows us
the defibrillators, the machines with the suction cups for pulmonary
ventilation (even a very small one, for newborns), oxygen tanks, various instruments for suturing, and so on. Dalia, who is rushing to a
call with three very calm nineteen-year-old volunteer women, is an
ambulance driver; in Israel this means being the team leader and the
person in charge in every respect. Dalia also has a son, Elisha, eighteen years of age, who is a volunteer: "I consider him old enough to
help in any situation. Besides, there's no question that he wants to
help. In Ben Yehuda after a bombing attack, he found a schoolmate
of his wounded. Do you understand? However, we try to avoid putting fifteen- to eighteen-year-old volunteers in extreme situations."

Elia, his blue eyes tired, his words few, his face unguarded, has a
tiny office that is bombarded with phone calls. His four children follow him on his chosen path: Yaacov, twenty-five, a paramedic, Rifka,
twenty-three, an ambulance driver, Aviad, twenty, a volunteer, and

even his youngest, a girl of thirteen, can't wait to enlist. "When I run into them in all the chaos, at massacres like the one at Moment Café, or Sbarro pizzeria, it's an enormous consolation." The volunteers take continuous refresher courses: "We actually have too many of them; as a minimum they must take a sixty-hour course. They are well prepared, but no one can relieve them of the terrible tension of the moment the ambulance races toward an inferno, when you don't know how it will be." Does he encounter many injured Arabs? "At Sbarro in particular, I found a pupil of mine, an ambulance driver. For me he was as dear as all the other wounded persons."

Zaka: Yehuda Meshizahav receives us in a kind of grotto in the religious quarter of Mea Shearim: there are plastic bags, gloves, scrapers, axes to hack through the rubble—all in excellent order though in the insufficient amounts typical of a volunteer association that few think about. "There are 604 of us, 80 of us in the capital. Wives were calling us saying 'my husband is acting crazy': so we decided to get a psychologist to help us. In group sessions, he helps us express the horror and tell about our day-to-day dealings with death. Think about it: we have to look into the pockets, at the date-books, letters, small pieces of jewelry of the people who are killed to identify them.

It's difficult to look at what an eighteen-year-old boy had in his pocket, or what was in a baby's carriage: up until a moment earlier there was a whole life to be lived. Many of us work and weep. And we are the ones who help the families find the bodies of their loved ones. Many parents faint, very many are in denial: impossible, I assure you it's not her. While we, on the other hand, are certain that it is indeed their daughter. Sometimes we tear children away from the lifeless body of their mother, or take a dead newborn from his mother's arms. In the morning, we see smiling photos of those whom we have gathered up in pieces. Then, too, we confront unspeakable horrors, with our hands, our bodies. I think that without believing in God, I wouldn't be able to do it." The men of Zaka also take courses to meticulously learn about the physiology of a human body. And what is it, in the end? "Something elusive, tragic, not guaranteed, that only becomes real again when I embrace my children at night."

# The Journalists and the Palestinians   JANUARY 2001

The information coming out of Israel these days is heavily influenced by the political imagination of the reporters and columnists
and cameramen who have flocked to the scene from the four corners
of the earth to cover this latest installment of violence in the ongoing
Middle East conflict. They tend—they are expected—to place those
clashes within an agreed-upon framework: the framework, roughly,
of David (the Palestinians) versus Goliath (the Israelis). It is only
when they fail to follow this paradigm that they, their editors, and
their readers or viewers become confused.

And no wonder. Imagine a weary journalist, getting back to his
office or press room in Jerusalem at the end of a hard day: how is he
to begin describing what he has seen? The events he must try to
present are, in truth, terribly complicated, and, when it comes to an
informed perspective, he himself is often wet behind the ears. As for
the subtle interplay between what in the swirl of events is cause and
what is effect, between the norms of Western and Eastern civilizations, between democracy and dictatorship, between the Judeo-
Christian world and the world of Islam—all this gets lost in the
confusion of daily armed clashes and terror bombings, so alien to the
normal rhythms of normal societies.

And so, like the morning mists that envelop the city of Jerusalem, the reality of the situation often dissipates into a fog made up
of the psychological impulses and fixed ideas of those observing it.
From an elevated spot like the suburb of Gilo, where I happen to
live, the local geography does in fact sometimes disappear in the
mist, and Jerusalem itself can seem transformed into a white lake.
My neighbors and I are left only with the explosions of firearms
aimed in our direction from the nearby Arab village of Beit Jalla, and
the furious responses of Israel's Apache helicopters.

And what about the view from East Jerusalem? In the Arab city,
from early morning on, the international media breathe the per-
fumed mist of something indescribably romantic and archaic min-
gled with the aroma of youthful furor. In the fog, the Jerusalem of
the Jews must loom in the imagination like a powerful machine, an
established mass pushing with its force and its money on a weaker,
newborn world. The fog offers an opportunity, a screen, against

which foreign correspondents project the attitudes they came with: their reflexive critiques of capitalism, of consumerism, of globalization, even of themselves and their own societies.

The American Colony, a lovely old hotel in East Jerusalem, is home to almost all the international journalists who have come here on temporary assignment. The ancient vine-covered stone is part of the hotel's charm, and so too is its storied past, redolent of travelers' tales, of miraculous reunions after shipwrecks at sea and near-escapes in faraway climes. Above all, its charm derives from the discreetness and quiet of the remote little street where it stands, a symbol of understatement amid the vertiginous passions of the surrounding environs.

Not far away runs Salah-al-Din, the central thoroughfare of Arab Jerusalem, all stores, noises, traffic jams. Here is where some of the Friday clashes take place, after morning prayers at the mosques. By evening, the restaurant at the American Colony has become packed with dusty, tired journalists, just back with their cell phones and notebooks from Gaza or Ramallah, from the areas of shooting. They are, most of them, between the ages of thirty-five and fifty, old enough to appreciate a moment of relaxation. In this comradely setting one feels the extraordinary informal power of the media—iconoclastic, sporty, ironic, virtually all of one mind.

The support crews are largely Arab, the stringers Palestinian and often the cameramen, too. The hotel waiters and staff are likewise Palestinian, as are the regular guests one runs into in the halls, left over from the time of the intifada of the late 1980s—the first intifada, the real one. The leaders of that uprising regard the American Colony as their private stomping ground, a place for keeping appointments, for conducting interviews, for jocularly confiding in foreign newsmen. An acquaintance amusedly tells me of overhearing a correspondent thanking his Palestinian source for supplying him with the precise hours of the next day's "spontaneous" clashes.

The American Colony—with its reassuring air of Arab refinement, the plashing of the fountain in the hotel's paradisiacal little garden where breakfast is served amid jasmine and roses, its white and blue Armenian tiles, its Eastern touches adjusted to Western tastes, the friendliness of its staff cloaked in courtesy and dignity— is much more than a hostelry: it is a metaphor for the sympathy the international press harbors for the Palestinian cause and, conversely, its complex animosity toward Israel. Slightly vain, many of the guests here still bask in memories of themselves at age twenty, Arab kaffiyehs around their necks, on the campuses of American or European universities: young rebels, young heroes, young upsetters of the hegemonic powers-that-be. For them, pro-Palestinian leanings are as natural, as elegant, and as correct as the American Colony's famous Saturday brunch.

The culture of the press is almost entirely left. These are people who feel the weakness of democratic values, their own values; who enjoy the frisson of sidling up to a threatening civilization that coddles them even while holding in disdain the system they represent. Twice a day the muezzin calls from the minaret right outside the wall of the hotel. Sitting by the pool, one feels very near Ramallah, only a few kilometers away, where the children sent to the head of the demonstrations are throwing stones at Israeli soldiers their own age or slightly older. The children are fixed in one's consciousness in all their touching humanity, while the Jewish inhabitants of nearby Psagot, showered with bullets nightly by Arafat's Tanzim in Ramallah, seem but so many insensate obstacles on the road to peace and justice.

Besides, settlers, like those in Psagot, by definition can never be victims, just as the Israeli army by definition never responds to fire but rather actively shoots at child demonstrators. BBC or CNN broadcasts begin: "Israeli helicopters attacked Beit Jalla tonight." Only then will they add: "Just before, shots from houses in the Palestinian village hit the neighborhood of Gilo." In some reports it has become customary to call Gilo itself, where 45,000 Jews dodge bullets, a settlement—that is, another colonial intrusion, another obstacle to peace and justice.

In the shelter of the American Colony, meanwhile, Palestinian spokesmen repeat their familiar themes of victimization and triumph, deploying the moral high cards of freedom, justice, and self-determination. Who is to question them? Because they come from an authoritarian society, they themselves are magically imbued with authority. European or American journalists pose respectful questions to representatives of the Palestinian Authority (PA) and note down their answers quite as if it were possible to investigate these statements or to check them against alternative Palestinian sources at any time. Since it is not possible, the only thing that makes news in the end is the ever-climbing number of dead and wounded. And that too is impossible to verify.

Not even the world-famous episode of the little boy killed by crossfire in Gaza, whose death, captured on film, was aired cease-lessly to demonstrate the barbarity of the Jews, was subject to inves-tigation by the world press. Although the Israeli army ultimately determined that the fatal bullet may well have originated not from the Israeli checkpoint but from one of the seven locations from which Palestinians were shooting, this could hardly be expected to gain traction against the idea that the child was a martyr, a shahid, murdered by the Jews. From the very beginning, the exact cause of his death was never considered worth investigating, lest it impinge on the axiom that Israel was committing "aggression against un-armed people" and causing "the daily massacre of children."

The most flagrant instance of this syndrome in action involved the journalist Ricardo Cristiano from RAI, the Italian state television network. On October 12, two Israeli reservists on their way through Ramallah were seized, beaten, lynched, and horrifically mutilated at the hands of Palestinian police and a civilian mob. PA forces on the scene promptly hunted down and confiscated film and videotape of the incident to prevent its being aired—but not before a crew from a private Italian television channel managed to send a clip of the atroc-ity to Rome that was soon broadcast around the world. Thereupon Cristiano published a letter of apology in the official Palestinian daily, *Al-Hayat Al-Jadida*. In it, he explained that he and RAI were not the ones at fault; blamed the misdeed on his colleagues at Mediaset, owned by Italy's right-wing opposition leader Silvio Berlusconi; re-iterated his commitment to respect the rules laid down by the Pales-tinian Authority—rules that presumably prohibit anti-PA reporting; and promised to bend every effort to prevent similar images being shown in the future.

A more explicit statement of fealty, or a more outrageous viola-tion of journalistic integrity, can scarcely be imagined. Yet, with one or two honorable exceptions, the reaction was muted both in Italy and elsewhere. Cristiano himself went back to Rome, and neither the directors of RAI nor its owners—that is, the Italian government—seemed to feel the need for further explanation. As for the commu-nity of journalists in Israel, at most they bestirred themselves to blame both the Palestinian Authority and the Israeli government for creating difficulties for the working press, with one Dutch correspondent taking the occasion to accuse the Israeli army, preposterously, of shooting at journalists.

But what else could be expected of a profession that does not even appear to know that it has struck a pact with Palestinian censorship? Every day, the rules that Cristiano declared he respected find a positive echo in the hearts of those who somehow cannot bring themselves to film, or to air, images of shooting by Tanzim or Palestinian police who have been positioned in the farther ranks of the demonstrating mobs, behind the stone-throwing children in the front rows. For such images would violate the tacit agreement by which Palestinians are to be seen always as victims, Israelis always as aggressors.

The stance of the media is, at bottom, simple. The reasons behind it, however, are complex. Not least among them, tragically, is the stance Israel takes toward itself. It is a country many of whose elites are insupportably suffused with a sense of guilt, lacerated by historical revisionism, starved for world sympathy, scarred by too many wars. Nowhere are the wounds more visible than in Israel's own press.

Just recently, the weekend insert of *Ha'aretz*, the country's equivalent of the *New York Times*, featured three main articles. The first, replete with a devastating caricature, focused on Ehud Ya'ari, a veteran television commentator who specializes in diplomatic and military matters and who happens to be less than enamored of Yasir Arafat; in it, this generally sensible and well-informed observer was accused of harboring a pathological antipathy that invalidated his right to speak as a professional commentator on Palestinian affairs. The second article was devoted to interviews with Palestinian mothers; but instead of asking why they send their underage children out to die—or at least why they do not prevent them from going—the author drew from their testimony of selfless dedication a profound and heartrending lesson that Israeli women in particular needed to heed. In the third, pilots who had taken part in helicopter attacks on Palestinian police headquarters after the lynching of the Israeli soldiers in Ramallah were invited to share their feelings; they duly voiced their remorse over any civilian casualties that might have occurred. (Like most citizens of advanced democratic countries, Israelis have a real horror of war and of killing in war.)

Even the army seems to lack the conviction to justify itself, thus reinforcing the impression that Israel is in the wrong and on the defensive. At a press briefing, one high-level general ruled out the possibility that anything could be done effectively to deter Arab aggression. The problem, he said, was technical: Palestinian civilians have been mixed in with riflemen, and so far the army has been at a loss to deal with this particular battle tactic. Not once did he state for the benefit of the assembled newsmen that (quite apart from such practical questions) Israel has an absolute right to protect itself against violence directed at its citizens and soldiers. By contrast, Palestinian spokesmen like Hanan Ashrawi or Ziad Abu Ziad or Saeb Erekat never miss an opportunity to begin their story from the top: this is our land, and ours alone, and the Jews who are occupying it are employing armed force against an unarmed people.

This, incidentally, may help explain, though it hardly excuses, the press's growing habit of viewing all of Israel as contested territory, not to mention its total lack of interest in Israel's painful and ultimately useless efforts over the last years to make territorial concessions to Arafat and the PLO. That, for example, in the latest negotiations at Camp David, Barak offered 92 percent of the West Bank, a sizable portion of Jerusalem, and a formula for international control of the Temple Mount seems to have done little to change the impression that Israel's "occupation" of age-old Arab lands is not a contingent fact rooted in particular historical circumstances but an innate character trait of the Jewish state, which in its entirety sits on "conquered Palestinian territory."

Occluded in this version of history, history as seen from the American Colony hotel, is the reality that Jerusalem is the established capital of the state of Israel, and that Hebrew, not Arabic or English, is the prevailing tongue in its streets. Only "in Jewish tradition," as Palestinian spokesmen like to put it, meaning in the imagination of the Jews, is the Temple Mount the site where the First and Second Temples stood. By such creeping semantic falsities, exactly as in the textbooks studied by Palestinian children, does the historical legitimacy of the Jewish presence in Jerusalem and Israel become, itself, a matter of contention.

It is difficult to believe that Israel's efforts to defend its actions before world opinion—necessary as such efforts are, weak and apologetic as they have been—can change matters in this respect, at least not in the short term. It is not just that we are talking about a profession, the world press, that is almost entirely uniform in its attitudes. The truth is that Israel, as the Jewish state, is also the object of a contemporary form of anti-Semitism that is no less real for being masked or even unconscious. (Arab Holocaust-denial, more violent and vulgar than anything in the West, is rarely if ever touched on in the mainstream media.)

And there is something else as well: looking into the heart of Arab regimes, preeminently including that of the Palestinians themselves, is simply too disturbing. For what one is likely to find there are disproportionate measures of religious and/or political fanaticism, bullying, corruption, lies, manipulation, and a carefully nurtured cult of victimhood that rationalizes every cruelty. On the streets and at the checkpoints, among the ardent stone-throwing youths facing the armed might of the Israeli "aggressor," it is possible for a newsman to forget such discordant realities; at the American Colony, it goes without saying, they are never allowed to intrude.

# How Suicide Bombers Are Made     SEPTEMBER 2001

During his historic visit to Syria last May, Pope John Paul II was unexpectedly upstaged by the country's young new president, Bashar al-Assad. Greeting the pontiff at the airport in Damascus, Assad used the occasion not to declare his own hopes for mutual understanding among the world's great faiths but—rather less in keeping with the spirit of the moment—to mount a vicious attack on the Jews. They have "tried," he inveighed in the presence of the Pope, "to kill the principles of all religions with the same mentality with which they betrayed Jesus Christ," and in "the same way they tried to betray and kill the prophet Muhammad."

So spectacular a venting of hate could hardly pass unnoted, and thus, for the duration of a news cycle, the usual fare of Middle East reporting—rock-throwers and settlers, bombings and retaliatory strikes, cease-fires and confidence-building measures—gave way to tongue-clucking over the charged words of the Syrian president. As the *New York Times* lamented, Assad had not only "marred" the Pope's visit but had reinforced his own "growing reputation for irresponsible leadership." So the coverage generally went, admonishing a new leader whose inexperience and immaturity had seemingly led him to embrace, as the *Times* put it, "bigotry."

Largely ignored amid all this was a far bigger story—a story not about a petty tyrant but about the poison that rose so readily to his lips. As few journalists either knew or thought it worthwhile to relate, such sentiments as Assad expressed are hardly uncommon in today's Arab world. Wherever one looks, from Cairo and Gaza to Damascus and Baghdad, from political and religious figures to writers and educators, from lawyers to pop stars, and in every organ of the media, the very people with whom the state of Israel is expected to live in peace have devoted themselves with ever-greater ingenuity to slandering and demonizing the Jewish state, the Jewish people, and Judaism itself—and calling openly for their annihilation. Only by turning a determinedly blind eye to this river of hatred is it possible to be persuaded that, after all, everybody in the Middle East really wants the same thing.

The anti-Semitic propaganda that circulates in such abundance in the Arab world draws its energy in large part from the technique of the big lie—that is, the insistent assertion of outrageous falsehoods about Israel or the Jews, the more outrageous the better. The examples are truly numberless. In Egypt and Jordan, news sources have repeatedly warned that Israel has distributed drug-laced chewing gum and candy, intended (it is said) to kill children and make women sexually corrupt. When foot-and-mouth disease broke out recently among cattle in the Palestinian Authority (PA), the Israelis were quickly accused of intentionally spreading the illness (despite the immediate mobilization of Israeli veterinary groups to treat the animals).

Especially garish have been the fabrications directed at Israel's response to the now year-old intifada. Earlier this year, at the world economic forum in Davos, Switzerland, a thunderstruck audience heard Yasir Arafat himself declare that Israel was using depleted uranium and nerve gas against Palestinian civilians. Official PA television obligingly furnished "evidence" for this charge, broadcasting scenes of hapless victims racked by vomiting and convulsions. Another recent film clip from Palestinian television offered a "reenactment" of an assault by the Israeli army on a Palestinian house, culminating in the staged rape and murder of a little girl in front of her horrified parents. As for Israeli victims of Arab terrorists, the PA's Voice of Palestine radio assured its listeners in April that Israel was lying about the assassination of a ten-month-old girl by a Palestinian sniper in Hebron; in fact, the commentator explained, the baby was retarded and had been smothered by her own mother.

The Arab press has also helped itself to the rich trove of classical European anti-Semitism. Outstanding in this regard has been Al-Ahram, Egypt's leading government-sponsored daily. One recent series related in great detail how Jews use the blood of Gentiles to make matzo for Passover. Not to be outdone, columnist Mustafa Mahmud informed his readers that, to understand the true intentions of the Jews, one must consult *The Protocols of the Elders of Zion*, in which the leaders of the international Jewish conspiracy acknowledge openly their "limitless ambitions, inexhaustible greed, merciless vengeance, and hatred beyond imagination. . . . Cunning," they allegedly declare, "is our approach, mystery is our way."

In a class of its own is the effort of Arab and Islamic spokesmen to distort or dismiss the record of Nazi genocide. Indeed, nowhere else in the world is Holocaust denial more warmly or widely espoused. A conference of "scholars" held in Amman in mid-May concluded that the scope of the Nazi war against the Jews had been greatly exaggerated, a claim enthusiastically parroted by the *Jordan Times*. On Palestinian television, Issam Sissalem of the Islamic University of Gaza recently asserted that, far from being extermination camps, Chelmo, Dachau, and Auschwitz were in fact mere "places of disinfection."

On April 13—observed in Israel as Holocaust Remembrance Day—the official Palestinian newspaper *Al-Hayat Al-Jadida* featured a column by Hiri Manzour titled "The Fable of the Holocaust." Among his claims: that "the figure of 6 million Jews cremated in the Nazi Auschwitz camps is a lie," promulgated by Jews to carry out their "operation of international marketing." A few weeks later, at a well-attended pan-Islamic conference in Teheran, Iran's supreme leader, the Ayatollah Khamenei, used his opening remarks to make a similar point. "There is proof," he declared, "that the Zionists had close ties with the German Nazis, and exaggerated all the data regarding the killing of the Jews . . . as an expedient to attract the solidarity of public opinion and smooth the way for the occupation of Palestine and the justification of Zionist crimes."

Occasionally, to be sure, the same organs of anti-Semitic opinion that deny the Holocaust do find it necessary to affirm that it took place—but only so that they can laud its perpetrators. A columnist in Egypt's government-sponsored *Al Akbar* thus expressed his "thanks to Hitler, of blessed memory, who on behalf of the Palestinians took revenge in advance on the most vile criminals on the face of the earth. Still, we do have a complaint against [Hitler], for his revenge on them was not enough."

Another variation on this theme is the now incessant comparison of Israel itself to Hitlerite Germany. In the eyes of *Al-Ahram*, "the atrocities committed by the Israeli army show . . . how those who complain about Nazi practices use the same methods against the Palestinians." For its sister Egyptian paper, *Al Akbar*, the ostensibly dovish Israeli foreign minister Shimon Peres is in actuality "a bird of prey, a master in the killing of the innocents," and a man responsible for deeds that "make Israel worse than the Nazis." In May, a columnist for Egypt's *Al-Arabi* wrote, "Zionism is not only another face of Nazism, but rather a double Nazism." Unsurprisingly, President Assad of Syria also favors such language, recently asserting that "Israel is racist, [Prime Minister] Sharon is racist, the Israelis are racist. They are more racist than the Nazis."

The effect of this relentless vilification is not difficult to discern. In the Arab world, where countervailing sources of information about Jews and the Jewish state are rare to nonexistent, Israel has been transformed into little more than a diabolical abstraction, not a country at all but a malignant force embodying every possible negative attribute—aggressor, usurper, sinner, occupier, corrupter, infidel, murderer, barbarian. As for Israelis themselves, they are seen not as citizens, workers, students, or parents but as the uniformed foot soldiers of that same dark force. The uncomplicated sentiment produced by these caricatures is neatly captured by the latest hit song in Cairo, Damascus, and East Jerusalem: "I Hate Israel."

From such hatred it is but a short step to incitement and acts of violence. Arab schools teach not just that Israel is evil, but that extirpating this evil is the noblest of callings. As a text for Syrian tenth graders puts it, "The logic of justice obligates the application of the single verdict [on the Jews] from which there is no escape: namely, that their criminal intentions be turned against them and that they be exterminated." In Gaza and the West Bank, textbooks at every grade level praise the young man who elects to become a shahid, a martyr for the cause of Palestine and Islam.

The lessons hardly stop at the classroom door. Palestinian television openly urges children to sacrifice themselves. In one much-aired film clip, an image of twelve-year-old Mohammed al-Dura—the boy killed last September in an exchange of fire between Israeli soldiers and Palestinian gunmen—appears in front of a landscape of paradise, replete with fountains and flowers, beckoning his peers to follow.

In early June, just two weeks after the fatal collapse of a Jerusalem wedding hall, PA television broadcast a sermon by Sheikh Ibrahim Madhi praying that "this oppressive Knesset will [similarly] collapse over the heads of the Jews" and calling down blessings upon "whoever has put a belt of explosives on his body or on his sons and plunged into the midst of the Jews." Slogan-chanting mass demonstrations, with Israeli and American flags aflame and masked gunmen firing shots into the air, reinforce the message. One need look no further to understand how children grow up wanting to be suicide bombers—a pursuit that won a fresh wave of media acclaim after a bombing at a Tel Aviv discothèque took twenty-one Israeli lives and that according to a recent poll has the approval of over three-quarters of Palestinians. "This missile," wrote an ecstatic Palestinian columnist, meaning the bomber himself, "carried a soul striving for martyrdom, a heart that embraces Palestine, and a body that treads over all the Zionist invaders."

Virulent anti-Semitism is no less essential in maintaining the region's most militant and totalitarian-minded regimes. Such standing as Syria's Bashar Assad now enjoys in the wider Arab world derives in large part from his unceasing denunciations of Israel and the Jews. For his part, Iraq's Saddam Hussein has repeatedly made known his readiness to destroy the "criminal Zionist entity." Should his own efforts not suffice, he has even sought divine aid, ending his speech at the recent Arab summit with the pithy entreaty, "God damn the Jews."

As for "moderates" like King Abdullah of Jordan and President Mubarak of Egypt, offering a wide latitude to anti-Semitic vituperation enables them to demonstrate their own populist bona fides, to show their sympathy with the Arab street. Do they themselves endorse such views? Of course not, they hasten to declare, disingenuously suggesting that nothing can be done about it since under their regimes even government-owned newspapers and television stations possess the right to speak their mind.

That moderate Arab leaders have remained mum in the face of rising anti-Semitism may be all too understandable, considering their overall records as statesmen. The West's moral and political leaders should be another matter, but they are not. In the days after Assad's anti-Semitic diatribe in Damascus, one waited in vain for the Pope—the same Pope who has recognized the state of Israel and visited the Holocaust memorial in Jerusalem—to utter a word of protest. The incident was, in many respects, a replay of then-First Lady Hillary Clinton's refusal to confront Suha Arafat when, at an event in Ramallah two years ago, the wife of the PA's president accused Israel of deliberately poisoning Palestinian air and water. And if any of the assembled leaders at the world economic conference in Davos thought to protest Yasir Arafat's lies publicly, their intervention has not been recorded.

One source of the general silence may be a subtle form of racism, or what George W. Bush in another context called "the soft bigotry of low expectations." The Arabs, it is implicitly suggested, are a backward people, not to be held to the civilized standards of the West. In this reading, rabid anti-Semitism is just another feature of Arab culture—the same ancient culture that is often also portrayed, with reason, as one of the world's most civilized and sophisticated.

Many Westerners who fastidiously ignore the Arabs' outrageous lies and insults about Jews also believe that the Arabs do, after all, have a legitimate grievance against Israel, however excessively they may at times express it. Once the substantive demands of the Palestinians or the Syrians are met, this line of thought goes, their hatred of Israel and the Jews will likewise subside, it being just a form of politics by other means. Throughout the Oslo years, the government of Israel itself seemed to share this attitude, systematically ignoring or explaining away the Arabs' unremitting verbal incitement.

But if we have learned nothing else from the latest intifada, it is that the Arab world's grievance against Israel has little to do with the minutiae of dividing up territory and political authority. It has to do instead with the entire Zionist project, with the very existence of a Jewish state in the Middle East. What Westerners (including some Israelis) dismiss as so much unfortunate rhetoric is an exact articulation of that grievance, whose goal is not to achieve but to prevent accommodation. For how can one accommodate a people who are nothing but murderers of children, instruments of world conspiracy, sworn enemies of religious and historical truth, and perfecters of Nazi brutality—a people who according to Islamic authorities must be driven out and killed, their body parts "spread all over the trees and electricity poles"? No, anti-Semitism in the Middle East is not just politics by other means; it is an end in itself.

# Israel's Last Line of Defense     JANUARY 2003

Almost every other day in Israel, it seems, an ordinary waiter, store guard, or bus driver, a twenty-year-old soldier on leave or a fifty-year-old businessman, will seize a terrorist by the arms and, while his explosive belt is still ticking, push him away from the scene, simultaneously shielding bystanders with his own body. He may save dozens of lives, and may forfeit his own in the process. He is a new kind of citizen-defender, and Israel's last line of defense. The Jewish state begets many like him, but he is also a unique type—very much a local product.

As the world knows, the Israeli army and police force have not succeeded in creating a hermetic seal against the catastrophic terrorism that has hit the country over the past two years. Barriers, checkpoints, and occasional armed forays into the occupied territories function only partially to deflect the lone suicide bomber armed with TNT and hate. Since September 2000, this latest strategic weapon of the Arabs has claimed 700 dead and thousands of wounded, in a country of only 5 million Jewish inhabitants. Everywhere, you see children in wheelchairs, disfigured victims of every age, not to mention the legions of mourners for family members and friends lost in a moment's horror.

All this has changed the face of civil society in Israel, if not the very concept of civilian life itself. For now, the most effective protection against such attacks, aside from periodic incursions into Palestinian cities, is this spontaneous form of civil defense, the only thing that works even when the terrorists from Jenin and Nablus manage to get past the barriers and show up at a café in Tel Aviv or a gas station in the West Bank town of Ariel. It seems to function naturally, on its own, but in truth it is a very strange phenomenon.

Noon. Emek Refaim, the long street that runs through Jerusalem's German Colony, where bougainvillaea and jasmine hang down from the weathered three- and four-story stone buildings. By this hour the daily racket has already reached its height: bus and car horns, mothers yelling at their children not to cross in the middle of the street, the din of rock music blasting from car stereos. In among the old Arab houses and the buildings of the Knights Templar—the cemetery of that medieval Christian order abuts the local supermarket and Burger Ranch, the boughs of its trees extending over the stone walls—are dozens of cafés, upscale wine bars, boutiques, sushi joints, vegetarian and Chinese restaurants. It is impossible to find a place to park; the police who patrol the area seem to have accommodated themselves to the prevailing chaos. The cafés are full, chic girls and boys are out walking their dogs, pretending they are in Tel Aviv. The large glassed-in terrace of Caffit, where people sit sipping cappuccino, completely exposed to the street, is an open invitation to a terrorist.

Our hero, Shlomi Harel, twenty-three and a waiter, is dressed in a white shirt and dark pants. His eyes are puffy. He was up late the night before: being a waiter, a guitarist, a student, and popular with the ladies will do that. He wears a ring in his left ear and two studs in his right, sports a tattoo on his arm and spiky hair. How many lives has this boy saved? Around fifty, but it doesn't show.

"On March 7 at 1:30 I saw a big fat guy trying to come into the place," he begins. "The guard had already stopped him, but I immediately rushed over. He was sweating a lot. I learned Arabic in the army so I asked him, 'What's your name? What do you want? Where are you going?'—anything to try and identify him, to try to understand. He had this lost look, he was sweating like crazy, and he said, 'I don't speak Hebrew,' in Hebrew. I pushed him into the corner, with the guard's help. I wasn't thinking about anything."

Shlomi has black eyes that his Iraqi-born mother might have painted on him with a paintbrush. He is well mannered, reserved though not exactly shy, dead tired. He would not let me pay for the coffee I drank at the bar, allowing me instead to admire his method of carrying several cups and saucers in one hand. His coworkers and the bar's owners like to laugh about the great Shlomi, whom the international press has made briefly famous. "Oh, you're the real Shlomi, the one and only, the big hero," they exclaim. Everyone seems to adore him.

A civilian hero is deprived of the incidental benefits, such as they are, of armed combat: the adrenaline rush of anticipated battle, the comforting presence of commanding officers and mates. Instead, he is alone with a bomb, his hands clutching a crazy man bent only on killing and being killed. But Shlomi is very cool. From the instant he shoved the sweating and stammering stranger into a corner, he says, the rest of the event unfolded "like a machine."

"I pulled the backpack off his shoulders and it fell onto the floor. I opened the flap and saw the wires sticking out. It didn't explode because something must have been broken. I was lucky. I picked up the backpack, I was still on automatic pilot, and I took it away while someone else pinned the guy down until the police came. Why did I carry it away? I said to myself, 'If someone has to die, better one than many.' And then I thought, 'If it blows up, we'll all die and I'll really look like an idiot.' But it worked out, and so I became a hero."

When he got home his mother screamed at him, hysterically: "You idiot!" She was lying on the sofa, a glass of water in her hand. "I ran home to warn her before she heard the news on the radio, but she raised her hand to slap me, crying about how I could have been killed." Shlomi laughs, but his eyes are still a little frightened at the thought of his enraged mother.

Shlomi is something of a Zionist, as Zionists go in real life. He was not a big believer in the Oslo peace process, but he was a little believer in it. He likes the idea of peace, and terrorism scares him more than war. But what is the alternative? Slowly, the dirty cups still balanced in his hand, Shlomi offers his ex-post-facto philosophy: "It went well, that's a sign that life goes on. If the backpack had blown up, I wouldn't be here to talk about it. So," he lapses into Arabic, "ya-Allah, we have to live. We move around, we keep going, nonstop. People do their best, they're walking on eggs."

In Gilo, the Jerusalem neighborhood where Shlomi lives, the whole area was under nonstop bombardment a year ago. "When a shell landed in my apartment building it was really scary. There, it was hard to plan: if it hit you, it hit you. But when you can do something, things go a lot better." For having done something, Shlomi came into $5,000, a prize from an American philanthropist. "I'm saving it," he says.

In the old days in Israel, heroism of the Shlomi type was both a national reality and a national ethic. It was part and parcel of the popular ideology of the ruling (mostly left-wing) elites, forged in the crucible of the 1948 war and, even earlier, in the age of the pioneering kibbutzniks and those who made the desert bloom. Driving it was an antiheroic dream: namely, the dream of a normal life in one's own land, among one's own people. This brand of valor had nothing to do with the outsized, myth-soaked heroism familiar to us from the propaganda and the statuary of fascism and Communism. It was not about gargantuan deeds by superhuman champions; it was family- and home-oriented, and rather intimate in tone. It was celebrated in lots of sad and even rueful songs but few marches.

No doubt to the astonishment of many, it is still alive, having survived even the era of rampant consumerism and the good life. There are still many yuppies in Israel, but their roots would appear to run only a few inches deep. That there are also deep political divisions concerning the country's future goes without saying, some of them reflected in emigration figures and even in desertions from army service; but considering the circumstances, these, too, are remarkably contained. As for the post-Zionist interpretation of Israel's history, which replaced the antiheroic hero with a bellicose, aggressive villain—the mythically rapacious, colonialist Jew who first oppressed and then drove out the native Palestinian inhabitants of the land—this mendacious reading likewise seems to have failed to take hold in Israeli consciousness, at least to anything like the extent once feared. The classic Zionist personality has assuredly gone through more than a few permutations over the last decades, but the essential character seems to have remained largely intact. Which is perhaps not so surprising, since it is unfortunately grounded in an implacable existential reality.

And it is evidently contagious. On October 12 of this year, Mikhail Sarkisov, a thirty-one-year-old recent immigrant from Turkmenistan, saved the lives of about forty people who were sitting in the Café Tayelet along the oceanfront in Tel Aviv. Sarkisov had been a guard for three weeks, his training having consisted mostly of a stint in the Russian army. He was living in a trailer, without a bathroom or a refrigerator, his only items of luxury being a well-groomed moustache and a gold—well, maybe gold—ring. He had been issued a fake pistol because he did not yet have a gun license. When an Arab terrorist, his jacket bulging, approached, Sarkisov confronted him even as the metal detector started to go off.

"What do you have there?" he asked. "It's mine," the terrorist responded. "I didn't ask whose it was," was Sarkisov's swift retort.

"I asked what you have there." As the Palestinian put his hand in his pocket, Sarkisov and two customers threw themselves at him and wrestled him down. "I understood that he was a terrorist because he spoke Hebrew very badly," says Sarkisov in a Hebrew flavored by a strong Turkmenistan accent.

Up until this day, Sarkisov had been treated very poorly by the company that hires guards for places like Tayelet and is linked to the worst criminal elements—whom it also recruits as guards. But now Sarkisov is smiling because they have given him a place to live. Also, he received $5,000 from the same American donor, and Prime Minister Sharon has presented him with an honorary plaque. Sarkisov the hero is a man without social or personal resources: recently separated from his wife, he lives alone; as if in a Charlie Chaplin film, he found himself armed with a fake pistol, required to act his part. But somehow he was prepared without question to give his life for his countrymen.

And how if not by some theory of positive contagion are we to understand the heroism of seventeen-year-old Rami Mahmoud Mahameed? This young Arab Israeli was at the bus station in Umm el Fahm in central Israel when he saw a Palestinian carrying a large black bag on his shoulders and wearing very dirty shoes. As the two were alone in the station, Rami politely asked to borrow the stranger's cell phone. Moving away, he quietly called the police. Then, instead of fleeing, he sat down next to the terrorist and waited. "I did what I wanted to do," Rami said later, as if surprised that anyone would find his actions peculiar. The police arrived in time to halt an arriving bus before it could enter the yard and grabbed the terrorist, who blew himself up. Rami was seriously injured. "Even if I had to die, I would have stayed there," Rami said later at the hospital, where at first he was under suspicion of having been an accomplice. "I thought to myself when I saw him, 'OK, if you want to kill yourself, go do it in Jenin.'"

Of course, it helps that Israel's regular army, the IDF, is a citizen army in the fullest sense, based on almost universal conscription and drawing much of its moral and cultural strength from a national mentality of preparedness and service that has been built up over the generations. It also helps, if in a grotesque way, that the enemy is so completely ruthless. "When I went into Jenin, I was astonished," says a reserve officer who participated in the operation in that West Bank city last April. "Under the beds, in the cabinets, in the kitchen, in the refrigerator there were explosives. The portraits of shahids [martyrs] were everywhere. It was sheer madness. Here were people who had built themselves a lovely city, who had been doing quite well financially, who had excellent rapport with their Jewish neighbors. We met a child carrying a bag of explosives. He must have been about seven years old." The terrible, sickening aggression of the enemy, the feeling of oppressiveness and rage that it induces in everyone who must face it, brings out a potent response. Besides, thanks to army training, the plain fact is that many people are used to reacting—when necessary, "like a machine."

A typical case is Eli Federman. If his family name is known in Israel, it is mostly on account of his brother, Noam, a former spokesman for Meir Kahane's extreme right-wing Kach movement, who has been arrested forty-five times. "My relationship with Noam is like my relationship with Yasir Arafat. To say we don't see eye to eye is an understatement," Eli asserts. On May 25, Eli saw in the distance a car driving much too quickly toward the Tel Aviv night club where he is a guard. With his imposing physique—he did his military service in a crack battalion—he started shoving people away and firing his gun. A bullet hit the oncoming terrorist, and the wildly careering car blew up.

Federman had lived in Thailand for a long time and had married there; that country holds a totemic place in the mentality of many young Israelis, whose post-army years often begin with a tour of the Asian hot spots. Today he lives with his family in a relatively leafy, lower-middle-class suburb. After the car blew up, he says matter-of-factly, he went over and "shot a few more bullets in [the terrorist's] head. We have to be as thorough as possible in the territories, not let them get as far as here." Benjamin ben Eliezer, then Israel's defense minister, inadvertently added a layer of complexity to the definition of the new Israeli hero when he hailed Federman as one "who deserves credit for defending the rights of people to get on with their daily routine and also have fun"—a hero who upholds a democracy's right to party.

I have not mentioned the bus drivers, who almost merit a category of their own as involuntary soldiers along Israel's civilian front line. They include Baruch Neuman, whose regular route runs from Petach Tikva to the Tel Hashomer hospital complex outside Tel Aviv.

At the stop near Bar Ilan University, he saw a man trying to enter through the rear exit. This is forbidden for security reasons. He slammed the door in the passenger's face, causing him to fall back bleeding to the pavement. Terrified that he had injured someone, Neuman got off, together with a passenger who was a doctor, to inspect the damage. Opening the wounded man's jacket, they saw the explosive belt and, in a flash, pinned the man's hands. He tried to resist and was kicking hard.

"He was big and strong, and he could have managed to activate the bomb at any moment," Neuman recalls. "We started to shout: 'It's a terrorist! Run! Run!' My only thought was, 'Hold onto those big arms.'" All the passengers except for one old lady managed to flee in time. "As the minutes went by he gained more and more movement, and we also understood that the bomb could be activated from afar, like with a cell phone. We decided to get away, and on the count of three we started to run. He blew up, but by that point there was hardly anyone around."

"A hero knows what he's doing," Neuman says in self-deprecation. "I acted out of pure instinct. I was doing my job and I was responsible for the safety of my passengers; I see them every day, you know. Are my wife and children proud of me? Yes—especially of the fact that I came home in one piece."

On February 1 of last year, another bus driver named Menashe Uriel broke up a major bomb attempt by pushing away a young man who was trying to get on his bus strapped with explosives. He rolled onto the ground with him. "The boy was sixteen years old, and he held his bag tight. I was sure I was going to die, but the bus was jam-packed with kids going to the Love Festival and with soldiers heading north"—a postmodern mix if ever there was one—"so I did what I had to do."

Not all who have done what they had to do have lived to talk about it. Yossef Twitto, the head of the response team in the West Bank community of Itamar, heard shots from a home one night last June but arrived too late to save the situation—three children dead, two wounded, all in the same family; when he burst in, the terrorist mowed him down, too. Another guard, Mordechai Tomer, nineteen, blond with a broad smile, was killed in Jerusalem when he stopped a car and asked to see identification papers; the driver blew himself up. And so it goes.

Sudden death, ever-present in the consciousness of Israelis, can lead to action, but also leads to a certain fatalism. Unlike in societies at peace, Israeli young people do not feel immortal. They live often to excess: dangerous trips, crazy nights, spur-of-the-moment impulses, exaggerated behavior punctuated by uncontrollable laughter and loud shouting. Beneath it looms the silence of death. "I knew perfectly well that he would have died to stop a terrorist. We'd discussed it many times," says the widow of Tamir Matan, forty-one, killed together with two young soldiers when the suicide bomber they were trying to stop blew himself up at a gas station.

This fatalism too is not new. In a 1947 novel by Moshe Shamir, *He Walked in the Fields*—a work much derided by later generations of intellectuals for its apotheosizing of the values of the old Zionist settlement in Palestine—the protagonist throws himself onto a bomb to save a comrade, even though his own girlfriend is pregnant with their child. Uri is a rural hero, torn between the dream of a quiet farmer's life and the ideal of service, of duty. For a man who would have preferred the countryside and love, duty wins out. He is like the boy in a famous ballad by the Zionist poet Natan Alterman, another self-sacrificing hero who gives his life to save his army buddies and does not even know why; or like the protagonist of another ballad about the terrible battle of Ammunition Hill in Jerusalem during the 1948–1949 War of Independence, who "between the grenades and shots . . . ran and laid the explosive. I do not know why I got the medal of honor. All I wanted was to go home quietly."

Not too far from the King David Hotel, a sumptuous new hotel is being built; a suicide bomber blew himself up there, splattering blood onto the pale blue windows. A mere hundred yards away, in a pedestrian mall, dozens of kids lost their lives to two suicide bombers as they sat drinking Coca-Cola and chatting while music wafted from the restaurant doorways. Not far from the Moment Café, where eleven young people were murdered in June, and from the Sbarro pizzeria, where fifteen were blown to bits, lies the big Mahanei Yehuda market, and not far from the market is the large building that houses my gym. Everything is near everything else in a city as small as Jerusalem. After class one day, the gym instructor, soaked in sweat, her voice barely audible above the exercise music, shouted: "Good for you, girls, coming to gym even with the way things are."

Good for you? Whom was she talking to? What was she talking

about? But as I looked around, at the Orthodox women, out of breath, carefully replacing their wigs or kerchiefs, at the rest of us pulling on our slacks before walking out the door to take our kids to school or shop in the supermarket or ride the city buses or sit and drink cappuccino as if mass murderers were not planning to murder us where we stood, my eyes welled with tears. Good for you. Really, well done.

## The Deheisheh Refugee Camp

The Deheisheh refugee camp near Bethlehem is like a massive warship flying black sails. It navigates the murky waters of an ever-stormy sea, carrying tens of thousands of people who refuse to dock even though dry land is in sight. For them, it is as if the longed-for shore weren't there. Those trees and houses in the distance? For them, they don't exist. Instead, the refugee camp is a fortress where militants are enlisted at birth in an endless war, the war for a free Palestine stretching from the Jordan River to the Mediterranean Sea. In exchange for this intractable ideology, they get a few kilos of rice, flour, and sugar provided by UNRWA (U.N. Relief and Works Agency).

Let us consider Shaladi, a young man I spoke to on the rough terrain of Deheisheh. Handsome and strong, with the eyes of a gazelle, he had an uncertain, ironical air. He wore a red American T-shirt and had gelled his hair into little spikes. "I'm twenty-two," he said. "I don't have plans for the future. What future? I was born in Deheisheh. My present and future are in Deheisheh. Outside, it's another world, but I'll never, ever leave here except to go back to Ajour, where my grandfather was thrown out in 1948, with my parents and aunts and uncles when they were little. We're all in Deheisheh, and we'll stay here until we go back to our house in Ajour." Don't you want to find a job? I asked him. "What job?" he said. "The only job is the Palestinian people's fight for its liberation." So you don't want to become a lawyer, or a computer expert, or a doctor? I pressed. "Maybe, but there's no time to think about that." No time? You have all the time in the world, I told him. And when you get married, you'll have the time of your children, too. I showed that I was exaggerating, and Shaladi became much more personable. He even smiled. "I'll get married in twenty, thirty, a hundred years," he said. "My life isn't mine until I go back to Ajour."

I asked him if he wanted peace—two states for two peoples. "Peace isn't possible with the Jews," he told me. "Maybe you don't understand, but my house is in Ajour, and they forced us out, violently. I don't care if Jews lived there, too. I don't care if I live close to them eventually." In the Jewish state? I asked. "Of course not. Not in a Jewish state, not even in a state where we both live. In time we'll see what will happen." Will you throw the Jews out? I asked. "They'll leave by themselves. Or if they stay, it'll be in a Muslim state," he answered. Will you eliminate them? I asked.."If they don't accept living in a Muslim state." Why a Muslim state? "Because there's no religious freedom among the Jews," he said. But don't you want to live in a nice apartment in Bethlehem, or Ramallah or Hebron, rather than living here in Deheisheh? Don't you want to live in a Palestinian state after we achieve peace? I asked. "There can be no Palestinian state unless it includes my house in Ajour," was his answer. I asked if he had ever been to Ajour. "No, but with God's help, I hope to go there," he said. Have you seen what it looks like? I asked. "I saw it in a film by a European director, but you could only see a few ruins, a few trees."

We spoke in front of a large, recently renovated low-slung building at the main entrance to the Deheisheh camp. A line of barbed wire used to run past here, stopping at a strange revolving gate. Since the gate was dismantled during the Oslo peace process, the entrance is now marked only by a monument to the martyrs of Deheisheh. This renders the sense of separation between.the camp and the outside more immediate, more a psychic fact than a physical one. Nearby, you can sense the street life of Bethlehem, with its noisy traffic and vendors cheerily selling their wares or food. But take a few steps, and the place might as well bear Dante's inscription to the Gate of Hell: "Through me the way into the woeful city." Here begins a labyrinth of little streets, the first houses where the residents of the first refugee camp lived. It was built in 1951, and its inhabitants now number more than eleven thousand.

The original refugees came from forty-five different villages whose names are venerated everywhere in Deheisheh, including on a large colorful mural at the entrance to the camp, which shows a map of Palestine. On the map's margins, Palestinians are depicted in traditional dress: calm men, women, and children herding their flocks, weaving, and tending the soil. This is paradise before the fall—the Nabka, the creation of the state of Israel. On their map, of course, Palestine encompasses all of Israel, with marks showing land the Palestinians lost. The implication is clear: This is land they can, will, and must one day reconquer.

The houses in Deheisheh get nicer the higher you climb through the little alleyways that have multiplied over time. Up here the buildings are better planned, and there are a few parked cars. The area looks cleaner, and there are also more television antennas. Still, things are definitely still rough. Children wander around in bands, the grim shops sell a only a few items, and the signs of unemployment are easily detected in the little groups of adults walking around, and on the faces of women in traditional dress who look weary and seem older than their years. But at the same time, Deheisheh doesn't entirely fit the description of a refugee camp either. It doesn't look like one of those temporary encampments where throngs of the unfortunate have been cast together in so many corners of the world so many times in the last century. And this is because UNRWA, the organization whose sole task is to oversee Palestinian refugees, has pursued a shrewd policy of allowing the refugees to settle down definitively, or at least semidefinitively. It has encouraged them to produce generations of refugees. It hasn't helped them resettle elsewhere or invest in new lives, but rather allowed them to remain refugees in perpetuity. This is the mentality that UNRWA has fostered—with the help of $300 million a year in American aid.

And this is how the children running around in groups and playing ball and going to school think of themselves. Some wear military uniforms. Others dress simply but not shabbily. The young people are well turned out and busy, and the crowds of people walking around don't look like a mass of desperate humanity. Instead, Deheisheh seems more like an organized little village, a community that's insular, but not starving or tattered or ill. Here barbers, bakers, teachers, and tire sellers work just as they would in any southern Italian or Greek village. In a social center called IBDAA, children play war games on different computers, whose colored screens show pictures of tanks and armies marching across green fields.

These computers—thirty-five in all—are also used for distance learning programs that put the children "in touch with different refugee communities and disseminate information through their Web sites," as IBDAA's brochure put it. IBDAA, to its credit, provides information about kindergartens, schools, theater, and dance classes. Yet even in the dance classes the memory of the places the refugees came from before 1948 and 1967 is kept alive. In some way, these places are no more than names. But the names—the same ones inscribed on the colorful map at the entrance to the camp—are part of every camp activity. They are an obsession, a focus of school activities at every stage of the children's education. Starting at a young age, the kids join groups named after Tal and el Safi, Falluja, Jora, Zakaria, Ashwa, Beit ha Tab, Ajoub. They talk about the towns, study pictures of them. If they can, they take field trips and look for the remains of their family's former houses in places like the Malha neighborhood in Jerusalem, or the area where the University of Tel Aviv now stands.

One of IBDAA's Web pages describes each village one by one, in great detail, and even provides a map of where its inhabitants wound up. Ajour, northwest of Hebron, is described as being situated between Zakaria and Deir Diban, today located inside the Green Line. The site also says that twenty-five different ruins can be found near Ajour, including wine and oil presses and the foundations of houses, mosques, and caves. The population was 3,730 in 1945, the Web page says. And in an emotional reminder, it informs today's youth that for the 1942–1943 school year, the highest grade taught was fourth. The implication is that the children's education was interrupted when the village was destroyed and its inhabitants dispersed. New Jewish settlements were built in its place, the Web page says. End of story—a tragic memory to pass down through the generations. The same goes for Al Burej, where the damage listed includes eight ruins, among them tombs and wine presses and Zakaria where, the Web page says, several citizens were "martyred," both in 1939 fighting against the English and in 1948 fighting against the Jews. The Web site helps construct a collective memory about these towns. It never once mentions any evidence of reconciliation between the Israelis and the Palestinians, perhaps because the current intifada has revealed a trait in the Palestinians that they might not want to talk about: their openness to terrorism.

To understand what happens to children caught up in this culture we need only look at a collection of letters posted on IBDAA's Web site and written in 1998 and 1999 by Palestinian children, many of whom are fourth-generation refugees. Here's what a ten-year-old boy named Ghassan L. wrote, "Do you know who I am? I am the child who was robbed of his homeland, who doesn't know what peace means. I say to all Palestinians: This land is our land. We must never give it up. Our right of return is a sacred right." Mualyad Hassan Qaraqeq, twelve, described the wonders of the village his family came from, Elar, and the hell inflicted on his people by the creation of the state of Israel. "The people of Elar were a tight-knit group, but families were separated and had their land taken. Among these were the Qaraqeq clan, the Assaf clan, the Zboun clan, and the Saraasra clan. We're all waiting to return to our villages. Our right of return is a sacred right." Many of the letters talk about the brutality of the Israeli soldiers and the violence the Palestinians faced at the hands of a fierce enemy. By exploiting these painful, indeed genuine memories of the past, the Palestinians have constructed a unique brand of political determination, built almost entirely on the demonization of the state of Israel. No one contests this way of looking at things. In fact, people in the camp told me privately that it would be scandalous to break away from the party line.

UNRWA contributes to this culture, too. It does everything it can to keep the Palestinians stuck, fostering a culture that binds them forever to the camp, rather than helping them resettle. It is in this way that the souls and lives of millions of people have been subsumed by a political imperative larger than themselves. The Palestinians who have grown up in the camps are like memorial candles. They are the body and soul of a lie that the whole world naively believes whenever the peace process is discussed. In fact, when the Palestinians say "restitution of lands," this means nothing less than their taking back the entire land of Israel. For them, it is both a political imperative and a religious one, as they, the descendants of refugees, are themselves considered refugees under the unusual rules of Waqf, Islam's rules for inheritance. Millions of Palestinians have stayed in refugee camps because the names of those hundred villages have for them become as flesh and blood. They are written into their hearts and fists, even though no one, except in the distant past, has ever seen substantial proof they existed. Some people even hold on to old, rusty keys in the hope they might one day open a door that no longer exists. To preserve the memory of these villages, millions of people have been deprived of the possibility of leading a normal life. Instead, they have resigned themselves to a life of endless war. Unlike any other refugees on earth, the Palestinians have heeded a declaration of war that is as psychological as it is practical and political. And it has prevented them from integrating, indeed creating, a society made up of home, work, and family, even of the joy of living—let alone the prospect of the creation of a Palestinian state.

You can't leave a refugee camp easily, even if you want to. In part, this is because the UNRWA works hard to maintain the status quo. It keeps people in the camps by providing meager but reliable services; food, education, and medical services are all free. But even as it provides for the refugees, it also encourages the seething anger that pervades the camps. The story of UNRWA would take a book to tell. It was created in 1949 as an entity inside the United Nations. But unlike the United Nations High Commission for Refugees, however, its aim is not to resettle refugees, but rather to preserve their refugee status. UNRWA has never fought to convince the Arab countries surrounding Israel—where some Palestinians wound up after the wars of 1948 and 1967—into resettling their brethren. Instead, all except Jordan refuse to recognize the Palestinians as citizens. In the beginning, UNRWA built its camps as temporary structures.

This, it bears noting, was part of a plan hatched by the Arab countries and the Palestinian leadership to perpetuate the refugee problem. In 1959, Dag Hammarskjold, then secretary general of the United Nations, tried to advance a plan to resettle Middle Eastern refugees, but it collapsed under the weight of Arab and Palestinian pressure against it. Over time, UNRWA took advantage of its collapse by becoming a vast bureaucracy. In 2003 it had 20,000 employees, 98 percent of whom are Palestinian, and an annual  budget of $300 million. Inside the UNRWA machine, the refugee is defined almost ontologically. He is a refugee because he fits a generally accepted definition of one, or he's considered a refugee by extraction, or because he's been moved from place to place for one reason or another. A Palestinian refugee doesn't think about himself in the future tense. He can't imagine himself living a normal life in an autonomous Palestinian city like Bethlehem or Ramallah or Nablus, because as a refugee he is not a person, but rather a pawn in a larger political strategy. Let us be clear: This strategy will never accept the idea of a two-state solution. Its only goal is for the Palestinians to reclaim all the land they believe was theirs and believe was taken by the Jews in the creation of the state of Israel—from the Jordan to the Sea.

And while the terrorist organizations feed on refugees everywhere, this is why they flourish particularly well in the camps. Thanks to the ties between UNRWA and the Palestinian Authority, secular extremists do especially well in the camps, including the Al Aqsa Martyrs' Brigade, which is connected to the Al-Fatah movement, or the Popular Front for the Liberation of Palestine. The refugees are the most important element in the Palestinians' war against Israel and in the strategy that led to the failure of the talks at Camp David in 2000.

As the historian Ephraim Karsh has written in the *Jerusalem Post* and elsewhere, the right of return is a euphemism for "the annihilation of Israel." The refugees are living proof of the lie contained in the statement "two states for two peoples," which is ultimately nothing more than a pious invention of the pacifist West. The idea isn't shared by the Palestinians or the Arab world, which has never asked Yasir Arafat to abandon his intransigence. The refugees are the Palestinian war machine. Looking back on it, it is quite remarkable that during the various phases of the Oslo peace process Israel and its American and European supporters believed that they could shelve the refugee problem and delay confronting an issue that ultimately translates into recognizing whether Israel has a right to exist or not. Anyone who visits a refugee camp immediately understands that the Palestinian right of return is not an issue that will go away through smiles and handshakes. One need only glance around a camp to understand that what they've been fed on, first and foremost by UNRWA, is completely indigestible. They cannot change their diet overnight. Four generations of refugees have been fed on UNRWA rice, flour, and sugar, and educated in schools where children don't just learn to read and write but are also taught to hate. The walls of Deheisheh aren't just plastered with images of martyrs, they are also painted with incredible murals that depict enormous Israeli soldiers shooting unarmed citizens and screaming children. Everywhere you turn, there are images of the dead and wounded terrorized by the *moloch* of the Israeli military machine.

The Palestinians may be the only refugees on earth who have

been institutionalized to be refugees, but what is even stranger is that, in the course of their political sanctification, no one ever remembers that in the same years around the creation of the state of Israel, the Arab countries exiled 800,000 Jews, threatening their lives and confiscating the property of generations. Although this was a devastating loss for these Jews, they were quickly resettled by their brethren in Israel and elsewhere. They moved into homes and schools and roles where it was possible for them to reintegrate into society. In short, they were restored to life. The Palestinian refugees were never considered owners of their own lives. Rather, they were defined only by their place in a group whose collective identity has been forged around an indomitable opposition to Israel's right to exist.

The number of Palestinian refugees created by the birth of the state of Israel is estimated at somewhere between 540,000 and 740,000. They now number around four million. That's almost equals the entire population of Jews in Israel, although some estimates halve the number of Palestinians. A document issued in 2000 by the refugee department in Ramallah put it candidly: "The Arab countries decided to preserve Palestinian identity by maintaining the Palestinians' refugee status (rather than naturalizing them or resettling them), in order to keep the refugee issue alive and to prevent Israel from shirking its responsibility." And so that is how the refugee theme has stayed alive, to the point that it has now become the most burning issue in the Middle East, more urgent than the question of Jerusalem itself. This development runs against all political logic and makes the Palestinian situation unique from any other analogous historical precedent.

Let's consider the history. Major conflicts the world over have created hundreds of thousands, if not millions, of refugees. In the twentieth century alone they numbered around 135 million. But of all these wandering and relocated souls only the Palestinians have remained refugees for more than fifty years. This is because their leadership considers them pawns, rather than human beings like everyone else, groups of families with personal histories, men and women who have the right to the pursuit of happiness and to live in peace. That is the desire that drove so many other refugees in the last century to return to their lands, be it in the Balkans or Rwanda, where they usually resettled in different cities in the same homeland or found refuge in other countries. The Palestinians have been far less alienated on a human level than other refugees, since neither their language nor their land, food, religion, or the sounds, smells, and colors of the places they had to leave are any different from those where they live now, considering that they mostly live on the outskirts of their former towns or in other Arab countries. And that would remain the case if a Palestinian state were created in the future. Indeed, the Palestinians have never moved more than several dozen kilometers, or at most one or two hundred. I certainly don't mean to underestimate the suffering caused by leaving their homes, but let's once again remember that all the refugees of the last century, including the nearly one million Jews cast out of Arab lands, were generally always resettled within one generation.

Apart from mass migration across the German-Polish border at the end of World War II, the most significant resettlement of the last century was certainly the one caused by the conflict that led to the creation of Pakistan in 1947. As the renowned historian Bernard Lewis told me in an interview, "In 1947, when England was disentangling itself from Palestine, it was also pulling out of India, thereby bringing about the birth of the states of India and Pakistan. But while the Arab-Israeli conflict created tens of thousands of refugees, the Indians and Pakistanis wisely agreed to transfer millions of people across the border in order to avoid ethnic and religious tension. India sent the Muslims to Pakistan, which in its turn sent the Hindus to India. Both these states granted citizenship to the refugees. It is a sad paradox that the smallest problem, and probably the easiest one to solve, has cost the Western world millions of dollars in humanitarian aid, only to perpetuate the demands of the refugees, who have monopolized media attention for more than half a century, when the alternative, a refugee exchange like that between India and Pakistan, has shown good results." Another important example is that of the estimated ten million ethnic Germans who were expelled from Poland, Czechoslovakia, Hungary, and Yugoslavia at the end of World War II. The truth is that if the German government had ever insisted on their right of return—something that never even remotely happened—it would have been clear that what West Germany was asking for was not a humanitarian solution for its dislocated citizens, but rather the annulment of the political results of Hitler's war.

Bearing this in mind, let us now return to Deheisheh. It is a city of martyrs, where the names of the *shahids*—the figures most honored by the Palestinians—are inscribed on schools and streets. These are the martyrs whom Mr. Arafat always exalts in his Arabic speeches, even as he condemns them in his English discourses. They are the role models that every Palestinian child wants to emulate. So far, three suicide terrorists have come from Deheisheh, but there are four martyrs, because they also count a fifteen-year-old boy who was killed by the Israeli army. Pictures of the suicide bombers cover the town, especially ones depicting Muhammed Darameh Ashouani, who blew himself up in March 2002, at the age of twenty. The Al Aqsa Martyrs' Brigade took responsibility for his attack. Such posters are plastered on the houses, on the town's few stores, and on its school. Sometimes local painters or activist teenagers paint big, realistic color pictures of the martyrs on the walls of houses, their faces rendered in black and blood-colored paint. It is clear that the suicide bomber is the local hero.

Muhammed Darameh is depicted armed, with strong muscles, a handsome boy like any other eighteen-year-old, which is just what he was before he killed dozens of people at a bar mitzvah party in Jerusalem's Orthodox Beit Yisrael neighborhood. The house he lived in is relatively comfortable and spacious and located in an area set apart from the oldest streets in the camp, the ones that were hastily built thirty years ago and still look nomadic today. In Darameh's neighborhood, the houses are more modern, the streets larger. The roofs all have big television antennas, which bring in stations from across the Arab world, not just Palestinian stations. A few people seem to be growing red flowers on their balconies. Everywhere the message is clear: The terrorist-as-idol has nothing to do with poverty, or even with religious fanaticism. Darameh is a modern, secular hero. He is used as a political example and to set a style. Indeed, Deheisheh isn't an area with a strong tradition of religious terrorism. Al-Fatah, the militant wing of the secular Palestinian Authority, reigns supreme here, and the Al Aqsa Martyrs' Brigades are also strong. People take pride in pointing out Darameh's house. And like priests upholding a politically correct norm, the local leadership wants to keep it that way. In spite of their grief for their dead brother, no one in Deheisheh expresses even the slightest doubt about suicide terrorism. For the Palestinians, killing Jews is considered an institutional duty, and those who do so are honored and boasted about. Their families even receive a monetary reward.

We go up a flight of stairs to sit with Amer, Darameh's twenty-five-year-old brother, on one of two sofas in a corner of the spacious living room on the second floor of the family's house. We could be in a living room anywhere, only we are sitting with a man whose brother carried out a genocidal pogrom, killing children, old people, and women dressed in their holiday best, including three generations of the same family, who have now vanished off the face of the earth. A young girl brings us coffee with cardamom. She is one of.Muhammed's nine siblings. Amer drives an ambulance for the Red Crescent. He looks like his brother and shares the athletic stance and modern look that come across in so many pictures of Muhammed. Amer immediately starts to talk about how a colleague of his was killed by the Israelis. "The Israelis stopped the ambulance with the wounded or sick inside. They didn't care what happened to them, only about security," he said. It was futile to try and talk to Amer about how the Israelis stop even their own ambulances on the street as they head toward the site of suicide bombings—like they did in September after the bombing in Jerusalem's German Colony—fearing that other suicide bombers might be hiding inside, waiting to inflict even more horror, as has happened before. Besides, wouldn't it be logical to suspect that the brother of a suicide bomber, a man who says he was always his brother's biggest supporter, might be a pretty reasonable target for a checkpoint, especially if he's driving an ambulance, a vehicle spacious enough to transport weapons hidden among the fake wounded?

Amer understandably chokes up at the mention of his brother, and his big, brown eyes well with tears. "No, I wouldn't scold him for anything, except for going off and dying," he begins. "If he were here today, I would tie him to the bed so he couldn't leave. Who would have ever imagined it? He was always so kind and sweet. The kids in the neighborhood worshipped him. He was always up for fun. We miss him. My mom really misses him, even if we're always busy with ceremonies in memory of the martyrs. They're always inviting us to them. They're really worried about us. It's not just Al-Fatah. All the parties call and ask us to say something in Muhammed's memory at their big events. We can hardly turn them down. No, even though we're devastated, I don't disapprove of what he did, even if I want to prevent the death of innocent people. Why? Because I've seen at all these ceremonies that what he did reflected people's thoughts, their desires. If he killed ten people, what's that compared to the massacres that happen every day in Gaza?"

Amer almost laughs when we ask him how one goes from being a refugee in Ashwa—a town a few kilometers outside Jerusalem where his family is from—to becoming a martyr. For him the answer is obvious. "To be a refugee in Deheisheh doesn't mean very much for you, but for us, it's our entire life. My grandfather, my father, my uncle, we're all heirs to something that's hard to express, but that's our whole life." But what if they had offered you a country, or if they do offer you one, that could be what Israel became for the Moroccan or Libyan Jews? I ask. "Never," Amer answers. "A few weeks ago I saw the cactuses and stones and walls and a stone wheel from Ashwa behind Rachel's Tomb. Like me, Muhammed felt that it was essential for us to stay attached to Deheisheh, to stay faithful to our rights. Of course, we talk a lot about being refugees, of how awful it is to be different, poor, without a future. My brother talked about it all the time. All the kids do. But I won't ever leave my village." He raised his head. "I wasn't cut out to be a martyr like my brother, but he was right," he boasted. "You only get out of here through the cemetery, or through Ashwa."

Little groups of terrorists started coming from the refugee camps during the Al Aqsa Intifada. But UNRWA, rather than trying to do something about it, or even make clear statements condemning it, opted to recuse itself from the debate. For an organization intent on preserving, not solving, the most explosive problem of the Middle East, coupled with its close ties to the Palestine Liberation Organization, the UNRWA's silence essentially translates into complicit support of extremism. As we have seen, young people, often unemployed, with a low standard of living and no hope for the future except their dream of defeating Israel and taking its place, have been fed a diet of extremism. This begins with elementary school textbooks, which deny the existence of the state of Israel, which don't even name it or show pictures of it, and instead praise Palestinian martyrs.

When a terrorist from the Jenin refugee camp blew himself up in Netanya in March 2000, leaving twenty-nine people dead, and the Israelis struck back at Jenin, the commissioner general of UNRWA,

Peter Hansen, had nothing but fiery words—against the Israelis. He told the international media that "it would not be an exaggeration to call" what Israel did to Jenin "a massacre." The reality, however, is that in a difficult three-day clash, the Israelis chose not to use heavy weaponry and instead fought door-to-door, losing twenty-three of its own soldiers and killing fifty-three Palestinians in a town completely planted with mines. In fact, the Jenin camp mounted a full-scale offensive against the Israelis, using well-armed militants from various groups. Indeed, many of the camps are cradles of terror like Jenin, and UNRWA hasn't done a thing to stop their proliferation.

Back in Deheisheh, we walk on the town's oldest streets and turn to the right into an improvised construction, its gray stones only partially joined with mortar. A covered patio stands above a cement platform, which is outfitted with a bed, a hookah, and a portable heater. The floor is covered by a large rug. A *rabana*, a kind of one-stringed violin, sits in the corner, alongside its bow and a wood and parchment case. On the rug sits the maestro of refugees himself, Mahmoud Ahmed Abeid. He wears a black-and-white kaffiyeh on his small, old head, and his vivacious eyes dart around above his noble, straight nose. His white moustache parts to show a smile. His face is clean-shaven. "I'm 107 years old," he says in answer to my question. (Others say he's probably ninety-five.) He tells his story from the beginning. He witnessed the Ottoman Empire. They treated the local Arabs dreadfully—they beat them up and exploited them, starved them and subjected them to wars that weren't their own. Then came the English. It was easy with the British; they liked the Palestinians. The Jordanians weren't any great shakes. And then came the Jews. The creation of the state of Israel brought about good things. It brought about work. They were friendly. Jews and Arabs, we often ate together in the fields, or at home during holidays, he said. Abeid stopped to roll a cigarette and kept trying to offer me one. At this point he skipped the entire story of the Palestinian refugees and instead jumped directly to the Al Aqsa Intifada, which he said started when Prime Minister Sharon wanted to take the Al Aqsa Mosque back from the Arabs.

But what about before that? I asked. Before that, Mahmoud said he lived in Zakaria but was thrown out. It was the Arab states who asked him to leave, promising that he could return, he said. Was he forced out at gunpoint? I asked. Abeid dropped the subject entirely and moved on to other stories. Maybe he didn't remember. From the time he fled his home until the 1960s, Abeid lived in Deheisheh. Then he moved to Oja, near Jericho, into the Abed Jaber refugee camp, with another wife. Then he and his wife and family went to Jordan. From there they moved back to Deheisheh, where his first wife had stayed. He remembers his house in Zakaria as a lovely place. He says the walls are still there, and that after all these pere-grinations, he's ready to fix the place up, if he could ever return. Even if the trees are no longer there, or the animals, Abeid said he'd rather to go back to Zakaria and "eat dirt" than live ill at ease any-where else. His twelve-year-old grandson, Khaled, was killed in this intifada by the Israeli army, he says. Another grandson, Milad Khaled, was sitting with us. He is thirteen years old and a good stu-dent, clean-cut and smiling. He said that maybe one day he'll be-come a martyr, too. His grandfather approves. The boy has been to see where their house once stood. He liked the place. Today, there are only rocks and scrub brush, but one day, who knows? Peace with the Jews is only possible if they recognize our rights, including the right of return, grandfather and grandson say. But these days I feel so small and weak, how can I fight? Abeid adds. Without his home and land a man becomes small. No one helps us, he says. The Arab governments don't help us; Arafat's government doesn't help us; the Europeans abandoned us; the YMCA only gives us medicine and a little food.

Mahmoud Abeid is a gentle man, with hands that seem large set against his small, thin body. They're the hands of a good peasant, proud of his profession and his honor. He remembers when he had a piece of land. If Palestinian aggression against Israel were less in-tense, or if UNRWA had been like any other refugee organization and resettled the refugees, if the Arab states had been benevolent and wanted to reach a solution, and if Arafat were a real politician, Abeid's long life would probably not have been so miserable. Nor would he have had to move around so much. Abeid would have had a field of his own to cultivate—a place to live for, rather than to die for. Instead, the refugee camp has eaten away the life of a centenar-ian. And it will do the same for Milad, who is only thirteen and whose whole life lies ahead of him.

# Anti-Americanism

On the eve of the beginning of Italy's presidency of the European Union in July 2003, Prime Minister Silvio Berlusconi chose a path of international daring by supporting the United States. He hoped that his determination to be a bridge between a malevolent Europe and the antiterrorist front would create a special role for Italy and also cover up with international support his serious internal problems, including an outstanding trial for corruption.

But he achieved the opposite result. The United States became hated even more in Italy, helped by the strong delegitimization that his enemies projected onto him. The left-wing political opposition found strong allies to form a large anti-American pacifist alliance based on long-held historically Italian views. Anti-Americanism has found entrée into the churches, the local sections of Forza Italia, Berlusconi's party, and mostly of La Lega, the populist rightist party, and the ex-Fascist right currently sitting in the government. It has created a bizarre situation in which intellectuals, the media, government, and much of public opinion view the United States with deep disapproval, intellectual contempt, envy, and even hate, while Italy's highest public official—one of the lone few in Europe—is pro-America. As during the era of Fascism and after 1945 in the environment of the Communist local headquarters or in the church parish, the United States arouses hostile feelings that few people dare to oppose publicly. The situation is identical to that which occurred in Italy after World War II, when the Christian Democrats led a pro-American government that subsisted on its connection with NATO and American aid, but in which anti-Americanism was the politically correct public opinion.

Italian anti-Americanism is historically rooted in Fascism, Communism, and Catholicism, all of which converge in the current antiglobal movement. After the war in Iraq started, colorful, striped peace flags could be seen hanging from windows from Sicily to Venice. (How ironic for a country which in its extremely postnational mood has renounced flags!) Several features characterize this anti-Americanism. First, it is a widespread religion, embraced by intellectuals and journalists, offering a strong widespread ideology that arms the future of the country itself. Second, Italy's anti-Americanism was born primarily during the twenty years of the Mussolini Fascist experience. Its current version represents this totalitarian origin and prolongs a substantial indifference toward democracy. Third, anti-Americanism is the only glue that a destroyed left can use to connect with people of the larger antiglobal movement. Fourth, at the European level, so lacking in common aims and common ground, anti-Americanism provides the only point of juncture where French President Jacques Chirac and German Chancellor Gerhard Schroeder can join in a sort of common struggle that many Italians desire to join. Fifth, an anti-Israeli and anti-Semitic attitude represents the most barbaric and hard-nosed face of anti-Americanism, to the extent that anti-Americanism is a version of anti-Semitism. This intellectually repulsive mix appears and operates at levels that defy the local anti-fascist national memory and ethos and even the law.

All these points have one common denominator: Italy doesn't have a deep tradition of democracy. Catholicism and Communism, its main cultural modern ideological components, care much more about social issues than about the civil and human rights guaranteed by democracy. But anti-Americanists are not so foolish as to present their cause as an unbridled, unqualified attack on the United States in its entirety. The Europeans in general, and Italy in particular, have an elaborate way of attacking the enemy by professing admiration for the United States' "great tradition of democracy," thus resorting to an intellectual invention that dates back to the fifties. The technique is to create the "Altra America"—the other America—of John F. Kennedy, Bill Clinton, Bob Dylan, Woody Allen, blacks, and feminists.

The Altra America, provides the left-wing Italian soul with a rationale for not condemning as a total monster and threat to humanity the nation that, after all, saved the country and all of Europe from Nazism and Stalinism. Even Enrico Berlinguer, secretary of the Communist Party, declared in the 1980s that he felt safer under the NATO umbrella, and the vast majority of Italians were never serious about becoming part of the Soviet bloc. Nor did Italy, with a weak post–World War II prime minister, Giulio Andreotti, divorce the United States as did France during the prime ministry of the powerful Charles de Gaulle. And while anti-Americanism in France is a basic and unchallenged instinct for a nation that sees itself as superior, in Italy, still grappling to establish a clear identity for itself, it is something to be debated. Moreover, the governments of Italy, for thirty years dominated by Democrazia Cristiana, the Catholic party, were still deeply engaged in the Cold War on the side of the United States, even if the Catholic Church was pushing against secularization and the emancipation of women, in a word, against any modernizing trend identified with the United States. Most Italians welcomed any sign of modernization in a country that had been dominated by the corrupt, parochial, secluded, ignorant, and hungry dictatorship of Fascism.

Italians saluted the Americans who entered Rome on June 4, 1944. They brought a fresh breath of culture, together with chocolate, toothpaste, soap, and blankets. The United States, through the Marshall Plan, gave Italians the money to finance a new age of democracy, the emancipation of women, boogie-woogie, American authors (F. Scott Fitzgerald and Ernest Hemingway), and role-model actors (Humphrey Bogart, Gary Cooper, and John Wayne). It was a real revolution, a liberation that the Italians registered in the deepest part of their subconscious. From the 1950s to 1970s, during the rise of the worst brand of imported Soviet anti-Americanism, Altra America was still loved and defended by Italian intellectuals as a sort of European American, soft and pacifist and basically anticapitalist whose worst enemy was the United States itself, its ruling class that wants to dominate the world and sends its youth to fight first in Vietnam and now in Iraq. I would argue that, as a matter of basic fact, this is a symptom of the unstructured nature of Italian anti-Americanism. Does this make the phenomenon of anti-Americanism less aggressive, less dangerous? No, because its power was magnified and exacerbated by the loss of a sense of identity experienced by Europe and its left.

Italian commentators often delight in the loss of American life. A famous Italian columnist and senior editor, Eugenio Scalfari, wrote in *La Repubblica*, a mainstream newspaper, on August 24, 2003, after the terrorist attack against the United Nations in Baghdad: "We have to sound the alarm [about the diffusion of a war of cultures] because the real, principal engine of the metastasis [of terrorism] is just the image of the marine sitting in his tank, ready to shoot any moving target that might appear suspicious; neurotic, because of the ambushes, because of the hostility, serving a tour of duty that he is not prepared for, that poor boy [the Altra America!] has already won a [limited] war but bought it with dollars, while he actually lost the [world] peace; he attracts all the terrorists without being able to kill them while after four months, Iraqi towns are still without water, medicine, aid. The primary mistake was not to make the peace between Israel and Palestine as the first priority and, just in case, to postpone the Iraqi war. But Bush and his hawks wanted the war; they needed it badly. So they made it and allowed the Palestinian priority to be forgotten. Now the government of the United States is asking the United Nations for a resolution that authorizes the influx of more troops and money [and that would give more power to the United Nations]. Powell has already said no; about Rumsfeld, there's no point in talking; those hawks use oil as a nutritive basis so the conflict will continue, the mullah will stir up the fires of fanaticism, while Bush from the decks of his many aircraft carriers will invoke the Christian God of the army of the righteous. Until such time as, just to prop up his political fortunes, President Bush starts another preventive war against Iran, which is right there, within reach of his cannons."

The article reiterates well-understood patterns of American behavior that don't even require any evidence. You just have to mention it, and the Italian public will repeat it on social occasions and teach it to their children. The pattern includes a conspiracy theory, where the genuine motives of America are very far from the declared ones, but are concealed in its ontological need to make war. In this case, that the war is motivated by greed—oil—and power games and that it will self-expand, from Iraq to Iran, for example, for the sake of power and of war itself. The poor but neurotic American soldier is a blind instrument of American power, a machine of death, ready to kill and be killed, because he is basically an idiot—again, the Altra America. Meanwhile a primitive Bush—who is also an idiot, but he is the boss, maybe even the dictator—uses a primitive God just as the mullah uses it, with no difference. Religion in the hands of the Americans becomes a cynical instrument of hatred.

On the same day, when the United Nations were attacked in Baghdad, *Il Manifesto*, a Communist antiglobal newspaper read mostly by students, defined the attack simply as "Bush's defeat." The United Nations is characterized surprisingly as something that in recent years has become "the back of the shop of the United States" that "after the embargo [on Iraq], slaughtered the Iraqi population and forbade reconstruction." It was struck by righteous terrorists because it helped the United States. And the results of the war? "America gave birth to a monster." The monster is the war, which America is obsessed with, and terrorism, which America invented and which is basically right in its struggle against imperialism.

More subtly, a very important columnist and intellectual, Barbara Spinelli, wrote on the same day a front-page article in *La Stampa* (my newspaper) where she bluntly asks: "Why is there a conflict? To defy terrorism? To convince the Arab population to distance itself from Islamic fundamentalism? Or maybe Bush's aim is another: to safeguard the image of an invulnerable superpower, to show the U.N. and Europe that the control of the entire world is firmly in American hands, to dominate from up close the regimes that own the resources that we all need, oil. But none of these aims has been achieved. . . . The war, like a drunk ship, sails toward shores that the American captain searches for with blind eyes."

This view of the United States took some time to develop fully after September 11, when the most venerable among the Italian newspapers, *Il Corriere della Sera*, declared "We are all Americans" on the front page, exactly like *Le Monde* did. For a few weeks, the horror prevailed and sympathy for the losses dominated the Italian general state of mind, just to lose ground at the very moment when it became clear that instead of accepting the role of victims, the United States was going to react and even to become the leading force in the war that Bush declared against terrorism. Spinelli writes in the aforementioned article that "Bush has chosen only one way, the military one [among many that could have been chosen]; it's the same choice adopted by the Israeli government, and nobody knows who is imitating whom, in this fatal belief in the indispensability of weapons."

War is the magic word that resurrects anti-Americanism, especially when it is coupled with the subject of the Israeli-Palestinian conflict. Peace in the Middle East was a sort of "call of the wild" for the tens of thousands of antiglobal, anti-imperialist youth who marched from Assisis to Perugia with the same leaders of the centrist-left government that in September 2001 had approved the participation of some military units in the war in Afghanistan on October 14, 2001. These antiglobal, Communist, and Catholic youth created a wave that the entire left was soon obliged to follow to avoid remaining isolated. The furious slogans were unfurled: "United States and Israel—the real terrorists"; "Yankee, be careful—

somebody could bomb you"; "Disarm the sky and the earth"; "Terrorism is the tragedy to avoid; war is the enemy to beat"; "No global war, neither with Bush, nor with bin Laden"; "War and terrorism are business for the rich."

The leading newspapers, the intellectuals, the left, and the populist right immediately got the message: either you join or you loose this colorful crowd of youth, nuns, priests, farmers, workers, and Arab émigrés waving red flags, peace flags, Palestinian flags, and flags with the faces of Che Guevara and Saddam Hussein. After many years of retreat and of attrition, of absence from the squares and the streets, after so many years of isolation and on the verge of being dispersed, the left suddenly found its way back to the mass movements and to the symbol of a flag, after the red flag had been buried, of anti-Americanism. It was an oversimplified, backward yet deeply Fascist and Communist anti-Americanism that gave up on the long road that led from the Cold War toward the acceptance of a new international scenario. The cowardice, envy, and parochialism of fascist anti-Americanism had returned, fueled by the desire of the left to find its piazza masses again and of the Catholic movement's belief that their battle for life in its mystical sense is fulfilled by pacifism. Third Worldism came back, dashing away all the crimes and the misdeeds of the dictators and the terrorists.

Concerning the war in Afghanistan, Tiziano Terzani, winner of many journalist awards, wrote: "Those B-52s are here not only to bomb the refuges of bin Laden, but to remind everyone who the new policemen, the new judges, the new owners and puppeteers are of this country. It's the Talibans' turn now to become the new victims of the Americans who want to avenge their dead, but most of all to establish the idea of their invulnerability."

The sources of this anti-Americanism are many indeed, but the central one is grounded in Fascism. Consider what Mussolini said in a dialogue about "the forces that threaten Europe": "I have a great sympathy for the [American] people. But I have no sympathy for their government. The American constitution brings to power, under the deceptive standard of democracy, authentic capitalistic oligarchies, which I call plutocracies. These are oligarchies made up of huge economic interests, more than of ideas and principles. American products . . . will need to glut the world market. Therefore, beyond business and in defense of business, it will not be inconsistent to find those products on a battleship or on the wings of a bomber."

Having explained the theory that pushes him to banish American products from the Italian Fascist marketplace, Mussolini ventures into the values that inspire his political attitudes: "It's out of the question that among the Italians there is a spread of American tastes and attitudes, certainly extraneous to our way of life: Negro music, awful cocktails, feet on the tables, chewing gum. . . . I raised my standard against Bolshevism. Now if necessary, I'll rally the Italians to an economic and spiritual autocracy."

Since then, from Julius Evola, the Fascist philosopher to today's Marcello Veneziani, the youngest of the deeply right-wing intellectuals, the political antagonism to the United States comes from a moral and aesthetic revulsion that Mussolini expressed completely with this conclusion: "The American imperialist pretense of dominating the world is not, as with many other imperialisms, the pretense of substituting an old power with a new one: it is the barbaric pretense of lowering human intelligence and dignity all over the world."

What is being said today by the anti-American democratic public opinion is not a pale shadow but a surprisingly mirror image of the words of the Fascist dictator. After the end of Fascism, there were still plenty of writings claiming that even the liberation of Italy and the Marshall Plan was a cynical business operation aimed to weaken Italian independence. And even if, as noted, the Christian Democrats pragmatically welcomed the American help and stood firmly on the side of the American military and of the NATO alliance, the Catholic Church still contributed the principal moral basis for the anti-American positions enumerated before and never changed them officially, even up until the present antiwar position of the Pope. There are hundreds of Catholic thinkers and several popes, including the last one, John Paul II, who see American society as a source of immoral secularization and modernity and as a guarantee of spiritual bankruptcy. According to this interpretation, the divinization of money made the governing class of America greedy and evil and the man in the street a pawn in the hands of a spurious democracy. The Church holds a long-lasting and enduring responsibility. It is responsible for the human issues just as much as totalitarian thought is responsible for the political ones.

Pius the XII, in his radio message on Christmas 1954, expressed his concern for Europe, the spirit of materialism and technology and (this from the man who was not able to utter a word about the problem of peace during World War II!) declared himself "worried about the materialistic view of the peace problem. We think particularly about those [the Americans] who judge the question of peace as a technical problem and regard the life of individuals in a technical, economical framework. With free trade, they think, will come eternal peace."

Such criticism cannot be defined as a rightist attitude, but rather was affected by and in turn affected the left: For instance, among Catholics, the criticism leveled by the right against mixed-pedigree America with its melting pot of blacks, Hispanics, and Chinese immigrants is seen from an opposite point of view. In the fifties and sixties in a series of articles in the prominent and respected monthly *La Civiltà Cattolica,* the United States is accused of favoring blond, North European immigrants and of indulging in racist standards. The Church in the years of reconstruction has offered the rising Communist Party a serious theoretical basis for its current agitation.

Consider this from Padre Brucculeri in the *La Civiltà Cattolica:* "The welfare of men [for the American] is similar to the welfare of a herd. . . . Our rich allies from beyond the Atlantic Ocean do not simply give us money and weapons, but, unsolicited, they also give us Malthusian advice . . . mediocre demographers and obtuse economists." They are, he adds, "Monstrous, animalesque, cruel." Or Father Baragli in the same periodical: "America is a civilization that will produce the next war just to make selfish use of the annihilating power of atomic energy, its last and most marvelous discovery."

These words were written during the years of an intensive process of Americanization, when the Fiat 600, television, the shower, urbanization, music, and the emancipation of women were changing rural and traditional Italian society. And with its strong intuitions, with its instinct for survival, the Church, looking for hegemony in Italian society, didn't choose the path of relating only to the backward right, but also speaks the language of the left. The Communist stereotypes of Americans that emerges in the voice of the historical leader of the Communist Party Palmiro Togliatti are a replica of the Church's portrayals: "Americans, a strongly selfish people who know no other God but the dollar." They are people who "are interested in producing and selling weapons all over the world to ignite a new world war."

The melding of these three cultures into one anti-American religion makes it an extremely strong cancer. Paradoxically, the historical disaster that beset the left with the fall of the Soviet Union and of the Berlin Wall has improved its fortunes. To whom, but the antiglobal pacifist movement would the left sell its newspapers, ask for votes, and preach from the television screen, since they were fortunate enough to meet on their way anti-Americanism and anti-Judaism as a cement for all the Italian extremism? When the left, immediately after the attack on Afghanistan, understood that their entire constituency was unifiable under the flag of peace, it didn't take them long to move beyond that position. We are all Americans, so we all have the right to become anti-American. The traditional Italian sympathy for the Arab world, which is reciprocated, is part of the anti-imperialist rhetoric. So, if it was a little embarrassing for them to be on the side of the Taliban and, afterwards, of Saddam, still it was very easy to discover that the real guilt of expropriations, domination, slaughters, deportation—in general, of all the international crimes that provoked terrorism—had actually originated in the imperialist politics of the United States. The responsibility for terrorism shifted from the perpetrators to the victims, exactly as it happened for Israel.

The emphasis on the value of life (Catholic philosophy), the value of the poor (Communist philosophy), and the value of a culturally independent society, as opposed to the assault of American culture, merged in Italy in an unreasonable and very dangerous movement that unites under the flag of a backward, miserable, and irrational culture. This is typical of a rural and primordially young industrial society with an anxious public in search of identity. The linking of Bush and Sharon shows how in the Italian mind they are connected in the most dangerous and condemnable nightmare for the easy Italian life—the outbreak of war.

Comparing both Bush and Sharon to Hitler has also been made in Italian demonstrations, on the radio, and in the extreme left-wing press. The idea of the Jewish lobby that pressures Bush to protect Israel from the just rage of the persecuted Palestinian is prevalent in Italy, too. A university professor told me: "Well, war on terror must certainly be fought, but if we ask ourselves where are its origins, everything points to Israel. So the [attack on the] Twin Towers are a consequence of that." When I asked, "Let's say you are right, then what would you do today?" His answer was crystal clear: "If the reason for this entire international clash is Israel, then the United States will also have to abandon it to its destiny and let it disappear. America, as usual, is imposing solutions on the world that are against any sense of justice. The Arabs are right: Israel is an extraneous body, a means of colonization by the United States, which must disappear."

This kind of attitude is one that justifies anti-Americanism and even terrorism. It creates a culture where the old world with all its values, with its basically fascist culture of the village and the church, feels historically counterposed to a culture that the old world considers rootless and in which economy, profit, and the expansion of welfare prevail over social cohesion. This old world fascist culture has the fantasy that in American society the ascendancy of a technical mindset brought mankind to a condition of stupidity, simplicity, and an inability to elaborate on the complexity of human life, accompanied by a greedy escalation of materialism that feeds its leadership. This culture is the same as that seen by the terrorists. It is a culture of illusions and of blaming others for our diseases. This culture provides the waters where terrorists can swim and find help, a harbor. It's the dangerous dream palace of the Europeans, similar to the dream palace that brought the Arab society to deep economical and ideological troubles and to a war against everybody.

## The Arabs: "No Recognition, No Negotiation, No Peace"

May 15, 1948: David Ben-Gurion reads the declaration of independence in a small room in the Tel Aviv Museum. The United Nations has finally given approval for the Jews to have a homeland. For the Jews it is a miraculous resurrection after Auschwitz. To his people wounded by the Holocaust and sorely tried by clashes with the Arabs, Palestinians, and Jordanians in the area, overwhelmed by numerous terrorist attacks on kibbutzim, markets, and buses, David Ben-Gurion announces that, according to international law, the Jewish people, after two thousand years, are "a free people in its own land." People dance in the streets. Even Ben-Gurion sings the "Ha Tikvà" (the hymn to hope), but immediately afterwards he hastens to call a meeting.

Leaving the room with him, faces pale, are the individuals who will be part of legend: Golda Meier, Moshe Dayan, Rabin, Peres, Yigal Allon, Moshe Sharett, Shamir. They don't agree among themselves; some have chosen violent, even terrorist, means to drive out the British and the Arabs, and Ben-Gurion will fight them to the death. But at this moment, the unity that arises from terrible moments comes into play because he has just received the declaration of a life-or-death war against the newly born nation: Five Arab nations have declared war against the newborn state of Israel, the armies of Egypt, Lebanon, Jordan, Syria, and Iraq will move concurrently to destroy it. Their radio networks call 700 million Muslims to an all-out war.

The Jews living in Israel at the time number approximately 750,000; for the most part they are just off the ships in the port of Haifa. Many come directly from the European death camps. One of them, Yaacov Sod, recounts today: "When we got off the boat, we looked around: all around us was an unfamiliar world, odors, colors, incomprehensible voices. We waited our turn in line. They gave me a rifle, an identification number. I was once again competing for survival. I was soldier number 24467." This is Israel's DNA. Weapons are scarce and inferior, especially those coming from countries in the Soviet bloc, like Czechoslovakia, or from France. But there are old weapons, mostly rifles, kept in secret cellars in the kibbutzim. There are two canons in all, which Ben-Gurion will station in front of Jerusalem.

With his British-style mustache and his love for daring acrobatics in the air, the future president of the state of Israel, Ezer Weitzman, at the time still a young man, establishes an air force from scratch. "I watched from the hill at Kibbutz Degania," Meir Davidson recounts. "I saw a sea of armored tanks and soldiers advancing toward us. An immense cloud. Hurriedly, I ran back to the huts. I warned that it was a matter of life or death. We hid the children, we grabbed the weapons. I don't know how we drove them back."

As Egyptian airplanes bomb Tel Aviv, the Jordanians invade Jerusalem, and the Iraqis, the north. The Arab nations imagine they can wipe out the Jewish state, and through flyers and radio broadcasts, they urge the Palestinians to leave: they will be able to return home soon, they promise.

Following this surge of flight, the Israelis, after having in vain urged the Palestinians to remain, instituted a firm policy of expulsion: the refugees, 600,000 of them, are the result of these two events, and it was this issue that made the Israeli-Palestinian peace talks blow up at Camp David. During the war, there was also a massacre at the hands of the Israelis at Der Yassin: 200 Palestinians dead, among them civilians. It remains on Israel's conscience; the first wrong committed by a people who had vowed never to have anything more to do with wrongs, a problem that is still deeply felt today at the checkpoints and in the occupation. And so many other problems also remain constant. Above all that of rejection by a large part of the Arab world, of widespread hatred, of terrorism, of fear.

Israel is the only democracy, a system in which war is ontologically forbidden, that has always been at war. For Europeans, war is only a memory. For the Israelis, burying their youth, grieving for their own people, feeling remorse for the grief of others, is everyday fare. The Jewish nation has known nothing but war, not only from the Palestinians, but from the entire Middle East. Only during brief intervals has it been able to construct a normal world, with universities, hospitals, and schools, a democratic parliament, and a legal system that treats everyone as equals. But war is the guest at every meal. The rejection of people from across the border, as well as that people's suffering, is a lump in Israel's throat. Strength and cunning are its indispensable companions. Young people killed in the war number 22,000, and the enemy too, in all, has suffered tens of thousands of deaths.

Burma Road is devised out of desperation, through the pines and white dust, parallel to the main road leading from the sea to Jerusalem, which is controlled by the Arabs—to break the Arabs' siege. In Jerusalem, Jews are now dying of hunger and thirst. Using stones and dynamite, struggling tooth and nail, working in secret, as relentless shooting continued in various corners of the country, Ben-Gurion's men construct a road for relief support (about eighty kilometers long, part of it along the plain where the Latrun Fortress, a Jordanian stronghold, was situated). And alongside the road, they build a long primitive aqueduct. Ben-Gurion calls every minute on the field telephones. They have to finish quickly, very quickly, so they can get to Jerusalem with weapons, food, water.

The Jordanians, led by Glubb Pashà, a mysterious Englishman, a new Lawrence of Arabia, set fire to the Old City where Jews had lived from time immemorial. Synagogues are burned, and people are driven from their homes. Jerusalem was much more than a famished city full of wounded people and Jewish refugees: it represented Jewish survival itself. For the Arabs, too, now that they had a state, it was symbolically essential to drive the Jews out of their most sacred place once and for all.

Israeli artillery, though paltry, comes by way of the Burma Road to attack Jerusalem, after four defeats on the plain of Latrun and after the furious battle at Castel Fortress. At this last engagement before Jerusalem, victory is achieved following the death of almost all the young soldiers as well as the killing of Feisal Hussein's valiant combatant father, Abed el Kadr el Hussein. Israel, after the initial shock, takes heart and changes its tactics, realizing that it has to rouse itself, to attack. Moshe Dayan, at that time a young officer, brings about the fall of Lydda and Ramle in July (the war had started in May), forcing tens of thousands of Palestinians to flee. Later he prevails in widespread victories, man to man, throughout all of Israel. There is fighting in every city and every kibbutz: children are evacuated during the night on the backs of older children, but their mothers remain in the front lines to fight against the imminent invasion. "When I saw wounded men at the Misgav Ladach Hospital get up out of bed on a glorious, moonlit, starry night and demand a rifle, I said to myself: I want to live at all costs," a nurse of that time, Ziva, recounts.

Yitzhak Rabin, then twenty years old, races along the dirt roads on his motorcycle to deliver orders, encourage his soldiers, provide a touch of support; Ariel Sharon, still a young man, is gravely wounded in the stomach at Latrun. With five nations against one, the war when it was won was a miracle of the will to survive: this time at least, after having earlier gone "as sheep to the slaughter" in Europe.

October 25, 1956: In the privacy of a villa on the outskirts of Paris, Ben-Gurion, the small man from Plonsk, Poland, with the e head of white hair, discusses action plans and arms supplies with representatives of France and Great Britain. Gamal Nasser, the raging Egyptian president who decided to reestablish Pan-Arabism in bold opposition to the Europeans and out of hatred for Israel, has nationalized the Suez Canal and threatened its closure. Nasser has deployed his troops in a position to attack to be ready for the West's reaction and also that of Israel.

At this point, Moshe Dayan enters the scene: the archeologist with the eye patch is ready with a deadly plan. Shimon Peres recounts that Dayan would mark up his maps for hours and hours with a red pencil and a blue pencil, depicting every possible variation. At a certain point the plan is ready: Israel wants to be one of the players, he tells France. By this time it has weapons, and Europe has an interest in aiding Israel. It is America who pulls back, in addition to Russia.

But by now the radio has announced the expected watchword, the one the army secretly knows and that is changed every week. Everyone is to leave at night to join their units, in silence. The newspapers will write "war" only after the war has begun. Israel has learned not to wait until the last minute: Operation Kadesh begins.

Nasser meanwhile has sunk many vessels in the canal to make it impassable. Dayan quickly takes the Sinai (which is later given back in its entirety in exchange for peace with Egypt) as far as Al Arish and then Sharm el Sheich: 45,000 Egyptians surrender, 6,000 are taken prisoner. The United Nations calls for a truce, but Israel does not stop until it reaches the end of the Sinai on November 5. It brings home the Egyptian war arsenal and obtains free passage through the Strait of Tiran and the port of Elat. That day twelve maritime powers obtain the right to pass freely through all the straits. Only 180 Israelis are killed. Dayan had discovered the secret: speed, resourcefulness, daring, the weapons of the Israeli army.

From January 1965 to June 1967, when the Six Day War begins, Israel undergoes one hundred twenty terrorist attacks at the hands of Arafat's PLO. Syria and Egypt declare that they would support the Palestinians in a war. Israel begins to prepare itself, while a Soviet lie ("Israel has already moved its tanks to the border") leads Nasser to think that the time has come to take revenge. The famous song of Umm Kalthum, the fine Egyptian singer, is heard, inciting from every radio: "Slit their throats, slit their throats." Nasser seems certain of succeeding. Russia persuades Syria as well to enter a general state of readiness; the United Nations removes its peace-keeping forces, clearing the way across the Sinai.

Moshe Dayan returns, and the magician once again performs a miracle: From the small, constantly threatened country it was, Israel becomes a feared military power in this war. Its victory this time, the conquest of the Golan and the territories, results in a cultural shift and provides unprecedented security. Paradoxically, it isn't long before the phenomenon of the settlements and of religious nationalism begins: The great joy that follows victory will become the anxiety of future years, the root of a strengthened Palestinian identity, prepared as never before for confrontation, and of the fragmentation of the internal political panorama.

Iraq, Jordan, Syria, and Egypt are already prepared. With the straits blocked again, Israel is isolated on all sides. De Gaulle abandons the field, and France declares an embargo; for the first time Europe leaves the Jews on their own. Shimon Peres, a great admirer of European culture, is particularly astonished. It is to this man, the young dreamer who is already talking about peace, that Ben-Gurion assigns the task of organizing the navy and planning for an atomic bomb. Once again, Israel feels its life is at stake. Dayan and Weitzman (who are brothers-in-law) realize that Israel's survival depends on acting quickly.

Israeli Mirages enable incredible raids on Iraqi, Jordanian, Syrian, and Egyptian military airports: in a single day, May 5, 1967, they destroy 367 planes. Meanwhile, King Hussein of Jordan bombards Israel from the heights, and Jerusalem again comes under fire. The "little king" once again dreams of taking the entire city, as in 1948.

Instead, the contrary happens: Israel occupies the West Bank in a decisive move; above all, it makes its way into Jerusalem. Led by Rabin, Dayan, and Uzi Narkiss, the soldiers tearfully touch the Wailing Wall. Before entering the city, Dayan, worldly and cynical as always, murmurs to Narkiss as they regard the walls from a distance: "What do we need it for, this Vatican?" Yet when rabbi-soldier Goren suggests that perhaps the Plain of the Mosques should be blown up: "That way we would resolve the problem." Dayan says to him: "Be quiet. I don't ever want to hear you say anything like that again."

Meanwhile, Jordan, which will lose control over Jerusalem entirely, also leads Iraqi troops to the Israeli border. This brings the total to 547,000 men deployed, together with the Egyptians. Prime Minister Levi Eshkol faints while speaking on the radio. Dayan becomes minister of defense. Rabin, chief of staff, feels a terrible, immense responsibility for what is happening: Israeli soldiers are dying; the enemy armies are gaining force; the occupied Territories are imposing a new imponderable destiny on Israel.

And the great general who supervises all the fronts together, perhaps in part as a result of the cigarettes he chain-smokes, collapses: he locks himself in a dark room with sleeping pills and no one is able to find him for twenty-four hours. The war of 1967 ends with a sweeping victory. But the Palestinian people find in the West Bank an element by which to identify and organize themselves. Israel tries various paths to open negotiations, but the Arab nations are angered to the extreme, and with their three "no's" at the Khartoum summit—no to recognition, no to negotiations, no to peace with Israel—declare their intent to destroy the Jewish state. Israel, having become inflexible in turn and proud of its victory, will require years to arrive at Oslo.

At 1:40 PM on October 6, 1973, on the day of Kippur, while everyone in Israel is fasting at the temple, the sirens sound for forty-five minutes announcing that the country has been attacked by Syria and Egypt. Golda Meier, the prime minister, though having gone to a secret meeting (disguised as an Arab) with King Hussein who wanted to inform her of the imminent attack, did not believe it: She never trusted him. It is she who coined the saying: "Peace will be possible when the Arabs love their children more than they hate the Jews."

Amid the total chaos, the reserves are not mobilized for several hours. The Syrian and Egyptian fronts advance unrelentingly, and along the borders the conscripted soldiers are dying, burned in their tanks by the Syrians and Egyptians. Abba Eban speaks of "a new Pearl Harbor." It was a war that killed 2,701 soldiers, wounded 7,500 of them, and took 300 as war prisoners, treated in the usual Syrian manner. One hundred airplanes and eight hundred tanks were destroyed. Moshe Dayan said: "We had to fight Soviet equipment more than the Arabs." For the first time the United States provides massive relief aid to Israel. When after eight days the Galaxy aircrafts arrive at the airport with supplies, the Israelis literally tip the planes over, with a system invented there on the spot, to unload them quickly. Once again, everyone mobilizes: blankets, transistors, newspapers, food, even the elderly hasten to bring them to the front. Meanwhile, Egypt is suffering from international pressures and poorly equipped soldiers who are in the desert without canteens.

Burt Lancaster and Ingrid Thulin, in addition to musicians such as Daniel Baremboim and Isaac Stern, hasten to raise morale. In short, there is a rallying. Shimon Peres mobilizes the navy against the Syrian coast. But the situation is finally turned around when Ariel Sharon, then a general, puts ashore at night on the other side of the Suez Canal, and with a maneuver that is hard to believe even today, surrounds the Egyptian ground forces. He is already well known for his toughness. He has carried out severe reprisals against Arab villages. But he saves Israel at the Egyptian front. Wounded in the head, he aids and encourages his soldiers one by one. Egypt is taken by surprise, and in a short time, even in the north, the Golan is occupied. At the end of the war, 8,301 Egyptian prisoners are exchanged for 241 Israelis.

But having been taken by surprise, Israel's faith is now shaken. Begin launches the campaign of 1982 at a time when the PLO has become an army that attacks the kibbutzim, schools, and towns of Galilee each day from Lebanon: "The Palestinians," the Lebanese representative to the United Nations accuses, "have transformed the refugee camps into military strongholds. They have smuggled heavy weaponry, imposed kickbacks." Operation Peace for Galilee is only supposed to occupy a safe zone in Lebanon. Instead, by orders of Sharon who is then defense minister, it becomes a definitive plan to eliminate the PLO. The war will become a quagmire in which the Hezbollah flourish even today and, in twenty years of occupation, will cause hundreds of deaths in the southern zone.

The war lasts eighty days. Gentle Prime Minister Yitzhak Navon does everything he can to prevent the army from striking civilians. The massacre of Sabra and Chatila, that is, the murderous attack by Lebanese Christian forces on a Palestinian camp and the subsequent accusation that Sharon was responsible for it, mark this war and leave a brand on Israel. It is the beginning of a great campaign of delegitimization that today is at its peak. Still, the PLO is driven out, and this is of vital importance to Israel, which finds incredible amounts of weapons hidden in its underground tunnels.

Arafat is saved. The ships that carry Arafat and his fedayeen to safety, amid the singing of the Palestinian anthem, amid flowers and signs of victory, are a salient part of the rais's epic. From there a surge of terrorist attacks is born, as well as the exile to Tunisia, and later the resurrection in the West Bank following the Oslo Accords.

Today, shut up at Ramallah, Arafat often cites Beirut to remind us of his ability to rise again. Arafat likes to exclaim that he is winning when he loses; it is a trait typical of the Arab world. Martyrdom, and even triumphalism, is preferred instead of progress, and it is considered progress.

Israel's second last war, the one in which Saddam, in 1991, showered Tel Aviv with missiles, was unfought. Yet because of this, it was Israel's most difficult battle—a nation that ten years earlier had destroyed the Iraqi nuclear reactor. This was the beginning of America's interdiction of Israel, which has lasted until today: at the time Yitzhak Shamir put his head in his hands and asked Colin Powell why on earth Israel should not respond. The reply seemed to follow quickly at Madrid, at the peace conference. And later on at Oslo, Washington, and Camp David. It seemed that Israel's destiny for war was over. Instead, we read about the last great war against suicide terrorism every day in the newspapers.

# CONCLUSION

In the Middle East the link between democratization, civil progress of the Arab countries' populations, and peace is a fact of everyday life. One sees at firsthand how the corrupt and self-centered management of twenty-two countries has led four hundred million people to misery. The terrorism that has bloodied Israel in the last few years is not just the product of the Israeli-Palestinian conflict. It is the quintessence of decades of internal fascist oppression, the essential component of which has been educating the young in death and aggression. Terrorism is the precipitate of this dictatorial culture, which exploits its young people, rather than thinking of their future, which earmarks them for chaos and death, rather than for life. There are another twenty-four Muslim countries, of which half are striving toward democracy. In Arab countries plus Iran, including the Palestinian Authority, tens of thousands die in prison or are summarily executed after laughable trials conducted by bands of militiamen. This economic and cultural disaster, testified by various U.N. reports and many Arab intellectuals, goes hand in hand with self-destructive political language and an international attitude that, albeit with different nuances, preserves a religious-cum-cultural-cum-military substructure that winks at terrorism or actively helps it.

In spring 2004, King Abdullah of Jordan accused Syria of having brought over the border vehicles containing chemical weapons and poisonous gases for use by an Al Qaeda terrorist conspiracy. Syria is also accused of having smuggled arms and terrorists inside and outside the frontier with Iraq and, moreover, of having sold Sudan components for missiles and weapons of mass destruction. In the meantime, after an extremely fierce soccer match in April 2004 in Qamoshli—a city with two hundred thousand inhabitants—there has been a big increase in clashes in northern Syria. There is talk of hundreds of dead and wounded, not reported by the press, while desperate demonstrations march through Damascus.

Syria—a country with a foreign policy that has brought it to the brink of foreign sanctions, and whose people have been held under the heel of the Alawite regime for so many years—is a country where newspapers' computers are set always to mention Israel, or anything concerning Israel, in quotes, as a way of indicating a virtual entity; that nearly always uses the adjective *criminal* for Israel or the term *apartheid state*; that keeps seventeen thousand men in Lebanon and does not even discuss the possibility of evacuating them, while it acts as a bridge between Iran, the Hezbollahs, Hamas, and the Shiite gangs in Iraq. In this country, which exemplifies the international risk posed by Middle Eastern dictatorships, even the words *reform* and *development* are, generally speaking, banned from newspapers and replaced by the word *change*, as if those other words have an overpositive meaning.

On April 16 at 9:54 AM, state radio broadcast a sermon of Sheikh Muhammad Abd Al Rahman Barakat that, while calling for Arab unity, asked people to close ranks in the face of the Zionist enemy and to help the Iraqi nation "to restore its security, stability, and prosperity." The sermon ended with praise of Assad's journey to Arab countries to "illuminate the Arab atmosphere and reactivate Arab and Islamic solidarity to recapture land from the Zionist enemy."

This combination of episodes, which underlines the servility of news media and hierarchies in general, together with instigation, anti-Semitism, anti-Americanism, and assistance to terrorism, forms a framework of international threats and of oppression against the people, as in many other cases.

Following the war in Iraq, we have been seeing numerous shake-ups in the world of Arab dictatorships. Since the time when the United States embarked on the path outlined by Bush in his June 2002 speech, we have been seeing a dance of fear, of steps forward and steps backward. Egypt, for example, seeks its usual guarantor role vis-à-vis Israel, but Mubarak keeps the frontiers closed to Israel. This leader is the only one who does not publicly reject (as do other leaders who call it "shameful") Sharon's withdrawal plan. But in March, he refused to celebrate the twenty-fifth anniversary of peace with Israel, the most significant in the area, and the anti-Americanism and anti-Semitism emanating from Egypt's newspapers, at the very time when he was visiting Bush, are perhaps the most virulent in the entire Arab world.

"Zionist Jews are behind every act of violence and terrorism throughout the world," Abd Al Wahhad Adas, a leading Egyptian journalist and deputy editor of the government newspaper *Al Jumhuriyya*, wrote on April 23: "It is the Jews, with their bloodied and stinking hands that are behind all the problems. . . . Their most recent operation was the Madrid attack."

Mubarak, who has recently made some moves indicating that he renounces establishing a dynasty in which his son would be his successor, is the Arab leader who, on the one hand, seeks to maintain a relationship with the United States—for example showing interest in a peace plan—but who, on the other hand, issued a document with Saudi Arabia, following announcement of the U.S. plan on Middle East democratization in June 2004, stating: "Our choice is to continue along the road of development of modernization and reforms, remaining faithful to the interests and values of our people." This flag of antiethnocentrism, also repeated at the May 2004 summit meeting, in reality covers the authoritarian Arab regimes' self-defense policy. When there is talk of their own values and lifestyles or interests, there are no substantive proposals, only defense of the status quo.

In 2003, shortly after Mubarak, the general secretary of the Arab League, Amru Mussa, declared: "This policy threatens the entire stability of the Middle East." It was true: The choices made by President Bush and the allies, besides Sharon's policy of unilateral exit, plus the relentless war against terrorism, have called the twenty Middle Eastern dictatorships into question. The war without quarter of spurious forces in Iraq must be set in this context, in the fear of change that, either peacefully or aggressively, is emerging in the Middle East like a tornado on the horizon. In Baghdad, Basra, and Nassiriya, both the remnants of the previous regime and the states that hate the idea of a flourishing democratic plant putting down roots in the area have made this into an appointment for international terrorism, of both a Shiite and Ba'athist matrix, and Al Qaeda superintends all the murderous combinations. If the democracy experiment were to succeed, for a great many it would be a disaster for terrorist organizations and for neighboring dictatorships. Terrorism, supported from over the border by Iran, Syria, and Saudi Arabia, is, according to many testimonies, strong. This, however, does not mean that success will not smile on the democratic side—simply that we are immersed in an indispensable world war that cannot spare us pain, confrontations, and terror.

Lack of intervention on the Arab side or our fear when we pull out and flee from the scene, as Spain did and as many others have threatened to do while terrorism pursues us right to our home ground, will only lead to future massacres, plus an intolerable tightening of the screws for the four hundred million Arab citizens. Moreover, this faint-heartedness means that the democratic heroes—the only pure heroes of today—are left isolated and alone, just as we once left Nathan Sharanksy or Sakharov isolated and alone. Today's heroes are called Sa'ad Al Din Ibrahim, Ali Salem, Hashem Aghajari, Lafif Lakhdar, Omar Karsou, Bassam Tibi,  Ahmad Chalabi, and now, fortunately, many others too.

We are ready to hope that democratic transformation can come about via a peaceful transition, but one has to look at Libya—the country that has become an example of how dictators can yield by virtue of persuasion, which first promised to free the dissident Fathi El Jatimi and then made him disappear—to understand what its real, not diplomatic, attitude is. Watch has to be kept over the fate of the ailing seventy-five-year old prisoner of Iran, the journalist Siamak Pourzand, to understand whether the policy of continuous appeasement vis-à-vis the ayatollahs is right. When at long last—and it took a lot of doing—we understood how important it was to free Sakharov and Sharansky, we also understood that the USSR, which seemed invincible, could fall. When Ronald Reagan maintained this, he aroused the pitying scorn and laughter of Europeans, who found him as stupid as they find Bush stupid today—let us not forget that.

The joint response of Hosni Mubarak and the Saudi rulers to the future democratization plan pretends, as does the document of the sixteenth summit meeting of the Arab League on May 23, to adopt democratic reforms but, de facto, is against the possibility of true internal change. When these two documents mention the "values of our people," the words *our people* in the Arab world do not mean an entity with a political will and power to choose, as in a democracy, but an entity dependent on and controlled by the wishes of the people's leader. Mubarak is the people; King Abdullah is the people—in the best of cases.

Critics of the plan believe that it is neocolonialistic in nature and will change the values of Arabian society and, above all, make Israel an integral part of Middle Eastern society. But the story of their "own culture" is an excuse. The American project proposed for the G-8 is compatible with all cultures because it is based on requesting aid to all industrialized countries and promoting freedom of the press, women's rights, free elections, expansion of the free market, increased use of the Internet, and new management systems. Generally speaking, the idea is to narrow the gap between the advanced world and a world where the illiteracy rate is as high as 40 percent and where, in 2010, fifty million people will enter the labor market.

It is remarkable that the summit document, while again indicating the desirability of compatible reforms and condemning violence against all civilians (therefore including Israeli civilians), does not condemn terrorism; instead, it claims that terrorism cannot be distinguished from the legitimate rights of a people combatting occupation. The debate on whether to accept the intervention of the West and the United States or whether instead to seek to reform "from within"—i.e., the debate that, according to the sources concerned, caused the failure of the Tunisian summit at the end of March—is a false debate. For most of the Arab countries plus Iran, it is not a question of triggering reforms from within, but of heading off the emerging revolution that is emerging—the rumbles of thunder coming from the Gulf countries, from Saudi Arabia, from democratic Turkey, from the growing Iranian opposition, and from Libya's renouncement of nuclear weapons.

Negotiations must happen when they are really effective and verifiable—such as the fortunate venture with Khaddafi who, in exchange for his regime's stability, offered his weapons of mass destruction. Otherwise, we will always find ourselves back at square one, until atomic weapons spread to rogue states such as Iran—the most active in fomenting confrontation and also one of the most oppressive, where prisoners are estimated to number thirty thousand, but also one that has a strong opposition, perhaps the largest, anxious to change the regime. But the democratic revolution is late in coming because the opposition, while we seek "moderate" counterparts, is not receiving sufficient support due to our fear of destabilizing the area.

But destabilization is already underway, and there is no doubt that, whether they like it or not, the Arab world's regimes have all had to put it on the agenda. In the Middle East, nothing happens "from within"—neither Israeli withdrawal from Sinai, as Muhammed Al Rahimi, a Kuwaiti commentator, wrote, nor the liberation of Iraq from Saddam Hussein's regime or Afghanistan from the Talibans.

The core values of these authoritarian cultures must be changed, and it is there that reformers' goodwill is put to the test: state education, which preaches aggression, must be reformed. The fear of a cultural invasion has become an excuse for fierce anti-Westernism, which, de facto, is an incitement to terrorist violence. For example, in Jordanian textbooks, which establish a code defining human rights and the concept of peace and universal values, one reads these questions: "What is the difference between a young Palestinian who performs a suicidal action as an act of resistance against the Zionist occupation and a person who hijacks an airplane and threatens to kill everyone on board if his friend arrested for drug pushing is not immediately released? What must the hijacker be called? What difference is there, in your own words, between legal resistance and terrorism?" This is the result of $450 million invested in educational reform in Jordan. The Islamist member of the Jordanian parliament, Abu Fars, retorts: "You have to wage war against those who war against you . . . and the entire educational reform aims solely to protect the Jews and the Israelis and to protect the boundaries of a country that has stolen the Arabs' rights." "Does the government want to spread the culture of subjection?"asked another Jordanian parliamentarian, Mahmoud Al Harabshe. "Does it want to spread the culture of normalization with the Zionist enemy?"

The greatest hurdle on the road to democratization—and this is a theoretical and political point that has not yet been sufficiently discussed—is that propaganda on Israel remains a formidable instrument for antireform Arab leaders. The myth of the "Israeli peril,"of the colonialist and imperialist design of the Israelis, or rather of the Jews, is one of the main weapons used by the regimes against democracy. People are free to take to the streets only to demonstrate against the United States and Israel and to burn their flags. The paradox constantly used by those Arab commentators who declare that they are left-wing critics of their governments is that, to solve their problems, Arab countries must first solve the Israeli-Palestinian problem, otherwise nothing can be done (and this is in fact one of the reasons why Assad and others caused the Tunisian summit to fail, saying that talk of democratization would have weakened the Palestinians). And so all summit meetings run aground on a useless maximalism where hatred of Israels acts as cement for nonexistent Arab unity.

In reality, one cannot understand what link there is between free elections, sensible education, respect of human rights, the battle against corruption, and law reforms and the solution of the Palestinian problem, particularly when the term *solution* means something that is not of this world, such as when the Arab constituency forgets Arafat's refusal at Camp David and Taba and when it interprets U.N. resolutions as it likes, imagining them as a pure mirror of Palestinian desires. Even the concept of "international legality" to which they refer, or that of the Geneva Convention, are fantasies that have little or nothing to do with legality. But current leaders, as always, offload all responsibilities for their peoples on Israel and by doing so forget their historical responsibility toward the Palestinians. The reality is that the situation has become extreme: the state of the economy, the culture, and the technical sector is simply tragic. Present reality can avail itself of anti-Americanism or of anti-Israeli hate up to a certain point—but this cannot be a full buffer against the state of things as it stands, which is becoming increasingly stormy.

Sharon, by proposing unilateral withdrawal from the territories while waging a war without quarter against terrorism, is, in fact, proposing a change of scenario, promoting a Palestinian leadership that must necessarily govern and, in this way, become a true partner in negotiations. This proposal has been met with a chorus of criticism in Europe, but it has a strong basis in reality. The current Palestinian leadership must produce and maintain a culture of hate to survive. It does not intend to combat terrorism and is impossible to negotiate with, even when Israel makes the best territorial offer. Therefore, it only remains to destabilize Arafat's policy, while at the same time seeking defensible borders and a turning point that could lead toward a different policy. In a certain sense, Sharon is the reflection of U.S. policy. With one hand he fights; with the other he offers self-determination.

The challenge is to overcome the shock of political transformation and return control to the hands of the reformers in Iraq, Syria, Libya, and, above all, in Iran. The reformers are the heroes and protagonists of the changes that are certainly underway.

But two—indeed three—points have to be remembered. First, the West must win the war on terrorism; the victory of democracy is indispensable. It is urgent to stop the vicious circle of shared ideologies and the funding of terrorism, which will perpetrate more horrifying massacres.

Second, Europe must abandon the myth of stability, when such stability means the growth of terrorism and suffering for the oppressed and also for us Westerners because this "stability" has created, and creates, terrorism. It is amazing how unconcerned the European public is that Saddam killed perhaps as many as four hundred thousand people and how concerned it is with underlining the errors of the U.S. administration or the misdeeds—real or presumed—of Sharon. What a strange world we live in if, instead of helping the Iranian opposition, Europe pushes for appeasement, hoping that will be of use, when any reasonable analysis tells us that there is no hope of moderate transformation and that three-quarters of the financing for terrorism comes from Iran. Few thoughts are spared for the thirty thousand people said to be detained in Iranian prisons and also for ourselves when, in one or two years' time, Iran will have the atomic bomb—constructed with European help.

This brings me to the third point. We are the ones who, first and foremost, must believe in the fight for democracy. If we think that it is a culture-related value—that infibulation or polygamy are equivalent to the Western woman's condition and that anything broadcast by television is all the same, even when the international broadcasts of the Palestinian Authority, Egypt, or the Hezbollahs' Al-Manar present children who want to become martyrs or sanguinary sermons, or when Syrian television presents forty episodes of a serial in which Theodor Herzl receives money from a brothel's prostitutes (besides the classic blood libel that accuses Jews of using Christian blood to prepare their Passover matzos)—we are in reality against democratization, regardless of whether it comes from outside or from within.

There cannot be any talk of "slightly" authoritarian regimes—their stability is the stability of horror. To think that it is possible to ask them to bring their solutions onto the stage, means asking for new despots, more courteous and affable, to talk with us in urbane tones. I am very suspicious of the Ba'athist rehabilitation in Iraq and amazed at the incredible treatment of Ahmad Chalabi, who for thirty years—in the midst of a thousand accusations of corruption, always with ulterior motives—has put himself, his family, and his fortune into play for the democratization of his country. The faces of hope are those of the oppressed, of the dissidents: It is not just their hope, it is the hope of all of us. The trouble is that their regimes know this, and their courage is directly proportional to the challenge.

It is April 22, 2004. Yesterday a suicide attack in Riyadh killed nine people, while once again in Saudi Arabia, U.S. Consul General

Gina Abercrombie-Winstanley, despite having been threatened, met with Saudi reformers, who in turn had been warned against meeting with her by the minister of the interior, Prince Nayaf. King Abdullah II of Jordan has suddenly postponed a meeting with George Bush, explaining that it seemed to him that the American president's positions prejudiced a negotiated solution of the Israeli-Palestinian conflict. In Basra, the terrorists have killed sixty-eight people, and the battle is raging. In Syria, after various items of news on clashes and demonstrations in the country, some with major bloodshed, prominent human rights activists are being tried by the security court on the charge of putting Syria's image at risk and of providing false information. They include Anwar Al Buni. In the meantime, the United States, according to the *Washington Times,* has decided that Syria is facilitating terrorism, like Iran and together with Iran, with the transit of jihadist militias who, for example, provide reserves for the fierce battle of Falluja. Moreover, in Damascus the foreign institutional bases of Hamas and of the Islamic Jihad find refuge and help. Bin Laden, too, has asked his followers to go to Iraq to fight the Westerners and demanded that the American side hand over power by June 30.

In Israel, Prime Minister Sharon has taken his program of unilateral withdrawal from Gaza and part of the West Bank to the Knesset, with U.S. approval. The majority of his own party voted against him because it is hard "to leave our own homes to terrorists," as the settlers in Gaza say. He is opposed by the extreme right and by the extreme left, and there is even unrestrained Palestinian opposition, which makes itself understood with a series of attacks, echoed in the Arab world in the hate not only of Sharon's idea—which after all proposes evacuating Jewish settlements after three years of terrorism—but also, and perhaps above all, of his alliance with Bush on this project. Evacuation that should leave the territory in the hands of a leadership more inclined toward peace could reopen negotiations and initiate a regime change. In other words, it is a choice that, like that of Iraq, seems to those who see it as an imperialistic move to be part of a brutal project for Western domination in the Middle East.

This is the repeated interpretation that, from the pages of the *Al Ayyam* newspaper, the Palestinian analyst Ali Sadek made of George Bush's June 2002 speech concerning changes of regime, when he accused Bush of "seeking an excuse to intimidate Arab governments and to force them to play a role functional to his imperialist policy" at Israel's service. He added that U.S. democracy was "arrogant and offensive." After the elimination of Sheikh Yassin and Rantisi, the heads of Hamas, Palestinian newspapers and television conveyed an identical message: The combination of the design for unilateral withdrawal and elimination of the two supreme heads of Hamas (which has undertaken 425 terrorist attacks, of which 53 were suicidal, with 289 dead and 1,649 wounded, and the two had devised the program and directed the actions) indicated the usual Israeli-American imperialism.

In a certain sense this is true. The theory of the change of regime is fundamental in the war on terrorism, as is disruption of the equilibrium of authoritarian political regimes in the Muslim world. It makes me smile as I remember when, last April, at Jerusalem's American Colony Hotel, I attended a meeting between the Palestinian leader, Professor Sari Nusseibeh, and his Israeli partner, Amy Ayalon, who described their courageous collection of signatures among Palestinians and Israelis. Among the many things said on that occasion was Nusseibeh's reply to a journalist who asked him what he thought of the targeted elimination of Sheikh Yassin in Gaza. Nusseibeh, with a mysterious and mischievous expression on his face, said just a few words: "It does not seem inconsistent to me with the prospect of the Israeli army's withdrawal from the area."

I might have misinterpreted it, but it appears to me that the background to this reply is the mindset of a reformer who observes, without prejudice and also hopefully, the extremely tough struggle to change regimes. Nusseibeh and Ayalon are attempting, via collection of signatures, to create bottom-up consensus for territorial division and the birth of a Palestinian state based on renouncing authoritarian and terror-mongering leaderships: that victimist/triumphalist ideology that, in the Palestinians' case, hinges on the impossible propaganda of the right to return. And it just so happens that Sharon and President Bush have established the possibility of going back to the road map on the basis of the path chosen by Nusseibeh, which undoubtedly also involves a change of leadership and relinquishing the fantasy of a Palestinian state from the river to the sea. This religious and political fantasy buoys up the present Palestinian leadership; it's a vision that relentlessly foments anti-Semitism and instigates the violence that flows out of the Arab world like burning magma.

Two quotations are clarifiers: one from the Egyptian professor, Gala Amin, who, in the *Al Ahram* weekly newspaper, asks himself which "opportunity" the Americans are talking about when they refer to the Great Middle East project: "An opportunity for what? For reforms? In which fields? Democracy, culture, women's emancipation? What right do they have to interfere in our affairs? Have we complained to you about our democracy, culture, women, and have we asked for help? What nonsense is this? How come you worry about it at this very time? The truth is that . . . the spread of terrorism threatens European and American security . . . and something has to be done . . . but who guarantees that a democratically elected government, which reflects its people's opinion, would not attack you with terrorism . . . or with culture? Are the terrorists not educated? And the women? Are the women Palestinian suicide terrorists not perhaps emancipated? They were educated, culturally independent, and very assured. And yet you see these deeds as acts of terrorism. Or maybe you want to see another type of emancipation?"

The conclusion is natural: exploiting the oil and crushing the regime to make it Israel's prey are the real reasons for the United States' desire for democratization. The Palestinian leader of the Islamic Jihad, Abdallah Shami, made a similar statement at the end of the first year of the war in Iraq, in early April 2004: "We condemn the United States for its war against children, women, mosques, and homes in Iraq. The American offensive has shown the brutal face of the United States, which veils itself in democracy and human rights." "Our message to the world," added Taisir Khaled, of the PLO's executive committee, "is praise for the Iraqi fighters' courageous resistance, hoping that Iraq recovers its role in the defense of Arab interests, in the face of the disgraceful, evil alliance between the radical right wing of the U.S. administration and the extremist, radical and expansionist government headed by Sharon." But we know the basis of the old relationship between Saddam's regime and the Israeli-Palestinian conflict. Saddam's most barefaced role vis-à-vis the Palestinians was to give $25,000 to the family of each suicide terrorist during the last intifada; his main function vis-à-vis his people—a glorious and ancient part of Arab history—was that of ruthlessly imprisoning, torturing, and decimating it.

Many of us—historians, journalists, authors, politicians, and members of very different groups and organizations—have spent the last three and a half years of the intifada discussing, with amazement and disappointment, the massive phenomenon of global anti-Semitism, which spreads like a weed, extending itself from Arab to European society and, to a lesser extent, also to American society. Many of our lives have changed. As a journalist and author of many works on the Middle East, I myself have observed a profound change in my friends and counterparts. I have not missed one war since 1967 when, as the young guest of a kibbutz, I became a traitor of the left wing, to which I naturally belonged as did nearly all young people at that time. Since that turning point, which resulted in the divorce between the left wing and Israel, it has become increasingly difficult to talk about the conflict in its true context: the Arabs' persistent denegation; the terrorist campaign after the Palestinian refusal at Camp David; the difficulty of fighting against the unconventional army of terrorists who hide themselves among civilians; and the incitement to genocidal hate that has accompanied the waves of terrorism. This hate against Israel and everything linked to it has created what Nathan Sharansky has defined as the "three d's"—demonization, double standards, and delegitimization (denial of the right to exist).

Not one Jew has escaped the new anti-Semitism of these four years. Several liberal intellectuals have discovered how the human rights culture of which they were a part rejected and abandoned them because they were Jews. Suddenly the state of Israel understood that one of the key purposes of its existence, putting an end to anti-Semitism, had failed and that its peace-inspired dreams had to be replaced by a strategy of intervention. Here I want to focus on what seems to me to be the new aspect of the phenomenon. In a word, anti-Semitism is part of the globalization crisis. We have fought hard, but to defeat anti-Semitism, we have to go deeper into its contradictions and lay them bare.

From a state of depression we have now passed to the counter-attack phase. All the theoretical effort I mentioned centers around what we did not want to believe: the existence of a new anti-Semitism—liberal, spread throughout the world, hypocritical, omnipresent, and genocidal. We have identified it. Hundreds and hundreds of articles, dozens of essays and books; tough reactions by Jewish institutions (such as the Anti-Defamation League, which has changed its line) and by democratic institutions in general; studies and conferences by scholars, politicians, and media observers; student campus activities; groups of Jews mobilizing themselves in the most varied ways; and, above all, serious involvement and commitment of the state of Israel (remember Sharon's words but also those of Benny Morris or A. B. Yehoshua; remember the struggle at The Hague, the taking of a stand by the Global Forum against government institutions' anti-Semitism; the Israeli foreign minister's meetings with the diplomatic corps)—all these efforts have made it clear that the attacks on the Jewish state with blood libels and prejudices are anti-Semitism.

But it is the first time in history that a Jewish state is able to fight anti-Semitism in the international arena, and this has changed things. The Jew is no longer alone. The Jewish state is a modern democratic body, influential and well organized, with a ministry expressly dedicated to anti-Semitism and whose voice is respected both morally and strategically by American presidents of any political color, be they Bill Clinton or George W. Bush. It is respected not because of the influence of a cabal or political lobby (the Arab lobby is more extensive and wealthier), but because of the Jews' moral heritage and because of Israel's incredible success in business and the arts and sciences, despite having to confront terrible enemies every day.

Never before has anti-Semitism been a diplomatic issue addressed at government level and by international forums. Today, for the first time, it has become a serious question, important for economic, military, or intelligence relations. Today, the elected representative of the Jewish people can officially point an accusing finger by means of resolutions and documents presented to the U.N. General Assembly or to the European Union, however hostile they might be. Furthermore, Israel has connected the anti-Semitic terrorist attacks against the state of Israel and against Jews in Djerba, Istanbul, Kenya, and elsewhere with global Islamist terrorism. This is a warning for European states: "Don't help the anti-Semites. They are also terrorists." In May 2004, the French Jews refused to take part in a demonstration whose organizers refused to connect anti-Semitism with anti-Zionism. Conversely, the OECD, at its global forum in Berlin in April 2004, linked the two terms.

Having a strong back is an unprecedented novelty for the Jews, which has given new strength to the Diaspora. The Jewish World Congress has written to the president of the European Union, several Israeli ministers have protested with ambassadors and presidents, and many traditionally left-wing intellectuals (Paul Berman, André Glucksmann, and Alain Finkielkraut) have stated their disgust at the anti-Semitism reemerging from the sewers of history to link itself with the ideology of terrorism.

Why did Israel and the international community remain surprised and confused by the new phenomenon for so long? Because the main theoretical problem was the identification of anti-Semitism as such. In practice, for a long time we argued whether and to what extent the attacks on Israel and Jews could, together, be identified as anti-Semitism. We did not want to believe it, and we were capable of realizing it only when we set the phenomenon in its global perspective. Useful in this respect have been the studies (for example by Robert Wistrich, Anne, Bayefsky, Nathan Sharansky, and Irwin Cotler) of Arab anti-Semitism and of the anti-Semitism of world institutions (headed by the United Nations) and the media (those by CAMERA [Committee for Accuracy of Middle East Reporting in America] and of Informazione Corretta [Honest Reporting], for example).

According to this new anti-Semite ideology, since Israel's alleged crimes are enormous (someone has made a comparison between the tragic battle of Rafah, in Gaza, for control of the area where the intifada weapons were smuggled from Egypt and the tortures at the Iraqi prison of Abu Ghraib), the punishment, too, must be like the one of sixty years ago, but this time the Jewish state, the "collective Jew," has to be eliminated. Emil Fakenheim has written that three messages characterize anti-Semitism. In the first stage, the message is: "You can't live among us as Jews"; in the second: "You can't live among us"; and in the third: "You can't live." Amnon Rubinstein has noted that, while in the 1930s the streets of Berlin were full of graffiti saying "Jews in Palestine" and "Jews out," today these are happily merged in the slogan "Jews out of Palestine"—almost a sort of "destination nowhere."

In the name of the supreme doctrine of human rights and equality, the global message that has become fashionable, also in Europe, is destruction of the state of Israel, the denial of Israel's right to belong to the family of nations. The new anti-Semitism, featuring the rejection of Israel's rights, and as so well defined by Irwin Cotler, has become exceedingly popular only because it is an element of unification—a simple, elementary bridge—between different cultures.

Its grim simplicity is like music based solely on rhythm, without any theme or melody, so that anyone can understand it. It is a bad rap song.

Groups of Islamist immigrants say, "Jews are bad," and the whole of a more sophisticated culture nods in agreement—a cheap way of gaining friendship, of showing sympathy to the new alleged outcasts, the immigrants, and perhaps of avoiding danger. For Europeans, the culture of "never again," a term once used to refer to the Holocaust and the culture of diversity, has been summed up, in the last three years, by the image of the little Muslim boy in Paris, an icon for liberal movements. This icon has replaced the little Jewish boy deported from the Warsaw ghetto. Indeed, denial of the Holocaust's existence has become popular, and some have said that the image of Muhammad Al Dura wiped out that of the little Jew with his oversized beret and hands held up in front of the guns.

We have seen an extraordinary distortion of concepts and language. Thanks also to the active collaboration of the United Nation's international consensus, the rejected and persecuted state of Israel—the little nation subject to an unprecedented wave of terrorist attacks—has been transformed into a Nazist colonialist persecutor. We have described the many aberrations, which go hand in hand with defamation of the United States. The left wing's cultural hegemony has spread immense wings on these themes. Its totalitarian roots on the one hand and the antidemocratic populist grafting of the Arab world on the other have given birth to a frankly fascist picture.

But the silence is not as total as it was half a century ago. There has been surprise, deep thought, protest, and even strength. The Israeli ambassador to Sweden successfully protested an artist's obscene admiration for a terrorist; an artist who was hosted, however, by state cultural institutions. Organizations such as CAMERA and Informazione Corretta have pressed journalists, and in universities professors have fought hard for a correct vision of Middle Eastern history. As I said, all this has helped denegation, one of the most important claims linked to the new anti-Semitism, to waver. It has finally been possible to shout in a chorus: The monster has returned.

But the very dynamics of globalization, which have had so much influence on the dissemination and spread of anti-Semitism, have been the most evident and biggest exhibition of the latter's destructive nature. The existence of anti-Semitism has been recognized and condemned. But how must one evaluate the response of European leaders, expressed mainly by recalling the memory of the Holocaust and by indicating that it should be taught in schools? Is it in this way that a little concern is expressed for living Jews? Or is it simply an attempt to restore those leaders' self-esteem as defenders of human rights?

In my opinion, even though the institutions' intentions (the OECD had been the most committed and also the most explicit) are superficial and hesitant, we nevertheless find ourselves with an important phenomenon. It is important because it is the start of the possibility of combating anti-Semitism with good chances of victory. The roots of the cancer growing in the heart of Europe are located within the very limits of globalization. A few years ago, globalization found its inspiration in the hopes of an integrated society in which the poor and the weak could merge in a democratic environment. Today, this seems part of a great illusion: This melting pot has been obstructed by crushing religious and cultural differences and, ultimately, by hate and, sometimes, by terrorism. The clash of Islamism with Western culture is the fundamental reason for the failure of globalization.

But big issues call for big responses. At first glance, European repentance is an attempt to recover quickly and easily from a foul disease by going over the past instead of facing the present. Anti-Semitism is not cured by simply declaring, in a conference or a visit to the local Jewish community, one's disgust with the fatal disease that afflicted Europe not so many years ago. Anti-Semitism has meant fundamental revolutions, ineffable perversions, wars, and fascism of various colors in Europe. I strongly feel that anti-Semitism is an indicator, a yellow flag signaling a pestilence that is spreading in the very heart of the globalization phenomenon, in its institutions (the United Nations, the NGOs, the European Union, and the media). It is here that the fight must take place. Institutions must be constantly, relentlessly faced with the truth. And the fulcrum of the claim must be the mistreatment suffered by Israel.

It has to be made clear how the sludge of the incredible quantity of falsehoods and international misunderstandings has become mixed with the smell of terrorist attackers' dynamite. This has given rise to the otherwise impossible amalgam of the Arabs' hate of the Jews and the new anti-Semitism of the post-Holocaust age in Europe. In the last year many people have been attacked or killed in various parts of the world for the mere fact that they were Jewish. Today in Turkey, Casablanca, Djerba, and Kenya, you die simply because you are Jewish, just as you do in Israel. The new anti-Semitism has genocidal traits—and even if not all victims are Jews, it would not be too rash to suggest that most of the terrorist attacks have been perpetrated by anti-Semites. This, I repeat, is the key link to be kept in mind.

Terrorism is a new, interesting form of globalization: Christians assassinated by Muslims in many parts of the world; Americans attacked wherever terrorists are able to get at them; and the dangerous expansion of terrorist cells in London, as in Milan or Paris. And below all this flows, like a well-channelled river, anti-Semitism. Terrorism itself undermines the dream of integration. It provides cover for any sort of destructive action against democracy, as in Madrid a few months ago. Europeans' fear and suspicion of the immigrant masses' violently anti-Western sentiments are no longer able to prevail over the ideological desire for integration. The historical memory of Europe, however sluggish and uncertain it may be, is still a dignified and decent social picture—albeit opportunistic—for democracy. After the experience of World War II, Europe, even though it wavers, is not in favor of authoritarian regimes or of uncontrollable Islamist alliances.

Consider France and the case of the head scarves; look at the demand of two political parties in the Netherlands (the populist LPF and the liberal VVD) to ban the pan-Islamic movement Hizb ut-Tahrir (HUT), stating that it was a threat to the Dutch legal system. Germany has already outlawed this group after the courts ruled that it was anti-Semitic and contrary to the German constitution. HUT wanted to hold its congress in a stadium but was prohibited from doing so. In the Netherlands there is also a demand to ban extremist Islamic parties. The Swiss government, usually so cold about these issues, is preparing a forum on anti-Semitism to be held in June, and Italy is too, in close collaboration with the Anti-Defamation League. In the Netherlands, in April 2004, the minister for integration, Rita Verdonk, asked the Dutch parliament to address the problem of Arab television stations broadcasting an anti-Semitic and inflammatory program. Cardinal Murphy O'Connor aligned himself with the ex-Archbishop of Canterbury, Lord Carey, in asking Muslims not to use Islam as a weapon.

I mention these episodes only to demonstrate that the phenomenon has been recognized and that we find traces of an effective awakening of conscience not so much in meetings, as in the admission by the EU president Romano Prodi that "criticism of the State of Israel is connected with anti-Semitism and is not totally founded," or in the visits of solidarity to Israel by the prime minister or deputy prime minister of the Italian government, or in the visit of Israel's President Moshe Katzav to the French president Chirac.

The acute and aggressive anti-Semitism that, among Europeans, is linked to the state of Israel was an outcome of the global idea of integration that undoubtedly grew from ancient Christian roots. In the last few years the Western part of the world has continued to try to demonstrate that the world is smaller and more united, more economically integrated, and better able to overcome differences. The Internet and McDonald's have become the symbols of a great hope that, in Europe, has included the millions of Muslims who live and work in London, Paris, and Rome. The great fear of Islam thus arrived almost simultaneously with the quest for a unified European soul, and while the search was underway for a new European unity open to globalism, a new fracture emerged in the world, a split that, a few years ago, was not there. The idea of a united humanity is a Western heritage and not necessarily the heritage of other cultures. Many Muslims have viewed the idea of unifying lifestyles and cultures as a sign of imperialist hegemony. Many have used their own experience of Western countries to fuel their disgust and contempt, and many as a means of finding a new outpost against an oppressive civilization. Homosexuality, social freedoms, sex, feminism, human rights, civil rights, the meaning of law and religion, and Western art and literature have become obstacles to realizing this global dream. I think that today, now that it has been recognized, anti-Semitism has become, or has the potential to become, one of the conceptual differences firmly wedged in the fracture.

When the war against terrorism was declared, the stench of the new anti-Semitism reached Europe's nostrils, and the union of sympathy for terror and anti-Semitism became clear in the crazy inventions about the role allegedly played by the Mossad on September 11. Linking Israel to everything that is bloodthirsty and part of a diabolical plan, where falsehood is the rule and killing for power is the natural tendency—just as in traditional anti-Semitism—cannot be part of an open society's aspiration to tolerance and universality. We are only at the beginning of the fight.

What is now clear is that the globalization culture, generally recognized, and the movements that claim to interpret its spirit, the human rights spirit, all have to be changed. The common sense of our times has to be changed. The possibility of Europe rebuilding its virginity on the past, while ignoring the present, must be avoided. The basis for acceptance of this repulsive anti-Semitism has indeed been created on the foundation of Europe's ill-willed political attitude to Israel.

For each European and each inhabitant of the planet who wants to combat antiterrorism, it must become impossible to separate Jews from their responsibilities vis-à-vis Israel. The damage that this attitude has caused is enormous, and the remedy must be proportional. Well, this proportionality is only possible via revision of human rights policy and lies in the idea of a radical fight against terrorism. There are no short cuts. The way to defeat anti-Semitism in Europe is to gain a deeper understanding of the contradictions of the open and globalized society. This means accepting the idea that (1) a large part of the demonization of Israel is an opportunity to incite violence and, in the final analysis, terrorism, (2) the memory of the Holocaust has not in itself succeeded in teaching the horror of anti-Semitism, when combined with ignorance of the history of Israel and Zionism, (3) grief for the death of a Jew does not in any way imply the will to save those who are still alive, and (4) mistaken identification of the victims and underestimation of religious hate and incitement is a sure recipe for a deluge of cultural misunderstandings. Globalized television networks such as Al-Manar or Al-Jazeera, which are also seen in Europe, must be forbidden to broadcast programs that incite. The meetings of the Islamic faithful in Europe, with all due respect for the freedom of religion, must respect the political and legal rules in force in their host countries and avoid any form of criminal incitement, even, and particularly, if those meetings take place in mosques.

Anti-Semitism is just a part, a symptom, of an erroneous international policy of underestimating the terrorist attack on the West, of standing against the United States, of misunderstanding the significance of global friendship, and of acknowledging and receiving the other. Giving hospitality to the other is the exact opposite of fearing and flattering him, of diminishing one's own personality, history, and morals. It is not even exchanging equality of rights and duties with moral equivalence.

We have been faced with the horrors of American tortures in the Abu Ghraib prisons and, on the other side, with the collection of butchered and dismembered people that started with the Ramallah lynching in 2000. Not by chance, the beheadings, the cruellest killings, shown live were those of Jews, Daniel Pearl and Nick Berg. The terrorists present them as an example to teach a lesson, to be an authentic advertisement. We have heard talk, by the usual progressives, of "the horrors of war," of the cycle of violence, of us like them. This is not so. "The horrors of war" exist, but in the case of Abu Ghraib and Nick Berg, the common factor between the two is that, in a certain sense, for the nth time they bring onto the stage, before our saddened eyes, the dark heart of human nature, when unleashed demons gain possession of a little power.

But there is power and power. There is the fascist political extolment of dark passions over reason, its strategic use in a jihadist war of conquest and hate. And, conversely, there is the shame of the *yetzer ha'ra*, the spirit of evil or evil instinct, the historical and institutional awareness of the Judeo-Christian civilization that, over the centuries, for the purpose of addressing the obscuring of reason, has produced an immense body of laws and rules that has constructed democracy and civilization based on human rights. Beware of betraying it out of fear, which has led to Fascism and Communism.

Today we are witnessing a phenomenon that we never wished to see: The voluntary erosion of our identity because the war is too difficult. But however difficult it is—and it is—we Europeans, like Israel, cannot avoid being there. First with the strength of our spirit and, only when necessary, with all the rest. Above all with the strength of life. Because it is true: we do love life a great deal—but it is our joy, our strength, and we want it for everyone.

# APPENDIX A

# A NOTE ON THE HISTORY OF THE MIDDLE EAST

## by Professor Marco Paganoni

As strange as this may seem at first, the Middle East is geographically and historically definable only in approximate terms. Perhaps the only element that gives us a unifying idea of it is the great Islamic majority that makes up its population. But the region's most celebrated historian, Bernard Lewis, leaves in doubt the question, for example, of whether Afghanistan is part of it or not. It is an inconclusive world, swept by external cultures, shaken by continual endogenic earthquakes, wars between countries, ethnic and religious conflicts that then become caught up in international movements that concern it and transcend it at the same time. It is a meeting place where, throughout the millennia, all civilizations have crossed paths only to later go on by. It is awe-inspiring for the eminence of the religious and cultural contributions it has made to world civilization—foremost that of monotheism—and yet it suffers from immense inferiority complexes. And at the same time, it is unable to break away from an acclaimed and at times belligerent Arab triumphalism.

It is the area of the world that is richest in oil and therefore capable, at present, of influencing the crucial energy market; yet not counting Israel, and not including its black gold, its volume of exports altogether is equal to that of Scandinavia. It has been a point of intersection and communication between the classic civilizations, Greece and Rome, and the rest of the world: Africa, India, and China. It gave birth to the three monotheistic religions, Judaism,

Christianity, and Islamism; it shared Hellenistic culture and Judeo-Christian culture with Europe, always bringing about some very fertile syncretisms with the legacy of its two very ancient, distant civilizations, Assyro-Babylonian and Egyptian.

The earliest political union of the villages that sprang up along the Nile dates from 3100 BC. The Assyrians conquered Mesopotamia at the end of the second millennium. The Jews left Egypt around the thirteenth century, giving rise to one of the greatest adventures of history and of the collective human imagination. The basic milestones of Middle Eastern history continued to leave a mark on the world with the birth of Christ and, later, in 570 with the birth of Mohammed in Mecca. And at its inception, Arab and Muslim civilization was a prodigious font of vitality and sociality. The Islamic world of the early Middle Ages marched triumphantly along the path of territorial conquest combined with creativity. It was multicultural, multiethnic, and intercontinental. The Middle East invented writing and numbers.

It should have merited the fate of becoming the richest civilization, one that would have been able to give the modern world a universal culture. Instead, this role fell to neighboring Europe, leaving the Middle East in a situation that, one might say, has all the problems of an autochthonous culture, Islam, together with those caused by too intimate a relationship with the West. This undesirable embrace is symbolized all too well by the presence—in the heart of the Middle East—of a country, Israel, whose characteristics are above all Western, a fact that dramatizes the local dynamics considerably. The fate of this region—and this is evident from the passion with which the entire world is following the peace process between Israel and the Palestinians—is important for everyone because it could produce a paradigm of the fate of relations between the Muslim world and Western democracies that are presently shifting. It is not so much the fate of the Israelis or the Arab countries that is at stake, as the prospect of peace between worlds that for the time being do not understand one other.

A precise definition of the boundaries of the Middle East is not simple. The term *Middle East* was used for the first time in 1902 by Alfred Thayer Mahan, a naval history specialist, to indicate the region between the Arabian peninsula and India, which has as its center the Persian Gulf. The term was taken up by the *Times* of London and later by the British government on various occasions, and so the region was baptized with this gray, anonymous name, devoid of any history or mythology (think of how charged with female mythological allure the name *Europe* is!)—a grouping of cultures, the main ones being Arab, Persian, and Turkish, and lands that history has designated in varying, disputed ways.

However, one can say that in our times the Middle East is made up of Turkey, Iran, and perhaps Afghanistan, Iraq and the Arabian peninsula, the four countries of the Near East (Syria, Lebanon, Israel, and Jordan), and Egypt, with variously definable extensions toward the south in Arabophonic Africa. The southern boundary is marked in Asia by the seas that bathe the coasts of Iran and the Arabian peninsula; in Africa by that border zone in which Arab Africa and Black Africa intermingle variedly. The only boundary line that can be traced in a natural way and therefore with a certain assurance is the one shared with the former Soviet Union to the north.

But in general the Middle East's borders are disputed and unreliable, derived with the help of a straightedge based on changing relations among the colonial powers and between the colonial and local powers. For that reason they are not readily acknowledged by leaders and populations, which almost always have higher aspirations regarding the regions assigned to them by history, and as a result they are contested. The defining criteria held by the various countries of the area are not in turn homogeneous.

Take, for example, the border dispute between Syria and Israel, in which Syria considers the 1948 borders or those of 1967 a parameter, depending on how it suits its game; or the authority issues of minorities seeking a precisely defined land of their own, such as the Kurds with respect to Syria, Turkey, and Iraq. It is nature, if anything, that gives us the unique characteristic that applies to the entire Middle East: aridness, the desert, the chronic lack of fresh water. The two great civilizations that arose in Egypt and what is now Iraq benefited from the valleys of the vast rivers along which the most ancient cities in the world evolved and developed administrative techniques that involved the use of writing and accounting.

For the rest, sand and stones: There is hardly a country in the Middle East where the desert doesn't cover a large part of the land. The Arabian peninsula is a desert zone, apart from the southwestern and southeastern corners; the Fertile Crescent is little more than a strip of arable land along the coast. Egypt is a big sandpit, except for the fissure of the Nile, which widens at the river's delta; a large part of North Africa is desert land, and the tablelands of Turkey and Iran are steppes, sand, and stones.

The miraculous resource that comes from this desolate land is oil, which has been a controversial venture for the region: in fact, the tendency of modern Muslim societies to develop without infrastructures and taxation, and accordingly without assemblies and democracies, has been reinforced by the oil economy. It is indeed difficult to say whether oil is an asset or a liability for the Middle East. Certainly, the elite have used it as a shortcut to wealth without modernization and without democracy—as the key to quick, personal enrichment from which the general population did not benefit. Entry into the market world has occurred without democratic checks, and the money has instead been used to modernize the means of social control.

Before oil, the Middle East had a pyramidal society regulated by honor codes; today, autocracy has often been replaced by despotism, and the corruption that has flourished around the wells has become one of the region's biggest problems. Where there is little or no oil, in Jordan, Tunisia, and Egypt, there are more signs of democratic development than elsewhere. Therefore, oil is not a friendly force for development. The other big obstacle to development is excessive population growth in disproportion to the growth of resources.

The basic languages of the Middle East are Arabic (used from Iraq to Morocco, varied when spoken, standardized as the literary and political language), Persian (standardized and not extensive), Turkish (extremely varied in its dialects, complicated by Kemal Atatürk's substitution and transliteration from the Arabic to the Latin alphabet), and one might say, by now perhaps, also Hebrew, a language that while limited geographically, has a decisive political-symbolic importance. Such languages overlap, jostle, and replace one another depending on the dominant powers in the area.

Creeds and power have always brought language with them. Aramaic, Coptic, Berber, and Neopunic of North Africa gave way to Arabic. The faith of the Koran became a rich base of communication between populations unified by the conquerors' language, which spread like an oil stain. With the influx of Islamic power from the border between Persia and Iraq through the entire Fertile Crescent as far as North Africa, Arabic supplanted the other official languages and was established thereafter as the common language. It was the period in which the Persians became Islamized. But their years-long experience of power allowed them to maintain their identity and language and play a large role in the management of the country, even under Arab control: the independent Persian dynasties that were born in the heart of the Arab world upheld a distinct Persian grouping, brilliant and cultured. Islamic Persian began to replace cultured Arabic in the tenth century, just as the vulgar languages replaced Latin. The cities of the Turks and Persians were prevailing over Cairo, Damascus, and Baghdad. Meanwhile, the Turks were making their appearance, taking military domination solidly in hand. In the eleventh century, they colonized the Middle East, establishing a center in Persia, incorporated Asia Minor into the Islam they had embraced, and pushed into Europe. All the dynasties from Syria to Egypt were Turkish: their hegemony lasted a millennium.

Muslim cultures supplanted those of the other two monotheistic religions: Christianity and Judaism. Christians and Jews (*dhimmi*), though protected by Islamic law under the conditions of domination, remained isolated and excluded from power. Christians once again found a role in the liberal, nationalistic patriotism that seemed to inspire the Middle East all of a sudden. Lebanon, an area of greater Christian concentration, was for a certain period of time a fortress of East-West mediation. But all this ended when Lebanon became a kind of Syrian province following a series of wars, the civil war of 1958, and a long-standing war with Israel. The Christian Crusaders are commonly seen as the first colonizers in the Middle East; a viewpoint that forgets the Crusades were part of a terrible clash between the West and Islam that had begun four centuries earlier.

The Jews, after a period of splendor highlighted by the brilliance of the Bible (the mother of all Western culture, religious and secular), clashed with the Persian Empire and with the Romans and were definitively defeated by the Romans in 135 AD, after having tried for fifty years to recover through daring rebellions and uprisings what they had lost for good in 70 AD, with the destruction of the great Temple of Jerusalem. The names *Jerusalem* and *Judea* were eliminated, and the names *Aelia* and *Palestine* applied to them.

The Arabs treated the Jews far better than the Romans and Christians had. The Jews continued to maintain a religious presence in Israel in any case, and it became vigorous with the Ottoman conquest of the sixteenth century. Three centuries later it became Zionist, that is, determined to reestablish the Jewish state at a time when European anti-Semitism was flaring up with the flourishing of nationalism and later with the advent of Nazism. By 1948, the year the state of Israel was born, the number of Jews in the Middle East had passed half a million. Meanwhile, the Jewish language had been restored and modernized and was commonly spoken again after centuries of religious use.

The history of the Middle East, whose thousands of twists and turns are impossible to follow in a few pages, shows its decisive importance for the entire world today in the hand-to-hand struggle between Islam and liberal democracy. After all, a community of more than a billion people resides here, whose history spans fifteen centuries and is shared among fifty-three different states (those united under the aegis of the OIC, the Organization of the Islamic Conference).

The relationship between Islam and the Middle East was born with the great Arab conquests of the seventh and eighth centuries, which for the first time since Alexander's time created a solid unity from northern Africa to the borders of India and China. Despite the Crusades, Western domination, and the defeats it endured, Islam, after having been obscured a number of times, became once again the region's most important unifying force. And it certainly took on an ideologically dominant tone with the advent in 1979 of the Islamic state in Iran, when the Ayatollah Khomenei took power and established the sharia, the law of the Koran, as state law.

It is notable, and an indication of the complexity of the process, that Khomeini incited the Islamic revolution in Iran from his exile in Paris, making decisive use of the telephone, fax, films, and cassettes, which were broadcast in the mosques on Fridays and from loudspeakers in the street, that is, using the very means typical of modern democratic development against which he has always directed the arrows of his condemnation. A sign of the intersection of two worlds, the West and the Middle East, which meet along the inevitable roads to (partial at least) modernization of the area, but which then make different, if not contrary, use of it.

Since the Iranian revolution, religion has become a dominant characteristic in the unification of the diverse identities of the region and has acquired a decidedly demanding trait, critical of Western democracy, with varying tones of revanchist triumphalism. It is interesting to note how secular leaders like Arafat or Saddam Hussein have over the years become increasingly sensitive to the themes of religion and in fact conduct their political campaigns in the name of Islam. The most intense of the many battles underway in the area, that of the Palestinians for a state of their own, became in 2000 the "Intifada of the Mosques." Whether Islam is compatible with democracy is a trenchant question because Islamic radicalism has now become part of the mainstream. The great intellectual creation of classical Islam, or the Islam of the Hadith, the pure Koranic tradition, have doors that are much more open according to experts.

In any case, only Turkey today in the Middle East is a democracy that has changed the government's majority in parliament a number of times. Yet, according to Western standards, even its system leaves much to be desired. In general, we find forms of autocracy more or less modernized, never liberal. According to Bernard Lewis, the concept of "citizen" is replaced in Arabic by that of "compatriot" or fellow countryman. The classical texts do not contain the idea of participation in the administration of the polis.

Given the long-standing contact between the Middle East and other cultures, why hasn't liberal democracy become a viable option? Several historical reasons can be cited here: Islam dominated the Christian world for the first thousand years of its life. As late as 1683, the Ottoman army was on the point of taking Vienna by storm.

After the profound disillusionment of defeat and colonization, the Muslim world struggled with an image of itself rooted in a triumphant Mohammed marching victoriously at the head of his army, founding cities and dictating law. For a long time, commentators sought solutions in all directions to explain this disillusionment. In the nineteenth century, the Muslims confronted as never before in their history the idea that to have a better future, to win again, they had to face democratization as the Christian universe, the victorious world, had done with its elective assemblies and democratically passed laws. After making a number of trips to carefully observe the flow of pluralistic information or the House of Commons in London, Islam began to make broad use of the word *liberty* instead of the word *justice*—liberty in a positive sense, a word that had been introduced in 1798 as a result of the Napoleonic conquest.

In addition to wearing Western clothing, the various local leaders charged the experts with designing new constitutions and reforming the armies. But democracy had a variable, uncertain fate: for example, in Turkey the parliament elected in 1876 was dissolved three years later, and in 1907 the revolution of the Young Turks took place ending in a military coup. Elections, including recent ones in Iran or in the Palestinian Authority, have remained in use almost everywhere since that time, but they mainly represent a means of ratifying existing balances of power.

Nonetheless, there are varying degrees of democracy: Jordan, Morocco, and Egypt are countries whose future envisions modernization measures, though limited, together with sporadic participation. On the other hand, the regimes of Saddam Hussein in Iraq, or of Bashar al-Assad, son of Hafez, in Syria take us directly back to the notion of fascism. Islamic extremist regimes, such as Iran or Sudan and even Afghanistan, are harsh regimes, not only deprived of internal liberty, but also predisposed to conversion or conquest of the external world.

This is where one of the most important phenomena of the Middle East began: international terrorism, particularly aimed at defeating the "Great Satan," the United States, and the "Little Satan," Israel. That's how the Ayatollah Khomeini baptized them. Iran and Syria finance movements like the Hezbollah in Lebanon or Hamas in the Palestinian Authority; Sudan and Afghanistan provide shelter to terrorist groups capable of launching attacks throughout the world with financing obtained in part through a vast opium trade. Their ability to produce or acquire chemical or biological weapons of vast lethal impact is new. Among these terrorist units, the most famous is Osama bin Laden's group in Afghanistan. This new phenomenon of worldwide import does not emanate exclusively from the Middle East, of course, but it has its headquarters and principal origin there.

The constitutional ideas that particularly in Turkey and Persia constituted a great hope at the beginning of the twentieth century failed, even though Turkey later showed that it never abandoned them entirely. The Ottoman Empire was destroyed along with all its dreams; Persia found itself squeezed between the Russian Empire and the British Empire; the French created constitutional monarchies of dubious success, the English, lame democracies. In general, therefore, over the years, the allure that the Middle Eastern world felt for democracy was contradicted by the difficulty of adapting to an ideology essentially relevant to the Judeo-Christian world, as well as by humiliations imposed by that world in various circumstances: the colonial relationship, and the imbalance of military power, per capita income, or simply scientific development.

This is what Muslim reformer Jamal al-Din al-Afgani had to say at a conference in Calcutta in 1882: "The Europeans have now laid hands on every part of the world. The English have reached Afghanistan; the French have appropriated Tunisia. But in reality these acts of usurpation, aggression, and conquest have not come from the French and from the English. It is science instead that manifests everywhere its greatness and power. Ignorance has no possibility of success: we must humbly acknowledge our weakness before science." And Egyptian educator Muhammad Abdu (1849–1905) pointed out an unfamiliar idea to his country's landowners, that of "European associations of farmers, industrialists and merchants, whose overall income, amounting to little more than thirty million pounds, is spent to impart knowledge, develop scientific research, and propagate arts and trades."

The frustration of the Arab world in its dealings with democratic countries was transformed over time into a search for political rapport, first with nationalism, and later with Soviet Russia. The Arabs particularly liked the Germans and their National Socialism rather than the Italians, since the latter had colonized them. Indeed in 1933, Jerusalem Muftì Haj Amin al-Huseyni approached the Germans and offered his help; and in 1941, Rashid Ali Al-Gaylani, supported by the military, offered the Axis a Syrian regime favorable to its policies.

But since the Axis, too, was defeated at the end of World War II, the new, more natural connection was Soviet Russia, which wholeheartedly reciprocated the fellow feeling. Pan-Arabism, especially in the years of the Cold War, became a springboard of anti-Western, anti-imperialist and anticapitalist claims, supported by the USSR with both rhetoric and arms. With Egypt at the center, the Arabs, free at last from colonial domination, came under the view of forced development, in which it was theorized that the world of the Middle East didn't have time for democracy, a system considered chaotic and risky in part due to the mechanism of competing in an untenable market. The memories of uncertainty and vulnerability left by the capitalistic countries that had withdrawn, provided a thrust toward socialist regimes imposed from above that in theory, as in the USSR, were supposed to promote forced industrialization and therefore enrich the region. In actuality the USSR used these regimes mainly as a form of domination against the West, and therefore against Israel, and certainly did not make them rich. Up until the recent powerful Islamic insurgence, all the experts agreed that the collapse of Communism signaled a hope of peace for a world that, except for brief periods, has always been at war.

The conflict between Arabs and Jews has characterized an enormous part of the history of the Middle East, with Egyptian testimonies that go back to biblical times, and that extend up to our own times, in which the conflict has reached its height. After the British Empire's unkept promises to the Arabs to support the birth of a vast Arab kingdom in exchange for help against Turkey, the English divided the Middle East region with the French, and in 1917, with the Balfour Declaration, recognized the right of the Zionist movement to make Palestine the national home of the Jewish people. Following this declaration, Jewish immigration grew in what was then the British Mandate, successor to the Ottoman Empire, and the conflict between the newly arrived Jews and the Palestinians was accentuated; according to U.N. surveys in 1948, at the time of the founding of the Jewish state, there were around 470,000 Palestinians in the region, subjects of the Ottoman Empire and then of the British. When the United Nations in 1947 recognized the new Jewish state with borders notably more limited than those of the present day, the surrounding Arab countries did not accept it and launched a concentric attack from which Israel emerged the winner.

That was the first of five wars (1948, 1956, 1967, 1973, and 1982) in which the Arab world time and again deluded itself that it would be able to eliminate Israel's very presence. Each war has given rise to new frustrations and new hatred, fed enormously by the awakening of the Palestinian nationalist movement that was organized in the sixties with the foundation of the PLO (Palestine Liberation Organization). The Palestinian war of independence is still underway, and after a brief period, from September 1993 (the Oslo Accords) to September 2000 (Intifada of the Mosques) in which an agreement between the two parties seemed to gain ground, the conflict, which then again is the dominant feature of the region, has flared up again.

By 1948, the process of identifying the national boundaries of the various peoples or dynasties of the region could be said to have been completed: Iraq, Egypt, Saudi Arabia, Turkey, Iran, and Afghanistan were defined in their current form more or less during the period between the two wars. In 1945, the League of Arab States was formed, consisting of Egypt, Iraq, Syria, Lebanon, Saudi Arabia, Yemen, and Transjordan. In 1946, Transjordan gained its independence. All of this came about as the result of the colonial powers' moving out. The movement to define new states continued with Libya in 1951 (the most artificial of all the entities of the area as far as its borders and cohesive history is concerned), the Sudan, Tunisia, and Morocco in 1956, Mauritania in 1960, Kuwait in 1961, Algeria in 1962, Southern Yemen in 1967, and the Gulf States in 1971.

Before returning to the conflict between Israel and the Arab world, we should keep in mind that, generally speaking, all the events that led to the recognition, independence, and self-definition of the Arab countries of the region were violent ones, accompanied by intense conflicts like the one between Iran and Iraq, and like the permanent state of tension and conflict that surrounds Turkey. The borders of the new states were often drawn artificially, leaving the door open to all kinds of territorial conflict: for years Algeria, Morocco, Egypt, Sudan, and Libya have been engaging in territorial diatribes concerning borders. The Syrians have resolute claims on Lebanon accompanied by military occupation; Egypt for many years has aspired to incorporate the Sudan. Iran wants Bahrein, Turkey Mosul, Libya Chad.

Dispossessed minorities are found in areas where they lack sovereignty, speak different languages, and practice religions extraneous to those of the population that rules them and often persecutes them. In Iraq there are numerous Persians and a million Turks, as well as many Kurds who are persecuted by the Turks and by the Syrians as well; Jews have been driven out of the majority of Arab countries. The Coptics are victims of the Egyptians, and all Christian denominations are in constant, apparent decline everywhere, even in Bethlehem and Nazareth. Lebanon is the most evident example of a country devoured and destroyed to its very foundations by ethnic-religious and territorial conflicts.

Oil, in turn, generates terrible clashes, like the one in 1991 between Saddam Hussein and Kuwait, which affected the entire world. In addition, there is a continual struggle for moral and historical predominance, for leadership of the Arab world, which is always anxiously in search of deliverance: Egypt, Syria, Iraq, and more discreetly Saudi Arabia compete for the honor, but Mubarak's Egypt seems in a better position to achieve it because of its more modern choices, even if this is precisely the reason why it is always in danger, threatened by Islamic fundamentalist resurgence.

The real apple of discord as everyone knows, however, is the Arab-Israeli conflict, which fueled by the Cold War in its day nevertheless has its own historical and psychological roots that at times seem insurmountable. Israel is a country whose institutions and economic development are entirely Western, even though the religious component with its Eastern ethnic origins has acquired prominent political importance in recent years and attempts to portray the Jewish state, that was born out of the secular, socialist Zionism of its founder David Ben-Gurion, as denominational as possible. Nonetheless, its flourishing democratic life, its economy characterized by a level of high-tech that can only be compared to that in the United States, its free customs and unrestrainedly pluralistic information, and, a fundamental fact, the emancipation of its women, make the Jewish nation unpopular in the region, where it is viewed as an element that corrupts the Muslim traditions. This, added to the territorial claims of the Palestinians, which over time have become more specific and extensive, as well as more closely focused on the city of Jerusalem—a city that has been a symbol for Jews, Christians, and Muslims in that chronological order—has created the idea that Israel is a Trojan Horse from the West whose charge is to inundate the Islamic world with spurious cultures and be the instrument of Western domination in the region. Zionism has never been recognized by the Arab world as a legitimate national movement, but has been seen instead as a product of Western imperialism.

In the end, despite the peace process that began in the seventies with Menahem Begin returning the Sinai to Egypt and the Oslo Accords of 1993, the situation has not improved much over time. The illusion that the disappearance of the USSR could bring about peace in the region shattered when it came up against Islamization and more generally on the irrational part of the conflict. President Anwar Sadat of Egypt, who came to Israel saying "Enough war," and Yitzhak Rabin, the general who later became prime minister and "father of peace," were assassinated by respective extremists. Shimon

Peres, the Israeli who, along with Rabin and Arafat, was awarded the Nobel Peace Prize in 1994, presented a plan for an integrated economy and culture in his book *A New Middle East* (Henry Holt & Company, 1993), a plan that does not seem destined to be realized—nor, for that matter, do the plans of any of our contemporaries.

# CHRONOLOGY

## 1947

**April 2.** Great Britain hands the Palestine problem over to the United Nations.

**November 29.** With Resolution 181, the United Nations provides for the creation of two independent states, Arab and Jewish, bound in an economic and customs union, with Jerusalem to be under international control for ten years. The partition plan is accepted by the Jewish side and rejected by the Arab side.

**December 8.** The Arab League decides to resort to war to prevent the implementation of U.N. Resolution 181.

**Autumn 1947–Spring 1948.** The conflicts intensify as the British gradually withdraw their troops. Palestinian notables and the ruling class leave the country before the actual eruption of the Arab-Israeli war.

## 1948

**January–February.** Penetration of the part of Palestine assigned to the Jews by irregular Arab troops from across the border. Attacks against Jewish villages multiply.

**March–June.** Siege of the Jewish districts of Jerusalem, ambushes against convoys arriving from the coast. The old Jewish district within the walls of Jerusalem falls: The Jews are all expelled.

**April.** Jewish extremist groups attack Deir Yassin, one of the Arab villages around Jerusalem, killing many civilians as well. Arabs attack a medical convoy in Jerusalem and massacre the inhabitants of Gush Etzion. The flight of Palestinian Arab refugees (ap-

proximately 700,000 of them) to areas under Arab control inten-
sifies; there they will be kept for decades in refugee camps, often
within Palestine itself. Another 160,000 Palestinian Arabs remain; they will become Israeli citizens.

**May 14.** Declaration of independence of the state of Israel. The
armies of Syria, Transjordan, Iraq, Egypt, Lebanon, and Saudi
Arabia attack—the first Arab-Israeli war. May 1948–January
1949. Israel drives Arab troops back beyond the partition lines.
With British restrictions abolished, there is mass immigration of
Jews from Europe (survivors of the Shoah), Asia, and North
Africa (approximately 600,000 Jewish refugees from the Arab
nations are admitted to Israel).

# 1949

**February–July.** Armistice agreements signed in Rhodes between Is-
rael and Egypt (February), Lebanon (March), Transjordan
(April), and Syria (July). Israel withdraws from Egyptian and
Lebanese areas. Gaza Strip occupied by Egypt, Cisjordan occu-
pied by Transjordan: an Arab state of Palestine is not created.
Jerusalem remains divided between Israel and Transjordan.
Jews are denied access to sacred sites. Jewish tombs and syna-
gogues are profaned and looted.

# 1950

**December 16.** Transjordan becomes the Hashemite Kingdom of
Jordan.

# 1951

**July 20.** King Abdullah of Jordan is assassinated by a Palestinian in
Jerusalem. His grandson Hussein succeeds him.

# 1955

First military accord between the USSR and Egypt: the Soviet
Union and the Cold War enter the Middle East.

# 1956

Attacks on Israel's borders, particularly from the Gaza Strip under
Egyptian control.
Egypt nationalizes the Suez Canal and blocks Israeli navigation to
and from Israel in the Strait of Tiran (Gulf of Elat).
**October.** Second Arab-Israeli war: campaign in the Sinai, Israel,
France, and Great Britain.
**November.** The United States and the USSR impose a cease-fire.

# 1957

Israel withdraws from the Sinai and Gaza Strip with assurance that
the border will be demilitarized and safeguarded by the United
Nations and that Israeli navigation will be guaranteed in the
Strait of Tiran and in the Suez Canal.

# 1959

Creation of the armed Palestinian organization Al-Fatah.

# 1964

Trial and conviction of Nazi party leader Adolf Eichmann: the only
death sentence carried out in Israel.
**January 4–6.** Pope Paul VI's pilgrimage to Christian sites in Israel.

**May.** The Palestine Liberation Organization (PLO) is formed on the initiative of the Arab League; its task is the destruction of Israel through armed conflict.

# 1965

**October 28.** Despite opposing campaigns from the Arab press and governments, the Second Vatican Council issues the Declaration *Nostra aetate* that revokes the accusation of deicide against the Jewish people and opens the door to Judeo-Christian dialogue.

# 1967

The Arab states complete their military, diplomatic, propagandist, economic, and terrorist siege of Israel and prepare for a decisive war.

**May.** Egypt calls for and achieves the removal of the U.N. blue berets from the Sinai. Israel warns that the navigational blockade will be considered a casus belli. The Arab countries block Israeli navigation from Tiran and the Suez. Nasser announces a war of extermination against Israel.

**May 30, June 4.** Military agreements among Egypt, Jordan, and Iraq.

**June 5.** Third Arab-Israeli war: premptive strike by Israel, which in six days takes control of Sinai, Golan, Cisjordan, and the Gaza Strip (referred to, from this time on, as the occupied territories). Jerusalem is reunited.

**September 1.** The Arab League meeting in Khartoum (Sudan) reasserts "no to recognition, no to negotiations, no to peace with Israel."

**November 22.** U.N. Resolution 242 establishes that peace must be negotiated among the parties on the basis of Israeli retreat from the occupied territories; respect for the sovereignty, territorial integrity, and independence of each country in the region within secure, acknowledged borders; a fair solution to the refugee problem; and navigational freedom.

# 1968

**May.** Arafat, leader of Al-Fatah, becomes head of the PLO. Modifications to the PLO Charter in a more nationalistic and less pan-Arab direction. The goal of destroying Israel is reaffirmed.

**December 26** Attack on an Israeli civilian plane in Athens marks the beginning of Palestinian international terrorism.

# 1969

**April.** Egypt launches a war of attrition against Israel along the Suez Canal.

# 1970

PLO forces use Jordan as a base for terrorist operations.

**September 6–27.** Following the hijacking of four airplanes in Jordan, King Hussein reacts with force (Black September); armed Palestinian groups retreat to Lebanon.

# 1972

**May 30.** Attack against passengers at Lod Airport (Tel Aviv) by Japanese terrorists affiliated with the PLO.

**September 5.** At the Olympics in Munich, the Israeli team is slaughtered by a Palestinian commando unit.

First wave of Jewish immigrants from the Soviet Union (100,000 in two years).

# 1973

**October 6.** On the Jewish holy day of Yom Kippur, Egypt and Syria attack Israel on two fronts. Breakthrough of Israeli lines in the

Sinai, strenuous resistance in the Golan. Airlift of Soviet military aid to Syria and Egypt, and American aid to Israel.

**October 14–15.** Having stopped the Syrians on the Golan, Israeli forces cross the Suez Canal and turn the tide of the war.

**October 17.** Oil-producing Arab states declare the first oil embargo against the West. In the following months, the Organization of African Unity, the Non-Aligned Countries, the European Union, and various U.N. bodies adopt anti-Israeli motions.

**October 22.** U.N. Resolution 338 requires the parties to negotiate to apply Resolution 242 of 1967.

**November 11.** Israeli forces are 101 kilometers from Cairo and 32 kilometers from Damascus when the Arabs accept the cease-fire.

**December 31.** Palestinian attack at Fiumicino (Rome).

# 1974

**January 18.** U.S. Secretary of State Henry Kissinger's "shuttle diplomacy" and disengagement agreements on the Egyptian front with Israeli withdrawal.

**April 11.** Palestinian attack on families in Kiryat Shmonà.

**May 15.** Palestinian attack on a school in Ma'alot Galilee.

**May.** Disengagement agreements on the Syrian front with Israeli withdrawal.

**June.** The PLO approves the "phased plan" for the liberation of all Palestine.

**December.** Terrorist attack in Jerusalem.

# 1975

**March 6.** Terrorist attack on a hotel in Tel Aviv.

**November 10.** U.N. Resolution 3379 equates Zionism to a form of racism.

Start of civil war in Lebanon.

# 1976

**June.** Hijacking of an airplane at Entebbe (Uganda): Israeli special forces free the hostages.

**July–August.** Syrian troops enter Lebanon. Siege and massacre of Palestinians in the Tal el-Zaatar camp at the hands of Syrians and Lebanese Christians.

# 1977

**May–June.** Electoral turning point in Israel, the conservative Likud Party's first government.

**November 19.** Egyptian President Sadat goes to Jerusalem and addresses the Knesset. Condemnation of Arabs and Palestinians.

# 1978

**January–March.** Wave of Palestinian terrorist attacks from Lebanon.

**March 11.** Palestinian commando attack against two Israeli buses on a coastal road. Israeli operation in southern Lebanon against Palestinian bases. U.N. Resolution 425 for Israeli withdrawal, restoration of Lebanese sovereignty, peace and border security. Dispatching of UNIFIL blue berets.

**September 5–17.** Camp David talks and accords between Israel and Egypt for a solution to the Arab-Israeli conflict (with Palestinian self-rule) and bilateral peace. Arab and Palestinian countries reject the Camp David peace accord.

# 1979

**January.** Khomeini revolution in Iran: the rise of Islamic fundamentalism begins.

**March 26.** Signing of peace treaty between Israel and Egypt.

**March 27.** Egypt is expelled from the Arab League.

**April 22.** Attacks against families in Naharya and Jewish sites in Paris.

**July 25.** Israel's phased withdrawal from the Sinai begins.

# 1980

**April 16.** Terrorist attack against a nursery school in the Misgav Am kibbutz (Israel).

**May 3.** Palestinian commandos attack Jewish faithful at the Tomb of the Patriarchs in Hebron (Cisjordan).

**July 27.** Palestinian attack against a Jewish school bus in Antwerp (Belgium).

**September 10.** Terrorist attack against a synagogue in Paris.

# 1981

**June 7.** Israeli aircraft destroy Iraqi nuclear reactor.

**October 6.** President Sadat assassinated by Egyptian fundamentalist soldiers. Hosni Mubarak succeeds him.

# 1982

**April.** Israeli completes withdrawal from Egyptian Sinai area in compliance with peace agreements.

**June 4.** After the nth terrorist attack, Israel launches Operation Peace in Galilee against the Palestinian bases in the Lebanon. PLO infrastructures destroyed and armed Palestinian groups leave the country.

**August.** Multinational peace force is deployed in Lebanon.

**September.** Israel signs a peace treaty with the Lebanese government headed by president Amin Gemayel. Gemayel assassinated. Retaliation of Lebanese Christians against the Palestinian camps of Sabra and Shatila, while Beirut is under the control of Israeli troops. Protests in Israel and institution of a commission of inquiry, which finds indirect responsibilities of the Defense Minister Sharon and of the chief of staff. Arafat flees from Beirut to Tripoli in Lebanon, from where he will be driven out by the Syrians in early 1983, after which he will establish his base in Tunisia.

**October 9.** Palestinian terrorist attack against the synagogue of Rome.

# 1984

Suicide attacks by Lebanese fundamentalist groups against multinational peace forces and against Israeli forces.

# 1985

**June.** Withdrawal of Israeli forces from Lebanon, except for the "security zone" on the border.

**September.** Terrorist attack against Israelis in Cyprus.

**October 1.** Israeli aircraft bomb the PLO headquarters in Tunis.

**October.** Hijacking of the ship *Achille Lauro* and assassination of a Jewish American tourist. The Americans arrest the executors and instigator (Abu Abbas). Italy gets them handed over (at Sigonella), but lets Abu Abbas get away.

# 1986

**September.** Terrorist attack on the synagogue of Istanbul.

# 1987

**December 8.** Outbreak of the intifada—a violent, popular uprising of Palestinians in the territories of Cisjordan and the Gaza Strip. It lasts until 1990–1991. Lacerating internal debate in Israel.

# 1988

**July.** King Hussein of Jordan renounces all claims on Cisjordan.

**August.** The Palestinian fundamentalist movement Hamas publishes its fundamental Charter invoking jihad (holy war) against Israel's existence.

**November 15.** In Algiers, the National Council of the PLO symbolically declares the independence of a Palestinian state and accepts U.N. Resolutions 181, 242, and 338. The United States recognizes the PLO.

# 1989

Start of mass immigration of Soviet Jews (almost a million in the next ten years).

**July 6.** Terrorist attack on a Tel Aviv–Jerusalem bus.

# 1990

**February.** Palestinian attack on a busload of Israeli tourists in Egypt.

**August 2.** Iraq invades Kuwait. U.N. censure. International coalition led by the United States. The PLO sides with Iraq.

# 1991

**January–February.** Gulf War against Iraq. Although it is not part of the conflict, Israel is hit by thirty-nine Iraqi Scud missiles.

**May.** "Pax Syriana" in Lebanon. All forces disarmed except anti-Israeli Hezbollah fundamentalists.

**October 30–November 3.** A peace conference, under the aegis of the United States and the USSR, with: Israel, Egypt, Jordan, Lebanon, Syria, and the Palestinians. Start of multilateral talks on regional problems (arms, the economy, water, the environment, refugees) and bilateral talks between Israel and its Arab neighbors.

**December 16.** The United Nations rescinds the resolution "Zionism equals racism."

# 1992

Diplomatic relations established between Israel and ex-Soviet bloc countries, China, and India.

**March 17.** Terrorist attack on the Israel embassy in Buenos Aires (Argentina).

**June.** Elections and a new government led by Labor Party leader Yitzhak Rabin.

# 1993

**February 26.** Fundamentalist car bombing at New York's World Trade Center.

**September 9–10.** Following secret negotiations in Oslo (Norway), an exchange of letters between Rabin and Arafat. Arafat recognizes the state of Israel in the name of the Palestinian people and accepts the method agreed to in the talks, renouncing the use of violence and pledging to modify the Palestinian National Charter toward this end. Rabin, in the name of Israel, recognizes the PLO as representative of the Palestinian people.

**September 13.** At the White House, Rabin and Arafat sign the Declaration of Principles for a gradual, negotiated solution to the conflict ("Oslo process").

**December 30.** Diplomatic relations established between Israel and the Holy See.

# 1994

**February 25.** Israeli extremist attack against Muslim followers at the Tomb of the Patriarchs in Hebron.

**March 31.** Israel and the PLO agree to a temporary international presence in Hebron and the resumption of talks.

**April.** Suicide attacks against Israeli buses in Afula and Hadera.

**April 29.** Paris economic accord between Israel and the PLO.

**May 4.** Cairo accord on the Gaza Strip and Jericho: start of the first form of Palestinian self-rule.

**July 18.** Car bombing at the offices of Jewish organizations in Buenos Aires.

**July 26.** Attacks in London against the Israeli embassy and Jewish offices.

**September–October.** Exchange of official delegations among Israel, Tunisia, and Morocco.

**October 9.** Terrorist attack on a crowd in Jerusalem.

**October 19.** Suicide terrorist attack on a bus in Tel Aviv.

**October 26.** Rabin and King Hussein sign a Peace Treaty between Israel and Jordan.

**November 1.** First economic conference of North Africa and the Middle East with Israel.

# 1995

**January 22.** Double suicide attack in Netanya.

**April–June.** Katyusha rockets fired at Israel by Lebanon.

**July 24.** Suicide terrorist attack on a bus in Ramat Gan.

**August 21.** Suicide terrorist attack on a bus in Jerusalem.

**September 28.** Signing of an Interim Accord regulating relations between Israel and the Palestinians until the future signing of an accord for definitive status. It provides for the formation of the Palestinian Authority and a Palestinian police force, Palestinian elections, the redeployment of Israeli forces in stages, joint patrols, and the temporary division of territories into zones: A (Palestinian control), B (joint control), and C (Israeli control).

**November 4.** At the end of a peace demonstration, Prime Minister Yitzhak Rabin is assassinated by an Israeli extremist. Arab leaders attend his funeral services in Jerusalem. Shimon Peres replaces him in office.

**December.** Israel accelerates its withdrawal from principal Palestinian cities.

# 1996

**January 20.** First elections for the Palestinian Authority's legislative council and President. Yasir Arafat is elected.

**February 25–March 3.** Series of suicide terrorist attacks on buses in Jerusalem and Ashqelon.

**March 4.** Terrorist attack in Tel Aviv.

**April.** Terrorist attacks by Hezbollah fundamentalists from Lebanon and Israeli reaction. A U.N. refuge is struck by mistake in Kana (Lebanon).

**April 24.** The PLO votes for an incomplete amendment of the Palestinian National Charter. Israeli-Palestinian talks on implementation of the accords resume in Taba. Exchange of official delegations among Israel, Oman and Qatar.

**May 29.** First direct election of the prime minister: Benjamin Netanyahu (Likud) is elected.

**September 4.** Meeting between Netanyahu and Arafat.

**September 26.** The false accusation that Israel was digging a tunnel underneath the mosques in Jerusalem unleashes Palestinian attacks against Israeli soldiers and civilians. For the first time, Palestinian police use regulation weapons against the Israelis.

# 1997

**January 15.** Netanyahu and Arafat sign the Hebron Protocol (dividing Hebron into zones H1 and H2). With Hebron, more than 95 percent of the Palestinians in the territories are now under self-rule.

**March.** Israeli schoolgirls killed by a Jordanian soldier. King Hussein personally pays his condolences to the stricken families. Palestinian suicide terrorist attack in Tel Aviv.

**July 30.** Double suicide terrorist attack in the Mahane Yehudah market in Jerusalem.

**September 5.** Suicide terrorist attack in Ben Yehudah in Jerusalem.

# 1998

**August.** Fundamentalist attacks against U.S. embassies in Kenya and Tanzania.

**October 23.** Netanyahu and Arafat sign the Wye Plantation Memorandum for the application of the interim accords.

**November 6.** Car bombing in the Mahane Yehudah market in Jerusalem.

**December 15.** The Palestinian National Council, meeting in the Gaza Strip in the presence of U.S. President Bill Clinton, officially approves the amendments to the PLO Charter promised by Arafat in his 1993 letter to Rabin.

# 1999

**February 7.** King Hussein of Jordan dies. He is succeeded by his son Abdullah II.

**May 17.** Early elections in Israel. Second direct election of the prime minister: Ehud Barak (Labor Party) is elected.

**July.** King Hassan II of Morocco dies. He is succeeded by his son Mohammed VI.

**September.** Barak and Arafat sign the Sharm el-Sheikh—memorandum establishing a timetable for implementing interim accords and for the start of talks concerning definitive status.

**October.** Syria rejects Israel's unofficial proposal to withdraw completely from the Golan.

**November 7.** Terrorist attack in Netanya.

# 2000

**March.** Pope John Paul II's official visit to Israel.

**May.** Israel's unilateral withdrawal from the "secure zone" (southern Lebanon).

**June.** Syrian President Hafez Assad dies. He is succeeded by his son Bashar.

**July.** Summit at Camp David. Barak presents Arafat with the most advanced proposal ever offered to the Palestinians to put an end to the conflict: nearly complete withdrawal from the occuied territories, a Palestinian state with a capital in the Arab section of Jerusalem, and a sharing of Sacred Sites. Arafat rejects it and threatens a unilateral declaration of independence on September 13, but does not find international supporters.

**September–October.** Using the pretext of opposition leader Ariel Sharon's visit to the Temple Mount in Jerusalem, the Palestinians unleash a wave of attacks and violence, with using firearms and terrorist bombing attacks. Security collaboration and economic cooperation blocked. Palestinian children in the front line against soldiers. Lynching of two Israel by Palestinian police in Ramallah. Destruction of Joseph's Tomb in Nablus. A civilian and three Israeli soldiers seized by Lebanese Hezbollah fundamentalists. The most serious crisis since the beginning of the peace process.

**December.** Barak's resignation.

# 2001

**January.** Clinton unveils his compromise proposal. Israel accepts in principle, the Palestinians set conditions. Israeli-Palestinian talks in Taba, the Palestinians reject a further Israeli proposal.

**February 6.** Early elections in Israel for the position of prime minister: Ariel Sharon (Likud) is elected.

**March 7.** Sharon's coalition government (Likud, Labor party, and others). The direct election of prime minister is repealed.

**May.** Report of the international Mitchell Commission providing for immediate, unconditional cessation of violence, a period of truce, mutual measures to re-create trust, resumption of peace talks.

**May 22.** Israel accepts the Mitchell report and announces a unilateral cease-fire. No truce on the part of the Palestinians.

**June 1.** Suicide terrorist attack at a Tel Aviv discothèque. Under pressure from the United States and German Minister Fischer, Arafat announces a cease-fire but violence continues. Mediation by CIA Director Tenet for application of a truce.

**June 13.** The Tenet truce officially takes effect, but Palestinian violence continues with road ambushes, mortars, explosive devices, grenades, and gunfire.

**August 9.** Suicide terrorist attack at Sbarro pizzeria in Jerusalem. Israeli blockade of Palestinian cities and actions aimed at those who plan and send out the suicide attack bombers.

**September 11.** Suicide terrorists hijack four civilian airplanes and fly two into the twin towers of the World Trade Center in New York and one into the Pentagon in Washington, D.C. International coalition led by the United States against international terrorism and those who support it.

**October 7.** Start of Anglo-American military operations against the Taliban regime in Afghanistan that protects Osama bin Laden and the terrorist network Al Qaeda, the main parties blamed for the attacks of September 11.

**October 17.** Terrorist attack in Jerusalem by George Habbash's PFLP (Popular Front for the Liberation of Palestine), which is based in Syria: Israeli parliamentarian and minister Rehavam Zeevi is assassinated. Israeli ultimatum to the Palestinian

Authority to take real antiterrorism measures. Israeli forces repeatedly penetrate areas in Palestinian Area A.

**November 12.** U.S. President Bush's speech at the United Nations: "We will spare no efforts to reach the day when two States, Israel and Palestine, will live peacefully together within secure, acknowledged borders."

**November 13.** Kabul falls: The Taliban abandon the Afghani capital after five years of an obscurantist regime.

**November 27.** Start of the first mission of new U.S. envoy to the Middle East, General Anthony Zinni.

**December 1–2.** Weekend of bloody violence in Israel: a double suicide attack and a car bombing in Jerusalem, a suicide attack in Haifa.

**December 3.** Israel destroys Arafat's helicopters and declares: "Arafat will not leave Ramallah until he has had Minister Zeevi's killers arrested."

**December 12–13.** Another wave of Palestinian terrorist attacks. The Israeli government declares Arafat's role irrelevant. Pressures on Arafat from the United States, Europe, and other Arab countries increase.

**December 16.** Arafat on Palestinian television orders an end to suicide bombings and armed attacks against Israel because "they are damaging to the Palestinian cause."

**December 24–25.** Held captive in Ramallah, Arafat cannot attend midnight mass in Bethlehem.

# 2002

**January 5.** In the Red Sea, Israeli air and naval forces seize Palestinian Authority freighter *Karine A* with fifty tons of weapons purchased in Iran.

**January 9.** A Palestinian attack against soldiers in Israel (near the Egyptian border) interrupts a period of relative calm following Arafat's television address. Attacks and counteroffensives resume.

**January 17.** Suicide terrorist attack in the Israeli city of Hadera.

**January 20.** Start of a vast antiterrorist operation by Israeli forces within the Palestinian city of Tulkarem.

# 2003

**January 5.** Two suicide attackers blow themselves up almost simultaneously in the Neve Sha'anan neighborhood, near the old bus station of Tel Aviv. Victims include many foreign workers.

**March 5.** Suicide attacker blows himself up on a bus in Haifa (Israel).

**March 9.** Phrases of an anti-Semitic tenor, targeting the president designate of the Italian public TV company RAI, Paolo Mieli, appear on the walls of the RAI premises in Corso Sempione in Milan.

**April 15**. Palestinian attacker opens fire at random at the Karni checkpoint between Israel and the Gaza Strip.

**April 30**. Pakistani suicide attacker with a British passport blows himself up on the sea promenade of Tel Aviv after trying unsuccessfully to enter a crowded bar. The body of a second Pakistani attacker with a British passport, whose explosive device had failed to work, is found two weeks later in the waters off Tel Aviv.

**May 16**. Five terrorist attacks are undertaken almost simultaneously in Casablanca by twelve suicide attackers. Targets include a Jewish community center and a Jewish-owned restaurant.

**May 17**. Suicide terrorist attack in the Jewish neighborhood of Hebron (Cisjordan).

**May 18**. Suicide attacker dressed as an Orthodox Jew blows himself up on a bus in Pisgat Ze'ev (Jerusalem). A second terrorist blows himself up half an hour later at the entrance of the Dahit Al Barid neighborhood in Jerusalem, without causing victims.

**May 19**. Female suicide attacker blows herself up at the entrance of a shopping mall in Afula (Israel).

**June 11.** Suicide attacker blows himself up on a normal scheduled bus in Jaffa Street in Jerusalem.

**June 19**. Suicide attacker blows himself up at the entrance of a store in Sde Trumot (Israel), killing the owner, who had stopped him outside.

**June 30**. The Anti-Defamation League (ADL) calls for an inquiry into Professor Andrew Wilkie, of the University of Oxford, who refused to accept Amit Duvshami as a postgraduate student simply because he was an Israeli citizen. On October 27, 2003,

Professor Wilkie is suspended from the university without pay for two weeks.

**July 7.** Suicide attacker blows himself up in the doorway of a house in Kfar Yavetz (Israel), killing the elderly woman who lived there.

**July 11.** Suicide attacker blows himself up during the rush hour on a bus in Jerusalem.

**August 10.** A sixteen-year-old Israeli boy is killed in Slomi (northern Israel) by rockets fired from Lebanese territory.

**August 12.** Suicide attacker blows himself up at the entrance of a supermarket in Rosh HaAyin (Israel).

**August 12.** Suicide attacker blows himself up at a bus stop on the outskirts of Ariel (Cisjordan).

**August 19.** Suicide attacker—a Muslim cleric (imam) and schoolmaster—blows himself up on a bus in Jerusalem full of families returning from prayers at the Western Wall.

**September 8.** Suicide attacker blows himself up at the entrance of the Café Hillel in the German Colony in Jerusalem.

**September 9.** Suicide attacker disguised as a soldier blows himself up at a bus stop between Zrifim and the Assaf Harofeh hospital (in the suburbs of Tel Aviv).

**September 18.** The Saudi Arabian Committee for the Propagation of Virtue and Prevention of Vice confirms the ban placed on the "Jewish Barbie doll, a symbol of the decadence of the perverted West." In April 2001 Saudi Arabian religious leaders had condemned Pokemon trading cards as part of a "Zionist conspiracy to lure Muslim children into immoral gambling."

**September 26.** Terrorist gets into a house in Negohot (Cisjordan) and shoots the family gathered for the Sabbath dinner.

**October 4.** Nineteen-year-old female suicide attacker blows herself up at the Maxim restaurant in Haifa (Israel), frequented by Jews and Israeli Arabs.

**October 15.** At the Beit Hanoun crossroad in the Gaza Strip a powerful bomb is detonated against a convoy of U.S. diplomats going to the Gaza Strip to award scholarships to Palestinian student.

**October 16.** Malaysian Prime Minister Mahathir Muhammad, when inaugurating in Putrajaya (the capital of Malaysia) the summit meeting of the Islamic Conference Organisation, which comprises Muslim leaders from fifty-seven countries, states: "The Europeans killed six million Jews out of twelve million [who were then living in Europe] and yet today the Jews rule the world by proxy. They get others to fight and die for them. They invented socialism, communism, human rights and democracy so that the persecutions against them seemed to be wrong. With these instruments they have gained control of the major powers, and so it is that this minute community has become a world power. 1.3 billion Muslims cannot be defeated by a few million Jews." The French President, Jacques Chirac blocks the draft of an EU position paper against Mahathir Muhammad's statements.

**November**. Egypt submits a resolution to the U.N. Third Committee (Social, Humanitarian, and Cultural Affairs) calling for protection "for Palestinian children, victims of Israeli aggression." Israel submits a resolution in which it expresses concern "due to the serious threat looming over Israeli children because of Palestinian terrorism and the grave consequences of the continuous direct attacks against Israeli civilians, children included." On November 6 the Committee approves (with eighty-eight votes in favor, four votes against, and fifty-eight abstentions) the Egyptian resolution defending Palestinian children. Twenty days later Israel is forced to withdraw its resolution because among the 191 countries represented on the Committee it is impossible to collect the quorum of adherents necessary to take it forward. Dan Gillerman, Israel's ambassador to the United Nations, states: "The incapacity of the international community to approve a resolution defending Israeli children deliberately hit by terrorism, after having approved a resolution defending Palestinian children unintentionally hit in confrontations, demonstrates that the U.N. General Assembly is an unreliable and prejudiced organism that lacks moral integrity."

**November**. During the month of Ramadan, Egyptian public TV repeats, as done the year before, the TV serial *Horseman with No Horse* based on the *The Protocols of the Elders of Zion*.

**November**. The Lebanese TV station Al-Manar (operated by the Hezbollah fundamentalists) broadcasts the Syrian-produced serial *The Diaspora* (Al-Shatat), which describes the plot of a "Jewish World Government" to dominate the world. The scenes also include the ritual murder of a non-Jewish boy whose blood is purported to be used to make matzo.

**November**. According to the results of a Eurobarometer poll, the majority of Europeans interviewed believe that Israel is the country that, more than any other, "is a threat to world peace."

**November 10**. According to an ISPO/Corriere della Sera poll, almost one out of five Italians has explicitly anti-Semitic feelings and two out of three Italians do not know the story of the state of Israel.

**November 12**. The famous Greek musician Mikis Theodorakis, in comparing Greeks and Jews, publicly states: "Today it can be said that this small people, full of stubbornness and presumptuousness, is the root of all evils."

**November 15**. Suicide attackers with a car bomb blow themselves up simultaneously in front of the Nevei Shalom and Beth Israel synagogues in Istanbul. In 1986 the same Nevei Shalom synagogue had been the scene of an attack by Palestinian attackers who killed twenty-two praying faithful.

**November 19**. A Jordanian soldier on guard at the border checkpoint between Aqaba (Jordan) and Eilat (Israel) fires his machine gun at a group of tourists in transit.

**November 23**. The *Financial Times* reveals that the European Observatory on Racism has avoided publishing a report on anti-Semitism, commissioned to the European Centre on Racism and Xenophobia (of Vienna), whose findings indicated that Muslim and pro-Palestinian groups were behind many of the manifestations of anti-Semitism examined. (After many protests, the report was officially published on March 31, 2004.)

**November 26**. A cartoon showing a caricature of Israeli Prime Minister Ariel Sharon while he devours a Palestinian child is awarded first prize in the annual competition of the British Political Cartoon Society. The cartoon—the work of Dave Brown—had been published by the daily newspaper *The Independent* some months earlier.

**December 2.** The U.N. General Assembly allows a resolution condemning anti-Semitism presented by Ireland to lapse without approval.

**December 25**. Suicide attacker blows himself up during the rush hour at a bus stop in Petah Tikva, east of Tel Aviv.

**December 30.** The 2003 report of the Israeli Co-ordination Forum for Countering Anti-Semitism finds an increase in anti-Jewish attacks (Istanbul, Morocco), physical aggression by individuals and groups, vandalism, threats, insults, and propaganda campaigns full of anti-Semite stereotypes that blame Jews and Israel for Middle Eastern crises and for the ills of the world, negate the Jews' right to an independent state and to freely express their identity (after various incidents, the Chief Rabbi of France was forced to advise Jews not to wear anything identifying them as such in public), and present theories of the Jewish/Zionist plot for world domination. Arab regimes grant ever-increasing legitimacy to anti-Semitic propaganda. Attempts continue to ostracize Israel and Israelis from academic, scientific, and cultural life. Conversely, there are signs of sensitivity to the problem among Western leaders and opinion-makers.

# 2004

**January 14.** Female suicide attacker pretending to be disabled blows herself up at the Erez checkpoint between Israel and the Gaza Strip just when some female soldiers came across to help her pass through the metal detector.

**January 19.** The photograph of Hanadi Jaradat, a Palestinian terrorist responsible for the massacre of Israelis (Jewish and Arab) at the Maxim restaurant of Haifa, flutters smilingly on the sail of a little white boat floating in a tank full of blood-red liquid, accompanied by a text justifying the gesture. It is the work of the artists Dror and Gunilla Skoeld Feiler called *Snow White and the Madness of Truth*, displayed at the Stockholm Historical Museum on the occasion of a conference on genocide. A gesture of protest is made by the Israeli ambassador in Sweden, who disconnects electrical cables to spotlights illuminating the display.

**January 29.** Suicide attacker blows himself up on a bus in Jerusalem at the crossroads between Gaza Street and Arlozorov Street.

**February 18.** The Anti-Defamation League (ADL) denounces Egyptian state-owned publishing companies that publish openly anti-Semitic books (including an edition of *The Protocols* *of the Elders of Zion* edited by Husein Abed Al Wahed, who gives credit to the text's arguments, and *The Jews' Crimes Against Monotheistic Religions* by Hanafi Al Mahlawi). The year before, the ADL had denounced the publication, under the patronage of the Egyptian president's wife, Suzanne Mubarak, of a series of children's books containing anti-Semitic themes.

**February 21.** Suicide attacker blows himself up on a bus in the centre of Jerusalem in the Liberty Bell Park.

**March 6.** Terrorists disguised as Israeli soldiers use machine guns and hand grenades to attack the Erez checkpoint between Israel and the Gaza Strip.

**March 14.** Two suicide attackers blow themselves up just a few minutes apart at the entrance into the port of Ashdod (Israel).

**March 19.** George Elias Khoury, a twenty-year-old Christian Arab of Beit Hanina (Israel), is killed by shots fired from a moving car while he is jogging in the French Hill neighborhood of Jerusalem.

**March.** Mel Gibson's film *The Passion of Christ* is used in some Arab countries to relaunch, with articles and cartoons, the accusation of deicide against the Jews. According to his close advisor Nabil Abu Rudeneh, Yasser Arafat, after seeing the film, states: "The Palestinians today still suffer the pains to which Jesus was subjected during the crucifixion."

**April 23.** Protest of the Anti-Defamation League (ADL) at the statement of the U.N. envoy in Iraq, Lakhdar Brahmi, according to whom "Israel is the greatest poison in the whole of the Middle East."

**May 2.** In Khan Yunes (southern Gaza Strip), a thirty-four-year-old Israeli mother, eight months pregnant, and her four children are hit in their car and then killed with shots in the head fired at point-blank range by Palestinian terrorists.

**May 2.** The Saudi crown prince, Abdullah bin Abed al-Aziz, speaking in Jeddah to a meeting of top government officials and academics about the recent terrorist attacks in Saudi Arabia, states: "It's known who is behind all this: the Zionists, followers of Satan." The accusation was repeated on May 4 by Saudi Foreign Minister Saud al-Faisal.

**May 6.** Lebanese Hezbollah fundamentalists fire artillery against military posts at the foot of Mount Dov (northern Israel).

**May 11**. In Gaza an Israeli armoured car blows up.

**May 11–13**. In the space of forty-eight hours, in two different incidents, eleven Israeli soldiers, hunting for tunnels used by terrorists to smuggle weapons and explosives, lose their lives when their armoured cars blow up on Palestinian mines in the southern Gaza Strip, on the border with Egypt. Members of Fatah, Hamas, and the Islamic Jihad mutilate the bodies of the soldiers killed, exhibit parts of the bodies in the street and in videos, and attempt to use them as something to trade in negotiations with the Israeli authorities. Three days later, another two Israeli soldiers are killed by Palestinian snipers while looking for the bodies of their fellow soldiers.

**May 19**. The Anti-Defamation League (ADL) protests a cartoon by Petar Pismestrovic published in the Austrian newspaper *Kleine Zeitung*, which identifies Israeli soldiers as Nazis "putting the Nazi policy of deliberate extermination of the Jews in Europe [the ADL writes in a letter to the editor] on exactly the same level as Palestinian victims accidentally caused within the framework of the Israeli-Palestinian conflict. Whatever one thinks of Israeli policy, this comparison is misleading and slanderous."

FIAMMA NIRENSTEIN is a columnist and Jerusalem-based correspondent for La Stampa, a daily paper based in Turin, Italy. She also writes for Panorama, an Italian magazine, covering events in Israel as they occur. Her books include: *Il razzista democratio* (*The Democratic Racist*), Mondadori 1992; *Israele: una pace in guerra* (*Israel: A Peace at War*), Il Mulino 1996; *Come le cinque dita di una mano* (*Like the Five Fingers of One Hand*), co-authored with her parents and sisters, Rizzoli 1998; and *Un solo Dio, tre verltà* (*One God, Three Truths*), co-authored with Giorgio Montefoschi, Mondadori, 2001.

ANNE MILANO APPEL specializes in the translation of fiction and non-fiction from Italian to English. Formerly a director of public libraries in California and New Jersey, she has also taught English, Italian, and English as a Second Language. In addition to an MLS in library studies, she holds and M.A. and a Ph.D. in Romance Languages and Literature from Rutgers University, where she specialized in Italian studies. Several of her book-length translations of contemporary Italian fiction and non-fiction have been published, and shorter works have appeared in other venues. Articles and reviews that she has written, edited, or translated have appeared in professional and literary journals, such as the *ATA Chronicle, Tradurre, Beacons: A Journal of Literary Translation,* and *Forum Italicum.*